VOICES OF
ORMONDE
HOUSE

Malcolm Phillips was born and brought up in Worksop in north Nottinghamshire in 1947. He was educated at Retford Grammar School and the universities of Cambridge, Newfoundland and Lancaster. His introduction to teaching in further education was in London after which he taught for a year in Canada. In 1975 he was appointed Lecturer in History at Newbury College, and in 1993 he was given responsibility for Student Services. Since his retirement from the college in 1999, he has lived in the Wye Valley on the border between England and Wales. This is his first major publication.

VOICES OF
ORMONDE HOUSE

A HISTORY OF THE EARLY YEARS OF NEWBURY COLLEGE

Malcolm Phillips

KERNE BRIDGE PRESS
2011

Kerne Bridge Press, Lydbrook, Glos. GL17 9SW

First published by Kerne Bridge Press 2011

Kerne Bridge Press, Hayes Knoll, Church Hill, Lydbrook,
Glos. GL17 9SW

British Library Cataloguing in Publication Data
A CIP catalogue record for this book is available from
the British Library

ISBN 978-0-9566490-0-3

Typeset in Sabon 10½ by
www.chandlerbookdesign.co.uk

Printed in Great Britain by the
MPG Books Group, Bodmin and King's Lynn

There is a tendency in some of us who place
a very high value on education to allow our
enthusiasm to run away at times

Eva Jarvis, Berkshire Education
Committee, 1949

CONTENTS

TABLES

FOREWORD

I n September 1948, a group of young building workers made
their way into Newbury. Many came on their bicycles, one
or two of the older ones had motorbikes and a few came by
bus. Their destination was the Oxford Road to the north of the
town. They were all boys, 15, 16, 17 years old. Some had known
each other since their time at school together; others had struck
up friendships at work. They were all apprentices: bricklayers,
carpenters, painters and plumbers. The Oxford Road climbed
gently out of the town through the parish of Speenhamland. A
little way along and there were three Victorian villas. They stood
some distance from one another, detached and enclosed within
large gardens. The boys stopped at the entrance to number 38,
which was called Ormonde House. Their bicycle wheels crunched
over the expanse of gravel in the driveway. Anxiously they made
their way towards the front door. Here they waited for a few
minutes. Some of them stood alone, while others gathered on the
grass alongside the drive in twos and threes and talked quietly
amongst themselves.

A few minutes passed, and they were met by an instructor
who came out of the house and down the three stone steps to meet
them. Some of the older boys recognised him, as the year before
he had taught them at the Technical Institute. The Institute was in
Northbrook Street, the busy thoroughfare which ran through the
centre of the town. Now, in the autumn of 1948, the instructor
was to carry on with their classes in Ormonde House. He was the

first teacher, and the young apprentices were the first students, of the Newbury Institute of Further Education.

The Institute at Ormonde House was welcomed by the local newspaper as 'something new'. It was set up by Berkshire County Council to take over the work of the Technical Institute which had been running classes in the town for many years. The new institute was to put on more courses and the building in Northbrook Street was too small for this anticipated expansion. When the property in Oxford Road came on the market, the County Council realised its potential, moved quickly and bought it. The house was on three floors. It had a number of rooms for classrooms and some of its sheds and outbuildings could also be used, as workshops for the more practical instruction. Two cottages, one with a garage, came with the property; and a site of four acres meant there was room for new buildings as well.

For a few weeks, the young builders had the house to themselves. Yet something new was happening in this quiet corner of Berkshire. Classes were organised, curiosity was awakened and the word spread. More students arrived in October and many more in early November. A steady stream of people made their way along the Oxford Road and by Christmas there were more than 1,000 men and women enrolled as students.

Three years later, in 1951, the Newbury Institute became the South Berks College of Further Education. Significant development occurred in the 1950s, an extensive curriculum was established and increasing numbers of lecturers and instructors were employed. This adventure into the changing landscape of further education in the Berkshire countryside is a story in which a wooden chicken hut and a lean-to greenhouse loom large. It is also a story about making the most of what was available, a constant narrative of changing rooms, of how a Victorian conservatory was used first for dressmaking, then as a drawing office and then as a chemistry laboratory. It is also about a continuing search for classroom space in the town, in rooms above shops and banks, in an Edwardian school building and in an old 17th-century chapel. But these were also years of the construction of a new college, blocks of brick buildings with lots of windows and flat roofs which emerged in the grounds at the back of the house on the Oxford Road.

With the new name in 1951 came new responsibilities. The college continued to organise courses in Newbury, but it was also made responsible for further education in the smaller towns and villages in the neighbourhood. This included the work of the institutes at Compton and East Ilsley, Hungerford and Lambourn, and Thatcham.

From 1975, the South Berks College was known as Newbury College, but the change of name was of little significance. The college remained the centre of further education in south and west Berkshire under the responsibility of Berkshire County Council.

In 1993 further education colleges in England and Wales were taken out of local authority control and were incorporated as independent and self-governing institutions. Berkshire County Council's control over Newbury College was over. A new era began in which the college was given the opportunity to shape its own future while maintaining the best traditions of further education which it had been developing since 1948. The association with the Victorian house continued. Indeed, for more than 50 years, Ormonde House remained the headquarters of further education in the Newbury district. This connection came to an end in 2002 when a new campus was built on the land of Sandleford Farm on the south side of the town. Nothing was to remain at number 38 Oxford Road and residential housing now covers the site.

Ormonde House has gone, but it is still fresh in Newbury's collective memory. This volume, an oral history of the college in its early years, is an attempt to keep the memory warm. It pieces together the recollections of some of those people who were involved in Ormonde House as it developed as a centre of further education. Most of the interviews were recorded around the time of the college's 50th anniversary in 1998, and everything quoted is, as far as is humanly possible, directly quoted from the person stated.

The stories are narrow in focus, somewhat modest and, on the whole, good-humoured. I interviewed 45 people, 37 of whom had been students between 1948 and 1960. Of these, 28 had studied part time, nine full time; 26 were men, 11 were women. Student memories predominate and I listened to the reasons why they went to college, what they remembered about their time there, and what they went on to do after they had finished. Six of the voices belong to college staff. Four of these were lecturers, one worked in the office and one was a technician. I have also included the recollections of two other people. One of these worked in Ormonde House when it was a family home before it became a further education institute. The other shared with me memories of his father who had been a college governor in these early years.

Most of the interviews took place individually but some people preferred to be interviewed together. Our conversations were unstructured. I did not have a list of questions to be answered. People told their stories in their own way, and most of my questions were in response to their own narratives. As we talked, blurred memories sharpened and became distinct. 'Yes! There was a greenhouse!' My task was to lend an ear to the voices and amplify them so that others might hear them as well.

Each one of these quieter voices of history has a story to tell and when the individual threads are woven together, a tapestry emerges. The conversations become a rich historical source and a bigger picture starts to come into focus. We are given an insight into some of the ways in which education developed in a small market town in the south of England in the years after the Second World War.

This was an important time in the history of further education. The 1944 Education Act encouraged its development and in the years that followed, old colleges were extended and new colleges and institutes were set up. In Berkshire the landscape of further education was transformed. The number of students and lecturers grew, as did that of the administrative and technical staff. 'It seems that every year in Further Education is a year of expansion', reported the Berkshire Education Committee in 1959; and this was happening all over the country. There was a lot more further education in Britain than there had been in the years before the war. The journey that started in Ormonde House was part of a much larger movement.

Yet while listening to these recollections unfold, I began to realise that what I was hearing was not just a story about further education. A local college helps define a local community. Ormonde House played a big part in the lives of many people and a record was emerging about life in Newbury in the middle years of the last century. These years of the college's history are set in a bygone age at a time when the country market town was on the cusp of changing into the business, commercial and distribution centre it is today. This ragbag of memory went beyond life at 38 Oxford Road. Splinters of everyday life, at rest and play, at school and work, were remembered. So was the look of the town 50 years ago, a bank of memory in which Newbury emerges as a peaceful and familiar place. The experiences recorded here, although somewhat parochial, are a chapter in this greater story of community.

This book has been long in the making and on the way I have acquired a multitude of debts. I would like to thank the following people, each one of whom has been important to the book's shaping: my wife Julia, and the younger members of my family, Jacob, Simon and Nick for their technical know-how, Clara and Nicola for their encouragement. This work has been a collaborative project and I hope I have conveyed my specific appreciation to each one of you.

I owe a special debt of gratitude to my editor Mary Armour for her work on the emerging manuscript. She has saved me from countless lapses and inconsistencies. Any inadequacies that remain are all my own work. I would also like to thank Sean O'Donoghue who has been a generous source of information and advice. To Odette, Sue Cocker, Gordon Bull and Jean Hart, my appreciation for their believing in the book from the beginning.

I would also like to thank those people and institutions for helping me find material and answer enquiries. The *Newbury Weekly News* kindly gave me permission to reproduce quotations, and Margaret Carruthers in the newspaper's library was of invaluable assistance. My thanks are also due to Anne Marshall and Kate Pyne at the Atomic Weapons Establishment at Aldermaston; Sue Connell at the United Kingdom Atomic Energy Authority at Harwell; Sue Matthews at Plenty of Newbury; Fiona Lees of Newbury College library; and Tom Rossiter of Penningtons Solicitors in Newbury for allowing me access to the deeds and conveyances relating to Ormonde House. I would also like to thank the staff at the Berkshire County Record Office, Newbury Library and Museum, and Reading Library. The OS map of Newbury, 1933 edition, is reproduced with the kind permission of Ordnance Survey. The painting of Ormonde by Alfred Wheeler is reproduced with the kind permission of the National Horseracing Museum, Newmarket.

At the South Berks College prize-giving evening in 1956, Principal Eric Lansley looked forward to the new buildings about to be erected. 'But fine buildings do not make fine colleges; it is the people in them who make fine colleges.' I would like to thank all those people who have worked with me in further education over the years and I am especially grateful to the many students whom I have enjoyed teaching and from whom I have learned much.

Finally, my particular thanks are to those men and women who were happy to share their memories with me and become the voices of Ormonde House. To some my thanks are, sadly, posthumous. It took patience and generosity to speak up. This book is for you.

Malcolm Phillips, Wye Valley, 2011

1

OVERTURE

What is further education?

> Education is not an affair of childhood and youth;
> it is the business of the whole life.[1]

Berkshire County Council, the local education authority (LEA), set up the Newbury Institute in 1948 to provide courses in further education. The term 'further education' (FE) includes all forms of post-school education except that provided by universities, usually referred to as 'higher education'. It is often seen as the poor and downtrodden relation of the education service, the 'Cinderella' who never arrives at the ball. In the education landscape, FE is low-lying. The higher land is occupied by schools and universities. Moreover, most people have a clear idea of what a school or university does. Yet a large part of the population is not that clear about what FE colleges do. Everybody has to go to school, but further education is voluntary. Nobody is legally obliged to continue their education beyond the school-leaving age.

The world of further education, then, is often far from the public mind. It is rarely high on the political agenda and plays a limited role in government planning. Few government

---

[1] James Hole, 19th-century social reformer and pioneer of adult education, quoted in J F C Harrison, *Learning and Living 1790-1960*, (London: Routledge & Kegan Paul, 1961), p.128.

ministers have experienced it themselves. Perhaps this is why FE colleges are too often neglected by those in power. Much of the work in FE is vocational and for many years there has been a divide between academic and practical education in our cultural heritage. We do not celebrate practical skills as well as we do academic qualifications, even though for years people have argued for an improvement in the status surrounding vocational study. The role that further education plays in social and economic life deserves better public recognition. It is important in giving opportunities to men and women and helping them to achieve their aspirations, whether to get on in the world or to enjoy the delights of cultural enrichment.

If there is a lack of clarity surrounding further education, this is because colleges serve a wide range of students with different needs. Around four million people pass through the doors of the 400 or so FE colleges in England and Wales every year. There are many more 16- to 18-year-olds working for their qualifications in colleges than in schools. There are more students in further education than there are in schools or universities. Some of these are young people; many are older, men and women for whom the approach of autumn coincides with a return to education. They are enrolled for part-time courses, paying tuition fees and with little financial support available to them. Some are senior citizens enjoying an active retirement. FE courses can provide an ageing population with mental stimulus and social contact with others.

Further education is diverse, but three broad types of provision can be identified. First, there are those courses which are essentially vocational in purpose, to develop the skills in the workforce needed by industry and commerce. This is part of the further education tradition, with roots going back into the nineteenth century. This was education for 'usefulness', practical and technical instruction, usually in the evening. Colleges have always recognised this economic imperative. The country needs highly trained builders, car mechanics, technicians, plumbers and countless other non-degreed professionals who keep the technological machine of a modern society in good working order. Colleges make an enormous contribution to getting young people qualified, from advertising and public relations to business management and veterinary nursing.

Today's FE colleges are the chief source of technical and vocational training, important engines of economic growth. They have to be responsive to the workplace. Employers expect the provision to be sensitive to their needs. Working together, colleges can meet the needs of employers to deliver a trained workforce and make the economy more productive and more competitive. Many colleges have a long association with the employers in their area. The training of apprentices and young people, and the retraining of older people, giving them the opportunity to update their skills, go to the heart of what FE is all about. It remains true that many of the people working in a particular locality will have been trained at their local college. Moreover, colleges have made substantial progress in the last decade. More people than ever before are using them and the traditional image of the FE college, full of machinery past its sell-by date, operated by men in greasy overalls, has been superseded by that of a dynamic and well equipped institution addressing the country's skill shortages. Where buildings were once run-down, today you are more likely to find a modern college with good facilities. Yet the aim remains vocational, providing work-related qualifications to millions of people every year.

Second, further education embraces non-vocational courses which provide opportunities for people to enrich their life with a leisure pursuit, a hobby, a spare-time occupation. This is not vocational training and many of the courses do not lead to examinations and certificates. Rather it is learning for the fun of it, to develop a particular interest. Sometimes the distinction between vocational and non-vocational can be blurred. The development of a particular interest and the skills involved can lead to increasing employability or self-employment. One person's flower arranging is another's floristry business. Be that as it may, learning for personal development is good for our health and terms such as 'adult', 'community' or 'continuing' education are used to describe such courses. They contribute to community wellbeing, cultural creativity and social solidarity. They are popular and there is a great swathe of programmes across the country enjoyed by people of all ages, all having a good time. The courses are provided by LEAs, by extramural departments of universities, by organisations such as the Women's Institutes

(WIs) and the Workers' Educational Association (WEA). In addition, there are a countless number of voluntary associations involved in such education, all contributing to an environment in which the work of the more formal organisations, such as colleges, can flourish.[2]

The third type of FE provision is that which is sometimes called 'general education'. This includes GCSEs, AS-levels and A-levels which remain at the heart of the secondary school curriculum. In 1948 the government announced that the General Certificate of Education was to replace the School and Higher School Certificates and the new O- and A-levels were soon offered by many FE colleges. General education courses also include those which have proliferated in the last 30 years: programmes for minority ethnic groups, for unemployed people, for people with learning difficulties and disabilities, classes in literacy and numeracy. Indeed the teaching of the three R's for those beyond school age was a main function of the adult education movement and this remedial role, making good the deficiencies in an earlier education, remains an important strand in contemporary FE.[3] Today's colleges cater for the disadvantaged and those disaffected with mainstream education, re-engaging those who have dropped out of learning. They work towards reducing a person's likelihood of unemployment and job instability. They aim to promote social inclusion and to help people fully participate in society. They are also important in helping people of all ages from 'untraditional' backgrounds gain a place at university. FE is a place where everyone has a chance – and a second and a third chance – to succeed.

Within these three types of FE provision, the range of courses is extensive, provided across a variety of institutions. The general colleges of further education, the technical colleges and the sixth form colleges, tend to offer a broad mix of courses. They sit alongside the more specialist institutions, such as the colleges

---

[2] Such a list for the 1950s could include churches and chapels with their clubs, fellowships and guilds; societies of business and professional people, Rotary Clubs, Round Tables, Soroptomists; branches of the British Legion and Toc H; political and internationalist organisations, the Fabian Society, United Nations Association, Young Conservatives; and literary and philosophical societies and local history groups.

[3] Harrison, *op.cit.*, p.42.

of art and agriculture, fashion and drama. Then there are the evening institutes in which a lot of the adult education takes place. Schools make up a relatively simple world, offering a small range of qualifications to a narrow range of individuals. The FE world is more complex, with thousands of vocational qualifications and millions of students of all ages. The curriculum of a large college today is most impressive and rivals that of some universities. 'The levels differ, of course, but response to known and, more important, suspected and potential needs is greater here than in any other part of the educational system.'[4] In the 1950s, colleges tended to be parochial in outlook, focusing on the needs of the local market. This has now changed, with colleges developing regional, national and even international dimensions.

It is difficult to construct a profile of the typical FE college. Local and regional variations have always been considerable. Today, no two colleges offer the same range of courses and each college is different from its neighbour down the road. Each one has a context reflecting the history and the social and economic character of the locality in which it is set.

In 1948, the LEA in Berkshire established FE institutes in the three towns of Maidenhead, Newbury and Windsor. It also set up an Institute of Agriculture at Burchett's Green outside Maidenhead. From the beginning, Newbury's Institute offered a mix of vocational and non-vocational work as well as a limited programme in general education. The courses were all part-time. The youngest student was at least 15 years old, the official school-leaving age.

The decision to set up the new institutes was most important. However, further education courses had been developing in Berkshire since the closing decade of the previous century.

'A veritable explosion of activity'

In Evening Institutes in Berkshire, classes have been held in various centres for many years and there has been a School of Art and Technical Institute at Maidenhead since 1895, but it is true that for the most part this work has

---

[4] Richard Hoggart, *The Way We Live Now*, (London: Pimlico, 1996), p.37.

been developed, often with a strong vocational bias, only in industrial towns.

Scheme of Further Education 1949

The history of further education in Britain goes back for at least 200 years, but it was in the second half of the 19th century that significant developments took place. From the late 18th century, Britain had been the first nation in the world to be transformed by an industrial revolution and for many years had led the world in economic growth. By the later 19th century, however, there was a growing concern that as other countries industrialised, Britain would lose its lead and fall behind its industrial rivals. New competitors were entering the world's markets. The poor showing made by British exhibits at the Paris Industrial Exhibition in 1867 dealt a blow to national pride and alarmed complacent manufacturers. From the early 1870s it was felt that sectors of the economy were falling behind. There was a growing unease as Britain began to lose its world predominance, overtaken by the USA in the 1880s in steel production, that Victorian symbol of economic virility. British markets became increasingly swamped with cheap manufactured goods labelled 'Made in Germany' and other recently industrialised nations. Free trade was held by many to be responsible and there were demands for protection of the home market with tariffs on imported goods.

It was in the face of this increasing competition that the later Victorians became interested in technical education. Inadequate education was holding back the British economy. Technical and scientific education was necessary for economic efficiency, not a new demand but now expressed with a new urgency. Twenty years of government investigations followed, including a Royal Commission on Technical Instruction which reported in 1884.

The investigations bore fruit. In 1889 the Technical Instruction Act allowed county councils and county borough councils – set up in the previous year – to use money from the rates to promote technical education in their areas. The following year the local authorities received money from the government in London and Berkshire County Council was given a grant of £6,478. In 1891 the Council set up a Technical Education Committee and there followed 'a veritable explosion of activity' in further education across the county.[5]

An administrative change came with the Education Act of 1902. County and borough councils became local education authorities, responsible for the schools, technical institutes and evening institutes in their areas. Berkshire County Council became the LEA. The newly formed Berkshire Education Committee took over the work of the Technical Education Committee, and a Higher Education Subcommittee was set up to look after technical education. This subcommittee remained responsible for the technical and evening institutes until the end of the Second World War. The Berkshire Education Committee was responsible for provision in Newbury. In Reading, education was the responsibility of the Borough Council, acting as the town's LEA.

The years before the First World War saw a significant growth in further education in Berkshire. Institutes were set up in two of the largest towns. In the east, the Maidenhead Technical Institute – offering 'Instruction in Art and Technical Subjects'– opened in Marlow Road in 1895.[6] Around the same time, in the west of the county, an institute opened in Northbrook Street in Newbury. It was financed by Berkshire County Council through an annual grant and the LEA employed a superintendent to organise the classes. This institute was the centre of further education in south and west Berkshire for the next 50 years. The courses at Ormonde House came out of this reservoir of education and training in Northbrook Street. The men and women who made their way along the Oxford Road in 1948 were a new chapter in an old story.

Newbury's Technical Institute was located on the main road running through the town. The building at 60 Northbrook Street had, for many years, been the meeting place for the Newbury Literary and Scientific Institution, a flourishing society which reflected the many interests of the Victorian townsfolk. Talks were

---

[5] Education in the Royal County of Berkshire 1967-70, Report by the Director of Education, pp.64-66.

[6] Since 1945, Education in Berkshire, A Report on the Work of the Berkshire Education Committee from 1945 to 1956, p.29. Hereinafter referred to as Since 1945.

given on a variety of subjects, ranging from biology, chemistry, physics and zoology to biography, literary criticism and travel. There were concerts, puppet shows and verse-speaking evenings; and there was a museum and a library which boasted 8,000 volumes and a librarian living in the house next door. For many years, Alice Hewitt's Ladies' School used the building as well. Importantly, it had been agreed that should the Institution ever close, then the property would be handed over to Newbury Council to be used for educational purposes.[7] When the Institution did cease to exist, its museum was moved to the Cloth Hall on the Wharf (1902) and its books were donated to the new library in Cheap Street (1905).

The Technical Institute was a 'commodious' building with two entrances, two sets of stairs and a number of rooms. The front door on Northbrook Street opened into an entrance hall, a room large enough for 72 chairs and the main staircase. The upstairs rooms were smaller and one was used as a laboratory for mechanical engineering students.[8] The rooms were lit by gas and downstairs there was a gentlemen's lavatory. The maintenance of the property was shared between Newbury Borough Council (external) and Berkshire County Council (internal).

The Technical Institute was a night school. Others used the accommodation during the day. It was here that the LEA opened the Newbury County Girls' School in 1904, with Esther Luker and her 38 pupils. 'The school is carried on in the Technical Institute and a boarding house is near it.' The school grew and in 1910 was moved to new and bigger premises on the Andover Road. After the First World War, the Institute was used by the boys of Newbury Grammar School for art classes; and in 1919 the War Pensions Committee was using the building.

The Liberal Club was the Institute's neighbour on the south side. The building on the north side from 1910 was used as a picture house, Newbury's white-painted Picture Palace. Its distinctive

---

[7] Vera Garlick, *The Newbury Scrapbook*, (Newbury: *Newbury Weekly News*, 1970), p.209. See also P Haynes, 'Some Notes on Victorian Northbrook Street 1850-1900' in Creative History Group, *Newbury Roundabout*, (Newbury: 1989), pp.57-64.

[8] Minutes of Berkshire Education Committee 22 October 1910. Hereinafter referred to as BEC.

overhanging upper floor housed the projection equipment which had to be separated from the auditorium because film was highly flammable. The films were silent screen showings with piano accompaniment, but the noise from the electric motor 'constituted a nuisance' as it could be heard in the classrooms next door.[9] The Picture Palace closed in 1931 because it could not be adapted to the new medium of talkies', and the LEA was pleased.

On the other side of the picture house were Albert Road, its junction with Northbrook Street, and the neat iron railings of Newbury's Methodist Church. The church stood back from the road. Along here was the Institute's side entrance leading to the back stairs and the upstairs rooms. Further down Albert Road was Elliott's Moulding and Joinery Company, the biggest employer in the town at this time.

The Institute was run by a small group of governors who were responsible to the education authority for managing the budget – £350 in 1911/12.[10] Some of the governors were appointed by the LEA, others by Newbury Borough Council. Around the time of the First World War these included Alfred Camp and Paul Hopson, the town's largest retailers, and Mr Plenty, Newbury's leading engineering employer.

The Institute's Superintendent, sometimes referred to as the 'head teacher', organised the classes for each session. A session was for two terms, autumn and spring; only very occasionally were classes taught for a third (summer) term. Many of the townsfolk were interested and lots of classes took place.

The 1910/11 session was a busy one, with 17 courses and 190 students – 99 women and 91 men – almost twice as many as in the previous year.[11] Prizes – not money – were awarded to the best students. All the classes were held in the Northbrook Street building except for cookery and woodwork which were organised in the Council School in Station Road. This LEA school had opened in 1909, with departments for boys and girls as well as a section for infants.

---

[9] *Ibid.*, 24 January 1913.

[10] Minutes of Newbury Technical Institute 18 October 1911. Hereinafter referred to as NTI.

[11] BEC 21 October 1911.

The Institute offered vocational and non-vocational courses. The co-operation of employers was sought and they were asked to let their errand boys and apprentices leave work in time to get to class. The classes were advertised in the *Newbury Weekly News*. Schoolchildren were not allowed to enrol but they were encouraged to join once they had left school. There was a natural link, through these evening continuation classes as they were called, between the education provided by the Council School and the more specialised instruction offered by the Technical Institute. The Superintendent worked with the schools 'to induce pupils who are leaving or who have left school to attend the evening classes'.

One of the problems facing the younger students who lived in the country districts was that of transport. Journeying into Newbury was difficult in the winter 'through inclemency of weather'.[12] Fifty years on, and the LEA found that the rural nature of much of the South Berks College catchment area meant 'serious travelling difficulties' for students, a problem partially remedied by the purchase of a minibus.

Table 1 Newbury Technical Institute: Classes 1910/11

Subject	Day	Hour
Art	Monday	6.15-8.15
Art	Thursday	6.00-8.00
Building Construction	Tuesday	7.00-9.00
Machine Construction	Thursday	7.00-9.00
Woodwork	Friday	7.00-9.00
Cookery	Tuesday	7.00-9.00
Dressmaking	Friday	7.00-8.30
Commercial Arithmetic	Monday	7.15-8.15
Commercial Geography	Monday	8.15-9.15
Bookkeeping	Tuesday	7.15-8.15
English	Tuesday	8.15-9.15
Needlework	Monday	8.15-9.15
Needlework	Wednesday	7.15-8.15
Singing	Wednesday	8.15-9.15
Shorthand and Typewriting	Thursday	7.00-9.00

NTI 14 September 1910

---

[12] NTI 5 April 1910.

When classes started, the students were enthusiastic but the attendance sometimes dropped off as the term unfolded.

Table 2 Newbury Technical Institute: Classes February 1911

Subject	Enrolment	Number Attending	Average Attendance
Art	40	–	17
Building Construction	15	–	7
Machine Construction	16	–	7
Woodwork	–	–	10
Cookery	19 in Autumn Term; Spring Term only 6	–	–
Dressmaking	21 in Autumn Term; Spring Term only 13	–	10
Commercial Arithmetic	51	31	22
Commercial Geography	30	21	12
Bookkeeping	50	32	21
Needlework	25	15	7
Shorthand and Typewriting	51	34	25

NTI 23 February 1911

The courses in building, commerce and engineering reflected the local economy. Workplace demand for such training fluctuated. In 1910 it was thought that the building and engineering classes 'might need to be duplicated', with an additional advanced course in machine construction. In the following year, applied mathematics was organised, with a lecturer from the University College of Reading paid a lucrative 17/6 (87 pence) for each evening class.[13] However by the winter of 1911, there were only four students in machine construction, with an average attendance of 1.6. Six young men had enrolled for building, but the average attendance was three. Commercial courses, on the other hand, were well supported. There were approximately 50 people doing arithmetic, bookkeeping, and shorthand and typewriting in 1910; and in 1911, there were classes in both elementary and advanced bookkeeping. French was added to the curriculum and in 1913 the teacher was paid 10/6 (52 pence) an evening plus travelling expenses.[14]

[13] BEC 3 March 1911.

[14] NTI 8 December 1911, 4 December 1913.

There were other vocational courses in agriculture and horticulture – farriery started in 1911 – and occasionally the Institute organised a teacher-training programme with certificates awarded to those who completed the course. 75 teachers, three of whom 'had a distance of over eight miles to cycle', enrolled in 1913 to learn about kindergarten teaching. The following year, 126 teachers attended a series of art lectures.[15] The Institute's non-vocational subjects included art, cookery, dressmaking, needlework, woodwork and singing; and the Newbury Amateur Orchestral Society used the Northbrook Street premises for rehearsals. Art and dressmaking were especially popular, with art classes sometimes running into a third term.

There were similar FE developments in the villages, where superintendents organised courses such as cookery, laundry and nursing. Sometimes, on Saturday afternoons, there were lectures on scientific subjects for teachers who could then return to their schools and teach their pupils basic science.

'Technical' and 'evening' schools were set up and instructors were taken on. The classes were usually held in LEA schools, and many of the FE instructors in the evening were schoolteachers during the day. In the west of the county, classes were held at Abingdon, Boxford, Bucklebury, Chaddleworth, Compton, Donnington, Great Shefford, Hermitage, Hungerford, Inkpen, Kintbury, Lambourn and Eastbury, Stockcross, Thatcham, Theale, Wallingford, Wantage, Welford and Wickham. There were 42 evening schools organised across Berkshire in 1913/14.[16] Each year the education authority decided which courses were to be advertised, and classes were not allowed to start without a minimum number of students registered, usually 12. If attendance fell once a class had started, the LEA could close it down. The evening school at Boxford was closed in 1912 and in 1913 the axe fell on woodwork at Thatcham, arithmetic and English at Inkpen and all the classes at Hungerford except those in carpentry and shorthand.

More than 100 students enrolled for practical subjects at the institute in Abingdon in 1892/93: building construction and ironwork, carpentry and plumbing, magnetism and electricity.

[15] NTI 2 August 1910, 14 September 1910; BEC 3 July 1913, 23 July 1914.
[16] BEC 20 January 1914.

The most popular class, however, was art. Other subjects 'useful' for engineers and metal workers were machine construction and applied mechanics taught at Compton and Wantage. Shorthand and typewriting were popular at Abingdon, Hungerford and Wantage. At Chaddleworth and Great Shefford there were classes in sickbed nursing for the wives and daughters of artisans and labourers. Popular recreational classes included cookery – when suitable premises could be found – dressmaking, needlework, physical exercise and woodwork. In 1911, the demand for woodwork was so great that a 'quantity of tools and benches' had to be ordered for many of the village institutes. Cookery classes were held in the school at Donnington and also at Thatcham, where the teacher was paid 9/6 (47 pence) an evening which covered travelling time. There were also general education classes, usually in arithmetic and English but also in geography, for which at Welford lantern slides were used as a visual aid.[17]

Agricultural education played an important part in these developments. Subjects included horticulture, poultry husbandry and dairying. In a predominantly rural county, the LEA organised a variety of classes: in crop-spraying, farriery, hedging and ditching, horticulture, and poultry-keeping. In many villages, agricultural science lectures were given during the winter months when rural workers were able to attend as there was little work to do on the land. There was fruit-culture instruction and potato-spraying demonstrations at Inkpen, and crop-spraying at Bradfield and Bucklebury, classes for farmers' sons, agricultural workers and schoolteachers. On one occasion 150 people turned up for a lecture at Thatcham. The LEA also supported other organisations involved in agricultural education. The Royal Counties Agricultural Society ran courses in dairying, the Berkshire Bee-Keepers Association taught people about the practicalities of bee-keeping. Indeed, the demand for classes was such that in 1913 Berkshire County Council appointed an agricultural organiser and a few months later the Agricultural Instruction Committee was set up. There was much to do once the First World War had started.

---

[17] *Ibid.*, 22 October 1910, 19 July 1911, 23 September 1911, 17 November 1911, 10 February 1912, 20 July 1912, 20 September 1912, 20 July 1913.

The further development of agricultural education at the present time (1915) is a task which cannot be dismissed lightly. On the contrary, it requires much consideration and in suggesting any scheme of new work the abnormal conditions now prevailing in the country on account of the European crisis have been constantly in mind. Therefore any means which might aid agriculture should be fostered to the last.

For the next 30 years, this committee was responsible for agricultural education across the county.[18]

The work of the Newbury Institute was cut back during the war. Its premises were in need of repair, with rain 'driving through the outside wall', the woodwork 'much decayed' and the floor 'dangerous to use'.[19] Fewer classes were organised and the budget was reduced to £245 in 1917/18.

Wartime classes included arithmetic, art, cookery, dressmaking, English, French, shorthand and typewriting, and woodwork. English and arithmetic were continuation classes for school leavers. When the attendance dropped in the winter of 1915, the schools were asked 'to be so good as to bring these classes to the notice of those scholars who were about to leave, or who had recently left school, and to use their influence to induce them to come to the evening classes'. Art, as usual, was popular, with 28 in the class in 1917. The teacher, Mr Barkas, was paid a fixed salary of £70; his assistant, Mr Nash, received £10. £20 was paid to Mr Stillman, who taught shorthand; and with 68 students in January 1916, his class was split into two groups. The following year, 'as many of the pupils were desirous to continue their attendance', the class continued into a third term, from April to July.[20]

The war affected the Institute's work in other ways. The English teacher was called up into the army, and was replaced by one from the Council School. There was some discussion about organising classes in cookery, saddlery and farriery for soldiers.

[18] Education in the Royal County of Berkshire 1967-70, *op.cit.*, pp.86-87.

[19] BEC 1 December 1917.

[20] NTI 27 March 1917, 6 November 1917; BEC 19 July 1917.

Meanwhile, a school for Belgian refugee children was opened on the premises, one of whom was given a 'free studentship' to study art without paying the course fee.

The military conflict of 1914-1918 put significant demands on the engineering industry. The Plenty factory was busy and wanted the Institute to put on classes in mathematics and mechanics. These would be 'invaluable' and it was anticipated that at least 20 of their apprentices would attend. The governors approved the request, university graduate Mr Mitchell was taken on as instructor, 54 young men enrolled and the classes were 'very satisfactory'.[21]

Once the war was over, classes picked up, the Institute's budget doubled and the pattern of further education which had emerged in the early years of the century continued. The LEA remained the most significant provider, working with its superintendents at Maidenhead and Newbury and those in the various institutes across the county. Maidenhead was the busiest and received the largest annual grant, around £900 in the 1920s; and it was the only centre where classes were held during the day. Windsor's budget was around £500 and Newbury was allocated around £400.[22] There were smaller 'urban centres' at Abingdon, Wallingford, Wantage and Wokingham; and there were the 'rural schools' in the villages. The students came in their own time and a few of them sat examinations leading to technical, commercial and professional qualifications.

J W Rosling was the Superintendent at Newbury for much of the interwar period. He was the borough's Education Secretary and had been the first librarian at the town's public library when it opened in 1905. He was paid according to the number of student hours registered at the Institute. Between 100 and 200 students enrolled each year.

---

[21] NTI 4 September 1917, 6 November 1917; BEC 22 September 1917, 1 December 1917, 16 July 1918.

[22] In 1922-23, the budget was £400; 1923-24, £400; 1924-25, £379; 1925-26, £407.

Table 3 Newbury Technical Institute:
Student Enrolment 1921/22; 24/25; 27/28; 33/34

Session	Enrolment
1921/22	119
1924/25	133
1927/28	166
1933/34	190

The classes were usually classified as 'elementary'. Those people who wanted 'advanced' courses had to go to colleges outside Berkshire's authority: to Reading, Oxford, or less frequently, London. They were called 'out-county' students: they lived in the county but studied courses not available locally. They could apply for financial assistance from Berkshire, however, usually to cover the cost of tuition.

The Institute's instructors worked part time, each one employed to take a particular class for a session. They did not have to be schoolteachers and many had daytime jobs in industry and commerce.[23] Each class was advertised in the Institute's prospectus and the *Newbury Weekly News*. A class would run with at least 12 enrolments and if the attendance dwindled, the education authority might close it. This happened frequently in the interwar years.

The classes were for those men and women 'whose ordinary occupation or employment occupies the greater part of their time and must not be attended by children who are at school'. The school-leaving age in the years between the wars was 14. The LEA's practice was 'to encourage pupils to remain at the Elementary School after attaining the age of 14 until they secure employment and the attendance of such pupils at Evening Classes should be encouraged'.[24]

To encourage school leavers, classes were offered to them free of charge within 12 months of their leaving school. In 1933, six Council School leavers enjoyed free tuition. Some young people went to the Institute while they were still at school. In 1922, of the 19 students in bookkeeping, seven were deemed 'ineligible'.

---

[23] BEC Regulations for Technical and Evening Institutes 1931-32.

[24] BEC 7 November 1925.

Six were of school-leaving age, 'only remaining at school until they find employment'.[25] Three years later, there were several ineligible students in commercial classes, but they were all 14 years old, or at least would be by the end of the term.

The main courses at the Technical Institute were in commerce, engineering and building, a vocational framework constructed in the years before 1914 and continued after 1945. The population of the town was growing steadily, from 12,295 in 1921 to 17,772 in 1951, a 45 per cent increase in 30 years. There were local job opportunities in clerical work: in businesses, in the offices of accountants and solicitors, in banks and estate agents. Commercial subjects were always in demand in FE: bookkeeping, shorthand and typewriting, English, arithmetic and commercial correspondence. Shorthand was so popular in 1921 that an assistant teacher was needed, two classes – elementary and advanced – were organised and 30 students enrolled. Three years later there were three shorthand classes, and 80 per cent of the Institute's students were doing commercial subjects.

Table 4 Newbury Technical Institute: Classes Autumn 1924

Subject	Enrolment	
Commercial Correspondence	17	13%
Bookkeeping - elementary	24	18%
Bookkeeping - advanced	8	6%
Shorthand - elementary - Thursday	22	17%
Shorthand - elementary - Friday	21	16%
Shorthand - advanced	14	10%
Mechanical Engineering	13	10%
Mathematics	14	10%
Total	**133**	**100%**

NTI 19 December 1924

This clerical demand continued: 62 of the 166 enrolments in 1927 were for shorthand, and by 1930 Royal Society of Arts (RSA) examinations were available. The interest in shorthand and typewriting was so consistent that there were both elementary and advanced classes, often taught over three terms. In the

---

[25] *Ibid.*, 28 October 1922.

1930s, younger students doing typewriting were expected to do commercial English as well: hints on grammar, style, planning and developing a composition, business letters, reports, prospectuses and précis writing.[26] In 1934, 13 bookkeeping students took RSA exams, five of whom passed. It was hoped that the 'unsuccessful students will re-form the class' and do the examination again.[27] For many years, shorthand was taught by a practising journalist. George Willis had started as a junior reporter with the *Newbury Weekly News* and was the proud holder of an RSA diploma, 140 words per minute, from the University of Reading. 'A capable teacher of shorthand' was Superintendent Rosling's verdict, whose students 'have had every opportunity given them of acquiring a knowledge of this essential commercial subject'.[28] As a town councillor, George Willis became one of the first governors in Ormonde House in 1948.[29]

We have seen how engineering classes were developed during the First World War at Plenty's request. In the same vein, building classes were started in 1925 at the request of the town's employers. The Newbury branch of the Reading and District Master Builders' Association wanted a programme for their apprentices. They suggested three subjects taught over three evenings each week: the theory of building construction – the employers said they could recruit a 'first-rate local man' as instructor – architectural drawing and 'suitable' mathematics. The governors and LEA representatives met with the builders, including Paul Hopson of Camp Hopson's building department, and Mr Hoskings of Hoskings & Pond. The employers were confident of getting enough students and the course started in the autumn of 1925. Numbers exceeded all expectations. Twenty students had been promised but more than 50 joined and the classes had to be split. There were so many students that a test was held at Christmas to

---

[26] NTI Prospectus 1933-34.

[27] NTI 3 August 1934.

[28] *Ibid.*, 30 March 1928.

[29] George Willis served on Newbury Council for 20 years. He was editor of the *Newbury Weekly News* from 1957 to 1965, and then became its managing director. In 1966 he was awarded the OBE for his services to journalism.

're-group' them into a 'first and second class according to ability'.

The Education Committee was delighted with the course, explaining its success with reasons which have stood the test of time as essential ingredients in the recipe for further education achievement. The 'interest' in the classes was 'well maintained, the students being very keen'. The employers 'loyally supported the establishment and working of the classes'. Finally, and most importantly, the 'fortunate choice of the instructors'; and the governors were to be congratulated on securing the services of 'such competent men'.[30]

Instructors/Salaries:

J Howe, Building Construction, 12/6 (62 pence) each class of two hours
F Brooks, Architectural Drawing, 12/6 (62 pence) each class of two hours
F Cox, Mathematics, 17/6 (87 pence) each class of two hours

Table 5 Newbury Technical Institute: Building Classes 1925

Classes		Enrolment	Meetings	Average Attendance
Building Construction	One	22	8	18
	Two	28	8	19
Architectural Drawing	One	25	7	19
	Two	23	7	16
Building Mathematics	One	21	7	17
	Two	19	7	15

NTI 20 November 1925

The training of building apprentices became part of the curriculum, accounting for over one third of student hours in 1926/27. The following year numbers dropped, the bad weather being partly to blame. Many students came from the country districts and it was not surprising that 'on some evenings they fail, through weather conditions, to put in an appearance'. Yet the governors remained convinced that 'every lad connected with the building

---

[30] NTI 8 May 1925, 26 June 1925, 20 November 1925; BEC 4 July 1925, 10 October 1925, 7 November 1925.

trade who has attended the course of instruction has had a splendid opportunity of gaining a considerable amount of useful knowledge regarding building construction'. For the future, they were going to look at the possibilities of certification, so that 'a definite course of work may be undertaken' leading to examinations.[31]

By the 1930s, the three classes a week had been reduced to two, building construction and practical drawing (geometry). In 1933, the 19 students were using 'models and bricks' provided by E A Bance & Sons of East Woodhay, the beginning of this company's long association with further education in Newbury. No doubt some of its apprentices were on the course in the 1930s, just as they were 15 years later in Ormonde House; and it was E A Bance who was awarded the contract to build the new college in the 1950s.

The building syllabus was practical and relevant to the workplace, covering foundations, brickwork, arches, parapet walls and copings, roofs and roofing, floors, framed partitions, shores and shoreing and gantries. The Institute provided the drawing boards and T-squares, the students brought their own pencils, set squares and instruments. Drawing paper could be bought on the premises for a halfpenny a sheet. The instructor, Mr Woolmer, had a first class City & Guilds Certificate in Builders' Quantity Surveying, and Superintendent Rosling felt that the way the teacher 'arranged the work and dealt with the students' was responsible for the success of the course.[32]

Building classes were more successful than those in mechanical engineering. The ongoing issue in engineering, on the surface at least, was one of poor attendance. In December 1919 the governors informed Mr Plenty that 'unless the attendance of pupils from his works was considerably better next term', the classes would be stopped. In reply, the employer pointed out that his apprentices did not find the teaching 'altogether satisfactory'. There followed a meeting between the employer and the instructors concerned. Unfortunately the outcome of these discussions is not recorded in the Institute's minutes. However, before the next session, the Institute was to make a concerted effort to get more students, 'to make inquiries amongst the

---

[31] NTI 30 March 1928.

[32] NTI Prospectus 1933-34; NTI 3 August 1934.

engineers and mechanics of the town regarding the probability of support for classes in mathematics and mechanics'. Without this support, the classes would be 'discontinued'. In the autumn the governors decided to go ahead with the course, but only one student turned up. Plenty was contacted to find out the reason for this lack of interest and this meeting must have had some effect. The classes went ahead, attendance picked up and the governors decided to take no further action.[33]

In 1921, 17 young men enrolled for mechanical engineering (drawing and theory) and mathematics, and the average attendance was 11. The following year, the classes were 'abandoned' owing to insufficient numbers, but two years later they were running again, this time with 13 students. The Institute persevered, but in the winter of 1925 attendance was 'disappointing'. Classes continued but, a few months later, the governors were again discussing the problem. This time they visited the employer at his Eagle Works in Cheap Street. Mr Plenty wanted the classes to carry on and he would write to the apprentices' parents 'with the view to obtaining students'. Significantly, it was agreed that Mr Corden, the company's chief draughtsman, would draw up the syllabus and organise the classes, to be held on two evenings a week, each one for two hours. This change, a good example of employer/Institute co-operation, should ensure that Plenty's needs would be met.

Organised by the company the course proceeded, but its future was not secure. It would run in 1928 'if sufficient support is forthcoming'. It was advertised in 1929, machine construction and drawing for people 'engaged in practical Engineering during the daytime'. Most of the classroom time would be spent on 'actual machine drawing'. The students did not materialise, however, and by the early 1930s engineering had been dropped from the curriculum.

As engineering stalled, so commerce and building remained the core of the Institute's work. Of the other courses, art was the only one taught regularly, occasionally extending into a third term. Numbers were healthy. There were 49 enrolled in 1921.[34]

---

[33] BEC 30 July 1920, 29 September 1920, 4 November 1920.

[34] NTI 5 December 1921.

The curriculum was not limited to recreational drawing and painting. When a new teacher was needed in 1924, it was felt that the person appointed should be able to move the course 'in the particular directions desirable owing to the nature of the local industries in which some artistic training of employees appears called for'.[35]

Teacher training remained an important part of the work at Northbrook Street. 'The Institute existed as a training centre for teachers, ordinary local primary and secondary teachers.'[36] In 1919 there were 'handwork' classes for teachers, in 1920 pupil teachers came in on Saturday mornings, and in 1933 rural pupil teachers were trained on Thursday evenings. Art was a popular subject. In 1927/28, 28 of the 49 art students (57 per cent) were pupil teachers from the Newbury district's elementary schools. In 1933/34, there were 38 art students, half of whom were pupil teachers attending a special class on Saturday afternoons.

The Institute occasionally organised other courses in the interwar years. French suffered from the lack of a teacher. During the First World War it had been taught by a Belgian refugee, but once the war was over Mademoiselle Castille returned home and the class had to be closed. A few years later Mr Beynon – purveyor of traditional warm winter clothing in his shop in Newbury's Market Place – wanted the class to resume, but the governors wanted him to guarantee enough students. This he could not do and nothing happened.

There were classes in hygiene (1919) and dressmaking (1925). In 1928 there was some discussion about cookery, and in 1934, there were plans for metalwork at the Council School. By this time, the infant section at the school had been closed, all the pupils were at least 11 years old and there were separate departments for boys and girls. A block for practical subjects had been set up with specially equipped rooms: woodwork and metalwork for boys, cookery, laundry and housewifery for girls.

Outside of Newbury, the LEA organised the work in the evening institutes. Abingdon and Wantage had the busiest of the 'urban' classes. In 1922, there were 75 enrolments at Wantage, in

---

[35] *Ibid.*, 19 December 1924.

[36] Interview with Roy Pocock.

applied mechanics, arithmetic, dressmaking, machine construction and drawing, and shorthand. Instruction in engineering had been organised during the war and classes were held in the Wantage Foundry where the students were employed. With over 40 people taking shorthand in 1923, the class had to be split. In the same year, a French class was started.

Fewer 'rural' classes were held, in places such as Arborfield, Boxford, Cold Ash, Didcot, Hermitage, Hungerford, Inkpen, Kintbury, Stockcross, Thatcham, Twyford, Welford and Wickham. In 1921, a total of £650 was allowed for rural evening schools across the county. In 1925, Twyford had a grant of £74, Kintbury and Thatcham £15 each, and Arborfield £4.

'Rural' classes were usually held in LEA schools. The regulations were similar to those in the urban centres. The Education Committee approved – or otherwise – the classes to be organised. The students had to have left elementary school, but secondary school pupils over 14 could attend with their school's permission. Usually there had to be 12 people enrolled before the class could start, and classes were discontinued if the attendance fell below 60 per cent. In the country districts, however, these rules were not always followed. The work at Hermitage was allowed to continue in 1919 with fewer than 12 in each class, while in 1925 classes in Boxford were allowed to start with 11 students. On the other hand, the LEA stopped the gardening classes at Inkpen in 1919 as the only people attending were the teachers from the village school. In 1922, Didcot's request to organise cookery for the British Red Cross Society was turned down. The following year poor attendance meant the closure of classes at Hungerford halfway through the term.

Many of the courses organised in the villages were either recreational or in general education. Cookery, woodwork, dressmaking and needlework were popular. At least 24 people enjoyed woodwork at Welford and Wickham in 1921, whilst two years later the Didcot class was so big it had to be split into two groups. The same happened to cookery at Wallingford. General education was usually arithmetic and English, but there were also classes in citizenship (Welford), geography, mensuration, rural mathematics (Cold Ash), and rural science (Boxford).

The LEA continued to work with other organisations. Much of the agricultural education was carried out by the University

College of Reading, which became the University of Reading in 1927. There were day classes, field trials and advisory visits. In Newbury in 1924, the University College ran a series of evening classes at the Institute.[37] Close co-operation also developed between the LEA and the Berkshire Farmers' Union, Young Farmers' clubs and other agricultural and horticultural societies.

The demands of Berkshire's rural economy meant that agricultural education continued to flourish. The Agricultural Instruction Committee organised training in the work of the farrier, and in the rural skills of hedging and ditching and thatching. There were classes in the production and preservation of farm and garden produce, and in butter- and cheese-making. Special assistance was given to milk producers. When the Second World War broke out the LEA concentrated its attention on agriculture as it had done 25 years before. The drive for self-sufficiency encouraged the production of fruit, vegetables, honey and eggs and the development of rural home economics. The women in the Land Army who volunteered to do farm work were given help and advice. By the end of the war, agricultural education had grown to such an extent that the LEA employed 14 instructors, in agriculture, bee-keeping, dairying, horticulture, poultry-keeping and the rural domestic economy. In 1946 the Agricultural Instruction Committee was wound up and its work given to the Education Committee.

The LEA also worked with the Women's Institutes, the Townswomen's Guilds and the Red Cross. Of these the WIs were by far the most important. The first Institutes had been set up during the First World War to encourage domestic food production, and they quickly spread to become the largest women's organisation in the country. In 1919 the Berkshire Federation was formed and WIs were organised in many villages. From the outset they had an educational purpose and they put on numerous classes in craft work: in basketry, glove-making, quilting, rug-making, slipper-making, toy-making and upholstery. Their meetings also provided women with educational and cultural opportunities in art, music and drama.

Two other organisations made significant contributions to

---

[37] NTI 22 January 1924.

further education opportunities. These were the Extramural Department of the University of Oxford and the WEA. Each of these ran courses in 'liberal' education. Very different from the typical WI class, and from the technical education at the Newbury Institute, their classes tended to be cultural rather than vocational. They were financially supported by the education authority which saw them as 'invaluable' and the partnership became a marked feature in adult education during the interwar years.[38]

The outbreak of war in 1939 severely disrupted the work of the Technical Institute and the next six years were a restless time. Military units moved into Newbury, to the large private houses in the neighbourhood and to premises in the town. The Northbrook Street building was requisitioned. Its rooms were 'unlikely to be available for some time' for teaching purposes. The Oxford & Bucks Light Infantry was billeted there for a while and later the Service Aviation Quartermaster Company used the building. Classes, however, could be organised elsewhere and Superintendent Swingler, who had succeeded Rosling as Education Secretary in 1937, invited the Newbury townsfolk 'who would attend such classes if they were organised' to send 'their names and addresses together with the details of the Class or Classes in which they are interested'.[39] They did, and from 1940, classes were held at the Council School, the Baptist Church premises in Cheap Street and at Mrs Spackman's Commercial School in the Market Place. It was only four years later that some classes were able to return to Northbrook Street.

Building construction (instructor, Mr E Roberts), metalwork and general art and modelling classes were held at the Council School. So were English (Mr J Swift), and bookkeeping (Miss I Partridge). Art was taken by Mr Boyes of the Central School of Arts & Crafts in London. There was also German taught by Miss Moses. The wartime emphasis on physical wellbeing encouraged keep fit activities. Physical training for women (1938) was followed by keep fit classes for women, men and girls. The courses started in the Council School and then transferred to the Baptist Church.

---

[38] Scheme of Further Education 1949, p.11.

[39] *Newbury Weekly News* 23 November 1939. Hereinafter referred to as *NWN*.

The men's class closed in 1941 – perhaps all eligible men had been called up – but the classes for women (instructor, Miss A Claxton) and girls (Miss D Humm) continued.[40]

Other classes shaped by the demands of wartime were 'make and mend', held with the Mothers' Welcome Club at the Lecture Hall in Cromwell Place, and Mrs Spackman's commercial course for men and women in the services. Mrs Spackman taught throughout the war years, her students took Pitman examinations and their successes were publicised in the press. At the end of the war she moved into the building known as The Litten, at the junction of Newtown Road and Pound Street.

In February 1943 the Council School was hit by enemy bombing. This proved to be a defining moment in the history of education in Newbury. The children were evacuated and when they returned to school, it was at Shaw House not Station Road. The Institute's German class eventually resumed at a house in Buckingham Road. Fortunately, the practical subjects block was not damaged, and its accommodation was put to a variety of uses. There were kitchen facilities and a large dining room, and within six months of the bombing raid, in August 1943, a British Restaurant had opened in the building. For the next few years, under the aegis of the Ministry of Food, this simply furnished cafeteria, manned by volunteers, provided cheap and healthy meals without the need for ration coupons.

Before the war was over, new FE courses had been started. Two of these were to be most important in future developments. In 1944 a course began for motor mechanics, two evenings of automobile engineering practice and three hours of English and mathematics on a Saturday morning.[41] The second course was in 'Technical Electricity' for those young men employed by the Wessex Electricity Company. In 1948 two of the courses in Ormonde House were in motor mechanics and electrical engineering. There were also classes in Northbrook Street in foremanship and organisation in industry, precursors of today's management training. Finally, in the autumn of 1945, a course for civil servants was started – English, mathematics, general

---

[40] *Ibid.*, 21 November 1940.

[41] *Ibid.*, 13 April 1944.

knowledge – with examinations. By this time, the war was over and a new superintendent, H G Runham, was in charge. The demand for classes picked up, the LEA saw the potential for FE expansion, and concluded that their part-time superintendents 'needed more time to develop the work'.[42]

Teaching had resumed at Northbrook Street in 1944. By 1947/48 there were 422 enrolments, over twice as many as had been customary in the interwar years. Since April 1946, the large downstairs room had been leased to Newbury Boys' Club so most of the FE classes were held upstairs. There was a similar increase in activity in the village institutes, and the picture was the same across Berkshire. The troops came home, life returned to normal and social activity resumed its peacetime pattern.

WI courses were flourishing as well. Their members had been active during the war, in billeting and welfare work; but their most important contribution was in food production, the same imperative which had led to the first Institutes being set up during the First World War. Fresh fruit and vegetables were sold at WI markets and with imported jam and sugar at a premium, jam-making became a patriotic duty.[43] The war also gave an impetus to rural crafts which in peacetime had been little more than interesting hobbies. Home weaving enjoyed a new popularity after 1945, as clothes were rationed. WI classes were in demand: slipper-making at Bucklebury, glove-making at Thatcham, embroidery at Woolhampton. The standards were high and the LEA was in no doubt of their significance. 'With a membership of over 700 in 137 Institutes, the (Berkshire) Federation exerts an influence over education in the widest sense which, in a mainly rural County, is of the greatest importance.'[44]

There was also a new organiser of further education in Newbury in the post-war years. This was the Community Centre.

In 1944 the Ministry of Labour had organised a conference in the town of representatives of business and voluntary

---

[42] Minutes of Further Education Subcommittee 12 December 1947. Hereinafter referred to as FESC.

[43] Norman Longmate, *How We Lived Then*, (London: Pimlico, 2002), pp.369-372.

[44] Scheme of Further Education 1949, p.11.

organisations. They were to set up a Social Centre 'to provide facilities for Social, Educational and Recreational interest open to all adult residents and transferred war workers in Newbury and District'. Decisions were quickly made and a centre opened in rooms over Marks & Spencer in Northbrook Street. Within a year over 750 people had joined, and there were groups/classes in country dancing, discussion, drama, first aid, 'make do and mend' – soon renamed dressmaking – and table tennis. Ballroom dancing, a cycling club, an orchestra and a choral society soon followed.[45] In the autumn of 1946 the Social Centre, now known as the Community Centre, was transferred to the two-storied practical subjects block at the former Council School, initially sharing the premises with the British Restaurant. From 1947, its cooking facilities were used for the LEA's school meals service. The Newbury Air Training Corps (ATC) squadron also used the building, renting a room on the first floor for one evening a week.

Mr Croker, the Community Centre warden, was not immediately enamoured with his new surroundings. The building had been a school and the 'effect' of this remained. However, he was confident that with 'modern methods' in interior decoration, 'this psychological reaction will fade away'. Evening classes were usually held in the rooms above the canteen. One of the most popular was Iris Brook's ballroom dancing class. There was also a demand for physical training, but without suitable accommodation, nothing was organised. The Community Centre worked closely with the Technical Institute and 'certain practical classes', including Mrs Runham's dressmaking, were held at Northbrook Street during 1946 and 1947.

'But somewhat indefinite and superficial'

It can be seen, then, that there was some growth of further education in Berkshire in the first half of the 20th century. The development was shaped by the social and economic environment, and Berkshire outside of Reading was a predominantly rural county.

---

[45] Social Service in a Country Market Town, Being the Annual Report of the Newbury and District Social Centre 1944-45. In Newbury Community Centre Records.

Many people worked in agriculture and its related industries, especially in the remoter western areas around Newbury. There were no large manufacturing towns as there were in the Midlands and the north of England. Indeed, there was an 'absence of major industries' in the county and the demand for 'instruction in technical subjects' was therefore restricted. The biggest towns, Maidenhead, Newbury and Windsor, had populations of less than 20,000. It is hard to avoid the conclusion that compared to developments in other parts of the country, further education in Berkshire had been limited. There had been some expansion since the 1890s; but most of the classes were in either agricultural or in recreational subjects distant from the world of the workplace. There had been only limited development in 'useful' and 'practical' education. There were successful courses in building and commerce at the Institute in Northbrook Street, less effective attempts at engineering. Moreover, Newbury's courses were usually at the elementary level and, with the exception of one or two commercial subjects, did not lead to qualifications. Not surprisingly, in 1949, the Berkshire Education Committee found the county's overall FE provision to be 'somewhat indefinite and superficial':

> In a mainly rural County, with no heavy industries, technical provision for further education has in the past been limited, and the Authority has tended to rely on facilities provided by other authorities (especially in Reading, Oxford and London) within comparatively easy reach outside their area.[46]

Many Berkshire students enrolled in colleges in Reading, Oxford and London. A few travelled further afield, to Guildford, High Wycombe, Slough and Swindon. Reading was the most popular destination. During 1947/48, about 600 students from Berkshire LEA were studying at Reading Technical College. Some of them were doing 'advanced' courses and, significantly, some were on day release, supported by their employers. There were another 450 Berkshire students at college in Oxford. Where students lived or worked usually determined their choice of college.

---

[46] Scheme of Further Education 1949, pp.6-7.

Many of those working in the London area 'naturally wish to take advantage of courses planned near their place of employment'. One such young man lived in Newbury, worked for the Great Western Railway in London, and took a course in bookkeeping at Marylebone College of Commerce.[47]

---

[47] FESC 12 December 1947.

2

AN ADVENTURE INTO
A LAND OF PROMISE

The Education Act of 1944

The new order in education created by the 1944 Act
was significant for many things. Not least was the
growing up of the 'Cinderella' of the service, that is to
say, Further Education. For a long time before 1944
Further Education had been for many an unwanted child
and most Authorities, although providing a number of
evening classes in their urban centres, had done little to
establish comprehensive systems of education for persons
who had left school. Since 1944, however, 'Cinderella'
has in Berkshire been led towards the fullness of life
which befits her new status; her two sisters, Primary and
Secondary Education, unlike the sisters in the story, have
given considerable help to her so that an educational
system may be established and maintained for people of
the County of all ages.

Since 1945, Education in Berkshire

The General Election of 1945 was a 'turning-point' election
of the 20th century. The landslide victory for the Labour
Party was, in part, the public's reaction to the 'hungry '30s'
when the Conservatives were in power. The feeling was that never
again should there be a return to mass unemployment. Britain's
first-ever Labour Government with an overall majority in the

House of Commons, led by Prime Minister Clement Attlee, was in power for six years. The years 1945 to 1951 are often referred to as an age of austerity. The pound was devalued and there were strikes and fuel shortages. Government controls over economic life set up during the war continued; so did conscription in the form of National Service. Wartime identity cards and ration books lasted deep into the peace. Clothes were rationed until 1949, petrol until 1950. Food rationing did not end until 1954 when, for the first time in many people's memories, they could buy what they liked.

Yet the Labour Government was elected on a radical manifesto and these were also years of far-reaching economic and social reform. The coal industry, the railways, the gas and electricity industries and the Bank of England were taken into public ownership. The familiar scaffolding of the welfare state was assembled. The 'new Jerusalem' was built as the government extended the social security system, provided thousands of council houses, established the National Health Service and worked to maintain full employment.

Attlee's radical government also introduced significant changes to the education system. The Education Act of 1944 was put together during the war by R A Butler, a leading Conservative reformer, and is widely known as the Butler Act. The Labour Government and the LEAs started to implement the legislation once the war was over. At last, it was felt by many that the criticisms of Britain's educational deficiencies in comparison to other European countries would be met. Vigorous action and advance were now expected and encouraged by the central government.[1]

The legislation is usually remembered for the reorganisation of primary and secondary education which it set in motion. Significantly, however, the Act was also responsible for the expansion of further education opportunities. Section 41 of the 1944 Act declared that: 'It shall be the duty of every local education authority to secure the provision for their area of *adequate facilities* [my italics] for further education.' Further education was defined as comprising: 'a) full-time and part-time education for persons over compulsory school age; and b) leisure-

---

[1] Kenneth Morgan, *The People's Peace*, (Oxford: Oxford University Press, 1992), p.40.

time occupation, in such organised cultural training and recreative activities as are suited to their requirements for any persons over compulsory school age who are able and willing to profit by the facilities provided for that purpose.'[2]

Section 41 was one of the least contentious parts of the act but its importance must not be underestimated. For the first time in the history of education in England and Wales, a statutory obligation was placed on local authorities to provide further education. In each LEA area, this meant an adequate range of courses to meet local needs organised either 'directly' or by the LEA working 'in co-operation with other bodies'. With all the financial resources of local government behind it, the LEA's potential to contribute to post-school learning was an exciting challenge.

Much of the thinking behind this extension of FE was to enable Britain to compete with its major industrial challengers by improving the education and training of the workforce. Thus were the arguments of the later 19th century heard again in the corridors of power. At the Board of Education between 1941 and 1945, R A Butler had been concerned about the lack of opportunities in vocational education for young people once they had left school. He had spoken to wartime Prime Minister Winston Churchill concerning the need for more industrial and technical training. At the annual conference of the National Union of Teachers he had argued for a 'more expert training for industry, with a revivified system of apprenticeship and with a practical form of continued education later to be called county colleges'. In a wireless broadcast to the nation, he had spoken of the importance of further education and the opportunity for young workers being released from industry to study. Butler wanted young people to 'continue under educational influence up to 18 years of age either by staying on at secondary school or by attending county colleges'.[3]

These sentiments were enshrined in the most ambitious proposal of his 1944 Act. Compulsory day release to what were to be called 'county colleges' was to be introduced for all 15- to

---

[2] Scheme of Further Education 1949, p.5.

[3] R A Butler, *The Art of the Possible*, (Harmondsworth: Penguin, 1973), pp. 95-97, 119-120.

18-year-olds who were not in full-time education. No longer was day release to be at the discretion of the employer; rather, all young people at work were to be entitled to it.

A national system, locally administered

With the 1944 Act, the Ministry of Education replaced the Board of Education. Schools and FE colleges and institutes were now under the direct supervision of a cabinet minister, recognition of the importance of education in the framework of government. The Ministry exerted a degree of control over the LEAs. It allocated money to the local authorities as the government's contribution to the cost of education in their areas. This supplemented the LEA revenue from the rates. The Ministry controlled educational building, deciding which authorities were to have new buildings, and when and where they were to be built. Ministry approval was necessary for an LEA to borrow money for a major building programme. More generally, through a stream of circulars and memoranda, the Ministry sometimes instructed, at other times advised, LEAs on a wide range of topics.

His/Her Majesty's Inspectors, the HMIs, were the Ministry's field force responsible for the regular inspection of the educational services. Small and streamlined, they worked alongside the local inspectors and were responsible for monitoring the quality of the provision in the schools and colleges. Unlike today, there were few targets set nationally or within institutions and little, if any, formal self-assessment of what was going on. The first county-wide HMI inspection of further education in Berkshire was in 1949. Six years later, in 1955, it was the turn of South Berks College in Newbury. Inspections were followed by HMI reports, the content of which would shape a college's future development. Less visibly, the HMIs acted as consultants, addressing problems in institutions and advising on a range of issues.

The local education authority was responsible for the day to day running of the education service. Berkshire's elected County Council, acting as the LEA, was the main engine of the county's provision. The principle of an earlier Education Act of 1902 was reaffirmed in 1944: locally elected representatives were best placed to decide on local needs. The LEA was responsible for the planning, building, opening and closing of schools and FE colleges and institutes, as well as for most of the other services including special education, school meals and school transport. W F Herbert was Berkshire's Director of Education until 1954, when he was succeeded by T D W Whitfield. Many of the LEA staff at Shire Hall in Reading worked with the schools, but some of them had specific responsibility for further education, as advisers, organisers and local inspectors.

With the new responsibilities of the 1944 Act, the Berkshire Education Committee set up several new subcommittees. The Further Education Subcommittee (FESC) was given responsibility for non-compulsory further education. Meeting about six times a year, its work was important and enabled 'Cinderella' to grow to maturity. It dealt with matters to do with buildings, courses, equipment and staffing. It was also in charge of the Youth Employment Service – the forerunner of the Careers Service – the Youth Service, teacher-training courses and county scholarships. It also took over responsibility for agricultural education.

The FESC met for the first time in September 1946. Some of its responsibilities went beyond the local authority area. One such issue was that of out-county students. Another was that of the duplication of courses which could become a problem once colleges started to expand. LEAs would need to co-operate with each other. In 1946, the Ministry of Education was aware of the problems caused by the proliferation of advanced vocational courses:

> It has often happened in the past that when a college, staffed and equipped for advanced technical studies, has been established in a town, it has attracted great numbers of students from far and near … In many cases, however, this attraction of students to a neighbouring college has led to confusion and duplication in the region concerned, with the result that small classes in advanced and specialised courses have been maintained in several centres within the area, with consequent waste of teaching effort and money.[4]

---

[4] Ministry of Education Pamphlet No. 8, 1946, in its advice to LEAs, in Southern Regional Council for Further Education 21st Anniversary 1947-1968, p.1. Hereinafter referred to as SRCFE.

The Ministry thought that one way forward was to put in place regional advisory councils which would maintain 'an effective and continuous survey of the educational needs of the area' and recommend 'sound and economic ways of meeting them'. Each council would advise the LEAs and colleges in its region, seeking to co-ordinate provision by identifying deficiencies and avoiding unnecessary duplication.

The Ministry had its way. FE advisory councils were set up by voluntary co-operation between education authorities, and they were financed by them. The Southern Regional Council for Further Education held its inaugural meeting in Reading in 1947. It represented the county councils of Berkshire, Dorset, Hampshire, the Isle of Wight, Oxfordshire, West Sussex and Wiltshire, and the county boroughs of Bournemouth, Oxford, Portsmouth, Reading and Southampton.

The Southern Regional Council influenced the provision of advanced courses: degree and postgraduate work, Higher National Diplomas/Certificates (HND/HNCs) and those courses, such as teacher-training, which led to professional qualifications. The Ministry's policy was to concentrate such programmes in a small number of the larger colleges; consequently, all the institutions within the region had to submit to its regional council any proposal for a new advanced course. For part-time advanced courses, such as the HNC, council members had the final say over whether or not the course should be allowed at a particular college. They would come to their decision based on the facilities available, the number of potential students and whether or not the qualification was available at a neighbouring institution.

Southern Regional Council decisions affected developments at South Berks College in the 1950s. Newbury's governors wanted to introduce HNC courses but permission was refused. From 1948 to 1960, all the FE work at Newbury remained non-advanced.

Also involved in the administration of education in Berkshire in the post-war years were the divisional education executives. Set up by the 1944 Act, in Maidenhead, Newbury and Windsor, they began their work in 1947 with responsibilities delegated to them by the LEA. The divisions kept the educational requirements of their district under review and advised the LEA. Most of their work was with the schools: the appointment of staff and governors, the use and maintenance of buildings, and matters such as pupil attendance, school transport, maintenance and travel allowances and the organisation of visits and games. However, the LEA wanted them to play a part in post-school education as well, and they were represented on the governing bodies of Berkshire's FE colleges.

The Scheme of Further Education 1949

> Since 1949 the progress of further education has been rapid and the service is very different from what it was 20 years ago. The main lines of development, however, were laid down in 1949.
>
> *Report on Education in Berkshire 1967-70*

Following Section 41 of the Butler Act, each local authority was required to submit a plan to the Ministry of Education showing how it intended to develop its 'adequate facilities' for further education. The plan was to cover a five-year period and was to include reference to county colleges and compulsory day release for school leavers. Berkshire's development plan was the work of the Further Education Subcommittee.

By the early summer of 1947, the preliminary arrangements for FE developments were under way. FESC members did not have to work in isolation. The Southern Regional Council wanted LEAs to confer with each other to ensure a 'measure of uniformity in the presentation of individual schemes'. Meetings took place between representatives from Berkshire, Buckinghamshire and Oxfordshire; and following a Berkshire LEA visit to Swindon in Wiltshire, an agreement was reached whereby the two authorities would accept each other's students on the same basis. There was a lot of discussion in Shire Hall about the provision of county colleges. Months of meetings took place. Berkshire's plan was to have been submitted to the Ministry by 31 March 1948 but the deadline was not met and an extension of six months was given. More time was needed, another six months passed, and still the work was not finished. There were discussions with HMIs about the results of a survey of the county's evening institutes during

1948/49;[5] and important talks were held with the Ministry about the prospect for new buildings.

In September 1949, 18 months after the original deadline, the plan was finished. Forty pages long, the Scheme of Further Education was sent off to London for approval. Months later, the LEA received the Minister's preliminary comments. As we shall see, much had already happened in the county by the time the Scheme was finally approved in 1952.[6]

The Scheme had to take account of what had been achieved in the preceding 50 years, but it is an important document as it would determine the shape of further education in Berkshire in the 1950s and beyond. Its eventual implementation meant that all parts of the county were provided with 'adequate' FE facilities. Across the Southern Region as a whole, these years were 'remarkable for the development of the Further Education service as the plans prepared by the local education authorities began to take effect'.[7]

Lucian Oldershaw, the chairman of Berkshire's Education Committee, wrote the foreword to the development plan, capturing both the excitement of the time and the challenges which lay ahead:

> Here is a preliminary plan for Further Education in the County of Berkshire for a period optimistically regarded as five years ahead. It is an adventure into a land of promise, charted for the first time in that great map of all the regions of the educational world, the Education Act of 1944. It is an adventure that we must make under the compulsion of a statutory 'shall' and it is an adventure that we should make gladly and hopefully, for we are now allowed officially to regard education as a process that is never finished and great opportunities are afforded in the new country for improving the talents and strengthening the morale of our people. We must do what we can to

---

[5] BEC 2 May 1947, 25 June 1948; FESC 9 April 1948, 14 May 1948, 31 May 1949.

[6] 'The Ministry of Education have now informed the Authority that the Minister approves their Scheme of FE, as amended.' FESC 14 March 1952.

[7] SRCFE 21st Anniversary, *op.cit.*, p.2.

take advantage of these new duties and to implement these new opportunities.

We can see vistas ahead and in them new Technical Institutes, and the County Colleges with their possibilities of a strengthened Youth Service and a wider adult education.

The excitement was genuine, but it was tempered with a little anxiety. 'Doubts are bound to arise', he wrote. 'County Colleges? Are they to remain castles in the air? Can we afford them?' Ahead lay uncharted waters, yet he was clear about the education authority's responsibility:

We have to assume that the Act will be carried out and plan accordingly, having regard to the particular needs of our own County. It is a Ministerial responsibility to correlate the ideal with the practical, to decide whether the gain to the Nation's efficiency outweighs the expense of securing it ... But we are only asked at present for a preliminary plan for our exciting adventure – and here it is.[8]

The Scheme's proposals were 'necessarily flexible'. This was because colleges were different from schools:

There can be no question of imposing a set pattern on any given number of individuals. The essence of further education (apart from County Colleges) is that it is voluntary and as such differs in character from primary and secondary education. The main need is that the interests of persons of varied ages, occupations and temperaments throughout the County should be appreciated and a quick response made to them. The machinery used will vary. It is always a question of finding the persons who as teachers or administrators will be most able to give encouragement.[9]

---

[8] Scheme of Further Education 1949, p.3.

[9] *Ibid.*, pp.6-7.

The Scheme's context was the county economy, the distribution of population, the importance of agriculture and the limited industrial development. Around 270,000 people lived in the LEA's area. It was mainly rural, the main occupation was agriculture and the people who worked on the land were 'scattered' throughout the county. There was no major town, although the county borough of Reading with its own LEA was a 'natural centre'. Beyond the county boundary were large towns with which there was 'naturally close connection'. For those people in the east of Berkshire, London was 'so near and so easily accessible' that in education, as in other activities, no local provision could hope 'fully to compete'. Moreover, many people who lived in the county worked in London, and it was 'natural that they should also take advantage of the further education facilities provided there'.

The LEA's largest towns were Maidenhead (26,000), and Windsor (21,000). Newbury, 'the town which is furthest in any direction from another large town', had a population of 18,000. Somewhat isolated, it was surrounded by downland where the 'population is sparse and communications poor'. The smaller towns, Abingdon, Didcot and Wokingham, had between 5,000 and 10,000 people. Bracknell, Faringdon, Wallingford and Wantage had between 1,000 and 5,000 inhabitants. There was 'growing development' at Harwell, where the Atomic Energy Research Establishment (AERE) had been set up in 1946, but few people at the time could have realised how significant this was to be in the growth of further education in the area in the years to come.

The county's industrial development was limited to 'pockets of engineering' at Maidenhead, Newbury, Abingdon and Woodley. There was no 'heavy industry' and no 'overwhelming local demand for a particular training'. This was a problem for the further education planners as it was 'all the more difficult to meet in one centre demands which tend to be both small and varied'.

Overall, the Scheme concluded, there were few vocational education opportunities and there was much work to do:

> In a mainly rural County, with no heavy industries, technical provision for further education has in the past been limited, and the Authority has tended to rely on facilities provided

by other authorities (especially in Reading, Oxford and London) within comparatively easy reach outside their area. There is also the difficulty that, as far as Secondary Technical Education is concerned, the description in the Development Plan of Berkshire as 'a rural County which in 1945 had no technical provision' still applies. If the present demand in the County is to be met, and if an effective contribution is to be made to the technical efficiency which the nation needs, the Authority realises that considerable development of technical education, especially with regard to equipment, is essential.

Yet the adventure had already started before the ink on the Scheme was dry. Classes had been disrupted between 1939 and 1945, but once the war was over, there was a rapid growth in evening classes. There was also the start of technical courses in the daytime and, crucially, the LEA wanted to develop this form of training.

Consequently, in 1948, while the FE Scheme was still under discussion, the Education Committee took an important decision. New institutes were to be set up in Maidenhead, Newbury and Windsor. Each centre was to be run by a newly appointed superintendent who was to develop courses in the town and give 'help and advice' in the surrounding village institutes. Crucially, these were to be full-time appointments, not part-time as in previous years. This was one of the ways by which the education authority was to meet its new FE responsibilities. A year into the job, and each superintendent was given the title of 'Principal', thereby underlining the importance of the work they were doing.

In 1948/49 the new institutes organised day-release courses in building, engineering and other subject areas. There was also a course in building, for half a day a week at least, at Wantage.

Table 6 Berkshire FE: Day-Release Enrolment 1948/49

FE Centre	Course	Under 18	Over 18
Maidenhead Technical Institute	Building	29	8
	Bakery	10	18
	Pre-nursing	48	2
	Motor Engineering	16	3
	Mech. Engineering	17	3
	Commerce	35	1
	Total	**155**	**35**
Newbury Institute of Further Education	Building	62	15
	Motor Engineering	12	–
	Elec. Engineering	42	27
	Total	**116**	**42**
Windsor Institute of Further Education	Building	23	2
	Motor Engineering	11	1
	General (GPO and Caley's)	88	–
	Total	**122**	**3**
Wantage	Building	13	–
	Total	**13**	**–**

Scheme of Further Education 1949

The plan for the future was expansion. Day release, observed the Scheme's authors, was 'meeting the need for better vocational training' and was to be extended 'until attendance at County Colleges becomes compulsory'.[10]

Maidenhead Institute opened in the same building in Marlow Road as the 50-year-old School of Art and Technical Institute. It had the biggest day-release programme in 1948/49, 190 students and six courses. Pre-nursing was the most popular programme, followed by building and commerce. All the work was part time but it was confidently expected that full-time courses would be developed 'especially in technical subjects for students of 15 to 16 years in order to lay a better foundation for courses of National Certificate standard'.

Within a year the education authority had purchased a second building in Maidenhead, Boyn Hill House, and this became the FE Institute's new home. The School of Art remained in Marlow

---

[10] *Ibid.*, p.16.

Road and developed as a specialist college with its own Principal. With no other art school between Maidenhead and London, it hoped to attract students from outside Berkshire, particularly from Oxfordshire and Buckinghamshire.

The Institute of Further Education in Newbury opened in 1948. Ormonde House was purchased to provide better accommodation than was available in the Northbrook Street property. Rooms in the old Institute continued to be used but most of the teaching was transferred to the Oxford Road. Day-release building and engineering courses had started and these were to be extended. Workshops were to be set up for technical subjects, and as in the east of the county, the intention was to start full-time courses for school leavers 'as the demand increases'.

The Windsor Institute also opened in 1948, but its launch was more protracted, so much so that 12 months went by with the LEA still looking for satisfactory accommodation. 'Attempts have been made to find a suitable house, which with the addition of temporary buildings could be adapted for use as a centre, but difficulties have arisen in each case, and after a thorough search throughout the town it does not seem that such a house is likely to be found in Windsor.' Schools were used in the evening but premises had to be hired for day-release courses. These arrangements were 'inconvenient' and it was hoped to build a permanent centre in 1950:

> A Further Education centre is needed in Windsor and for this a small building is proposed as a nucleus round which huts can be grouped ... In a town the size of Windsor where there is less specialised demand for technical courses it seems that a building of this character, to which huts could be added for workshops and additional classrooms, would appropriately meet local requirements for some time.[11]

The Institutes at Maidenhead, Newbury and Windsor were at the centre of the county's FE developments in the 1950s. Each one had a governing body, with representatives from the LEA, the borough and rural district councils, the education division,

[11] *Ibid.,* pp.9, 33.

the chamber of commerce and the trades' council. The governors were to 'review and encourage demands for further education' and 'make as effective provision as possible to meet them'. Advisory committees gave employers the opportunity to get involved and shape developments. Employer participation was also encouraged by the necessary liaison over day-release arrangements. The School of Art at Maidenhead had its own governing body.

The new centres, particularly at Newbury and Maidenhead, did well in their first year. However, the LEA felt that a fourth institute was necessary because of the 'growing importance' of the AERE at Harwell and the consequent housing developments in nearby towns. Steventon was thought to be the ideal place, near enough to Abingdon, Didcot, Wallingford and Wantage. Many people in the northern parts of the county were 'naturally drawn to Oxford' and students would continue to go there for 'advanced' courses. However, 'the demands from all sources on the Oxford Schools of Technology, Art and Commerce' were becoming 'increasingly heavy'; hence the need for a new institute in north-west Berkshire.

The authors of the 1949 Scheme felt that the demand for vocational courses would remain 'scattered', while the 'more specialised courses and equipment' could only be provided in the 'larger centres'. The new institutes, then, were to concentrate on non-advanced work. 'Fuller provision' was intended 'for pre-Senior and Senior 1 work and for particular courses (eg Inter-BSc at Newbury) for which there is sufficient local demand'. Senior courses were the Ordinary National Certificates (ONCs). With more workshops, it was intended to provide second-year ONC courses at Newbury and Maidenhead in 1949 and a third-year programme in 1950. This would allow all three years to be completed without the students having to transfer elsewhere. A course in workshop practice was also planned for 1949. This would enable students 'to take progressive and systematic courses in preparation for National Certificate and City & Guilds courses in the County, which would be linked where necessary with Institutions of other areas, and in particular with Reading Technical College'.

Such non-advanced ONC and City & Guilds work was to be at the heart of Berkshire FE. For advanced courses, students would continue to go out-county. Indeed, the number going to Oxford and Reading would increase as those colleges in their turn developed their curriculum. In addition, some students would continue to go to London where the courses were 'generally of a high standard, the demands for which the Authority would never be in a position to satisfy within its own area'.

'Further education courses are hampered unless there is in any given locality a person able and willing to stimulate interest and organise classes.' One of the significant breaks with the past in the post-war years was the increasing number of people in FE who were employed 'whole time'. Full-time superintendents were not restricted to the new institutes and the School of Art. In 1949 four more were appointed, to the evening institutes at Abingdon, Didcot, Wokingham and Woodley. This meant that all the main centres of population had full-time officers and in the smaller centres, as at Woodley, full-time appointments were to combine organising the work with teaching duties. Two years later, as we shall see, there were full-time area superintendents covering the whole of the county.

During 1948/49 evening courses were held at 76 institutes in Berkshire. The larger institutes had advisory committees of men and women from industry and commerce. Traditionally, evening courses had a 'strong vocational (mainly commercial) bias'. Now the curriculum was broadened. The policy in the post-war years, 'in accordance with local demand', was to offer education in the 'widest' sense. 'Both the vocational and non-vocational aspects of continued education will be included, but rather than a sharp distinction being made between them, a balanced programme of further education is the aim.' The broad and balanced curriculum became a characteristic of further education in the 1950s.

The FE Development Plan did not want to restrict the Institutes exclusively to teaching. 'No hard and fast line can be, or should be drawn between education and social and recreational provision.' Institutes were to develop a 'strong social side' with dramatic and musical societies, sports clubs and 'holiday and other visits'.

The anticipated expansion of evening work was to be encouraged in a number of ways. Course publicity was to be 'fuller and more attractive', classroom accommodation 'more adequate and comfortable'. Most importantly, the number of instructors and organisers was to be increased. Teachers were to be appointed, 'especially experienced in further education' and able to give their 'whole time' to it. A laudable aim, but recruitment could be difficult and advertisements for part-time instructors met with mixed results. 'Evening Institute work is handicapped by the fact that the present rates of payment have not attracted some of the more competent instructors.'

LEA schools – empty in the evenings with a caretaker on hand to turn out the lights and lock up – remained the venue for many of the night classes. Community Centres were also used. Some of these, like the one in Newbury, had begun during the war to provide recreational activities; now their educational side was to be developed. The County Council financially supported the centres at Dedworth, Didcot, Lambourn, Maidenhead and Newbury. It paid the rent and the warden's salary and also contributed towards the wages of a caretaker/cleaner. It was hoped to improve such centres and in any new development, buildings were to 'attract by having the atmosphere of the home rather than of an institution'.

Evening classes were also held in village halls. The 1920s had been a great era for village hall building in England. By 1949, there were 134 such halls in Berkshire, and there were plans to build more with money from the government. The LEA was 'fully alive' to the importance of the village hall in making available FE opportunities across its rural heartland:

> Although to some extent people can be drawn to the market towns to participate in education activities, each village should be encouraged to develop its own Further Education activities, and these demand in the village no less than in the towns their own home.

The LEA was to continue to support those organisations which had been active in FE in the interwar years. Of these the WIs remained the most important. In 1948/49, there were 7,642 students in 420 classes held at 76 centres in Berkshire:

> Women's Institute classes are organised through Evening Institutes and there is the closest co-operation with regard to instruction in subjects relating to agriculture, horticulture

and rural domestic economy. The Federation also holds its own courses, residential and otherwise, and takes an active interest in all matters affecting village life. [12]

In 1948, Denman College outside Abingdon opened as a residential college for WI members. Named after Lady Trudie Denman, the first chairwoman of the national federation, 1,000 students passed through its doors in the first 12 months.

The University of Oxford's Extramural Department and the WEA continued to organise FE classes. The Extramural Department had a resident tutor in Berkshire and the WEA employed an organiser in the Reading district. 'It is anticipated that their activities in both stimulating and in meeting requests will grow in the coming years, and that co-operation with the Authority will be increasingly close.'[13] Other organisations whose activities would continue to be 'welcomed' by the LEA included the Townswomen's Guilds and the Red Cross.

Agricultural education, which had played a significant part in Berkshire FE in the first half of the twentieth century, was to be extended in the post-war years. At its centre was a new agricultural institute.

Hall Place Estate, with its large Georgian mansion, lay in a 'well-wooded and pleasant district' in the village of Burchett's Green, near Maidenhead. In 1948 the County Council bought the house, its farm buildings and part of the estate and it became the home of the Berkshire Institute of Agriculture. This was a residential college with room for up to 40 students – from Berkshire, Buckinghamshire and Oxfordshire – and the teaching and domestic staff. It opened in 1949 with a one-year full-time course in general agriculture and dairy farming, for people with 'at least one year's practical farm experience'. Thirty-two students moved into the house, looked after by a matron. Outside on the

---

[12] WI classes were held at Appleton, Barkham, Bisham, Blewbury, Botley, Bucklebury, Cockpole Green, Compton, Cookham Dean, Crowthorne, Cumnor, Eastbury, Embrook, Fernham, Great Coxwell, Hagbourne, Hermitage, Marcham, Northcourt, Old Windsor, Priestwood, Shrivenham, Steventon, Sunningwell, Thatcham, Uffington, and Wittenham. *Ibid.,* pp.11-12.

[13] *Ibid..*

farm were six Jersey cows, some beef cattle, two horses and a few pigs.[14]

The Institute developed as the county's centre for agricultural education. It is true that by the end of the 1950s agriculture was no longer the mainstay of Berkshire's economy, and the number of people depending on the land for their livelihood had declined. Yet farming remained important and the demand for courses continued at Burchett's Green, in the FE colleges and in the evening institutes.

The county's agricultural programme was a varied one. There were part-time day and evening courses in agriculture, horticulture, fruit preservation, bee-keeping and poultry-keeping. There were classes in bookkeeping, farm calculations and land measurement. In the later '50s, a course in general agriculture was taught at night school. Young farmers learned how to drive tractors and as machines replaced manual work, there were classes in repair and maintenance engineering. At the same time, the LEA continued to work closely with the Farmers' Union and the Young Farmers, while staff from Shire Hall made frequent visits to agricultural and horticultural societies, allotment holders and village produce associations.

Many of the attitudes towards food production, which the government had encouraged during the war years, continued into peacetime. There was much interest in the rural domestic economy with classes on the 'utilisation' of home-grown food, including bacon-curing, and lectures on the 'care and preservation of clothing'. In 1951, the Rural Domestic Economy Centre opened in the grounds of Denman College. People went to the Centre – affectionately known as Homeacres – to learn about bee-keeping, poultry and home-produced food.

The Institute of Agriculture was one of two residential colleges set up at this time. The other was a teacher-training college for women in the former home of the Marquis of Downshire at Easthampstead Park outside Wokingham. This was Berkshire LEA's first higher education establishment. It opened in 1948 with 41 students.

---

[14] Education in the Royal County of Berkshire 1967-70, *op.cit.*, p.87; Scheme of Further Education 1949, p.17.

County colleges or castles in the air?

The most ambitious proposal of the 1944 Education Act was that of compulsory day release to county colleges for all those 15- to 18-year-olds who were in work. This underlined the importance of vocational training for the youngest strata of the nation's workforce. The Ministry of Education was to make the ultimate decision about this new and radical idea; all the LEA could do was work out the number of such colleges considered to be necessary in Berkshire and wait to see what happened.[15] The Ministry did not specify when the programme was to start but the LEA assumed that it would be within five years; hence the full title of the 1949 document was the 'Scheme of Further Education and Plan for County Colleges'.

Berkshire planned for five such colleges, at Maidenhead, Newbury, Steventon, Windsor and Wokingham. The buildings would be new, with 'well equipped rooms for class and practical work' and 'facilities for physical training and recreation'. At Steventon, the college for 350 would also be used as the county's fourth FE Institute. One of the colleges, 'preferably in the western part of the County', would require halls of residence. This was because some young people might find it difficult to attend for one day a week over a long period of time, but they would be able to attend every day for a number of weeks over a shorter period. Such a pattern of study would suit farm workers in the winter months. For this residential college, a new building was not necessary. Rather, it was hoped 'to purchase and adapt existing properties with adequate grounds for development of recreational activities'.[16]

A lot went on in further education in the 1950s but the county colleges never emerged. They remained 'castles in the air'. Yet the idea lingered on. When in 1956 the LEA reviewed its achievements since 1945, it included the following comment:

> With the possible exception of further buildings for the initiation of new senior and advanced technical courses required by industry, there will remain only the building

---

[15] Lucian Oldershaw in *NWN* 27 October 1949.

[16] Scheme of Further Education 1949, pp.14-16, 33.

of accommodation specifically required for County College attendance when the release from work on one day a week, or its equivalent, becomes a legal obligation under the 1944 Act for all young persons between the ages of 15 and 18.[17]

It did not happen. Neither did compulsory day release. Although the number of companies releasing their young workers increased, it remained at the employer's discretion.

Most importantly, however, many of the other commitments in Berkshire's Scheme of Further Education were realised. The pace of change quickened, the adventure into the land of promise began for an increasing number of men and women. One of the most reliable indicators of progress in further education is the annual student hour total: the number of hours spent by students in FE classes during the academic year. In the three years from 1948/49 to 1950/51, the county's student hour total increased from 268,000 to 420,000.[18] At the institutes at Newbury, Maidenhead and Windsor new courses were started, more accommodation was found, and full-time lecturers were employed. Students completed ONCs locally and did not have to go out-county. Work was also developed at the specialist establishments, the School of Art and the Institute of Agriculture; and the evening institutes were busy with both vocational and non-vocational programmes.

One of the LEA's proposals in 1949 was to organise its FE work by geographical area. This was considered the best way of meeting the needs of the post-school population. Two years later, this area organisation was achieved. At its centre were two colleges of further education.

The reorganisation of 1951

In 1951 the institutes at Maidenhead and Windsor were joined together as the *East Berks College of Further Education*. The college remained responsible for further education in the two towns, and it was also given control over the work in the

---

[17] Since 1945, *op.cit.*, p.32.

[18] *Ibid.*, p.31.

outlying districts. Evening institutes, such as those at Crookham, Cranborne and Sunningdale, were affiliated to the college. At the other end of the county, Newbury Institute became the *South Berks College of Further Education.* Its work, too, was extended into the surrounding area, in its affiliated institutes at Compton, Hungerford, Lambourn and Thatcham. From now on, East Berks and South Berks were to be known as area colleges. They each had an area Principal although it remained to be seen whether the work of supervising the affiliated institutes would be 'best undertaken by the Principal himself or by a full-time member of his staff'.[19]

To complete this reorganisation, there remained those parts of the county beyond the catchment area of the colleges. Since 1949 there had been full-time superintendents at Abingdon, Didcot, Wokingham and Woodley. The other evening institutes were run by part-timers working independently of the full-time superintendents and without 'local committees to guide and co-ordinate their activities'.

In 1951 those parts of the county beyond the two colleges were divided into four administrative areas. The *North Berks* area included Abingdon, Botley, Faringdon and those villages to the north of the Didcot/Swindon railway line. At Abingdon – not Steventon – an institute opened in 1950. *West Berks* included Didcot, Wallingford and Wantage. *Central Berks* was a semicircular area around Reading extending from Basildon in the west to the county boundary in the south, and to Woodley, Twyford and Wargrave in the east. The *South-East Berks* area included Bracknell, Crowthorne, Sandhurst and Wokingham, where the LEA bought Montague House to use as a further education centre.

The classes in these areas were organised by full-time area superintendents, each working with an advisory committee which kept the education and training needs of the area under review. The four superintendents liaised with each other to avoid the duplication of classes in adjacent districts.

So from 1951, Berkshire was divided into six FE areas. With the two area Principals and the four area superintendents, each part of the county now had a full-time organiser. Separate

---

[19] FESC 1 December 1950, 19 January 1951.

prospectuses were issued by each Principal and superintendent and the LEA co-ordinated the overall provision. Area organisation was complete.

The colleges and institutes organised courses for people in their areas; the two specialist institutions continued to recruit students from across the county and beyond. In 1967 the Institute of Agriculture became the Berkshire College of Agriculture. The County Council's Art School at Maidenhead developed as a centre of advanced and specialised work. Reading College, controlled by Reading Borough Council, also had an Art Department. In 1958 the two authorities co-operated to establish a federation between Maidenhead School of Art and the Art Department of Reading College. This became the Berkshire College of Art, maintained by both authorities under one Principal. The building in Marlow Road was the home of its Maidenhead branch.

There were some changes in detail, but this area organisation continued for many years. As the 1950s drew to a close, planning started for two more FE colleges. One of these was at Abingdon. This was the *North Berks College* and its first instalment opened in 1963. At the same time the *South-East Berks College* was planned for Bracknell, where the building of the new town had created a 'great potential demand' for further education.

Principals

The LEA had overall control of each college but the day to day management was in the hands of the Principal who worked closely with the board of governors. The Principal was the most important member of the college staff. Academic Boards did not appear in colleges until the 1970s, the concept of team management did not take hold until a decade or so after that. 'We didn't have many meetings in the early days, not like there became.' Moreover, it was generally the case that FE Principals and governors were given more freedom of manoeuvre than headteachers and governors in schools.[20] The 1950s college Principal was a powerful figure, as long as he had the support of the governors.

---

[20] L M Cantor and I F Roberts, *Further Education Today*, (London: Routledge & Kegan Paul, 1979), p.22.

One of the Principal's most important responsibilities was the appointment and management of the staff. Most of these were lecturers. However, there were also the technicians, indispensable for an engineering and science curriculum which involved the constant use of workshop and laboratory equipment; and there were the administrative staff working as receptionists and secretaries, answering the telephone, handling enquiries, organising enrolments and examinations. There was also the caretaker looking after the building and its security. Caretaker Harry Whiting was the Superintendent's first full-time appointment at Newbury in 1948. 'In the very beginning he was caretaker-cum-gardener-cum-everything else.'

Another responsibility of the FE Principal was to develop relationships with local employers. The success of day release rested on their support. 'It is very difficult for anyone outside a further education establishment to realise the importance of good relations with industry and commerce.' At South Berks College, 'we are indeed fortunate that almost all local industry has been education- and training-conscious and college courses have been established with local co-operation and filled with local students'.[21]

The Principal also had to make the work of the college known to the community. 'Cinderella' had to be seen, explained and understood. Part of the public image of further education, then and now, is that some people are never quite sure what it does or what it is meant to be about. 'People don't know what goes on up here today. Only a very small part of the population really knows anything about the place. When we tell people what we're doing, they say, oh, can you do that?'[22] Communication and clarity is all-important.

In the 1950s, the message was spread by word of mouth, through the local newspaper and by Open Days, but one of the key vehicles of publicity was the college prospectus.

And one more important point. It may well be that the class you want is not scheduled. This is because only those

---

[21] South Berks College of Further Education 25 Years, Anniversary Publication. Hereinafter referred to as SBCFE 25 Years.

[22] Interview with Pat Harte (in 1998).

classes for which there has been a past demand or a specific request have been included in the Prospectus. So, if **your** class has been omitted, raise your voice and let us know. If the demand is strong enough, efforts will be made to meet it.

When you have read this Prospectus and if you are still not interested, please give it to your next-door neighbour, or your brother, or your mother-in-law, or even your grandmother (our oldest student last year was around the 80 mark!), in fact to anyone who may make use of it.[23]

For the most part, the publicity was local. The horizons of a Berkshire FE college did not stretch beyond its local area.

The FE Principal would meet regularly with the heads of department. The work of each college was usually divided into departments, each one with its advisory committee. Departments were hierarchical. At the top was the head, and then came the lecturers and the assistant lecturers of different grades. Last but not least were the part-time assistants/instructors.

National Certificates, City & Guilds, RSA and all that

Berkshire's area colleges offered a broad curriculum. The majority of the courses were vocational, leading to recognised examinations and qualifications. This was similar to FE colleges elsewhere. 'Local colleges provide on the vocational side courses, mainly part-time, up to the level of ONC or its equivalent.'[24] In Berkshire there was more engineering than science provision although, significantly, South Berks had a Science Department. The work was non-advanced, with the two colleges acting as feeders to the advanced work at Reading and Oxford. Most of the curriculum was organised into part-time courses. However each college provided a small number of full-time programmes for school leavers: commercial and secretarial, domestic science and Pre-Apprenticeship courses in building and engineering.

---

[23] SBCFE Prospectus 1951-52, p.7.

[24] BEC 14 September 1956, from a government White Paper on Technical Education.

The bread-and-butter vocational qualifications were the National Certificates, the awards provided by the City & Guilds of London Institute and those qualifications offered by professional associations. The Ministry of Education was responsible for the National Certificates. The ONC was widely taught in subjects such as engineering and applied physics. Its vocational and practical flavour proved attractive to countless numbers of students, and left a good taste in the mouths of employers.

City & Guilds courses were also highly regarded. The City & Guilds Institute was the main awarding body in work-related subjects such as bricklaying, carpentry, plumbing, electrical installations and mechanical engineering. There were also qualifications for electrical and laboratory technicians and motor vehicle mechanics. The programmes for craftsmen were practical; those for technicians were more theoretical. The courses were of recognised quality, and the qualifications had prestige across the industrial landscape.

In the commercial world, shorthand and typewriting were always in demand with qualifications offered by Pitman, the London Chamber of Commerce and the Royal Society of Arts. The typewriter in the office of the 1950s was as important as the computer is in the modern office of today. Typewriting was so popular that it was taught in virtually every college in the country. Berkshire LEA was always buying typewriters, 280 of them between 1948 and 1956, most of which were new, a few of which had been rebuilt.[25]

Less common in FE in the '50s were general education courses. Berkshire colleges and some of the evening institutes offered GCE O- and A-levels but the big expansion of GCE work in FE came after 1960.

---

[25] FESC 15 May 1953, 14 May 1954, 16 November 1956.

Table 7 Berkshire FE: Examinations 1958/59

Qualification	Entries	Passes
Ordinary National Certificate	780	537
Royal Society of Arts (Commerce)	835	471
Others	2,831	1,667

Report on Education in Berkshire 1959-60

For most of the students the further education experience was a part-time one. There were few full-time students in the 1950s. However, the institutes at Newbury and Maidenhead had only been open for a few months when discussions were started about full-time courses for school leavers. There was some confusion as to whether such provision belonged to colleges or schools. The distinction was important and the issue was referred to the Ministry of Education, which decided that such courses could be taught in colleges. Full-time programmes started at South Berks in 1951 and at East Berks a year later.

The expansion of vocational work in the colleges affected courses at the evening institutes. The institutes were no longer under pressure to cater for the vocational needs of young people as they had been in the interwar years. The result was that such classes declined, while the number of recreational classes grew. This was accompanied by a changing student profile in the night school of the 1950s. Students were older and there were many more women than in previous years. Hence the popularity of women's subjects: basketwork, cookery, dressmaking and needlework, glove-making, handloom weaving, leatherwork, millinery, soft furnishings and tailoring. Also in demand were classes in keep fit and dancing, drawing and painting, music and drama. Such courses did not usually lead to qualifications; but they were good fun and enriched the lives of many people.

'It seems that every year in Further Education is a year of expansion'

The years of austerity came to an end in Britain in the early 1950s. In the years that followed, the feeling grew that the country was starting to enjoy a period of affluence and progress. The Conservatives won the 1951 General Election and they remained in power for the next 13 years. In the summer of 1957, Prime Minister Harold MacMillan memorably announced: 'Let's be frank about it, most of our people have never had it so good'.

Economic growth was one of the main reasons for the development of further education in these years. There was significant expansion in the Southern Region, in engineering and agricultural machinery, aircraft manufacture, atomic research, electronics, the motor vehicle industry and oil refining. Industry – and people – moved from London into the overspill areas to the south and west of the capital. By the end of the decade, the tempo of industrial activity had risen steadily and the 'high level of demand and full order books' had stimulated the production of both 'consumer and capital goods'.[26] The growing interest in scientific research meant an increase in the number and size of research establishments. Industry wanted scientists and technicians; and there was an exciting new industry, atomic energy and nuclear power, with its 'consequent growing demand for specialised manpower'.

In Berkshire, the population increased, towns grew and there was 'noticeable industrial development' in what had been, a few years before, rural areas. Fewer people were dependent on the land for their livelihood. The first report on the work of the Education Committee since the Butler Act was written in 1956. 'The period since 1944 is one in which Berkshire has changed greatly in many respects. The development of the county by industry and by Government and allied departments has brought about a remarkable increase in population ... The boundaries of rural Berkshire have receded and urban areas have developed.' Bracknell was beginning its transformation from a country town of 5,000 people into a new town of concrete and chrome, light industry and uniform office blocks, roundabouts and ring roads. Its eventual population was estimated to exceed 50,000. Such development put pressure on Berkshire's education resources, both schools and FE. The atomic energy establishments at Harwell in north Berkshire and Aldermaston just over the county

---

[26] See SRCFE Annual Reports 1956, 1957 and 1960.

boundary in the south brought about a considerable increase in the population of the nearby urban areas while industrial development in other parts of the county meant more education provision was needed. According to the LEA, there were few parts of the county unaffected by economic development.

This was the background to the reports produced by the LEA and the Southern Regional Council. In FE, at least, they had never had it so good. In 1959, the Education Committee proudly declared: 'It seems that every year in Further Education is a year of expansion.' Between 1948 and 1960, student hours increased by almost 325 per cent. Following the reorganisation of 1951, there was an 'impressive expansion' in the range of courses. There were more students, particularly full-time and day-release. In the eight years between 1952/53 and 1959/60, full-time student numbers increased by 151 per cent, part-time by 47 per cent.[27] The biggest increase was in the autumn of 1956, when full-time enrolments were 27 per cent more than in the previous year. As the decade drew to a close, further expansion was confidently predicted as the post-war bulge of boys and girls was about to reach the school-leaving age of 15 'and make its presence felt in Further Education'.[28]

More and more people were employed in post-school education, more administrators in Shire Hall, more lecturers and support staff in the colleges. Teaching hours increased by 45 per cent between 1955 and 1960 with many lecturers now employed full-time, in contrast with the pre-war years when part-time work had been the norm.[29] By 1960, the number of people working in FE in Berkshire was much, much larger than in the years before the war.

The great adventure into a land of promise meant a constant struggle for the LEA to keep up with the ever increasing demand for courses and the changing needs of industry while simultaneously trying to maintain and improve standards. At the same time it

---

[27] FESC 13 November 1959; Education in the Royal County of Berkshire 1957-58/1958-59/1959-60, Report by the Director of Education.

[28] In the bulge year 1961/62, 5,300 additional students were anticipated. See SRCFE 21st Anniversary, *op.cit.*, p.3.

[29] FESC 13 November 1959.

had to accommodate changes in government policy. Inevitably there was a steady rise in expenditure, so much so that the money spent on FE grew more rapidly than on any other part of Berkshire's education service. Between 1954/55 and 1958/59, the increase in spending was 87 per cent. Such was the cost of providing 'adequate facilities' for post-school education.

Table 8 Berkshire FE: Costs 1954/55 to 1958/59

Session	Costs
1954/55	£90,681
1955/56	£100,790
1956/57	£125,009
1957/58	£154,286
1958/59	£169,503

FESC 13 November 1959

The single biggest reason for the rise in spending was lecturers' salaries caused, in part at least, by the increasing number of full-time appointments. There were, however, other factors at work such as the increase in salary scales and the equal pay instalments to women so that, by the end of the decade, they were paid the same as their male colleagues. There was also the furnishing of new buildings and the rising cost of equipment and materials.

Accommodation was always needed to ensure that classroom and workshop space kept pace with student numbers. Between 1954 and 1956 although the volume of work increased, few new courses were approved because of the lack of suitable accommodation.[30] Progress was being held back although, by 1958, the Education Committee was sounding a cautious note of optimism sensing, for technical education at least, 'a growing public realisation of the need for better facilities'.[31]

---

[30] *Ibid.*, 14 September 1956.

[31] Education in the Royal County of Berkshire 1957-58, Report by the Director of Education, p.23.

In the later 1940s the County Council had bought residential properties such as Boyn Hill House in Maidenhead, Hall Place in Burchett's Green and Ormonde House in Newbury and given them makeovers. Bedrooms were transformed into classrooms, dining rooms became offices. In the years that followed there was 'continued planning and building of new accommodation'. Prefabricated structures and Nissen huts were assembled and used as workshops and laboratories while other premises were hired as and when required. But this was not enough. Further education 'extended to such proportions' that the LEA decided to build new colleges 'to replace hired accommodation and premises which have become unsuitable because of the large numbers of students seeking instruction in technical subjects'.[32] New colleges were built at Newbury and Windsor, then at Abingdon and Bracknell. What was happening in Berkshire was mirrored across the Southern Region with new buildings at Bournemouth, Farnborough, Henley, the Isle of Wight, Oxford, Reading, Southampton and West Sussex.[33]

Staff

Table 9 Berkshire FE: Lecturers 1954/55 to 1958/59

Session	Lecturers FT	Lecturers PT	Teaching Hours
1954/55	49	564	84,783
1955/56	55	576	86,210
1956/57	61	578	95,303
1957/58	71	545	101,529
1958/59	77	542	107,139

FESC 13 November 1959

'The Berkshire Education Committee appointed a number of full-time teachers in Maidenhead, Newbury and Windsor and their numbers grew as the demands for technical courses became evident.' In 1955, there were 49 full-time FE lecturers; by 1959, the

---

[32] Since 1945, op.cit., p.31.

[33] SRCFE 21st Anniversary, op.cit., p.3.

number had risen to 77, an increase of 57 per cent. Those working full time were greatly outnumbered by part-timers. Many of these, of course, were only responsible for one class for a couple of hours a week. Yet they remained a most valuable part of the teaching force, as they had been since the beginning of the century. Part-time numbers fell slightly towards the end of the decade, although there was more teaching to be done. This was because their hours were being absorbed by their full-time colleagues.

There was an important difference between teachers in schools and those in further education. Schoolteachers had to have completed a professional course of training before entering the classroom. This was not a requirement in further education, where tutors were often 'engaged in industry and commerce'. The employment of men and women 'not ordinarily experienced in teaching method' was as common in FE after the war as it had been before.[34] Such people brought with them invaluable experience of the workplace – and recreational skills in the non-vocational curriculum – but many remained without a teaching qualification. Moreover, there were few development opportunities to enable them to get such a qualification, little of what was to become known as in-service training. Some work, however, was done by the Regional Council which, from its earliest days, organised short courses and conferences for those working in FE.

A teaching qualification was not necessary, but recruitment of lecturers was not easy. In 1955 it was 'extremely difficult, and at times impossible, to secure staff replacements when vacancies occur', particularly in science and engineering in which 'few, if any, applications have been received in response to recent advertisements'.[35] Five years on and staffing was still a problem. 'Well qualified applicants' were not coming forward for the 'lower graded posts'. Moreover, it was not just teaching positions that were difficult to fill. There was a similar problem in finding invigilators for examinations, for which the pay in Berkshire was lower than in some other education authorities.[36]

---

[34] FESC 1 December 1950.

[35] *Ibid.*, 28 November 1955.

[36] *Ibid.*, 16 July 1954.

Students

Table 10 Southern Region FE: Student Enrolment
1947/48, 1957/58

Session	FT	PT Day	Evening	Total
1947/48	2,266	7,415	19,442	29,123
1957/58	3,894	24,345	24,710	52,949

SRCFE 21st Anniversary 1947-1968

In the decade from 1948, the number of FE students in the Southern Region almost doubled. The most significant increase, an impressive 228 per cent, was in the growth of part-time day students. In the same 10-year period, for the country as a whole, the part-time day figures had doubled. In the Southern Region they had more than trebled, a 'remarkable achievement' for the education authorities. Full-time numbers grew by 72 per cent, which meant a lot of student hours. Night-school students grew by 27 per cent.

The success of the Berkshire adventure can be seen by looking back to the interwar years. Before 1939, the maximum number of annual student hours in the county was never more than 100,000. Each year there were about 3,000 people going to evening classes. Only a few students were on courses which led to public examinations. Furthermore, only a few attended advanced courses out-county. In contrast, by 1955/56, student hours approached one million. There were over 11,000 students, 90 per cent of whom were on examination courses. In addition, a further 2,000 were studying advanced courses in Reading, Oxford and London.[37] By 1959/60 there were more than 14,000 FE students in Berkshire.

---

[37] Since 1945, *op.cit.*, p.29.

Table 11 Berkshire FE: Student Enrolment 1955/56, 1959/60

Session	PT	FT	Total
1955/56	10,904	197	11,101
1959/60	13,973	296	14,269

Report on Education in Berkshire 1959-60

With the area organisation in 1951, East Berks became the biggest college: 2,680 students in its first year compared to 1,788 at South Berks. East Berks grew 'much more rapidly' than its neighbour, its Principal had more responsibilities, and he was paid more. By the mid-'50s, it had almost twice as many enrolments as South Berks and over seven times more than the Maidenhead School of Art. It had more full-time students, more part-time day and noticeably more evening students than South Berks. Consequently, its volume of work was much greater, 320,000 student hours compared to 250,000 hours at Newbury.[38] The Art School was the smallest of the three, but a quarter of its students were full time.

Table 12 Berkshire FE: Student Distribution 1956

FE College	FT	PT Day	Evening	Total
Maidenhead Art School	25%	6%	9%	(8%)
South Berks College	33%	35%	31%	(33%)
East Berks College	41%	59%	60%	(59%)
Total	**99%**	**100%**	**100%**	**(100%)**

FESC 16 November 1956

Table 13 Berkshire FE: Modes of Study 1951, 1956

FE College	Year	FT	% change	PT Day	% change	Evening	% change	Total	% change
Maidenhead	1951	20		33		338		391	
Art School	1956	42	110%	109	230%	255	-25%	406	4%
South Berks	1951	26		351		2,069		2,446	
College	1956	55	112%	631	80%	901	-56%	1,587	-35%
East Berks	1951	-		405		2,435		2,840	
College	1956	68		1,072	165%	1,701	-30%	2,841	0%

FESC 23 May 1952, 16 November 1956

---

[38] FESC 14 September 1956.

Between 1951 and 1956, enrolments at the School of Art increased by four per cent, those at East Berks stayed the same, while those at South Berks dropped by 35 per cent. Raw enrolment figures, however, do not reveal the important changes which were taking place in the modes of study. More and more students were coming to classes during the day; fewer were coming in the evening. While there was little or no increase in enrolments at the School of Art and East Berks, and while there was a significant drop in the number of students at South Berks, further education was expanding with more classes, more student hours and more teaching.

There was a big increase in the number of full-time students. East Berks did not have any in 1951, but there were 68 in 1956. At South Berks, the increase in the same five-year period was 112 per cent; at the School of Art, 110 per cent. The increase in part-time day students was just as significant: 230 per cent at the Art School, 165 per cent at East Berks, 80 per cent at South Berks. These were years of growth, although paradoxically there was a steep decline in evening class numbers. This decline was greatest at South Berks, where it was 56 per cent. At East Berks, the numbers dropped by 30 per cent, at the School of Art by 25 per cent.

Part-time day students were those usually released by their employers. Most of them were boys. This reflected the fact that major industries, such as building and engineering, which employed principally boys, were more generous in releasing their young workers than the offices and the shops which employed mainly girls. Girls had considerably fewer opportunities than boys and their chances of apprenticeship and day release were much smaller. Also, the opportunities for full- and part-time study fell off markedly as people grew older. There were few chances for 'delayed' students to try again or retrain. Restrictions on apprenticeship were one cause of this difficulty – they were intended for young people – but the reluctance of employers to release older workers was also important. Some evening classes were designed to remedy this shortcoming.

Some students found day release difficult. The demands of the course meant that on their day in college they were studying from nine in the morning until seven o'clock at night. In some cases, they also had to attend classes on another evening during the week. National Certificate students in particular had a lot of homework. They had to learn to balance their work with study and social and family life.

We have seen that the county college commitment for 15- to 18-year-olds was never realised and day release was not made compulsory. Although opportunities were more common than they had been in previous years, college-based training provision for young workers was far from universal. In 1960, Berkshire Education Committee ruefully observed that there were still some employers, especially in building and commerce, 'who appear to be extremely reluctant to allow their staff to take advantage of day-release facilities'.[39] Nationally, the percentage of young people obtaining release remained low, with many employers reluctant to support this form of training. This was part of a bigger problem: the employers' comparatively low level of investment in developing the skills of their workforce.

The majority of FE students went to night school. Vocational students often had no choice but to attend college in their own time to further their careers. Many were young women, doing typewriting and shorthand. Some found this way of studying difficult. Going to an evening class after a day at work was tiring, and a vocational course often required homework.

The following table shows the number of students enrolled in Berkshire's FE areas in 1956.

Table 14 Berkshire FE: Student Enrolment by Area 1956

FE Area	FT	PT Day	Evening	Total
South-East Berks	17	18	731	766
West Berks	–	59	898	957
Central Berks	–	32	973	1,005
North Berks	49	169	1,521	1,739
Total	**66**	**278**	**4,123**	**4,467**

FESC 16 November 1956

---

[39] Education in the Royal County of Berkshire 1959-60, Report by the Director of Education, p.32.

The North Berks area around Abingdon had the most students followed by the Central Berks area around Reading. South-East Berks and West Berks had fewer students. Nearly all the classes were in the evening, and 92 per cent of the students were in night school. However, particularly in North Berks, there were some classes during the day. This was because of the demand from AERE Harwell.

3

SOMETHING NEW AT ORMONDE HOUSE

Newbury in 1948

> Newbury, at the present time, is the ideal country market town, large enough to provide everything needed in the way of markets, shops, education, culture, entertainment and sport, both for itself and for the huge rural area dependent upon the town; but not too large, so that a wonderful spirit of friendliness and good comradeship pervades everything.
>
> *Newbury Guide 1948*

Newbury lies in the valley of the River Kennet, the main tributary of the Thames, in south-west Berkshire. It is set in the heart of the countryside, a landscape of downland, farms and hedgebound country roads. For centuries corn has been grown on the lowlands, sheep have grazed on the slopes of the higher grassland. The town was a centre for the buying and selling of agricultural produce and livestock. It was granted a market charter in the 16th century, but the market began long before. The place was popular with medieval traders, a crossroads town where ancient roads met. The road from London to Bath and Bristol met the road from the south, from Winchester and Southampton, leading to Oxford and the Midlands. Newbury's early prosperity was due to this favourable position on the road network.

Years ago, the manufacture of woollen cloth was at the heart of the town's prosperity. Newbury became famous for its weaving and was one of the richest towns in the country. Wool from the Cotswolds was spun and woven and the cloth trade produced the town's greatest hero, Jack of Newbury, with his 'factory' of 200 looms and 1,000 workers. Wool money built the parish church of St Nicolas', and it was a cloth merchant who built the red-brick Elizabethan mansion of Shaw House.

When the cloth trade declined, new industries took its place. The River Kennet was straightened and made navigable between Newbury and Reading. The Kennet and Avon Canal was completed in the early 19th century linking London to Bristol by waterway. Newbury's wharf area was developed and the town became an inland port. There was work in iron foundries and in brick-making yards and at the gas works. William Plenty, a wheelwright from Southampton, arrived at the end of the 18th century and set himself up as an agricultural engineer and metal founder. His Eagle Iron Works built the Plenty plough and the country's first lifeboat. Within a few years it was steam engines to drive machinery and to power coastal shipping. The company grew to enjoy a worldwide reputation as marine engineers exporting to all parts of the British Empire. The Plenty family lived over their works in Cheap Street in the middle of the town. Their foundry was a short distance away, in King's Road. Close by, Newbury Diesel, another manufacturer of marine engines, was set up early in the 20th century as a Plenty's subsidiary.

Samuel Elliott started another business in the town around 1870. The Albert Steam Joinery Works was in Albert Road. Elliott's were high class joiners, doing quality carving for churches and country houses, making ammunition boxes during the First World War and furniture, bedroom and dining-room suites in the years that followed.

Yet much of the town's economic activity in the 19th and early 20th centuries remained connected to agriculture. There were jobs in farming and its related industries and the great estates, such as Benham Park, and the grand houses, such as Donnington Grove and Sandleford Priory, employed many staff. A few miles to the south of the town, shaded by giant cedar trees, was Highclere Castle, the family home of the Earls of Carnarvon.

In and around the town there were water mills grinding corn and animal feed, maltings roasting barley and breweries making beer. West Mills and Town Mills, owned by Hovis from the early 1920s, were on the banks of the Kennet. Grain and seed merchants had their shops and warehouses and both Dolton and Midwinter were in business from the 19th century. Corn was sold at the weekly market in the Corn Exchange and sheep and cattle were bought and sold at the cattle market opened by the Earl of Carnarvon in 1873. Agricultural equipment was manufactured and distributed. Newbury's businesses worked for the farming community and they were all represented at the Agricultural Show, organised every year by the Newbury and District Agricultural Society. At Christmas time there was another long established tradition when the Craven Hunt gathered in the Market Place for its Boxing Day meet.

In 1948, Newbury was a medium-sized country market town with a population of around 18,000. It provided services for the local community and enjoyed a significant passing trade as well. Half-day closing, religiously observed, was on Wednesday. Thursday was market day, the busiest day of the week. People came in from the villages to buy their produce and mingle with the townsfolk and farmers brought their livestock to the cattle market. Agriculture was still important. Some families had farmed the same land for generations and many village people either worked on the land or had experience of working on it. In Farnborough, high on the downs to the north, nearly all the men in the village worked on one of three farms and lived with their families in the tied cottages that went with the job. 'People in the village knew everything there was to know about the fields. The land was a sacred thing.'[1] In 1949, a grain-drying plant was opened in Newbury for farmers in Berkshire and the neighbouring counties, the first agricultural co-operative of its kind in the south of England. The town's corn market continued, although on a small scale, and the Corn Exchange was increasingly used as a venue for social events. The Michaelmas Fair was no longer a hiring fair where those looking for work hoped to attract the attention of a prospective employer.

---

[1] Candida Lycett Green, *The Dangerous Edge of Things*, (London: Doubleday, 2005), p.38.

In post-war Newbury it was purely entertainment, no longer held in the Market Place on the first Thursday after Michaelmas Day but on a field by the river in Northcroft. The Agricultural Show was held further away, at Elcot Park near Kintbury. Anthony Hurd, a sheep farmer at Winterbourne Holt, was the town's Conservative Member of Parliament from 1945. A journalist and broadcaster on agriculture, and champion of the farming industry, he also served as chairman of the Conservative Agricultural Committee.

Newbury had good road communications in 1948. The spine of the town was the road which ran north and south of the River Kennet, the A34 from the south coast to the Midlands. The approach from the south was down Newtown Road and along Bartholomew Street. The narrow stone bridge over the river led into Northbrook Street and at the northern end, the street widened into the Broadway. It was here that the A4, the Great West Road, crossed from east to west.

The Clock Tower stood at this important junction, forming a roundabout. This local landmark was built in 1929, its six stone pillars supporting an oak roof complete with turret, inside which was a large electric clock. Plates were displayed on the fascia boards directing travellers south to Winchester, east to London and west to Bath. Under cover were a public telephone and an oak bench for passengers as they waited for the buses which stopped nearby.

In 1948 Newbury was a busy commercial place, 'more of a business town than an industrial centre'. There were 'no huge factories giving employment to hosts of hands'. Trade was 'largely concerned with distribution from wholesale manufacture'.[2] Commercial life flowed through the shops and businesses in Bartholomew Street, Cheap Street, the Market Place, Northbrook Street and the Broadway; and with its 250 members, the town's Chamber of Commerce was 'very active and efficient'.

Northbrook Street was the great shopping thoroughfare. A 'fine street', declared the town's directory, with 'some lovely old houses', though in nearly every case by 1948 the ground floors had been 'cut out for shop fronts' with their colourful canopies.[3]

---

[2] Newbury Official Guide 1938, p.39.
[3] Newbury Rural District Guide c.1948, p.19.

Above were the attractive, gabled upper storeys. 'It must have been a swagger street before shops invaded it and traffic killed it stone-dead.' This was Nikolaus Pevsner's caustic verdict in 1958.[4]

Long and straight, Northbrook Street was where shops, estate agents, garages and public houses clustered together. There was a balance of locally owned businesses and chain stores. Nationwide retail outlets had arrived in the years between the wars. Alongside F W Woolworth and Marks & Spencer there were chemists (Boot's, Timothy White & Taylor); booksellers (W H Smith); food shops (J H Dewhurst, David Greig, MacFisheries); tailors (J Hepworth, Montague Burton); shoe shops (Freeman, Hardy & Willis, Lilley & Skinner, Milward, Barratt); and cycle shops (Curry's, Halford). Yet many of the shops and services were still independent and owned by local families. This gave the town its individual character. 'In these days of ever increasing multiple shops and chain stores, it is refreshing to find a town such as Newbury with a large number of good businesses still owned and being run by private enterprise.'[5] Their money remained in the local economy, and their owners worked for the community as councillors, mayors and magistrates. The owners of family businesses played an important part in FE developments in the town.

The hardware store, the House of Toomer, stood at one end of Northbrook Street. Founded in 1692, this was one of the town's oldest retail businesses. J J Davies, the china shop, opened in the middle of the 19th century. On the Kennet and Avon Canal the family kept their narrowboat, used to collect their wares from the potteries of Derbyshire and Staffordshire. Other local family businesses included Metcalf and Hewitt – studio, wedding and polyfoto photographers – and outfitters G S Paine.

The biggest of the retail outlets in 1948 was Camp Hopson. Years before, Joseph Hopson had been a commercial photographer who also ran a decorating business and worked in the furniture trade. Alfred Camp came to Newbury, took over a rather old-fashioned business and transformed it into the popular Drapery Bazaar. In 1920, Joseph Hopson's grandson Paul returned from

---

[4] Nikolaus Pevsner, *The Buildings of England, Berkshire*, (Harmondsworth: Penguin, 1966), p.182.

[5] Newbury Official Guide 1938, p.52.

the First World War and married Alfred Camp's daughter. Shortly afterwards, Camp Hopson was born. This was the start of a new chapter in the business life of the town. In 1948 Newbury's largest retailer occupied a row of shops stretching from numbers 6 to 14 Northbrook Street, selling a wide range of merchandise: clothes and fashion, millinery and hosiery, sportswear, furniture and furnishings. There was also a building department, a removals and warehousing business and a funeral service.

A lot of Newbury people in 1948 were employed in clerical and commercial work, in shops and banks and in the offices of accountants, auctioneers, estate agents and solicitors. Many of these continued to do business with the farming community. They included A W Neate, land agents, surveyors, and estate agents; Day, Shergold and Herbert who, after the First World War, had held a weekly auction of eggs, poultry, butter and vegetables; and Dreweatt, Watson and Barton, estate agents who ran the auctions at the cattle market.

The Second World War had led to changes in many of the town's manufacturing businesses but by 1948 normal service had been resumed. In the autumn of that year Newbury celebrated Civic Week with an exhibition of employers in the Corn Exchange. There were the old established firms – Elliott's, Plenty and Newbury Diesel – alongside the newcomers – Opperman Gears, Vickers Armstrong and Southern Electricity.

Elliott's was still one of the biggest of the local manufacturers. Horace Buckingham was chairman and managing director. He lived at White Lodge on the Bath Road, overlooking his works which during the war had been commissioned by the government for aircraft production. He dedicated himself to the war effort making components for Spitfire fighter aircraft and gliders. Such was the output – the company had 600 people on the payroll – that Stafford Cripps, wartime Minister of Aircraft Production, paid a visit to the factory to thank all concerned. The war over, it was back to furniture production at the Albert Works.

'There weren't many what you'd call heavy engineering companies.' Plenty remained the biggest of the engineers in 1948. During the war they had been busy making engines, including submarine engines, for the Royal Navy. This continued in the post-war years, but they also 'established themselves' in the manufacture of pumps, filters and mixers. Newbury Diesel was smaller. It was no longer owned by Plenty but continued to make spare parts for diesel engines.[6] The gear-cutters firm, Opperman Gears, was one of the newcomers. It had moved from London – the capital was a prime target for enemy bombing – to Hambridge Road in the early months of the war. Vickers Armstrong also came to Newbury when its Supermarine Works in Southampton was heavily bombed. A factory was built on the Turnpike Road in Shaw which made fuselages for Spitfire aircraft.[7]

Another significant employer in the town was the electricity industry – taken into public ownership by the post-war Labour Government – under the regional authority of the Southern Electricity Board (SEB). Many of the downland villages were still awaiting electricity when the SEB was formed.

Newbury was served by three railway lines in 1948. At the beginning of the year the railways were nationalised and British Rail was formed. The station was a short walk from the town centre, along Bartholomew Street and over Blackboys Bridge. It was on the main Great Western line from London Paddington to the West Country. There were also two branch lines. One of these ran north to Didcot through Hermitage, Hampstead Norreys, Compton, Churn, Upton and Blewbury. The other, the Lambourn Valley line, went through Speen, Boxford, Welford, Great Shefford, East Garston and Eastbury on its way to Lambourn.

Since the early years of the century, Newbury had been famous for horse racing. During the Second World War its racecourse had been requisitioned and handed over to the US army. This was the beginning of Newbury's American connection. The racecourse became a huge supply depot, its precious turf disappearing under

---

[6] 'In 1955, by which time steam engines were no more wanted, even by the most dyed-in-the-wool shipowners, we had established ourselves in three principal spheres – positive displacement pumps; filters for liquids and glass; and mixers for laboratory and industrial purposes.' G T Shoosmith, *Mostly Plenty*, Unpublished MSS, p.29.

[7] With the extensive bombing of Southampton in the autumn of 1940, the government ordered the dispersal of Spitfire production over the south of England. Newbury and Reading became centres for the manufacture of Spitfire components – which were taken to the airfield at Aldermaston for final assembly.

miles of concrete roads and railway track. Reinstating the course once the war was over was a mammoth undertaking and racing was not resumed until 1949. There were also American servicemen stationed during the war at Greenham Common. An RAF airfield had been developed, control passed to the USA and Greenham Common became a base for the US 101st Airborne Division. There were also American troops at Snelsmore Common which was used as a fuel dump and vehicle supply depot.

The area round Newbury was horseracing country. In northern Hampshire, there were stables at Kingsclere and Highclere. In Berkshire, the training of horses was important to the village economies in Compton, East Garston, East and West Ilsley, and especially in Lambourn, the valley of the racehorse. The downland turf was the attraction and with the opening of the Lambourn Valley Railway, racehorse preparation became a thriving industry. In 1948 the stables were the biggest employer in the village and formed the backbone of the local community. Early in the morning, residents woke to the sound of the horses as they made their way to the gallops. It is still the same today. 'If you live in Lambourn and are not connected to a stable, the odds are that you know somebody who is.'[8]

By 1948 there had been some development at Thatcham a few miles to the east of Newbury. Its population was around 5,000. Assuming the 'size of a town', it was the largest shopping centre between Newbury and Reading.[9] New industries were 'springing up', but the biggest employer was an old industry in the water meadows by the River Kennet round Colthrop. This was the Colthrop Board & Paper Mills, manufacturer of cardboard boxes and paper bags.

The most significant economic developments in the post-war years, however, were occurring to the north and the south of Newbury. In 1945 the government announced it was going to set up a research centre for atomic energy. The decision grew out of the wartime research into nuclear fission which culminated in the atomic bombs used with such devastating effect at Hiroshima and

---

[8] Robin Oakley, *Valley of the Racehorse*, (London: Headline Book Publishing, 2000), p.84.

[9] Newbury Rural District Guide c.1948, p.42.

Nagasaki in Japan in 1945. In 1946 the Atomic Energy Research Establishment was set up. The site chosen by the Ministry of Supply was an RAF airfield – with a nucleus of accommodation, large hangars and a road network – on the north Berkshire downland at Harwell. This was a sparsely populated area but close to Oxford and not too far from London, thereby enabling university contacts to be maintained by the scientists and research staff.[10]

A few miles away, the poet John Betjeman's daughter, Candida Lycett Green, was growing up in the rectory at Farnborough. Her childhood was spent in the shadow of the Atomic Establishment. She and her friends were fascinated by the top secret developments on the airfield with its high-wire perimeter fence, its spread-eagled hangars and its 200-foot high skyscraping chimney. There were rumours about a bomb being built, the biggest bomb in the world, and there were worries about personal safety. Everyone at Harwell had been issued with extra milk rations. If you drank enough milk, you were safe from radiation; this was an 'absolute fact'. Playing on the downs the children could see the research site below them, 'laid out like a map with all its rough winding roads between the big unwieldy buildings and the massive BEPO stack towering over it all'. Set out in 'rigid rows' were the new prefabs that had 'sprouted up overnight on the bare, bleak downland ... shining like white field mushrooms'.[11]

In the spring of 1950 the government opened a second atomic energy centre a few miles to the south of Newbury on another disused airfield. This was the Atomic Weapons Establishment (AWE) at Aldermaston.

The economic and social effects of these developments, on Newbury and the neighbouring towns and villages in west Berkshire, south Oxfordshire and north Hampshire, were profound. The Ministry of Supply became the biggest employer in the area and opportunities in technical and scientific work opened up for thousands of men and women. The Ministry's work was the single biggest influence on the development of FE in Newbury in the post-war years.

---

[10] *Harwell: The British Atomic Energy Research Establishment 1946-1951*, (London: HMSO, 1952), pp.9-10.

[11] Lycett Green, *op.cit.*, p.176.

Schools in 1948

We have seen how the Education Act of 1944 encouraged the expansion of further education, but the legislation is usually remembered for the changes it led to in schools rather than colleges. The Act established the break between the primary and secondary stages of education by ensuring that children would, at the age of 11, move on to the secondary stage in a different school. This would continue until at least the age of 15, the new school-leaving age from April 1947.

There were to be three types of secondary school: grammar, technical and modern. Each one was to offer a different curriculum, but they were all to be of 'equal standing'. Entry to secondary school was by an examination, and the shadow of the eleven-plus fell across pupils in their final year at primary school. Those who passed would go to a grammar or technical school, those who failed would go to the secondary modern.

Ormond Postgate was appointed Newbury's Education Officer at the beginning of 1947. Explaining the new system to the Newbury townsfolk, the grammar school, he said, was for those children 'who are attracted by a more abstract approach to learning', with a curriculum which focused on books and ideas. 'Such a course requires a high measure of general intelligence, combined with an interest in abstract ideas, and involves stern intellectual discipline.' There were two such schools in Newbury. Newbury Grammar School for boys (St Bartholomew's) was the oldest school in the town, proud of its 15th-century foundation, its history and its traditions. In the later 19th century, its new school was built on the Enborne Road. In the past the school had taken in boarders but by 1948 there were only day pupils. The County Girls' School was much newer. It had opened in Northbrook Street in 1904 and moved to the Andover Road a few years later. In 1948, the pupils of both these schools would stay on beyond the leaving age, probably until they were 18, and many would go on to university or, at the very least, into white-collar and professional occupations.

The technical school was to provide 'more specialised courses for children with particular aptitudes in science and mathematics who wish to take up engineering and agriculture'. The curriculum would also include art, commerce and other special subjects.

Like the grammar school, the pupils would get in by passing the eleven-plus and would probably stay on beyond the age of 15. However, there was no technical school in the Newbury district and although there was some discussion about building one, nothing was done. Newbury was not unique here. A lot of LEAs neglected the technical school and, nationwide, not many were set up. This gap in secondary education in the Newbury area, however, had an important effect on further education developments.

The third type of secondary school was the modern school. 'The majority of children learn most easily by dealing with concrete things and these will go to secondary modern schools which provide a good, all-round education.' The origins of such education in Newbury go back to the Council School. In the 1930s it became a school for older pupils. There were two buildings, each with its own entrance. The boys' entrance was on Station Road. Round the corner, on Bartholomew Street, were the gates for the girls' school. Frederick Ball was the boys' headmaster. 'He gave the older boys the privileges of more advanced education, training them in the practical subjects of horticulture and woodwork while giving them an inspiring knowledge of the more literary subjects.'[12]

The implementation of the 1944 Education Act began a quiet revolution in the schools in the Newbury district. As we have seen, developments were shaped by an event which happened on the afternoon of 10 February 1943. The country had been at war for three years, Newbury's air raid sirens had sounded on many occasions and there had been some enemy bombing in and around the town. None of this, however, had been very serious. However, on that fateful winter afternoon, a single German bomber broke out of the clouds and approached the town from the south-west direction. There had been no warning of its approach. It opened fire with its machine guns as it flew over Newtown Road and dropped a number of bombs. It left 15 people dead and many more injured. St John's Church was destroyed and the main building of the Council School was 'partially demolished'.[13] Three

---

[12] *NWN* 1 July 1954.

[13] Once the war was over, the War Damages Commission agreed to regard the building as a total loss and in 1950 Berkshire County Council was awarded damages of over £30,000. BEC 10 March 1950.

of the people killed were schoolchildren, and the headmaster and his wife were badly injured. Fortunately it was late afternoon and most of the pupils had gone home.

The Council School was closed and new premises had to be found. As a temporary measure, the pupils operated a shift system with Newbury's younger schoolchildren. The boys went to Speenhamland School in the afternoons; the girls went to St Nicolas'. A few weeks later, accommodation became available in a grand old house on the edge of the town. A new phase in Newbury's educational history was about to begin.

Shaw House was an Elizabethan mansion in the parish of Shaw-cum-Donnington. For more than 350 years it had been an illustrious family dwelling, improved in the 18th century when the Duke of Chandos had laid out a carriage drive entrance from the London Road. Early in the 20th century, the house passed to the Farquhar family and with the advent of the Second World War, like many big houses at the time, it was taken over by the military. For some weeks an Airlanding Reconnaissance Squadron lived in it and trained on its lawns. The building was subsequently occupied by American and Canadian soldiers, and then its use changed again. On 3 May 1943 it opened as a school for Newbury's older pupils who had been bombed out of the Council School. A nearby field, The Paddock, became the school's playing field.

Once hostilities were over, the Farquhar family decided to sell up and Berkshire County Council bought the house and 21 acres of ground to secure its continued use as a school. The Council also acquired the rest of the Shaw estate and 100 acres were designated for house building.

In 1947, the 27 teachers at Shaw House were responsible for more than 650 boys and girls in rooms filled with furniture loaned from London County Council.[14] This was not to last. The boys were to have their own school. Park House was on the south side of the town on the road towards Andover. During the war the house had been used as a hospital for wounded servicemen. When it came up for sale in 1947, the County Council bought it and its

---

[14] There were 335 girls and 330 boys. See Secondary Schools Subcommittee 24 October 1947.

eight acres for just under £9,000.[15]   Park House School opened in 1948 with the older boys transferred from Shaw House. Over the next few years, all the boys were gradually moved into their new surroundings, leaving only girls at Shaw, a process which was complete by the summer of 1955. As the boys' school developed, additional accommodation was built in the grounds.

By 1948, then, the reorganisation of education in Newbury was well under way. There were four primary, two grammar and two secondary modern schools. In the country districts, however, the changes took longer to implement. Some of the church and LEA schools were all-age schools with pupils from the age of five to 15. This was to continue for the time being at Chieveley (LEA), Compton (C of E), Hermitage (LEA), Hungerford (LEA), Lambourn (C of E) and Thatcham (C of E and LEA). Those children in the all-age schools who passed the eleven-plus went to the grammar or high school in Newbury; the rest stayed put.

However, other village schools were being reorganised into primary schools with children leaving when they were 11. From September 1948 older children were transferred from East Ilsley School to Compton, from Leckhampstead and Peasemore to Chieveley, and from Brimpton to Thatcham. Such reorganisation continued for a few years. It was not until 1956, for instance, that the all-age school at Hermitage became primary and its older pupils started going to secondary school in Newbury.

There were other schools in the area set up in the immediate post-war years. St Gabriel's was a private school for girls which had been evacuated to Newbury and decided to stay in the town once the war was over, moving into Sandleford Priory in 1948. A Special School for the Deaf opened in Donnington Lodge in 1949. At Snelsmore, the residential Mary Hare Grammar School for Deaf Children opened in Arlington Manor in 1950, the first school of its type in England.

Finally there was a school beyond Berkshire which had special links with Newbury. Christ's Hospital was a public school with a charitable charter and substantial endowments, and John West, a wealthy Newbury clothier in the 18th century, had set up a foundation for the town's children. The girls' school was at

---

[15] Co-ordination Subcommittee 16 January 1948.

Hertford, the boys' at Horsham in Sussex. The children of anyone related to John West were entitled to go to Christ's Hospital School and enjoy a private education with the fees paid out of the charitable foundation.

A walk along the Oxford Road

Travellers journeying from Newbury to Bath in the west, or Oxford to the north, left the Clock Tower on the Broadway by way of Oxford Street. This was the parish of Speen, and that part of it which took in the northern end of Northbrook Street was called Speenhamland. This area of the town lay beyond the north brook, the stream which ran from a pond by Elliott's Albert Works and flowed under Northbrook Street to surface in Victoria Park. In 1878 Newbury Borough had been extended to take in Speenhamland and the area beyond it known as Donnington Square.

The Broadway, London Road, Oxford Street – this was the busiest part of Speenhamland. Before the age of the railway, this part of the town had been full of coaching inns. The horse-drawn journey from London to the fashionable city of Bath used to take two long days, and Newbury was the halfway point where the horses were rested and the travellers put up for the night. Up to 60 coaches a day passed through the town, the inns were kept busy and one of them became famous for another reason. It was at the George & Pelican that the Berkshire magistrates met in 1795 and devised a new way of allocating poor relief which became universally known as the Speenhamland System.

In 1948 two of Newbury's garages were situated in this busy area. Wheeler's Garage was on the Broadway. Run by a local family for many years, its premises had been used during the war to train army mechanics. Across the road in Oxford Street was Martin & Chillingworth.

Two coaching inns, the Chequers Hotel and the Bacon Arms on Oxford Street, served as a solid reminder of the earlier age. It was here that the road forked. As you left the town, to the left was the Bath Road, straight ahead was the Oxford Road. At the junction stood what was formerly a toll house. Years before, this had been a stretch of turnpike road and money from the tolls was used to improve the potholed surface. In 1948 the smell of the freshly baked bread of the Wells bakery came out of the building which had once been a toll house.

The Oxford Road climbed gently through Speenhamland towards Shaw-cum-Donnington. A little way along and there was Pelican Lane, down which were Speenhamland School and the police station. In the evening this main road to the north was lit by gaslight.[16] It passed through a residential area of quiet respectability. The houses were Victorian and private, some with large gardens. On the west side stood Donnington Villas, a row of six semi-detached houses of red brick. A little further along was Donnington Square. This was a square in name only; it was actually a crescent of imposing town houses dating from the middle years of the 19th century. Further along was Grove Road, and the Gothic-styled Donnington Grove could be seen in the distance. This was a most attractive Georgian house recently bought by Daisy Fellowes, a well known society figure and president of the London Fashion Designers. Gently uphill, and a bridge carried the road over the River Lambourn to the 'beautifully situated' village of Donnington. The medieval hospital buildings by the river were now used as almshouses. High on a hill, overlooking the village from the west, stood the ruined gatehouse of Donnington Castle.

On the east side of the Oxford Road, beyond the turning for Pelican Lane, there was a small house close to the roadside. Number 36 had at one time been the Gardener's Arms public house, then Gardener Cottage and the home of an artist with his studio. In 1948 it was called Wayside, the home of schoolteachers Sarah, Dorothy and Ethel Keep. The sisters had bought it in 1938 for £650. Then came three large houses, each one set in acres of grounds. Number 38 stood opposite Donnington Villas. This was Ormonde House. Over the trees, beyond a paddock, was Marlborough House, another solid Victorian building. A little further along was Chacombe, formerly the parsonage for St Mary's Church in London Road but now a private family home. On towards Donnington, there was a field beyond which was a

---

[16] There were nine gas lamps on Oxford Street and along the Oxford Road to the northern end of Donnington Square. Newbury Borough Council 27 November 1953.

large house, Donnington Priory, occupying the site of a medieval priory. Across the River Lambourn, at the top of the hill, stood the imposing Donnington Lodge, a house which had been occupied by RAF pilots a few years before and was now being turned into a special school.

Ormonde House

> When the Newbury racecourse scheme began to take shape ... I bought my present home at Newbury which, in honour of the greatest horse I or anyone else ever trained, I called 'Ormonde House'.[17]

Number 38 Oxford Road stood in four acres, an attractive double-fronted residence reflecting owners of substance. It had been built in 1861 on a piece of land known as Horsepool Field. The main part of the house was two storeys, but the northern side had a third storey. The facade was solid rather than imposing. Age had softened the harshness of the white brick. The grey slate roof, with its four tall chimney stacks, plunged at various angles over the rooms and passageways below. A large conservatory was attached to the sunny south side of the house. Above it was a metal grille fixed to the guttering to protect the glass from melting snow. The house stood well back from the road, partially hidden behind trees and flowering shrubs. The six sets of windows at the front looked out across the Oxford Road to the terrace of red-brick villas. At the back of the house were gardens with shrubs, flower beds and vegetable plots. Access to the rear was down a side drive from the main road. The drive passed by a lean-to greenhouse supported by a brick wall, turned a corner and led to two small cottages. There was a garage next to one of them. The grounds were cluttered with sheds and outhouses – and there was a tennis court.

The entrance porch with its three heavy stone steps to the front door was approached down a gravel drive, set in lawns bordered with rhodendrons and clipped yew bushes. Along the drive fir trees had been planted, dark green and grey, sheltering the north side

---

[17] John Porter, *John Porter of Kingsclere, An Autobiography*, (London: Grant Richards, 1919), p.446.

of the house. Appropriately, the property was originally known as The Firs. In 1901 John Mason, Newbury grocer and provision dealer, was living there with his family, a cook and a housemaid.[18] A few years later, there was a new owner and the house was given a new name.

John Porter was a celebrated Victorian racehorse trainer. He turned out a string of winners from his stables at Kingsclere and he is still regarded in racing circles today as one of the greatest names in the history of the turf. He trained over a thousand winners and won prize money of almost £800,000. His horses won the Derby seven times, the St Leger Stakes six times and the 2,000 Guineas on five occasions. By the time he retired, he had trained 23 classics winners. When his career drew to a close, he left Kingsclere and came to live in Newbury. He was 67 years old, but this man of vision still had work to do. He was busy setting up Newbury Racecourse on land owned by the lord of the manor of Greenham. The initial opposition of the Jockey Club was overcome through the personal intervention of King Edward VII, who, as Prince Edward, had been a patron of the Kingsclere stables. A license was granted and the scheme went ahead under Porter's 'constant, experienced supervision'.[19] The course was laid out, a palatial grandstand was built and racegoers decanted at their own railway station. John Porter was 'pretty fully occupied' as managing director of the course, 'especially while it was in the construction stage'. The first meeting was held in 1905 in front of 15,000 people and its future was assured. A race named in John Porter's honour is run at Newbury to this day.

It was around this time that the famous trainer bought The Firs in the Oxford Road. As a tribute to the memory of one of his most successful horses, he decided to change the name of his new residence. From now on it was to be known as Ormonde House.

Ormonde was a powerful colt, reddish-brown in colour with a black mane and tail. The horse was owned by the Duke of Westminster and first appeared on the turf in 1885. In a short career of only three years, he won an amazing 15 races and more than £27,000 in prize money. His unbeaten exploits made 1886

---

[18] 1901 Census.

[19] *NWN* 29 September 1955.

the racing *annus mirabilis*. Ormonde was acclaimed as 'the horse of the century' as he raced to victory in the 2,000 Guineas at Newmarket, the Derby at Epsom and the St Leger at Doncaster.[20] His usual jockey, Fred Archer, was one of the greatest of riders, who, with self-effacing modesty, claimed that Ormonde could be ridden by anybody and still come back a winner.[21]

The season of glittering triumph, however, was marred by an unfortunate ending. One misty morning, on the downs above Kingsclere, trainer John Porter heard an unwelcome sound. As Ormonde galloped past him, there was a whistling noise. The three-year-old had 'gone' in his wind. Porter was dumbfounded and, years later, could still vividly recall his feelings on that sad morning. 'The idea that the horse I almost worshipped was afflicted with wind infirmity distressed me in a way I cannot describe. I hardly slept at all the following night. My mind would dwell on the fact that Ormonde had become a victim of that scourge roaring!' The winter came, the electric sponge was applied, but by the time the horse was back in training, he had become a pronounced whistler. 'One morning, when there was a thick fog on the downs, we could hear him breathing when he was nearly half a mile away.' His last race – he won it in spite of his problem – was in the summer of 1887. After that, there was one more public appearance. During the celebrations for Queen Victoria's Jubilee, the Duke of Westminster held a reception at Grosvenor House in London. It was a most royal occasion. 'The Prince and Princess of Wales were there, together with four kings, two queens, several other princes and princesses, and a number of Indian potentates.' Yet it was Ormonde who was the centre of attention as he was paraded round the garden. The great horse bowed out in style, politely consuming the carnations offered him by the Queen of Belgium and the geraniums handed him by the Indian princes.

Although Ormonde was put out to stud as was customary for champion   racehorses, his usefulness had been permanently impaired by his affliction. Yet when the Duke of Westminster

---

[20] Porter, *op.cit.*, chapter entitled 'The Career of Ormonde', pp.245-283.

[21] Peter Gill, *Cheltenham's Racing Heroes*, (Stroud: Sutton Publishing, 1998), p.11.

sold him to a breeder in Argentina, the racing fraternity criticised him for letting such a great horse leave the country. Yet he was convinced that the decision was the right one. 'Ormonde was a roarer and a descendant of roarers; and to keep him in England might well prove detrimental to British bloodstock.'[22] A few years later, and Ormonde was sold again, this time to a breeder in California. He was finally put to sleep in 1904, but his skeleton was returned to England and reassembled in the Natural History Museum in London.

When John Porter sat down in the library of his Oxford Road home to write his autobiography, he devoted a whole chapter to this remarkable horse. 'I am anxious,' he wrote, 'to honour the memory of Ormonde by relating the story of his career in the fullest possible detail, so that future generations may be able to understand why he gained such worldwide renown'.[23] The memoirs were published in 1919 and the author kept 'a few hairs' from the horse's mane and tail to remind him of such a 'great and noble creature'. These have long gone, but a painting of Ormonde remains on display in the National Horseracing Museum at Newmarket. In the saddle is another Victorian sporting hero, champion jockey Fred Archer.[24]

John Porter and his wife Isabel lived in style in Ormonde House for almost 20 years. They had three servants living with them, a cook and a parlourmaid from Woodhay, and a young housemaid.[25] When the trainer died in 1922, his final journey was back to Kingsclere to be buried within a few feet of the west door of St Mary's Church in the village. The property at 38 Oxford Road was offered for sale by a firm of Newbury estate agents.

---

[22] R Mortimer, R Onslow and P Willett, *The Biographical Encyclopaedia of British Flat Racing*, (London: Macdonald & Janes, 1978), p.430.

[23] Porter, *op.cit.*, p.245.

[24] Fred Archer was 13 times champion jockey, winning 2,748 races of which 22 were classics. His career ended tragically when, at the age of 29, he killed himself while suffering from a fever brought on by constant weight-watching.

[25] 1911 Census.

'An attractive small freehold residential property with grounds of four acres'

A W Neate's publicity described Ormonde House as a 'well-appointed comfortable and medium-sized residence' standing 'well back and screened from the road'. The approach was by a carriage drive, enclosed by a pair of 'handsome wrought iron gates'. Inside, the house was fitted out with 'thoroughly modern' services: electric lighting, company's water, mains drainage, central heating with radiators and coal fires, gas for cooking, and a telephone. Through the porch, the front door opened into an attractive hall with an ornamental tiled floor and open-tiled fireplace. From here was access to four reception rooms: the dining room, drawing room, library and morning room. Across the hall a door opened into the library. The dining room and drawing room were neat and of good size, 21 feet by 16 feet. In the drawing room a 'French casement' opened into the 'excellent conservatory'. At 41 feet long and 18 feet wide, with mosaic floor, hot water pipes and radiators, the conservatory was the biggest room in the house. At the back of the house, 'complete and conveniently placed', was a large kitchen with a double oven range, dresser, store cupboards and serving hatch. At the bottom of a flight of stone steps leading from the kitchen were two wine cellars. Off the kitchen on the north side was the scullery, with a copper, a sink with hot and cold water, and a fireplace. This room was designed for the wet and dirty kitchen tasks, the preparation of vegetables and the washing up. Adjoining it was a 'fitted butler's pantry'. Outside through a 'covered passage' were the servants' WC, a wood and coal house and the 'knife and boothouse'.

The centrepiece of the entrance hall was the 'wide easy staircase' with its gleaming banister rail. The curved stairs opened on the first floor to a 'spacious landing', 25 feet by nine feet, heated by radiator. Here were the five principal bedrooms, each one with its own fireplace. The largest one, 17 feet by 16 feet, was almost square. There were two 'excellent' bathrooms, 'one having lavatory basin, WC and linen cupboard, which is heated'. The domestic staff had their own WC and the use of a 'secondary staircase'. These stairs led to their living quarters on the second floor at the top of the house, three servants' bedrooms of good size – the largest was 17 feet by 13 feet – with 'hanging cupboards and modern grates'. There was also a 'housemaid's closet with sink and supply taps for hot and cold water'.[26]

This delightful family home stood in four acres, 'a pleasing feature, being very private and most attractively laid out in the well known taste of the late owner'. At the front were lawns and flower beds. Immediately behind the house was a 'productive' kitchen garden with an 'excellent south wall with peach and nectarine trees'. On the wall along the side drive was a 'three-division greenhouse with stove house, heating apparatus and staging' and a 'range of 16 glazed pits'. Next to the kitchen garden was a rose bed, a rock garden and an attractive herbaceous border. There was also a lawn for tennis or croquet, an arbour of yew trees, a rustic summer house and a sundial.

At a little distance away from the house, 'conveniently placed' down the side road, were the outbuildings. These were hidden from the Oxford Road. The stabling included 'two capital loose boxes' with a loft above, the groom's living room and bedroom, and a double coach house. Other buildings included the garage complete with pit, a traphouse, store room, and potting shed. There was also a yard with tool shed and pigsty and a small enclosed paddock.

Thomas Garlick bought Ormonde House in 1923 and lived there for 13 years. He was a watchmaker and jeweller with a long established business in Northbrook Street.[27] In 1936, the house came on the market again. This time it was bought by the Waldron family. A few years later, Mrs Waldron took on a young girl to help in the house. Her name was Vera Chandler.

'It's a lovely old house, isn't it?'

Along the River Lambourn beyond Donnington lies the picturesque village of Bagnor. Its old corn mill is now the home of the Watermill Theatre. Next to The Blackbird public house stands a row of cottages, and it was here that **Vera Chandler** lived as a child. There was no school in the village, so the young girl went

---

[26] Ormonde House Sales Brochure 1923.

[27] T H Garlick & Co., Jewellers & Opticians, 46 Northbrook Street.

to the school in Love Lane in Shaw where some of her classmates during the Second World War were evacuees from London. Vera stayed at school until she was nearly 15. It was 1941 and her mother found her a job as a housemaid at 38 Oxford Road. Vera was paid 15 shillings (75 pence) a week. She gave her mother 10 shillings (50 pence) for her keep, her father two shillings (10 pence) for his beer and she kept the rest for herself.

> Ormonde House was my first job. I think my mother knew the cook or somebody there and she just said to me, 'You're going there to work.' I had to do as I was told. I didn't live in the house – I came on my bicycle from Bagnor. I worked from eight or nine o'clock in the morning until after lunch, about two o'clock. Mrs Waldron was there on her own. She was quite elderly. Her son was a serving officer, a captain in the army, coming back on leave very occasionally. In the short time I was there, I only saw him once or twice.

The house was quiet, but Vera was not alone as Mrs Waldron employed two other young women, both of whom lived in. Kate and Emily Whitelands were sisters from Winterbourne, 'the next village along from Bagnor'. One worked as the cook, the other as housekeeper, and they lived in the rooms at the top of the house. 'The one at the front was the cook's bedroom; the one at the back was her sister's room.' Mrs Waldron also employed two other people who lived in a couple of the outbuildings, which had by this time been made into cottages.

> The chauffeur lived in one, the gardener in the other. The chauffeur's name was Mr Cooper. There was a garage down there next to the cottages – that's where the family car was kept. It was a big black car, but it wasn't used much. The gardener's wife used to come in the house and help do the cleaning jobs. There would have been more than one gardener there but during the war they cut it down to just the one. The men had to go to war. The gardener was over call-up age, say 60, the same as with the chauffeur, 50 to 60.

It was wartime and I used to do whatever they wanted me
to do, but I didn't scrub floors or anything like that. We
had a little Ewbank and you had to sweep round the floors
with that. I used to go in the room if they rang the bell. I
used to take coffee into them in the morning and worked
some afternoons taking tea in if there was anybody there. I
made the tea and took it into the drawing room, especially
when the housekeeper was off – she had one day off a
week. The cook and housekeeper had a uniform, but all I
had was a white hat and a white apron which my mother
used to wash and starch.

They were lovely big rooms. The dining room had an oak
dining table and a long sideboard with all the decanters on
it. That's all there was in there, just this long sideboard
and this enormous big table with two carver chairs and six
other chairs round. It was all oak in the dining room. They
did entertain occasionally at weekends, but during the war
they couldn't do much of that. In the drawing room they
had a bell, a big pull-cord. Mrs Waldron used to pull the
cord. They used to have lovely big log fires. The gardener
used to bring all the big polished scuttles with logs and
coal. Round the fireplace they used to have all the long
shiny fire tools. There was a conservatory going off the
drawing room. It was oval-shaped, all glass. The room
was lovely because of all the flowers, and there was a vine
in there. The conservatory had wicker armchairs. They
used to sit there in the afternoons and have their tea. At
the back was the study, not as large as these other rooms.
It had French doors going outside into the garden. It had
a fireplace. The gentlemen used to sit in the study a lot.
The kitchen was next to the study at the back of the house.
There was an Aga stove. There was no sink – you didn't
wash up in there. All the dishes were taken through to the
scullery to be washed – that was quite a big room as well.
At the back there was another little room which was the
maids' sitting room, and there was a pantry where they
used to do the silver. You went down a passage and down
some steps. Next to the pantry there was a cloakroom.

A flight of stone steps went from the kitchen to the cellars, where wine bottles and odds and ends were stored. However, it was wartime, and the cellars had another use. Newbury's air raid siren was located on the Wharf by the River Kennet. 'When it sounded, we all went down the cellars, the cook, the parlour maid, Mrs Waldron. The chauffeur and the gardener joined us. It was horrible and dark.'

The grand staircase was in the hall but 'round where the kitchen was there was another staircase where the maids used to go up'. These were the narrow and dark back stairs which went up to the second floor 'where there were two bedrooms and a bathroom' for the cook and the housekeeper. The stairs in the hall, with the 'lovely red carpet', opened on to the wide landing. In 1941, most of the rooms on this floor were empty.

> The first floor was all bedrooms and a bathroom. It was the middle of the war, the men were away fighting and few of the bedrooms were being used. One room was the son's bedroom and he also had a dressing room with all his clothes hanging up there. At the time I was there, only the lady's room was used, and her bathroom. Mrs Waldron's bedroom was at the front of the house and it was her bathroom off the landing. It was a large bathroom.

The family and their friends used the front entrance to the house. There were iron railings round the garden. 'These were taken down during the war, to be melted down, like the ones were in Victoria Park.' The government launched its scrap metal drive early in the war and all over the country railings from public parks and private gardens were dismantled. Ormonde House lost its railings and Newbury lost its Crimean Gun, taken from Victoria Park and melted down by Plenty.

On one side of the gravel drive entrance were the 'lovely clipped yew bushes in the lawn'. On the other side were 'big high shrubs', beyond which was the tradesmen's entrance, the side drive, used by Vera and the domestic staff. There was no access at the rear of the property. 'You couldn't get into Ormonde House any other way except from the Oxford Road. That's the way I used to go to work. There was a gate across because I used to get off my bicycle to open it. There was a back door in the house and you went straight into the scullery.'

At the back of the house were the gardens, quite private, with 'high hedges all the way round'. There was a large kitchen garden with vegetables – 'you had to do that during the war, grow more vegetables' – and lots of fruit bushes. 'There were apple trees, pears and peaches in these really big cages. I used to go down and help pick the fruit and the cook used to give me some to take home.' If the flower garden was maintained principally for visual effect, the kitchen garden was expected to earn its keep and play a part in the domestic economy.

Vera Chandler worked at Ormonde House for almost a year. When she left, Mrs Waldron gave her a present, a copy of *Little Women* by the American writer Louisa May Alcott. A few months passed, and the Waldron family also moved away. It was the end of an era. In the winter of 1942, Ormonde House was sold for £5,000.[28] Its days as a family home were over.

The girls move in

The war years were a restless time. Enemy bombing was a real threat in London, the sea ports and the great manufacturing cities. Rural areas were considered safer and almost every organisation of any size sent at least some of its departments out into the countryside. Newbury was seen as a relatively safe place and relocated office workers could find themselves in strange surroundings. The staff of the Great Western Railway moved from their Paddington headquarters to restaurant cars parked at the racecourse. Also from London came employees from the Shell petroleum company. Many strangers arrived in the market town, people from urban areas in England deemed unsafe, as well as refugees from the continent. In Britain as a whole, more than a million children were evacuated and Newbury took its share, from London, Kent and Southampton. Newbury-born writer Norman Longmate vividly remembers the crocodile of small boys and girls 'laden with cases and gas masks' arriving at the railway station

---

[28] Ormonde House Deeds, Land Certificate BK1166.

and making their way two by two up the road to the reception centre at the nearby Council School.[29] Two private girls' schools were relocated to Newbury from London. The Godolphin and Latymer School shared the County Girls' School, one school using the rooms in the mornings, the other in the afternoons. St Gabriel's School did not have to share. Their home from 1942 was Ormonde House. Across the road, they opened a kindergarten at 6 Donnington Square.

St Gabriel's was a private girls' school run by a teaching order of Anglican nuns called the Companions of Jesus the Good Shepherd. The school stayed in Ormonde House for six years. Twenty women were registered as living there in 1945.[30] Some alterations had to be made to the property recently vacated by the Waldrons. Living rooms were used as classrooms and the chatter of voices and shrieks of laughter could be heard coming from a chicken hut converted into a gymnasium. Two other wooden huts were joined together to make a chapel where the girls could assemble for prayers and Bible-readings.

It was at this time that the young **Roy Crocker** was training to be a carpenter, and one of his first jobs took him to Ormonde House.

> The chicken hut was a whacking great big long building. The firm that I worked for, Eggleton & Tallin, erected the thing in the first place. When I first started with them, a gang of carpenters went up there and lined the place out on the inside with studded plasterboard to make it more suitable. It was to be the girls' gymnasium. When they found the place wasn't high enough, Eggleton & Tallin had the chance of going down there, taking the roof off and lifting it up, making it two feet higher. But they couldn't cope with the job and Camp Hopson went up there and did it. They took the roof off and made it two feet higher so they had enough room for their gym. There were two more chicken huts round the back which they used for a chapel. I went up there soon after I started work, me and

---

[29] Longmate, *op.cit.*, p.51. Norman Longmate was born in Newbury and educated at Christ's Hospital School in Sussex.

[30] Newbury Civilian Register of Electors 1945.

this other carpenter, and we knocked these two chicken houses into one so that they had a bigger church. They were two side by side or end on end, and we cut the wall out so they had more room.

Once the war was over, the sisters of St Gabriel's started to look for new and bigger premises for their school. They wanted to stay in Newbury and they unsuccessfully tried to buy Shaw House. Their interest was alerted again when Sandleford Priory came on the market. This property was on the south side of the town alongside the Winchester road. The former medieval priory had long been used as a private house. It became fashionable in the late 18th century when architect James Wyatt remodelled it as a Gothic country house, 'Capability' Brown laid out the gardens and hostess Elizabeth Montagu entertained the literary and artistic celebrities of the day. It remained a family house until the Second World War, when it was used as a convalescent hospital for wounded servicemen.

St Gabriel's bought Sandleford Priory in 1948. It was set in 30 acres, significantly bigger than their home on the Oxford Road. The girls and their teachers moved in, again alterations were necessary, and again Camp Hopson did much of the work. One of their bricklayers remembers working there for a while. 'One of the old bricklayers was doing the alterations up there – I wasn't up there very long, 'cos that's what they used to threaten you with if you didn't behave.' One of the young painters remembers spending time there as well. 'They were nuns there you know, and when we'd finished, they gave us a party!'[31]

The Institute moves in

The Institute of Further Education at Ormonde House, Newbury, was established in 1948 and replaced the Newbury Evening Institute which had its headquarters in the old Technical Institute in Northbrook Street.

FESC 19 January 1951

---

[31] Interviews with Graham Tillen and Alan Lawrence.

By the spring of 1948, with St Gabriel's getting ready to move to Sandleford, Berkshire LEA had already decided to purchase a building in Newbury to use as an FE institute. When Ormonde House came on the market, it was interested. The premises, after all, 'had been used by an evacuated school and might, therefore, be suitable for the Authority's purposes'.

Further investigation showed that the house was, indeed, suitable – and there was much potential. It was estimated that the conservatory could take up to 60 students while smaller classes could be accommodated in the bedrooms. The rooms at the top of the house could be used as living quarters for a superintendent while other staff could live in the cottages round the back.[32] The gymnasium and chapel – the wooden chicken huts – could be used for lessons and the lean-to greenhouse and the garage for practical work. There was scope to make use of the other outbuildings as well. Furthermore, if there was money available, there was space for new buildings.

So in March 1948, the LEA started negotiations to buy the property. The members of the Further Education Subcommittee were excited. They were so convinced of the suitability of Ormonde House that if agreement on the price could not be reached, they wanted to use a compulsory purchase order. It did not come to that. The price was agreed. Berkshire County Council bought Ormonde House and its 4.1 acres for £8,000.[33] The Victorian building on the Oxford Road in Speenhamland was to become the headquarters of the Newbury Institute of Further Education.

'The last thing we did down at the Boys' Club would have been in the spring of 1948'

Local boy **Roy Crocker** (b.1931) was expecting to go to the Council School at the age of 11; instead he found himself among the first group of pupils to be sent to Shaw House. A few years later, his schooldays over, he had to find himself a job.

---

[32] BEC 30 July 1948.

[33] Ormonde House Deeds, Land Certificate BK1166; FESC 14 May 1948.

I started school at St John's which was up Newtown Road, then I went to St Nicholas' School which was up Enborne Road, and then we had to go up to Shaw because the school in Station Road had been bombed. There were two buildings. One was supposed to be for the boys and one for the girls, but it didn't work out quite like that. Some of the girls were in the boys' part and some of the boys were in the girls' part. One of the buildings had a direct hit with a bomb in the war.

I left school after my 14th birthday on 5th December 1945 and started work on 7th January 1946. I was with a firm called Eggleton & Tallin in Berkeley Road. I walked into the office and said, 'Do you want an apprentice?' I was in carpentry. We had to do 12 months before we could be signed on. We were some of the last people to leave school when we were 14, and they said you can't be signed on until you're 15. So everybody in our year did a year at work before we could be signed on. It was very unfair really to make us wait a year when we were getting paid hardly anything.

The apprenticeship started in January 1947. We signed the indentures in a building in Craven Road behind the Coopers Arms. It was called the Oddfellows Hall.[34] It was the Ministry of Labour and National Service. It was where you had to go when you were 18 to sign on for National Service – you had to go along there on a Saturday afternoon.

The apprenticeship was for five years. The war was over, council house building was picking up and Newbury builders started to take on more apprentices. Much of the training was on site, with the apprentices working alongside skilled craftsmen, but there was also an opportunity to go to classes. In 1946, the classes were held in an upstairs room in the Council School building.

---

[34] The Oddfellows Hall was at 2 Craven Road.

I started work at the beginning of January 1946 and we started the evening class in the springtime of that year. We did one evening a week for two hours at the old Council School in Station Road. We did general building, you know, just lectures on general building. It was only for a few months we were up at Station Road. When we finished there, we went down to what was part of the Boys' Club in Northbrook Street. This had been going a long time. We did two years down there, one afternoon a week definitely, and I have got an idea we did an evening as well. The last thing we did down at the Boys' Club would have been in the spring of 1948 – you didn't do any courses or things during the summer months. I won a prize which was reported in the *Newbury Weekly News*. We had a book token and I bought two books with it.

Roy and the other young men finished at the Institute – 'the Boys' Club' – in the spring of 1948. By the time classes started again in the autumn, Ormonde House was ready.

Superintendent Owthwaite arrives

Mr A H Owthwaite has been appointed Superintendent of the Institute of Technical and Further Education, Newbury. It is anticipated that Mr Owthwaite will take up his duties early in July.

NWN 3 June 1948

The FE institutes set up in 1948 at Maidenhead, Newbury and Windsor each had a Superintendent responsible for 'the development of Technical and Evening School Work'. The establishment of day-release classes had 'increased the need for such appointments'. It was anticipated that 'at least half their time' would be taken up by evening work and the rest given over 'preferably to the Day Release work or possibly to Secondary School teaching'. Their students would come from the three towns and the immediate neighbourhood.[35]

---

[35] FESC 20 February 1948; BEC 30 April 1948, 25 June 1948.

In the first instance, the Superintendents were only to be responsible for classes in the towns. The institutes were to develop initially by meeting the needs of the immediate locality. They were not given responsibility for the work in their neighbouring villages. In those parts of the county, for 1948/49 at least, the existing arrangements with part-time superintendents were to continue. However, the new Superintendents would be 'expected to give any help and encouragement which seems desirable, especially in the formation of new centres'.[36] In other words, the new arrangements were to complement the existing ones.

LEA members expressed a note of caution while discussing the detail of the new appointments. If the Superintendents did not have a full working week, 'some teaching in schools may be required, in order to make up full-time service'.[37] This serves as a gentle reminder that the outcome of the adventure into a land of promise was not known. With hindsight, it is easy to look back at the growth of Newbury College, and the other Berkshire colleges, and assume that expansion was in some ways inevitable. This would be a mistake. There is a danger of reading too much into the story too soon. What started in 1948 was, in a literal sense, a voyage of adventure, destination unknown.

When the journey began, the country was struggling with the economic difficulties and the financial constraints of the years of austerity. Furthermore, discoveries were made once the journey was under way. It was always difficult to predict the demand for further education, which remained, after all, non-compulsory. Moreover, the nature of FE work, with its large number of short courses and part-time students who could, potentially, drop out at any time, made the situation volatile. Again, the dynamic of the further education adventure was continually influenced by social trends, by demographic factors, by the movement of peoples and the growth of towns. Development was planned for Newbury. The population was to increase by 5,000 in the early 1950s and roads were to be built to relieve the anticipated traffic congestion. Thatcham was also earmarked for development. Population expansion was likely to increase the demand for FE

---

[36] FESC 4 June 1948.

[37] BEC 25 June 1948.

opportunities. There were other factors influencing post-school education as well. Government policy was always important, whether it be to do with apprenticeship training and day release or the public commitment to non-vocational courses. The money available for new buildings, laboratories and workshops was always an issue, especially in the early years in the grey bleakness of post-war Britain, while LEA support was influenced by the ratepayers, by the results of local elections and by the policies of whichever political party was in power.

As it turned out, the transformation of Newbury from the market town of 1948 into the dynamic commercial centre of today enabled its college to grow. Moreover, the growth of Thatcham was meteoric. Housing estates mushroomed and green fields gave way to red brick as the population rose from fewer than 5,000 in 1948 to more than 10,000 in 1971 – and exceeding 20,000 by 1991. There were also rapid developments at Harwell and Aldermaston, especially in the 1950s. Further afield was the economic activity along the M4 motorway and the Thames Valley, what became popularly known as 'Silicon Valley'. Yet none of this was certain when the new head of the Newbury Institute arrived in Ormonde House in the summer of 1948.

On Tuesday, 27 April 1948, the LEA interviewed ten applicants for the three Superintendent posts. Of the successful candidates, two came from technical colleges, one from a school. F W Tweddell, from Hinkley Technical College in Leicestershire, was appointed to Maidenhead and J Martin, from the County Boys' School in Maidenhead, was given the job at Windsor. Albert Owthwaite from Blackpool Technical College was to be in charge in Newbury.[38]

Albert Owthwaite was to work at Ormonde House for seven years. An honours graduate in French (Sheffield, Poitiers and Lille universities), he came to Newbury with an impressive track record, having worked in technical and grammar schools as well as FE centres.

> After spending a year in France on research and lecturing at a French college, he successively served as senior French

---

[38] FESC 14 May 1948.

and commerce master at the Priestman Technical School, Bradford; handicraft, art and commerce master at the Grammar School, Llanfyllin, Mont.; handicraft and sixth form economics master at Grove Park Grammar School, Wrexham; master in charge of the Day Commercial School and headmaster of the Wilsden Evening Institute, Bingley, Yorks; and Head of the Modern Languages Department, Palatine Technical School, Blackpool, and Lecturer in Commerce, Blackpool Technical College.

During the war he had worked as a buyer for Rolls Royce and as a technical officer on explosives for the Ministry of Supply. In 1945 he was awarded his MA for research into commercial and technical education.[39]

The Superintendent's salary was between £300 and £555. In comparison, the salary of the headmistress of the County Girls' School was £944, while the headmaster of Newbury Grammar School enjoyed a salary of £1,195.[40] Albert Owthwaite started at the Newbury Institute on 1 July 1948. His office was at the back of the house at the end of the landing on the first floor. Its windows looked out onto the rose garden and the orchard.

The Institute was due to open in less than three months, and he had much work to do. His immediate responsibility was to decide which courses to put on for the coming session. The previous year's classes would guide him here, the education authority had a view as to what should be on offer and ideas were exchanged with his colleagues at Maidenhead and Windsor. Most important of all, however, were discussions with the town's employers. Those who were already training apprentices – the builders, Plenty, the SEB, garages like Marchant's – had to be persuaded of the value of enhancing their training by the day-release mode of study. Other employers without a formal arrangement in place had to be convinced of its value. The Superintendent had to persuade them of the benefits of day release, and he needed to know what they wanted from the curriculum. After all, Ormonde House was a local institute to meet the needs of local firms.

---

[39] *NWN* 3 June 1948.

[40] Secondary Schools Subcommittee 19 December 1947; FESC 15 July 1949.

Once classes had been agreed, Albert Owthwaite had to find teachers and publicise the information so that the townsfolk could be kept abreast of what was happening. Working closely with the LEA, decisions were taken about the curriculum, to be advertised in the *Newbury Weekly News* in September and October.

Instructors had to be employed. Some of these would have been teaching the previous year; others would be new. It was expected, in the first instance at least, that they would continue to be employed part time. The Education Committee had advertised in May, inviting people to join 'the Panel of Part-time Instructors in Courses for Adults in Towns and Villages throughout the County'. Most of the teaching would be in the evening. However, day-release courses for 15- to 18-year-olds were anticipated; as were afternoon classes for women.[41] Commercial subjects – bookkeeping, shorthand and typewriting – and technical subjects, such as building, mathematics, motor engineering and technical drawing, were planned. So were recreational classes in ballroom dancing, civics and current affairs, cookery, dramatics, dressmaking, folk dancing, handicrafts and home decoration, metalwork, music appreciation, physical training and woodwork.

The Superintendent also had to organise the teaching accommodation. The rooms in Northbrook Street would continue to be used but most of the classes were to be at Oxford Road where, over the summer, urgent work was done. Rooms were decorated, power points installed, heating and lighting facilities improved. The LEA spent £525 getting the house ready for September. It was a busy time, and work was still being done when the first students arrived. A few weeks later, and more money was needed as further work had to be done.[42]

Some of the alterations were for the living quarters for Albert and Elsie Owthwaite. They had no family living with them. Their flat consisted of the two rooms at the top of the house and two of the rooms on the first floor. The rent was 15 shillings (75 pence) a week, increased twelve months later to 18 shillings (90 pence), inclusive of rates and repairs. The Superintendent had to

---

[41] *NWN* 6 May 1948.

[42] Building and Works Subcommittee 16 July 1948; FESC 30 July 1948; Education Finance Subcommittee 1 October 1948.

provide 'his own fuel for the hot water system should he desire to use this when it was not required for school purposes'. The flat had its own gas and electricity meters. The Owthwaites moved in to Ormonde House on 1 September 1948. It was to be their home for three years.

Something new at Ormonde House

The opening of Ormonde House was eagerly anticipated and it was ready on time. The Newbury Institute of Further Education welcomed its first students on Monday, 13 September 1948.

LESSONS AND LEISURE
At New Educational Institute

Something new in the way of educational facilities for students and adults will be provided by the Institute of Further Education, opening shortly at Ormonde House, Oxford-road, Newbury.

Intended as a centre for technical and non-vocational training, the courses planned include day release sessions for building, electrical engineering and mechanical engineering apprentices, advanced evening classes in electrical, mechanical and automobile engineering, commerce, economics and banking. There will also be trade classes for butchers and grocers, and the syllabus includes languages, matriculation, agriculture, horticulture, arts and crafts, dressmaking, leatherwork and cookery.

It is hoped to combine lessons and leisure in a manner that will make the Institute a social centre for those attending classes. A students' union is being planned, with common room, canteen and table tennis, so

that people attending evening classes can
finish up with social activity and dancing.

Age limit is 15 and upwards. The Institute
opens with a day release course for building
apprentices on September 13th.

NWN 9 September 1948

Roy Crocker was now a second-year apprentice. Most of his
classes so far had been in the evenings with only the occasional
afternoon. From now on, it was to be very different. 'We never did
a whole day release until we went to Ormonde House.' Roy and
his friends were about to make a little piece of educational history.

4

THERE WERE BRICKLAYERS, CARPENTERS, PAINTERS AND PLUMBERS

'There was a lot of building going on in Newbury. All these companies had apprentices, and all these apprentices had to come to the college.'

'We went right in at the start so it wasn't really organised. Everybody used to roar in on push bikes – very few had motorbikes and I didn't know anybody who had a car.'

'I reckon that if you took all five years, there would be over 200 building apprentices. I bet every builder in the town had four apprentices working for them, besides all the ones that was out in the country.'

The young men who gathered outside Ormonde House on that autumn morning in 1948 were all in the building trade: bricklayers, carpenters, plumbers and painters. A couple of them were plastering apprentices. 'They were a bit thin on the ground because that was a hard, monotonous job. It's worse than brickwork.' The construction industry was strongly associated with apprenticeships and training. Building classes had been taught in the years before the First World War and a programme for apprentices had been organised from the mid-1920s. The association between the Institute and the Newbury builders lasted for over 50 years and it played an important part in the growth of further education in the town.

At the end of the Second World War there was a lot of pressure on the construction industry. In London, the ports and the industrial towns, there was much work to be done repairing the damage caused by bombing. Moreover, in the 1945 election campaign, Labour had promised a massive house building programme. There was urgency about the training of building workers and government departments and public authorities were urged to play their part as 'good employers' in training apprentices under approved agreements.[1]

In 1948 Newbury's builders agreed to release their apprentices for one day each week to Ormonde House. The day-release students were typically between 15 and 18 years old and they were paid as though it was a normal working day. At 18, the pattern of study changed. From then on it was night school, one or two evenings a week in their own time for which they were not paid. The training was thorough and there were examinations and City & Guilds certificates to be gained. This was a big change: previous courses, in Newbury at least, had not included opportunities to achieve nationally recognised qualifications.

The young building workers and most of the other apprentices who came to Ormonde House were part of the traditional indentured apprenticeship scheme which has been superseded by the kinds of training provision common today.[2] The indentured scheme was a contractual agreement between the employer and the apprentice. The employer was contracted to train the individual to a particular standard, sometimes but not always measured by passing examinations. The apprentice on his part agreed to undergo the training and fulfil the requirements of the contract, and would potentially be in breach of the agreement if he failed to attend classes.

'It was absolute bloody bedlam!'

Roy Crocker was one of the young men at Ormonde House when it opened and at least three others from Eggleton & Tallin came with him. Roy lived in Jubilee Road, cycling to the Institute in the

---

[1] FESC 20 February 1948.

[2] The modern apprenticeship common today is usually a tripartite arrangement between employer, apprentice and training provider.

daytime – he lived close enough to go home for lunch – walking there in the evening. Most of the apprentices came on their bicycles. A few, particularly those who lived outside Newbury, had motorbikes. 'The only person I knew that had a car was the plumber from Woolton Hill – he used to use his dad's.'

Roy was not happy at the thought of 'going back to school'. He had left Shaw House some years before and English, mathematics and current affairs reminded him of his schooldays. This was a common feeling: 'Everybody would rather have been at work than at college.'

> When we first went up to Ormonde House, they used to start treating us like school kids: 'You can't do this' and 'You can't do that'. Of course, blokes rebelled against that. We'd been at work three years and we didn't want to be treated like bloody children again. We certainly weren't having any of that. When they came up with the English lesson, when this woman was supposed to teach us, that put the cat amongst the pigeons. It was absolute bloody bedlam! There was nobody in the class interested in English – we just didn't want to know. It was as if you were at school with 11-year-olds.

> That English class – it wasn't literature – was often the first one of the day. When we'd finished, there used to be a nice old chap come along to take us for maths. He was a retired teacher from up at the Grammar School. Maths didn't worry me.

Current affairs lessons were in a wooden shed. 'About six foot away from the conservatory there was a chicken house, a biggish building, which we used as a classroom.' The teacher was 'something to do with the printing industry – he used to talk about printing and things'. He used to come 'in the afternoons' but usually the timetable after lunch was filled with building classes. 'When we first went, we used to go up there and do this practical in the afternoon. We used to take our own tools with us because they never had any. But later on, towards the time when we were getting ready to finish, they did get some tools.' For the practical work, they were grouped into their trades. Roy and the carpenters had lessons in carpentry, general building, woodwork and technical drawing. All the builders did drawing. So did the engineers, and technical drawing was the single most popular subject taught at Ormonde House.

There were four wooden huts in the garden: one by the conservatory, two out the back which had been used as the chapel, and a 'big one which was down at the bottom'.

> That was a whacking great big long building that used to be St Gabriel's gymnasium. It was divided in half. The carpenters had half of it for their benches and their practical work, the other half was a classroom. One of the panes of glass was missing for months and months during the winter time, and they had this wire over. Old Arthur Owen used to say, 'It's bloody cold in here!' And one bloke used to say, 'You don't want to worry. That wire's cutting it all up into little bits!' We had some 'slow but sures', tortoise stoves in the middle of the floor. It wasn't too bad during the day when you was doing practical.

> Arthur Owen was the only full-time lecturer that was up there on the building. In 1948 he did a lesson in estimating. I don't know what they called it, but it was a lesson where you had to find out how much material you wanted on a job and how much it would cost, pricing it all up like quantity surveying, that sort of thing. Then in the afternoons he took practical woodwork.

Arthur Owen 'was out of the building industry – he was born into it'. His father was managing director of E B Hitchman in Speenhamland, where Arthur worked as a carpenter and site foreman. 'Over the years, nine times out of ten, the carpenter becomes a general foreman. The carpenters are normally a bit more methodical than the trowel men. I've worked under bricklayer generals, but you always find that the carpenter ones are a bit more switched on.'[3] Arthur Owen had been teaching

---

[3] Interview with Graham Tillen.

the apprentices before 1948, and when they were transferred to Ormonde House, he came with them. He was the tutor who welcomed them when they arrived and he was the one who organised their course. Initially paid by the builders, he was soon moved over to the LEA's payroll. The post was not advertised. He was already doing the job.[4]

Arthur Owen was the only full-timer, so Roy Crocker and his friends were usually taught by part-timers.

> You didn't have the same person for the same class all the time. You swapped and moved about. Somebody would come for a term and teach you and then they'd vanish. A lot of the people that taught were only part time – they only came for a couple of years. They were not trained teachers – they were just people that they could get to do the job. We had this bloke for drawing that was an architect, and there was a bloke from Camp Hopson used to come and teach us in the evenings. He was a very good carpenter, ever such a tidy sort of bloke. Another chap that we had took us for practical woodwork. He used to run a sports shop over the top of Etherington's paper shop in Cheap Street. I could never see him working on the building.

After two years, a second full-time building lecturer was taken on. J Forster (brickwork) finished at teacher-training college at the end of June in 1950, and he was appointed to Ormonde House from 1 July. Interestingly, the education authority was concerned as to what he was going to do during the two summer months. Consequently the Newbury Division found him work until he started at the Institute on 1 September.[5]

Spending a whole day at the Institute each week encouraged the apprentices to become friends with one another. Those who did not go home for lunch, and that was most of them, often walked down the Oxford Road into town. They also got to know some of the staff. 'When we were there during the day we met all these people, but when you finished days and you only went evenings,

---

[4] FESC 17 February 1949.

[5] *Ibid.*, 21 July 1950.

you never saw anybody else. It was dark but you knew where you had to go for your classes. You just went in and you only met the lecturer that was taking that particular subject. You never met all these other people, like the office staff and that.' Early in 1949, the builders were taken to the Ideal Homes Exhibition in London, a pioneering educational visit. The Superintendent asked the LEA for a grant towards the costs but the request was turned down. 'Such a visit would only be indirectly concerned with the work of the day release courses.'[6]

Evening classes were often held in the rooms in the house. The conservatory was 'like walking into a bloody fridge'. There was some heating, 'but you know what a place is like which is all glass – there's nothing to keep the heat in is there?'

Within a year or so a rudimentary canteen service was in operation. The kitchen facilities were used for mid-morning refreshments – the caretaker and his wife were responsible for this – but Superintendent Albert Owthwaite was surprised by the students' reaction:

> Another thing which happened – the way they treated us like kids – it was NAAFI break in the middle of the morning. Peter's, the cake shop, was in Oxford Road, almost opposite the Bacon Arms. They ran a café as well so we all used to go down to Peter's and get a cake and whatever we wanted. We used to walk down there some mornings, buy a Swiss roll and eat that, and at other times, six cream doughnuts and eat them. Then they started having tea and coffee and biscuits in what they called the canteen in Ormonde House – that was the room on the left hand side of the entrance hall. The Principal stood up and told us that we wasn't to go down the road to Peter's.
>
> 'That's got to stop. If you want tea and coffee, you've got to buy it from the thing here.'
>
> 'We're not buying bloody tea and coffee off you up there. We're still going down to Peter's!'

---

[6] *Ibid.*, 17 February 1949.

Any absence was promptly reported to the employers; so 'most people' attended 'most of the time'. An occasional absence meant a telling-off, but anyone who missed a lot of classes could be excluded from the Institute and might have his apprenticeship terminated.

> The other carpenter apprentice with me absolutely hated going to these evening classes. He used to miss quite a lot of them and at eight o'clock the next morning, the governor used to walk out of the office with a letter in his hand. 'You never went to school last night did you?' How the hell they got it up there so bloomin' quick, goodness only knows. If he never went there in the evening, the next morning at eight o'clock the governor had that letter in his hand as he walked out of the office.

> I was one of those who never missed many classes, but I had the bloody jaws ache one day and couldn't bloody go. And the governor came to me at eight o'clock and said, 'You never went last night Roy?' I never said anything, but I thought, if they ask you anything, tell them you had the jaws ache. And I thought, well it's not a lie 'cos I did have the jaws ache. How these governors got these things by the first post the next morning, goodness only knows, but they did. Eight o'clock, that's the honest truth. They called the registers at seven o'clock and if you weren't there, they got the letters out.

> Our bricklayer wouldn't behave himself and go to school. He was missing classes. They finished his apprenticeship and told him to 'sling yer hook'. He was the only person I can remember being kicked out, though a lot of them didn't like going.

Roy Crocker went to the Institute for three years. He left in 1951. 'As soon as my birthday arrived on 5th December, I said cheerio. That was it. I'd finished with it. I didn't want any more to do with it.' His apprenticeship was over. Two months later he joined His Majesty's Armed Forces and was on his way to London.

'You prefer to have been on the tools really'

George Milsom lived in Thatcham and went to one of the all-age schools 'all the way through from five to 14'. Thatcham Council School had opened on the Bath Road just before the First World War. The other school in the village was older. St Mary's on Park Lane had begun as a National School (C of E) in the mid-19th century. Both schools gave the children an 'elementary education' until their reorganisation following Butler's Act.[7]

In 1948 George was training to be a plumber, but when he had left school 18 months before, he had been heading for the board mills at Colthrop. His father, however, had other ideas.

> I left school at 13. I was nearly 14 – my birthday is on 27th December, and you always left before Christmas. Dad came out of the Royal Marines and went down to Colthrop mill on maintenance, and of course, the Council School fed the mill. You had people come in as you were about to leave school, suggesting what you were to do. This lady came in one day and said, 'I think Dick and Harry would be just right for the mill.' And she gave me this card to go down there. Dad came home and there's this card on the mantelpiece. 'What's this then, boy?' I said, 'Well, they suggested I go down the mill and ...' He said, 'If I catch you down the bloody mill I'll kick your arsehole!' So that was that.

Fortunately George's father did not leave the matter there. He had a friend who worked for F J Reynolds, the local builders, and he went to see him.

> 'Do they want any apprentices?'
> And he said, 'I could do with a boy with me.'
> So dad called in on a Saturday dinner time on the way home from work.

---

[7] The existing school accommodation remained for a while after the 1944 Act but by the mid-'50s the Council School – built for 350 – had 545 pupils. The Kennet School (secondary) opened in September 1957 and the village schools became primary schools for pupils aged five to 11.
The Council School was renamed Francis Baily School in 1964.

And they said, 'Tell him to come down on Monday.'
And he said to me, 'Well boy, there's a job for you.'
So that was that. That's how I started.

George's experience in starting work was typical of many boys at this time, fathers taking responsibility for getting their sons a start in life.

George was just 14 years old when he cycled out to Cold Ash early one morning to start his first job. 'It was an outhouse, a big flat roof place, down Bucklebury Alley. It had had a fire and they were renovating the place.' A year later he signed his indentures. Ormonde House opened and he was sent there on day release. He was not overenthusiastic.

> Ormonde House was like school, and you had had enough of school. You wanted to get out into the wide world and make a living. When current affairs and all that came along, at that age you're not terribly impressed. You prefer to have been on the tools really. During the day we were doing technical drawing, English, current affairs and things like that. I was looking at a book not so long ago – I done some smashing drawings. The same people used to take us for English and current affairs. We were all together then. We kept to our own trades in the evening – then we were doing our plumbing.

> When the Institute first went up there, there wasn't so much land as what they got later. There was an old house at the side of it, on Oxford Road, which they bought later and pulled down for extra space. The side drive used to go straight the way down to our chicken house and round the back of the house and its garden. There was a high wall on one side of the drive. These lean-to greenhouses used to go down the other side of that – originally that would have been the vegetable garden for the main house. The tennis courts were just behind the chicken house. They were hard courts. We had a carpenter working with us and he used to go up there in the evenings and play on them. One of our friends was sat on top of the fence one day and ripped

his trousers all open. The caretaker had to take him into the cottage down there and sew his trousers up.

The plumbing workshop was the 'big garage, next door to the cottage where the caretaker lived, opposite the chicken house, down the bottom'. It had 'big sliding doors which went back round the side – there was room for two cars in there'.

The plumbers were in one half of the garage, the bricklayers in the other. 'Ernie Newport took us for plumbing.' A registered plumber, he had his own business on the London Road in the town, opposite the Cross Keys public house.

> He used to tell us tales about the old toilets they used to have with the flaps at the bottom. He had a lot of tales to tell after a lifetime in plumbing, with all the different things. You can go on talking about different jobs for hours, especially in the building trade, blimey!

> When we first went to college they had nothing. It was 'make do and mend'. Even the people that taught us, they were all part-timers then. People from other jobs used to come in. Sully used to take us for something – he was an engineer on the cars. But at that time, when it was new, we used to see different people for different things.

> I never missed a day release. Every year in February I used to get tonsillitis – I used to have it when I went to school. That would have meant I missed a day release, but I gradually grew out of it. But an evening, that was different. I missed, if there was a girl to meet or something like that.

George Milsom went to the Institute for three years. He finished his apprenticeship at the end of 1951. Two months later he started his National Service. Many of the generation of apprentices at Ormonde House between 1948 and 1960 were called up for National Service. During the Second World War people had accepted conscription but its continuance into peacetime was unprecedented. Yet Britain was a world power, the small professional forces could not meet the huge demands placed upon them, and the army generals were demanding more and more men. Manpower was important in the government's strategic thinking and there was an expectation that you had to do your bit for the country. The result was that, for more than a decade, thousands of young men in their late teens and early 20s were recruited into National Service. Conscription was initially for 18 months but when the Korean War broke out in 1950, it was extended to two years. After two years in the barracks, where many later reckoned the humour and companionship had done them good, the servicemen became civilians again in their old workplace. 'They had to give you your job back.' The return to 'Civvy Street' could be difficult and in 1955 MP Anthony Hurd voiced his concerns about the difficulties some of them were facing.

'It was well known that you very seldom got where you wanted to in National Service. If you wanted to go in the RAF you usually ended up in the army.' Most of the peacetime conscripts became soldiers, some became airmen, and fewer became sailors. Many of the soldiers never left Britain and did not hear a shot fired in anger. However, some spent their time in West Germany, a highly desirable posting, while a small number experienced action in such hot spots of conflict as Korea, Egypt, Malaya and Cyprus.

At its peak, in the early '50s, there were 6,000 recruits every fortnight. Then, in the mid-'50s, government defence thinking began to change. Future strategy was to be based on the nuclear deterrent rather than big labour-intensive armies. In 1957 British H-bomb tests started on Christmas Island in the Indian Ocean and a White Paper on defence argued that the country could reduce her conventional forces and rely to a greater extent on nuclear weapons. This new strategy led to cuts in the armed forces and the phasing-out of National Service. The final call-up papers were sent out at the beginning of 1961 and the last conscripts were demobbed two years later.

Young men were liable to be called up when they reached the age of 18 and in Newbury, registration took place in the Ministry of Labour offices in Craven Road. It was difficult to get out of it, unless you were deemed medically unfit. However, those on a five-year apprenticeship could defer their call-up until after their training. To be deferred it was important to follow the correct procedure and it seems that not everybody was aware of this. The town's builders were concerned.

> Many parents of boys entering the building industry fail to realise that for their boys to complete their five years training and obtain the advantages of deferment of National Service it is necessary for them to become properly indentured apprentices not later than their 17th birthday.
>
> This entails attendance at Day Release and evening classes from the commencement of their employment and unless this condition is complied with the Local Joint Apprenticeship Committee for the Building Industry are unable to endorse their indentures.
>
> Many cases have come before the Committee recently where parents (and even employers when these are not members of one of the building organisations) pleaded ignorance of their obligations, and asked for emergency action to prevent interruption of apprenticeship by call-up.
>
> May I be permitted to stress the importance of entering into proper indentures preferably on attaining the age of 16, failing which it may not be possible to obtain deferment when the boy registers for National Service?
>
> RUSSELL H. RADCLIFFE,
> Chairman, Local Joint Apprenticeship Committee for the Building Industry.[8]

Nine of the young men who feature in this volume were conscripted, two others failed the medical. Six of them joined the army, three became airmen, and none of them went into the navy. When it was over, six returned to their former workplace, the other three decided to look for new jobs.

---

[8] *NWN* 30 November 1950. Russell Radcliffe was a governor at Ormonde House from 1951 to 1958.

Life in National Service began with basic training, 'eight weeks square-bashing', which finished with the passing-out parade. Then came the posting, which seems to have been very much a matter of luck. Six of our nine recruits stayed in Britain and three were posted overseas. Two of these went to West Germany and the other one was sent to North Africa. This was George Milsom.

'Some of the stuff at college I had quite a job to grasp'

Graham Tillen was a 'brickie' from a family whose connections with building went back at least two generations. His grandfather, 'a good tradesman, slow and methodical', had worked for Hoskings & Pond, builders of St Joseph's Catholic Church. A foreman, complete with bowler hat, he had the power to hire and fire. Graham's father was a carpenter. So was one of his uncles; and another uncle had a spell as a general foreman for Bosley 'which was quite a big firm'. Lots of Graham's family worked on the building and he was pleased to do the same.

Graham was born in Newbury, moved to Bucklebury and when he was five, moved again, this time to Thatcham. This is where Graham grew up, going to St Mary's School where his mother had once been a pupil. 'We had to march down to church on certain days.'

> The education that we had was very, very basic, you know, the old reciting of times tables and all that. There were a couple that couldn't read or write when they left. I'm not complaining about it – it served me very well. The teachers were very, very kind. They persevered with you and they got it out of you. The education was very basic unless you were good enough or clever enough to go to Newbury Grammar School. There were no schools like the Kennet. The standard of education has changed tremendously in the last 50 years. Even at primary now, my great nieces and nephews are so switched on. With the world they're going to be living in, they've got to be, haven't they?

When he left school, Graham got a job with Camp Hopson. It was the summer of 1946, and he was 14. The job was 'for a month or a trial period', 40 hours a week, Monday to Friday. 'Camp Hopson was a reputable builder with a big staff in those days.' They were building council houses in Newport Road, off the London Road to the north of the town. Graham was filled with pride as he was taken on to the site by Paul Hopson himself.

> I'd seen Mr Paul Hopson 'cos my father took me in there and we got the job. I had to go in on the Monday. I went into the office and Mr Hopson said to me, 'Do you know where Newport Road is my boy?'
> I said, 'Yes sir, yes sir, I know.'

> 'Well,' he said, 'you get on your bicycle and you go on down there. I'll give you a start and then I will catch you up and take you down.' So I got on this bloody bike and I pedalled as fast as I could down there. He had this big old Wolseley car and he passed me going down Newport Road. He said to old Harry White, our foreman, 'I've brought you this new lad.'

> He was a very fair man Mr Hopson, although you didn't have that much to do with him. Although he ran the building, Mr Bates was the actual manager. But Mr Hopson gave me the job and he took me down there.

> You had to work for a year before you could be an apprentice, but as a matter of fact, that first 12 months was part of your training. You got an extra year. Now I think they do about two at the most – that's something else. We did six, so we were lucky really.

Graham's trial period went well and when he was 15, he was taken on as an apprentice at 16 shillings (80 pence) a week. 'Whatever the bricklayers were on, you got a percentage. If their rate went up, your rate went up. That's how they worked it out.' The rate increased each year 'as you got more experience and better in the job'. Graham was a quick learner. 'I was laying bricks alongside the bricklayers time I was 16. I was on the outside with our foreman.'

During the first year of his training in 1947, Camp Hopson encouraged him to go to Arthur Owen's evening classes which were part of the local apprenticeship programme.

> Before the formation of the college, Arthur Owen took this building construction at the British Restaurant, which was up by the railway station. It was a great long building opposite the railway line, right next door to where the Council School was that was bombed during the war. As you were going up towards St John's, there was a gate opposite Pound Street. We went in round the back. It was in the upstairs part; we had a room up there. We had to climb these bloody fire escape steps, metal steps.

> We were told that this instruction was going to take place. It was all voluntary; you just went along. All trades went. There was carpenters, bricklayers, painters and plumbers. It was just once a week. You would pop in seven to nine or something like that. Arthur Owen was taking building construction in this room up the stairs. It covered the basic things of the trade. He was working as a joiner in those days and he was doing this in a part-time capacity. He was a very quiet-spoken, methodical sort of chap, the sort of chap you could listen to. The instruction was very good. Arthur Owen was obviously capable of doing that and he'd been asked to do it.

A year later and this voluntary attendance for a couple of hours a week was all changed.

> When they got it organised from Ormonde House, we had to do two evenings and a day-release course. We had to go – that was part of the agreement. They said your indentures will be cancelled or summat and you'll be going into the army. You've signed this agreement and you have to go. You had to attend. They reported back to the builders, who used to get a report of our progress, how we were getting on, if we were misbehaving or whatever. And your parents backed it up in those days.

When we were first up there at Ormonde House, it was all a bit alien to us. But this day-release course was well organised and it went on into the evening. If the day release was on a Wednesday, you might have to go, say, to building technology on a Monday night from seven to nine. It made sense to do one of your evenings the same as the day; otherwise you would have to have gone to college three times a week.

Going to classes in the daytime required little effort. 'You were getting your weekly wage; you were paid to go to school.' Turning out in the evening, however, required a little more discipline. 'After all, we could be playing football or something interesting.'

Graham spent four years at Ormonde House, studying building technology, construction, practical brickwork, English and mathematics 'with lots of geometry'.

Taking a mental picture of Ormonde House, you had the back of the house, which would be the east elevation. Out the back you had these wooden buildings that were known as chicken huts – that's where some of the instruction took place. There was a track down and it went round to the left. Moving on down to the bottom – it was quite a big piece of land – there was a garage which is where we used to do the practical brickwork. Each side of that there were a couple of oblong outbuildings. The one on the right hand side was used. I remember going in there to do geometry classes.

Albert Owthwaite did some teaching, 'a bit of English or something like that', but not as a 'regular thing'. Sometimes Charles Sully taught mathematics, 'a bit of geometry or something like that'.

He didn't take us very often. Perhaps he was standing in for somebody and they stuck us in there to try and teach us something that we weren't getting elsewhere. I think they used him, if 'used' is the word, in the early stages. He knew what he was talking about because I sat in several of his sessions. Mr Moore was employed as a part-time instructor. He had this little sports shop in town just opposite the Post Office, next to Penn's shoe shop. It was a queer old place with a window on the angle.[9] He was what I call an 'all-rounder', using a cricketing term. He was a very clever man. He used to do geometry and maths.

Geometry was important. The bricklayers had to build arches and corners and they needed to know about angles.

Obviously the geometry was the start of that. The carpenters were the brains behind the arches 'cos they had to make all the centres – you had to have a support. The carpenters always made the pieces, and that's where the geometry comes in. All we had to do was run the brickwork over. We were doing corners. Sometimes you would do some angles and they'd say, 'This one is not coming off at 90 degrees. It's going to be something else.' They were trying to help us. Moore was giving us all this, if you were listening all the time, which we weren't always. He drew all these lines and different things. You picked all that up if you were a carpenter because it's all about angles, isn't it? We had a drawing board and a couple of the old T-squares and a few of the old protractors to draw whatever we was trying to draw. I wasn't always sure what we were doing. I was thinking about the football on a Saturday.

The 'fellow Moore' also taught brickwork technology and practical brickwork 'because they didn't have anybody else to take it'.[10]

The brickwork was down in the garage. There we built these piers and corners, put them up and took them down, and cleaned the bricks and all this sort of stuff. Moore

---

[9] Sportcraft, (J R Moore, proprietor), sports dealer, 30a Cheap Street.

[10] The first full-time lecturer in brickwork at Ormonde House was J Forster (1950-51) followed by C Taylor (1951-52), Ken Morton (1952-53) and Bill Parrott (1953-67).

was lumbered with us on the practical brickwork until this fellow Barnett arrived. He was a north-country man, a bricklayer by trade. He was employed on a part-time basis to instruct brickwork. He was a little bit sergeant-majorish, but he was a very helpful sort of bloke. I came across him in later years because he was employed by the education authority as a clerk of works. He used to go out to the schools and supervise the works and that.

The college provided us with half a dozen trowels, three or four club hammers, a couple of bolsters and chisels, a couple of levels and brick lines, and a square, which is the basic things. We had a wooden square that one of the carpenters had to make as part of his training. If you didn't have a square, it was easy for you to make it yourself. They provided a cheaper sort of trowel because, let's be fair, we didn't have full control of it in them days. We weren't an expert with it. We were learning.

Sometimes the students themselves did work for the Institute. The carpenters made T-squares for the bricklayers; the bricklayers built a workshop for the plumbers.

We were told we were going to do this bit of wall. We built this brickwork along. We had to brick up the door and we built in a couple of these old metal casement windows to make this workshop. We put these window frames on this old existing outbuilding to make it habitable.

Occasionally an instructor might offer his students work in the evening or at the weekend.

There's another little story about our friend Moore. In those days people used to keep pigs and he said to me about building these pigsties at Greenham Common. I said no, I didn't fancy that. I got all these excuses in. 'When are we going to do it?' 'We're playing football.' 'We've got to bike up there.' But we actually did go up there and we started this job. I went up there two or three times.

Sometimes the lessons were difficult to follow and the apprentices would help each other out. Graham Tillen cycled from Thatcham with George Milsom. 'He helped me out a bit if I hadn't been listening.' Sometimes there was simply too much information to absorb. 'The subjects that we were taught they never even talked about at school.' Mathematics was difficult. Basic arithmetic suddenly became geometry, fractions and decimals, a little bewildering at times.

> If they thought you wasn't bloody listening, they'd ask you something, wouldn't they? That's the normal trick I found. When I wasn't bloody concentrating they'd ask me summat. When I was bloody concentrating, it never used to happen. I was quite disappointed then 'cos I had the bloody answer. When I got home my father used to ask me what I'd done, and sometimes I couldn't remember. I didn't come out of there confused, but sometimes your mind wasn't on it like it should have been, which you can understand at that age. I'll be quite honest, some of the stuff I had quite a job to grasp. Some of us were all in the same boat because we didn't get it at school.

> We were supposed to be doing building and you would think, what the hell am I doing up here talking about these things which I'd never heard anything about? But the standard was very good. The information and the knowledge was there if you took it all in. The instructors used to try, although at 15, 16, you didn't always take all of it in like you should do. But they were very helpful. Even in those days they tried to help us. That was the object of the exercise.

Graham Tillen finished in 1952. He was 20 years old and National Service could no longer be delayed. 'I was called to jump into the khaki.'

'We used to get a master decorator to come all the way from Oxford'

Alan Lawrence started at Ormonde House 12 months after it had opened. Born in Chieveley, Alan went to the village school 'right up until I was 15'. He left in 1948.

> I was humming and hawing; I didn't know what I wanted to do. In the village they had a chap who was a decorator. He was a painter on his own and a friend of my father's. He said to my father, 'Ask Alan if he'd like to come on with me and work in the village.' I thought, I don't want to go and work for him but I might have a go at decorating and see if I can get a job in Newbury. In those days, in the building trade, apprenticeship, that was the thing you had to have and that's when I went to Camp Hopson. I went and saw Mr Paul Hopson for an interview. They took me on for a six-month period to see if I was suitable, then after six months they enrolled me and signed my apprenticeship papers. I started at college in 1949. I was 16.

Alan was paid about a pound a week. Five years later, as a qualified craftsman, he could earn 'top money, about £10 a week'.[11] For three years he went on day release, with classes in English, geometry, mathematics, painting technology, practical painting and science. In the mornings he caught the workmen's bus from Chieveley; after night school, he went home on the service bus.

> At the front of Ormonde House was just a drive and all shrubs and trees. When I first started it was just the main building and two or three chicken sheds at the back. We used to use those.

> Day release was a new thing at the time. It was a change to take it a bit easy. I preferred the days to the evenings. I used to get a bit cheesed off in the evening after working all day and then having to go back for a couple of hours.

---

[11] In 1951 average weekly earnings of men over 21 was £8.30. A decade later the figure had almost doubled to £15.35. Arthur Marwick, *British Society Since 1945*, (London: Penguin, 2003), p.88.

They used to have a little restaurant where you could get a meal in the evening. You could get pie and chips and things like that, nothing very flash but it was there if you wanted it. Sometimes we'd be there all day and then have a break for an hour and then start again in the evening.

We were taught in the house itself. The office was downstairs – there was only one woman in there – and the other rooms were all classrooms. Evening times we used to be up at the main building. There would be 15, 16 of us, something like that. They used to have a couple of classrooms down Albert Road, by the Methodist Church there, where it used to go up to Elliott's factory. They used to have two classrooms at the back and we used to go there for lessons.

Practical painting was in a wooden shed, usually in the afternoons. The instructor lived thirty miles away.

There were two what used to be chicken sheds, wooden sheds. That's where we used to go for the practical side of it. We used to get a master decorator to come all the way from Oxford. He was getting on a bit and he used to come on the bus every week. He was a signwriter, grainer, the lot he could do. He worked for himself, one of the old boys.

Another instructor travelled from Southampton. One of the teachers worked with Alan at Camp Hopson. 'We used to have a joiner, Pat Wyatt, who used to do a bit of evening teaching at the college. He used to live over the top of where Halford Cycles was in Northbrook Street.'[12]

There was homework, usually drawing, and progress was monitored. In practical painting 'we used to have tests, a questionnaire we had to fill out, how to do this, how to do that, what we should do with this.' The examinations were City & Guilds, the intermediate certificate at the end of the third year, the final at the end of the fifth. All the way through, Camp Hopson

---

[12] J P Wyatt is listed in the 1951-52 Prospectus as a part-time assistant.

was kept informed. 'If you didn't turn up, they would soon have you in the office. Oh yes, they would know. I did miss once or twice and they called me in and said, "I hear you're not going into college. What's the trouble?" And they give me a bit of a stripping down. Oh yes, they kept you on the ball. Still, they were good days. We had some good times there.'

'It was nice going back into the school ways again'

Fifteen-year-old plumbing apprentice **Chris Green** started a year after Alan Lawrence. He worked for Cooke Brothers in Northbrook Street – the yard was in Park Way – and started on 17/6 (87 pence) a week. By the time he was 18 his earnings were around £3. When he finished and went into National Service he was on 'a full tradesman's wage' of around £8 a week.

> I started at Shaw before Park House was opened. We were all at Shaw originally. It wasn't mixed. There were two schools there, a boys' school and a girls' school. The girls had their own playground and everything, and the boys had their own at the front of the house. We used to go up to the Community Centre for metalwork. They used that as a classroom because there wasn't enough room at Shaw. It was Mr Parker that used to teach metalwork, 'Nosey Parker' they called him. And then Park House opened and, in the first instance, we used to do three days at Shaw and two days at Park. We used to come out sometimes and didn't know which school we were in. Then the A-stream moved up permanently into Park House and gradually all the boys moved up in the end.

> I started at Ormonde House in 1950. I was a day-release student and we went one day and two evenings a week. I did plumbing and was there for five years as an apprentice. There were painters, builders and plumbers. We were all together for parts of the course but then split up into our separate trades for the practical. Cooke Brothers had five apprentices on the course. We all came to college on our bikes; I would say 90 per cent of us. I remember getting

30 shillings bonus (£1.50) on a job and I went and bought myself a new dynamo set. There weren't a lot of luxuries, but we all had good bikes. It was 17/6 (87 pence) a week I started with but it didn't seem to matter much. Some boys who had left school the same time as us were earning double, treble that at Colthrop and places like that if they were on shift work. But the building trade wasn't too clever, while in the early days, some of the engineers that worked for Plenty and places like that actually had to pay to be apprenticed.

Ernie Newport did the plumbing. We did what was called lead burning. It's like lead welding – you do it with a torch. There was one particular chap who was an apprentice at Harwell. They actually had lead roofs and he would weld on the ceiling upside down. He came to the school and he said to old Ernie Newport, lead burning on the bench, 'Have you ever tried it upside down?' Ernie said, 'You can't do it upside down.' But he actually got a piece of lead and he nailed it on the ceiling and he got up there and welded it.

There's a lot of skill in lead work. I was lucky. I was apprenticed under a chap who was brilliant at it. He could do anything with a piece of lead. There's not much lead used today but it was all lead in the early days. I came in on the end of lead really. Copper was coming in, but we still did some houses with lead and a lot of lead roof work, gutters and valleys. Lead is still used for that today, but they are specialists that do it now. Everybody did it in those days. It's amazing how many people ring me up and ask if I will do it for them. I still do some for a nephew of mine who renovates and builds oak buildings – they want traditional stuff.

Arthur Owen was in charge of the building. Ernie would put his order into him, what we needed for the plumbing side. The materials, the lead pipes and all the gear, so to speak, we kept in the greenhouse. That was funny because if you were in the workshop Ernie would send two or three lads to get a piece of lead and you'd have to walk up through the garden in the dark. They used to go up there and never come back. They used to get on their bikes and go home.

We were also taught in what we called the chicken hut, a long hut used for chickens because it had the chicken hatches. While we were waiting for a class we used to watch people playing tennis, and the caretaker used to sell us windfall apples for a penny each.

The maths teacher was a strange character. His maths was beyond me, some of the things he used to do. He set us some homework at times but usually there wasn't any. Sometimes we would cycle down to the place we had behind the Boys' Club. We took science down there with Pocock. The Boys' Club faced Northbrook Street. There was a big window and behind it were the billiard tables and things. The building was one up from the corner of Albert Road. We went down the road and round the back. It was a tatty old room – it wasn't anything special at all. It was only the one room which we ever used. We were down there until I was 18. Then they stopped the day release. In the evenings we just went up to the college; so we would only have been down at the Boys' Club two or three years at the most. That was normal. That was the agreement as far as the building was concerned, to stop the day release as soon as you were 18. And then, well, they wouldn't have to pay you any more to have a day off.

We were in our own little cocoon really. It was an enjoyable time even though we thought we had left permanent school. But it was nice going back after a while, back into the school ways again. It certainly didn't do any harm, and having the day off from work was useful.

It was pretty easy going really but you could get into trouble. I was threatened. I was late for class when I was courting. There was one or two expelled from the college for some reason and if they were expelled, they cancelled their indentures. You used to have to go before the Joint

Apprenticeship Committee which consisted of builders and employers. They used to meet in Craven Road behind the Coopers Arms. You used to have to go in there and sign before this committee.

On the building

'If you work on the building, you've got to be a bit on the crude side. If you start talking posh, you have the mickey taken out of you. We talk a language of our own.'

'It's a terrible trade for anyone innocent going in that's led a sheltered life. You learn very quickly.'

The construction industry was busy everywhere in post-war Britain, one of the largest employers in the country, and there was a lot of building going on in and around Newbury. The town had not experienced much damage although St John's Church had to be completely rebuilt. It was the demand for housing which kept the builders busy and the brickies and the chippies, the painters and the plumbers, were a familiar sight round the town. Private houses were built for people with money to buy and Ministry of Supply houses were built for those who worked at the atomic energy establishments. However, most of the houses were for people to rent from the local authority.

The building of council houses between 1945 and 1960 changed the landscape of Britain. Housing estates mushroomed all over the country and the council house became one of the most powerful symbols of the post-war welfare state. Decent homes – semi-detached, three bedrooms, bathroom – were provided at a rent people could afford.

Council house building in Newbury was not new. Nearly 400 such houses had been built in the interwar years. Most of these were in St George's Avenue, Camp Close and Skyllings; but there were others in St Michael's Road, Monks Lane, Speenhamland, Remembrance Road and Essex Street.[13] However, from 1945

---

[13] Borough of Newbury Official Year Book 1947-48, p.10.

onwards, the programme was much expanded. Housing had been one of the big issues in the General Election. Norman Longmate remembers his Labour-supporting sister at an election meeting in Newbury demanding of the Tory candidate, 'What do you expect us to live in? Glider boxes?' This was a reference to the discarded crates littering the racecourse at the end of the war.[14] The country market town did not have anything like the housing problems facing the larger urban centres, but Newbury Council became more and more involved in house building.

The prefabricated bungalows erected immediately after the war soon gave way to more permanent dwellings. In 1946 houses were built along Newport Road, Cromwell Road and Doveton Way and before the year was out, work had started on the Shaw House estate. Prisoners of war were used to lay out the roads and construct the sewers and over the next few years, the biggest housing estate in the town took shape. 60 houses were occupied when Ormonde House opened, and the building of another 26 – scaffolding, skeleton roofs and salmon-pink window frames – was under way.[15] The new houses were celebrated during Civic Week in October 1948:

> All the houses constructed since the war have hot and cold running water, bathrooms and all modern conveniences, and are of the traditional brick and tile construction. The layout of the new estates is a considerable improvement on the old type of council houses, and every endeavour has been made to construct them on attractive lines. Seven local building contractors are engaged in the work with approximately 150 men.[16]

By early 1952, there were 284 houses at Shaw. By the end of 1953 there were more than 300 and the estate was finished. Winchcombe School was built, the juniors' section opened in September 1951, the infants' a few months later. Most of the children were transferred from the overcrowded Speenhamland School. On the edge of the estate was a new fire and ambulance station.

---

[14] Longmate, *op.cit.*, p.506.

[15] *NWN* 10 May, 8 July 1948, 10 February 1949.

[16] *A Handbook for the Citizens of Newbury, Civic Week 1948*, p.11.

Newbury Council also bought land belonging to Donnington Priory to the north of Shaw and more houses were built around Love Lane. There were 96 under construction by early 1952, 120 by the time this estate was finished. By 1953, 500 council houses had been built and the landscape of the north-eastern rim of the town had been transformed.

There were also Ministry of Supply houses, 200 or so built for Aldermaston and Harwell employees. They were on estates to the south of the town. The Valley Road estate included Garford Crescent, Henshaw Crescent, Home Mead Close and Sidestrand Road as well as the houses on Valley Road itself. Nearby was the Wendan Road estate which included Culver Road, Roebut's Close, The Glade and Three Acre Road. These houses were built in the early '50s. The new John Rankin School was in use by 1955, officially opened by the Director of AWE Aldermaston, William Penney. Then, in the mid-'50s, the Valley Road estate was extended and more council houses were built. As the decade drew to a close, another housing estate was started. This one was at Speen, to the west of the town.

Similar developments were taking place in the villages around Newbury for which the Rural District Council was responsible.

'If you were in the building trade and had an apprenticeship, you had a job for life'

The Newbury builders, then, built hundreds of houses. The bigger employers included Camp Hopson, A J Chivers, Cooke Brothers, Eggleton & Tallin, Hoskings & Pond, J W Palmer and T C Pembroke. Smaller companies included E B Hitchman, E Lipscomb and R A Wickens. Round and about there was E A Bance at East Woodhay, F J Reynolds at Thatcham and J Wooldridge at Hungerford. 'They were all reputable business people. Cooke Brothers were the biggest, the leading firm in the town. Hoskings & Pond run Cooke close to being a biggish firm. They were the two big boys.' Camp Hopson was another of the 'big boys'. When Alan Lawrence did his day release, there were five others with him, two painters, two carpenters and a bricklayer.

Camp Hopson were a very big firm. At one time they
had 17 painters alone, plus about 12 carpenters and four
or five bricklayers and plumbers. The builders' yard
was at the back of the shop, where the new furniture
shop is now. It used to be a big carpenters' and joiners'
shop all through there at one time. They had 12 or 14
work benches. They used to make their own coffins and
everything 'cos they did the funerals.

On the estates 'there was nobody about that was big enough to
take on the whole job.' So the construction was shared between a
number of firms all under contract to Newbury Council. 'They were
allocated so many houses each. If on the first phase, say, you've got
twenty pairs of houses to build, then Cooke had eight pairs, Camp
Hopson got four, Hoskings & Pond four. Pembroke, who were
smaller, and Eggleton & Tallin, they just had a couple of pairs each.'
Graham Tillen started work with Camp Hopson in Newport
Road and was then moved to the Shaw estate.

There's not all that many council houses in Newport Road
– it's not a big site. When I got there we were right down
the bottom by the river. We had two pairs to do, so we
were only there about a twelvemonth. There's not many
at Cromwell Road but there is a few at the back there, the
ones that are terylene, that yellow stuff. They built them in
flims and then they sprayed this old terylene stuff on them.
It was put on with the hurdy-gurdies as we say. It was all
bagged up; they just flushed the joints up and rubbed the
bag over it. They didn't mess about pointing them. It was
all filled up. We called it government pointing, or sack
finish – in other words, if you didn't do it right, you'd get
the sack. They're still standing, those houses.

I was on the Shaw estate when it was just a field. The
houses backed on to the old Dower House on the London
Road, a big rambling old house with a long garden where
Wheeler's Garage is now.[17] The gardens of the houses back

---

[17] Dower House was closed in 1954 and demolished shortly afterwards.

on to there. Those were the first phase of council houses. Cooke built them.

Access to the estate was from the London Road at the end of the Dower House gardens. 'They cut an entrance in to get to the Shaw estate. They were all concrete roads in there. As you go in, the first pair on the right hand side, Camp Hopson built those.' A little further down the London Road going away from the town stood a reminder of the old entrance to Shaw House which had been landscaped two hundred years before.

> There was a big pair of gate piers by the side of the road, and there was an old lodge next to them. The avenue of trees was still there. When we were building the early houses, the girls used to walk to the school up the avenue. It came out where it does now, almost opposite the big gates at Shaw House.

A few years later, another entrance into the estate was made, this time from the Oxford Road, a little to the north of Ormonde House. 'Castle Grove, you come into the Shaw estate from there. All private houses down so far and then you've got police houses. You go on down towards the Shaw Club and there's a little cul-de-sac on the right hand side. We built four pairs of houses in there. I worked on them.' Then Graham was moved again, this time to Love Lane. 'We moved over the other side of the river. In Love Lane, going towards Donnington, over the A34, and those two on the left hand side that drops down in, we built the first two. The first pair was in LVC rustics and one of them was pebble-dashed – the old rendering with the stones on. Then they made an entrance in and they started to build behind that.'

F J Reynolds of Thatcham and E A Bance of East Woodhay built for the Rural District Council.

> In Cold Ash it was at the top end. One builder was normally in charge of all the others. Although Reynolds would come in and build two pairs, the main contractor would be Bance we'll say – that's how they used to do it.

We built some along at Woolhampton. I always remember a bloke digging a soakaway. They said, 'Where's old what's his name?' They had to go and look for him. He had dug this old soak and he couldn't get out. They had to give him a ladder.[18]

There was also work in the private sector as new houses were built and old houses were improved. Some of the housing around Newbury was very grand.

Camp Hopson did a lot of work on these great big country houses, you know, East Woodhay or down at Stype at Hungerford. And they also used to provide them with furniture and everything, and then when the time came they used to carry out their last.[19]

Camp Hopson did some very good work. They used to work for Lord Carnarvon, and Mrs Vera Lilley of Lilley & Skinner who lived at Woolton House, and all the Wills', the tobacco people, and people like that. It used to be a regular thing, out at Highclere Castle every winter time, 'cos Lord Carnarvon used to go to the Bahamas and places like that for the winter. We went over one year and done the bedroom and the bathroom suite when the Queen stopped there – 1952, 1953, something like that. Lord Carnarvon's son is her racing manager now. He's well in with the royals.

I can remember working out at the son's when he first got married. We done the big house, Milford Lake House – it's got a massive lake in front of it – where he used to live. It was in a bit of a state after being let to the army during the war. We were there for weeks and weeks doing that up. He had a firm of interior decorators come down from London to supervise and say what colours he should have for this room and for that room, and what he should have

---

[18] Interview with George Milsom.

[19] Interview with Graham Tillen.

here, and all that sort of thing. They were there for two or three days, wasting paint left, right and centre, trying to get these colours. Then they came to the foreman painter and said, 'Well, that's what we want in that room, and that's what we want in that room.'[20]

The massive demand for housing in these years put pressure on the supply of raw materials. Timber was scarce. 'That's why you see a lot of council houses with quarry tile windowsills.'

> Timber was on license. You couldn't just go and say I want 50 ten-foot lengths of four-by-two. It was allocated. And when we built Shaw estate, bricks, believe me, they were like gold dust. They used to deliver Saturday mornings, 'cos it was a short run in from the nearest LBC depot, just the other side of Oxford. Six and a half thousand the big ones carried, a lorry and a trailer. You used to have to unload them by hand. There was none of this business now where they just take 'em off with this machine. We were never out of bricks, but a lot of those houses on Shaw estate have got these hollow pots, like a clay pot. If you got in the hollow bit, you were in space. You couldn't cut them like a brick because they would just go to pieces; but they were alright when they were plastered.

Most of the workers were local but some came from further afield. 'Before the war bricklayers used to do the tiling, but after the war the tiler came through, which is common practice now. Collins from Slough used to send these guys down to do the tiling. Some of them were cor blimeys, as we call Londoners.' Occasionally, to meet the demand for labour, older apprentices, known as improvers, were taken on.

> They were guys that had been in the army in the latter stages of the war. They were young fellows. They went up to Slough on a six-month course, they gave them a bag of tools and they came and worked for local builders.

---

[20] Interview with Alan Lawrence.

We had three or four of them on, not just bricklayers. They got a percentage of the tradesman's wage.[21]

The young apprentices spent a day at the Institute and the rest of the week they were trained on site by a craftsman, amongst the handcarts, the wooden wheelbarrows and the water-cooled cement mixers. They went to work on their bicycles; an occasional luxury was to travel on the back of a lorry under canvas. The work itself was physical and tiring, with hours spent mixing paint or sawing wood. Lunchtime was a chance to rest, sit on a bag of cement, eat a sandwich and read the newspaper.

Graham Tillen: I lived in Thatcham and cycled to work. Nobody would ever pinch 'em in them days. The town was quiet in 1948. We used to bike into the yard. I was on site a lot of the time, so I biked to Shaw estate. Camp Hopson had handcarts for some of the town jobs. You would go up to St Michael's Road or somewhere with a handcart and a couple of bags of sand to put a manhole cover on, or if the old brickie had to put a chimney pot on. They even had wooden barrows in the yard. If you went on some of the smaller jobs, what we call 'jobbing', you didn't have a mixer, but on the bigger site we had the water-cooled mixer. It had a brass tap on it. You used to drain it out at night so it didn't freeze. She used to start straightaway, the old girl. She'd go all day you know. You had to top it up with water every so often.

They'd put this bloody canvas thing on the back of a lorry. If there were nine or ten blokes you'd get on the back. They'd drop you off and pick you up at night. Then in the early '50s, when they had an extra van or so, a couple of bricklayers and a mate would probably go out in a little pickup van. All the sand and that was delivered to the site by these little petrol Bedfords. They could get anywhere. Four cubic yards they used to carry. They gradually got bigger and they'd bring six cubic yards. Now, of course,

---

[21] Interview with Graham Tillen.

they bring about 20 bloody tons, these bloody great things which can't get in on the site.

George Milsom: The only paid holiday when we started was the two-minute silence. People laugh at that but it was true; there was no paid holiday at all. Then they brought in the holiday stamps which the firm paid for. That's why we say, 'Give me my money and my card.' The cards were the stamps as well as your employment thing. Food was still rationed. Being in the building trade, we had an extra cheese ration for sandwiches. Mum used to swap my cheese for more bacon. You could do that unofficially with the shopkeeper. He wasn't worried as long as he got the coupons.

Alan Lawrence: When I first started work, I used to cycle from Chieveley into Newbury every morning, all weathers – that's about five miles. And you'd get to work and they would say, 'We want you to go to Highclere this morning.' And we used to cycle to Highclere. We used to get three pence (1 penny) a mile cycle money. If you asked people to do it today, they would tell you where to get off, but it was the norm in them days. Then it got better and they had a couple of lorries and the vans used to take you out there.

As an apprentice you were not doing a lot of painting because you were only a boy. The boy's job was the preparation: rubbing down, washing off the ceilings, washing the floors and things like that. Occasionally, if the foreman was in a good mood, you might get to paint the radiators. You never used to be classed as a decorator until you'd served your time. After two or three years, I suppose, I was doing the whole thing.

There was no colours like there is today. You couldn't just go and show the card and the chap knock it up in five minutes on one of those machines like they have got today. Now it's all done computer-wise; you can get any colour you want. But in those days, you had the creams, whites, one or two blues. Mostly people wanted colours to match the curtains or the carpet. You could spend hours trying to get these colours. You used to have the stainers, greens, blues and all that sort of thing. It took you an hour to knock a tin of paint up because of all the lead. It used to settle at the bottom. It was like concrete. You could be there for hours stirring a tin of paint. The gloss paint could take two days to dry if the wood was really hard. In fact, there used to be a special thing you could put in the paint to make it dry quicker.

5

A GOOD START 1948-1949

Consequent upon the appointment of full-time Superintendents of Further Education in the Maidenhead, Newbury and Windsor areas, demand for the provision of evening classes and courses has shown a considerable increase, as also has the demand for day-release courses.

BEC 15 October 1948

The founding fathers

The LEA appointed a local committee to look after the Institute, the founding fathers of Ormonde House. These were the first college governors. Their role was strategic. Their purpose was 'to develop interest in the classes and in particular to maintain contact with local schools, employers and trades councils'. The committee was made up of representatives from the Berkshire Education Committee, Newbury's Borough or District Council, the Chamber of Commerce or Employers' Association, and Newbury Trades Council. The fifth member was a head teacher. Up to seven other people with a special interest in FE could be co-opted, giving a maximum membership of 12. Committee members were to serve for three years, until April 1952.[1]

Most of those appointed lived in the town. They enjoyed a comfortable middle-class life style and their social circle was made

---

[1] BEC 18 November 1949.

up of families from a similar background. They included Dick Greet, Maurice Paine, Harry Metcalf, Oliver Brown, George Willis and the Revd Bertram Russell. Responsible for the developments in Ormonde House, they were untrained and unpaid but had a strong sense of civic responsibility. Energetic Newbury worthies, they were committed supporters of the fledgling Institute and most of them continued as governors in the 1950s. Ormonde House grew strong roots in the local community.

Richard Hynson Greet (b.1912) of the House of Toomer, Dick Greet as he was usually known, was one of the most important of the founding fathers. A bachelor who lived at Long Acres on the Andover Road, he came from one of the town's oldest families. Educated privately, he was a graduate of the London School of Economics where he had been the treasurer of the students' union. During the war, he served with the Royal Berkshire Regiment, rising to the rank of major. When he came home to succeed his father as the managing director of the town's biggest hardware store, he took over a family business going back 250 years. There was also a tradition of community involvement: Greet family members had served as mayors on many occasions in the 18th and 19th centuries. More recently, Dick Greet's father had been mayor and president of both the Chamber of Commerce and the National Federation of Ironmongers.

Dick Greet continued this tradition. Particularly interested in education, he was a leader at Ormonde House and was chairman of the local committee. He continued as chairman of the reconstituted governing body in 1951. He was a county councillor (Conservative) for a brief period, and vice-chairman of the Education Committee. As a member of the FESC – and chairman 1951-54 – he helped produce the Scheme of Further Education. He was also one of the founder members of the Newbury Division. A dedicated public servant, Dick Greet was a governor of Newbury Grammar School (1949-52, 1955-58), and Reading Technical College (1951-52), and a member of the Southern Regional Council for FE (1953-54) and the Youth Employment Service (1952, 1955-61). When he died (1984) he left an estate of nearly one million pounds and an impressive legacy to education in Newbury.

Dick Greet's House of Toomer stood at one end of Northbrook Street by the stone bridge over the River Kennet. Further along at number 21, next to Marks & Spencer, was G S Paine, gentlemen's outfitters. Maurice Paine (b.1906) went to Newbury Grammar School and then joined the family's retail business which he ran with his brother. Rejected for military service during the war he joined the Air Raid Precautions instead. In 1947 he was elected to the Borough Council and this turned out to be the beginning of a 'remarkable' journey of 'almost unparalleled voluntary service to the town'. It was as council representative that he became an FE governor the following year and he continued this into the 1950s.

Maurice Paine was a town councillor for nearly 30 years and education was one of his 'keenest interests'. With Dick Greet he was a founder member of the Newbury Division, served on it for many years, was chairman for four years and represented it on the county's Education Committee. At one time or another, he was on the governing body of six Newbury schools and for one of them, Park House, he developed a 'deep interest and great affection' which lasted 'until the end of his days'. A hard-working community servant, it was largely due to his efforts that the Citizens' Advice Bureau began in the town in 1963. He was an active churchgoer at St Nicolas' (churchwarden, sidesman, church council member), and he was involved in many other activities including a long association with the Rotary Club and the Newbury Trustee Savings Bank.[2]

Maurice Paine never spared himself 'to work with enthusiasm for objects and ideas' which were of 'inestimable benefit' to the people of Newbury. Public recognition came with the award of an MBE and when he was made an honorary freeman of the borough.

Harry Metcalf was another of the governors with an independent business in the town, an ophthalmic optician's practice. He, too, was an active public servant dedicated to young people and education. He was a member of the FESC, was chairman of the Newbury Division and helped run the Community Centre. He was also on the local Employment Committee, was a governor of the Grammar School and was involved in the work of educational charities.

Founding father Oliver Brown was a builder like his father, chairman and managing director of J Wooldridge in Hungerford,

---

[2] *NWN* 1 November 1979.

a firm with 'a hundred years reputation for good work'. A town councillor since the mid-'30s, his 'technical knowledge' of building was of the 'greatest value' to the town. He was chairman of the Estates and Town Planning Committee and in 1948 he became mayor. Two years later he was made a magistrate. He was also a governor of the Grammar School and sat on the Newbury Division. He remained a governor at Ormonde House for most of the '50s while also serving at Park House and Shaw House schools. His technical knowledge was invaluable in Ormonde House, where he was involved in the development of the building courses. 'He has a quiet speaking voice, but carries weight with anything he says, as this is always fortified with knowledge.'[3]

Other committee members included one from the local newspaper and one from the parish church. George Willis was a *Newbury Weekly News* journalist who had taught at the Technical Institute before the war. Durham University-educated Revd Bertram Russell was rector of St Nicolas' Church for eight years from 1946 to 1954. He also sat on the County Council, was another of the founder members of the Newbury Division and its first chairman. For nine years he was vice-chairman of the County Council's Co-ordination Subcommittee.

'Rooms have been allotted to every subject in an extensive curriculum'

When the Institute opened, Albert and Elsie Owthwaite, Arthur Owen with a part-time assistant or two, and the building apprentices had Ormonde House to themselves. This lasted for a few weeks. The ONC courses started in October, the others in November. This meant that for many students, that first Autumn Term only lasted for six weeks.

On 16 September the *Newbury Weekly News* advertised the courses and the newspaper remained the Institute's most important publicity vehicle. It also carried details about enrolment, the procedure whereby men and women signed on and paid to join the course of their choice. Anybody who wished to enrol had to go to Ormonde House on specified evenings between seven and

---

[3] *Ibid.*, 6 November 1947, 20 November 1947.

nine o'clock. The Institute's prospectus was another important means of communication, available in Ormonde House and in the public library in Cheap Street. There were also copies available at the exhibition in the Corn Exchange held as part of the Civic Week celebrations.

The curriculum of 1948 set the pattern for FE development for years to come. As there was no overwhelming demand for a single sort of training, a broad range was offered: 67 classes in technical, commercial, handicraft and general subjects.[4] This mix of vocational and non-vocational work was there in the beginning and has remained a characteristic of the further education undergrowth in the Newbury area ever since.

Building, engineering and commerce were at the heart of the vocational programme with certificates awarded by the City & Guilds, the RSA and the Union of Educational Institutions (UEI). Evening classes in electrical and mechanical engineering were the first year of the ONC.

Most of the courses were held at night but two new day-release programmes started after Christmas. The one in electrical engineering, ONC and City & Guilds, was initially for the SEB apprentices but it was open to others and a group of employers were brought together to advise on course content. There was also a day release in automobile engineering. Garage employers were willing to support the programme with its City & Guilds and National Craftsman certificates. An advisory committee was put together before the course started. The members represented 'several local firms' which had begun formal apprentice training.[5]

Many of the other subjects offered in 1948 had been taught in previous years. Banking was new, but, as we have seen, typewriting and shorthand had been popular in the interwar years as had classes in agriculture, horticulture and poultry-keeping.

This was also true for much of the non-vocational work. Many of the recreational courses were aimed at women rather than men. In these years of austerity many items remained rationed and the British housewife continued to practise the skills she had developed in wartime, learning how to cope with shortages and how to juggle

---

[4] FESC 17 September 1948.

[5] *NWN* 16 December 1948.

points and coupons. With clothes in short supply, making your own was an attractive proposition. At the same time, once the war was over, many married women no longer had jobs outside the home. They had the time and the energy to study and craft courses were popular, especially those in tailoring and dressmaking.

Other creative subjects included art (and commercial art), handicrafts (woodwork) and photography. For young men, all of whom would have a medical examination when called up for National Service, there was physical training.

This, then, was the curriculum of Ormonde House in 1948. The LEA also organised a variety of work at the Community Centre – dancing, gardening, handicraft, judo, lip-reading and music – while the part-time superintendents continued to arrange classes for village folk as they had done in previous years, including country dancing at Hamstead Marshall, needlework, musical appreciation and country dancing in Kintbury's Coronation Hall, and brass band music at Inkpen.[6]

---

[6] FESC 17 September 1948, 12 November 1948.

BERKSHIRE COUNTY COUNCIL EDUCATION COMMITTEE
INSTITUTE OF FURTHER EDUCATION
OXFORD ROAD, NEWBURY
SESSION 1948-1949

The Institute offers Courses of Study in the following Subjects or Group of Subjects:

MECHANICAL ENGINEERING
ELECTRICAL ENGINEERING
AUTOMOBILE ENGINEERING
PRELIMINARY TECHNICAL COURSE
BUILDING APPRENTICES (DAY-RELEASE)
ELECTRICAL APPRENTICES (DAY-RELEASE)
CITY AND GUILDS HANDICRAFT TEACHERS
NATIONAL CERTIFICATE IN COMMERCE
PRELIMINARY COMMERCIAL COURSE
SHORTHAND TYPIST COURSES
BANKING AND SECRETARIAL
MATRICULATION
INTER BSc (ECON)
INTER B COM
LANGUAGES

WOMEN'S CRAFTS: -	POULTRY KEEPING
DRESSMAKING	AGRICULTURE
HOMECRAFTS	HORTICULTURE
MILLINERY	HANDICRAFT
LADIES' TAILORING	ART CRAFTS
	COMMERCIAL ART
	PHYSICAL TRAINING
	PHOTOGRAPHY

CLASSES COMMENCE:
NATIONAL CERTIFICATE COURSES: 4 October 1948
ALL OTHER CLASSES: 8 November 1948

ENROLMENT FOR CLASSES:
NATIONAL CERTIFICATE (ELECT): 27 Sept. 1948, 7-9 pm
NATIONAL CERTIFICATE (MECH): 28 Sept. 1948, 7-9 pm
ALL OTHER COURSES: 11-15 October, 7-9 pm

NWN 16 September 1948

Rooms filled to overflowing

> Eight short months have seen a complete transformation at Ormonde House, Oxford Road which, from an empty country house has become Newbury's Institute of Further Education, filled to overflowing with students.
>
> *NWN 30 June 1949*

The first transformation of the Victorian country house had started with the arrival of the convent girls during the war. Now there occurred a second transformation; and this time, 38 Oxford Road was changed beyond all recognition. Every year between 1948 and 1960, somewhere on the site, building work was taking place. The house itself looked much the same from the outside, but inside it was very different. More dramatically, the outbuildings were altered, used as classrooms and then taken down. In their place a new college was built.

The work which had started in the summer of 1948 continued into the autumn. A sum of £685 was spent to make the property 'suitable for immediate use'. Some of this went on 'sanitary equipment' in the house; the rest was spent on the outbuildings and the cottages.[7] A few months later, a further £1,105 was used for 'interior adaptations, outside painting, etc.' Most of the renovation was done by contractors but the building students did some of the work using 'second-hand timber'.[8]

The house was the Institute's office and its main teaching centre. The office/reception was at the end of the hall, but other ground floor rooms were used as classrooms. Above was the Superintendent's office and flat. The conservatory was used for dressmaking; the wooden hut which could be seen through its windows was a general classroom. Behind the house, the two huts which had been used as a chapel were changed into something more secular. The nave became a classroom, the vestry – 'electrically heated and quite snug'– a tutorial room.[9] The 'whacking, big long hut', the girls' gymnasium, was altered again. This time it

---

[7] BEC 15 October 1948; FESC 12 November 1948.

[8] Vera Garlick in *NWN* Supplement 6 September 1973.

[9] SBCFE 25 Years.

was partitioned; one half was a classroom, the other a workshop for the carpenters.

This was the chicken hut, with its rafters, wooden walls and splintering floorboards. The hut is snagged in the Ormonde House memory, that part of their habitat which staff and students still speak of today with warmth and affection. With its 'high louvred glass and wire mesh windows', the elevated chicken hut was hot in summer and cold in winter. Every morning, caretaker Harry Whiting slid a scuttle of anthracite into its great black cast iron stoves; but the 'skirts' around the bottoms 'did not prevent the wind howling underneath and, even with tortoise stoves red-hot, it was never cosy'. Mornings frequently saw temperatures below freezing on the desks.[10]

Beyond the chicken hut, the two cottages were never used as classrooms. They became the family homes of the first two members of Owthwaite's staff.

Within a few weeks of the Institute's opening, the FESC was arguing for more room for practical work so that Newbury could provide 'systematic and progressive' courses, the second-year engineering ONC in 1949/50, the third year in 1950/51. Six prefabricated huts were needed, three for engineering – two 'production shops' and one for 'heat engines' – and two for laboratories, in electrical work and science. The sixth hut would be for domestic science; there was nowhere on site suitable for this. The cost of the huts would be 'relatively high', so they could be phased in over three years. The education authority listened to the arguments, agreed to provide three and hoped to have them ready by Easter 1950.[11]

The lack of accommodation was a serious matter. There was a 'general shortage of premises' and the FESC spent a lot of time discussing the problem. In addition to the Oxford Road property, the County Council owned the Technical Institute and the Council School building; and the new Institute used both of these.

Early in 1949, a conference was held at Ormonde House to discuss the best use which could be made of the premises available in the town. Albert Owthwaite met with Education Committee

---

[10] *Ibid.*.

[11] FESC 12 November 1948; NWN 30 June 1949.

members and other interested parties: the Youth Service, the Community Association, the Boys' Club and the Air Training Corps. Once the three prefabs were erected, it was anticipated that the Institute would be 'reasonably self-sufficient'. Rooms in the old Institute in Northbrook Street would no longer be needed and other organisations could use them.[12] At the Community Centre, if new premises for the school meals service were found, its cooking facilities could be used for FE cookery classes.

In the event, the school meals service moved out of Station Road and cookery classes started there in 1951. The Air Training Corps stayed there with the Community Association, renting part of the first floor and a hut in the playground. The Newbury Institute held classes there until 1954. In addition, the Institute continued to use the upstairs rooms at 60 Northbrook Street until 1960 – it was, in effect, an annex of Ormonde House – while the Boys' Club stayed in the large room downstairs.

Technical education was expensive, with its budget-guzzling demands for machinery, equipment and materials. Building students needed a continuous supply of bricks and mortar, timber and piping; engineers needed electrical and welding equipment, lathes and milling machines; car mechanics needed engines to work on; and an ever increasing number of typewriters was needed for commercial courses. At the start, the LEA allowed more than £2,000 for 'initial equipment', but in the first few weeks of the Institute's history, resources were put together in a somewhat piecemeal fashion. The building apprentices assembled for their first morning, and a set of borrowed chairs and tables arrived in the afternoon. Tools followed a few weeks later. Blackboards were loaned from the schools, and for the annex in Northbrook Street, the bulk of the electrical equipment was bought 'in hundredweight lots from RAF surpluses.'[13]

Ormonde House had only been open a month when it was used as the venue for a two-week course in childcare for nursery school staff. A nursery school had opened in Newbury in 1942 in Victoria Park, to allow mothers to be employed in the war effort at Plenty, Elliott's and Vickers Armstrong. The LEA continued to run

[12] FESC 17 February 1949.

[13] Vera Garlick in *NWN* Supplement 6 September 1973; SBCFE 25 Years.

the school after the war and no doubt some of its staff went to the course in Ormonde House. There were lectures and discussions, opportunities for craft work and visits to nursery schools. HMIs visited and thought the course 'thoroughly successful'.[14] It was held from 18 October to 3 November, finishing five days before the majority of the Institute's classes were scheduled to start.

Whole-time instructors

All the classes for the Autumn Term had started by early November, and Harry Whiting had been taken on as caretaker. A most important job, the day (and night) of a caretaker in a further education institute was a long one. Newbury's caretaker was soon working a 55-hour week and, during term-time at least, it was suggested that he was paid an additional five shillings (25 pence) a week.[15] The unsocial hours meant that it was convenient for him to live on site, and Harry and his family moved into number one cottage.

Harry Whiting lived and worked at 38 Oxford Road for more than 20 years. When his cottage was demolished to make way for new buildings, he moved into a newly built bungalow on the site. He was still working at the college when he died in 1969.

Before the Institute opened, it was anticipated that the first whole-time instructors would be in building and English for the day-release courses. If there was not enough work for them to do – and full-time staff was expected to teach 27½ hours a week – then some additional schoolteaching would be arranged. Once the Institute had opened, the FESC wanted full-time appointments in building and engineering. Arthur Owen developed the work he was already doing on behalf of the district's Building Federation; and from 3 January 1949 he was employed whole time by the LEA and not the Federation.[16] He had lots of experience but was without formal qualifications; so in 1952 he sat the examination for the City & Guilds final certificate in carpentry and joinery with

---

[14] FESC 12 November 1948.

[15] *Ibid.*, 17 February 1949.

[16] *Ibid.*, 10 December 1948.

his own students. Not surprisingly, he was rewarded with a first class pass. In charge of building, he remained a lecturer but was paid a special responsibility allowance.[17] In 1964, the importance of building was belatedly recognised by the establishment of a separate department with Arthur Owen at its head. Six years later the department was closed down but he stayed on, completing almost 30 years at Ormonde House before retirement.

By the time the LEA had assumed responsibility for Arthur Owen's work, another whole-time appointment was in place. The number of engineering students warranted a full-time lecturer and an advertisement was placed in the *Newbury Weekly News*.

BERKSHIRE
EDUCATION COMMITTEE
INSTRUCTOR IN ENGINEERING
Applications are invited for the
Post of Full-time Instructor at
the Institute of Further Education,
Ormonde House, Newbury. The
Instructor will be required to teach
in Day and Evening Courses in
Mechanical and Electrical Engineering, and probably also in
Mathematics or English. Salary –
Burnham Technical Scale for Assistants. No special forms are issued,
but applications giving details of age,
qualifications and experience, and the
names of two referees should be sent
to the undersigned by 6 November,
1948.

W F HERBERT
Director of Education
Shire Hall, Reading.
NWN 21 October 1948

---

[17] The allowance of 9/6 (47 pence) a week for 30 weeks was for the 'storage and issue of timber for all practical woodwork classes.' SBCFE 25 Years.

Charles Sully got the job and he started on 1 December 1948. He knew a lot about engineering 'and was involved in the first tanks, as a mechanic or whatever, in the First War'. He was familiar with teaching as he had worked as an RAF instructor 'at Nias training servicemen during the Second War.' 'He was qualified to teach in some sort of engine training. If you were any good at aero engines, it automatically meant you were very good at car engines.'[18]

Finding suitable housing for teachers in the post-war years could be difficult. Their numbers were growing and affordable accommodation in some areas – and Berkshire was one – was in short supply. Charles Sully was happy to live in number two cottage, next door to the Whitings. The Institute was only using it for storage. Alterations were made, £140 was spent, a bedroom was partitioned and a bathroom installed. On 13 August 1949, nine months after starting work, Charles and his family moved in. The rent was 15 shillings (75 pence) a week inclusive of rates and repairs.

Charles Sully taught many subjects, but it was motor engineering which he made his own. Twelve young men started on day release early in 1949, the garages supported the Institute, the course was established and he was the man in charge. Like Arthur Owen, he was given a responsibility allowance.[19] In 1952 he sat down with his students and took the City & Guilds final in Motor Mechanics, passing with the top mark.

'As a Socialist I believe in the greatest good for the greatest number'

The students remember Charles Sully not only because of his outstanding teaching but also because of his passion for politics.[20] He was an active Labour Party supporter and stood as a candidate in the local elections in 1953. The returning officer on election night was governor Harry Metcalf. The 'technical master' from Ormonde House was not elected that year, or the following year when one of his opponents was governor Maurice Paine.

---

[18] Interview with Roy Pocock.

[19] FESC 27 January 1950.

[20] 'His salty advice on modes of living, motor vehicle technology and politics were much appreciated by staff and students.' SBCFE 25 Years.

TO THE ELECTORS OF THE EAST WARD

Once again I have been invited to stand as a Candidate for the East Ward. Mr Lovegrove, your present Member, is the only Labour member on the Council and it is essential for good Government that other Labour members be elected to assist him in his endeavours. The ordinary worker has little representation on our present Council and it is time that your problems receive more attention.

National Legislation has increased the financial burdens of Local Authorities and impending national legislation is likely to increase your rents. It is essential that you should have a critical representative to watch over your interests in the coming years. The ideal of fair shares for all must be preserved in local Government, in spite of the attack upon this principle by the Tory Government.

As a Socialist I believe in the greatest good for the greatest number and I hope you will support me on May 13th to enable me to carry out my ideals, for your benefit.

Yours sincerely,
CHARLES SULLY
No. 2 Cottage, Ormonde House,
Oxford Road, Newbury

NWN 6 May 1954

Albert Owthwaite, Harry Whiting, Charles Sully, Arthur Owen – the first year of the Newbury Institute ended with four whole-time staff, three of whom lived on site. Only two of these were lecturers, so it was part-time staff that carried out most of the teaching.

And part-time assistants

During the Institute's first year, 33 part-time staff was used.[21] The part-time assistant was employed to teach a particular class for a few hours a week. Payment was on an hourly basis and varied according to the level, or grade, of the work taught.

---

[21] Vera Garlick in *NWN* Supplement 6 September 1973.

**BERKSHIRE
EDUCATION COMMITTEE**
INSTITUTE OF FURTHER
EDUCATION, NEWBURY

Applications are invited for
the following PART-TIME
INSTRUCTORS:–
PHYSICAL TRAINING (MEN),
    Wed. 11-12
MILLINERY, ECONOMICS,
    Wed. 7-9
PHOTOGRAPHY, WOMEN'S
CRAFTS, HOMECRAFTS,
LADIES' TAILORING
    (afternoon or evening)
SHORTHAND, PRACTICAL
BRICKWORK and MASONRY,
    Wed. 2.15 - 4.15
ENGLISH
Detailed applications, stating age,
qualifications (if any) and experience,
to be sent as soon as possible to:
A H Owthwaite, Superintendent,
Ormonde House, Oxford Road,
Newbury.

NWN 9 September 1948

Plumber Ernie Newport was one of the part-time assistants from the beginning. So was G Hughson, a teacher at Shaw and then Park House. He taught woodwork at school and technical drawing – 'that's what he was more interested in' – in the evening at Station Road. His head teacher at Park House was Derek Turnbull, whose wife Kay was another part-timer at the Institute. She taught dressmaking and her classes were so popular that the FESC wanted her to be paid a preparation allowance.[22]

---

[22] FESC 17 February 1949.

1,500 enrolments

The (FE) subcommittee regards these requests for additional facilities for Further Education an encouraging sign of the public interest in this part of their work.

BEC 15 October 1948

Public interest in the transformation of the country house was most encouraging, 50 classes and more than 1,000 enrolments in the first term. By the end of the first year, there were over 1,500 enrolments; and the total of 48,522 student hours far exceeded that at the Technical Institute 12 months previously.[23]

Day-release was the most exciting development. Following the lead taken by the building companies, more employers began to release their apprentices. In January 1949, 69 enrolled for electrical engineering, 12 for motor engineering. Although there was an evening course in mechanical engineering, there was no day release in the first year. This was started 12 months later.

Table 15 Newbury Institute: Day-Release Enrolment 1948/49

Course	Under 18	Over 18	Total	
Building	62	15	77	(49%)
Electrical Engineering	42	27	69	(44%)
Motor Engineering	12	–	12	(7%)
Total	**116**	**42**	**158**	**(100%)**

BEC 23 September 1949

Building was the most popular with nearly half of all day-release students. Most of the others were electricians and the SEB's support was most significant. The recently nationalised industry needed a continuous supply of craft apprentices to work as electricians, electrical fitters, jointers and meter mechanics. The SEB was keen to promote training. Indeed, it had a statutory requirement to provide training and education and to advance the skills of its workforce 'in consultation with appropriate organisations'. The Board had a 'real business need for craft

---

[23] *NWN* 16 December 1948; SBCFE Prospectus 1973-74, p.12.

apprentices, recruited to ensure the future availability of the skills needed for the hands-on work of maintaining the supply of electricity'. Its first education and training officer was appointed early in 1949 and all over its area - from Newbury to Southall in west London down to Portsmouth and Bournemouth on the south coast – electrical engineering apprentices were trained on approved college courses.[24] This commitment from the SEB secured a reliable supply of students to Ormonde House for many years.

The motor mechanics made up the smallest group of day-release students, yet their number could be expected to grow. Newbury's roads served local as well as regional and national needs, its garages were busy, and the great expansion in private car ownership which characterised the '50s was about to begin.

In previous years, in Newbury at least, the most common method of obtaining qualifications for people at work had been confined to night school. Some young people had been encouraged to join this 'after-tea' training culture; but this had had mixed results and not many had participated. Now, from 1948, studying during the working day was to become more acceptable. Relations between the Institute and employers were nurtured and more companies were attracted to day release. Employers' attitudes shaped developments at Ormonde House. 'Initially a lot of the companies around really didn't go with day release because, as you can appreciate, kids away from work one day a week, they only had them for four days, so they felt that they were being paid for spending a day in college.'[25] Those industries with a tradition of apprenticeship, like engineering, and those now in public ownership, such as the electricity industry, as well as the Ministry of Supply establishments where there was an emphasis on training, were the ones most attracted to the scheme. On the other hand, those industries without such a tradition or where the work was not especially skilled were reluctant to get involved. Elliott's furniture manufacturing was essentially semi-skilled work which was learnt on the job. There was no comprehensive apprenticeship. Moreover, smaller businesses with staffing and financial constraints could not afford to get involved.

---

[24] Clive Collier, *Southern Electric: A History*, (Maidenhead: Southern Electric, 1992), pp.47-48.

[25] Interview with Robin Morris.

The importance of Newbury's day-release programmes must not be under-estimated. Yet most of the 1,500 enrolments in 1948/49 were for night school, with the 71 evening courses accounting for 1,350 of them. This represented three times as many evening enrolments as the 422 of the previous year.

Table 16 Newbury Institute: Evening Enrolment 1948/49

Under 18	532	(39%)
Over 18	818	(61%)
Total	**1,350**	**(100%)**

Under 18			Over 18		
Male	351	(66%)	Male	441	(54%)
Female	181	(34%)	Female	377	(46%)
Total	**532**	**(100%)**	**Total**	**818**	**(100%)**

In the evenings, building and engineering were taught alongside art, ballroom dancing, commerce, English and history, homecraft, music and drama, physical training, woodwork and metalwork. Young and old, men and women, sat side by side in this medley of learning. Such variety is at the heart of further education and is deeply satisfying to those teaching in it. Sixty-one per cent of night-school students were adults over 18, 39 per cent were young people. In comparison to the daytime, evening class students were more mature, and a lot of them were women. All the daytime apprentices were young men, but 41 per cent of night-school students were women and 46 per cent of all those students over 18 were women.

'There was no fanfare or official opening – I just turned up and that was it'

In September 1948, the bricklayers and the carpenters were pleasantly surprised to find two young women sitting in some of their lessons. One of them was training to be an architect; the other was still at school.

Sheila Smith was at the County Girls' School. She had recently passed her School Certificate and had just started in the sixth form. 'I was in the science lower sixth, doing maths, chemistry and biology – we didn't do physics in those days.' Sheila had ambitions to become an architect and the school arranged for her to take drawing for one morning a week at the FE Institute.

> I was more or less sent down to Ormonde House to do drawing. There must have been some collusion between the college and the school because they wanted some pupils to come down and do things. I came in the morning, walked to the college and walked back to school at lunchtime. I had to miss domestic science or something in order to be able to do building drawing. It was in a room in the old house, upstairs on the first floor, above the front door. There couldn't have been more than 15 in the group, all sitting at long tables.

> In those days, to become an architect you had to find someone to take you on as an apprentice in an architect's office. Now you would go to university, but it was different then. It was very rare for anybody to go to university. My parents would have had to have kept me for another year at school and they couldn't have afforded to have done so. This other lady, the year before me, had wanted to do the same thing. She got the only job that was going.

During that autumn, Sheila Smith learned to draw under the watchful eye of Arthur Owen. Then, at Christmas, she left school. She was 16, and her plans had changed. Realising how difficult it was going to be to qualify as an architect, she began to think about working in a drawing office instead and early in the New Year, she got a job with Plenty. A few months later, she returned to Ormonde House to study mechanical engineering.

'I just heard about it and decided'

Alan Gibbs (b.1924) was one of the students in the Institute's first night school. His employer did not tell him to go; rather, Alan made the decision himself, eager for a qualification to help him in his career. He was typical of a lot of evening students in these years. For many of them, formal education had finished at 14. Some had seen active service during the war. Many were now in their 20s or 30s with full-time jobs. Some were recently married and about to start a family. All of them would find night school a challenge. The classes could take up three evenings a week, and there was homework to fit in. Some of the students would have been encouraged by their employers; others, like Alan, would have taken the initiative themselves. What they all had in common was a desire to achieve a qualification.

Alan lived in Boxford and through his family's links with the family of John West, he could have gone to Christ's Hospital School in Sussex. He did not go and stayed in the village instead.

> I had an elementary school education in Boxford. It was an all-age school, five to 14, just two big classrooms. I always did well there. I used to do my homework with a candle and a paraffin lamp in the middle of the table. I passed the exam to go to the Grammar School, but my mother couldn't afford the train fare or the uniform.

In 1938 Alan started an apprenticeship in electrical engineering. All the training was on the job. In 1939 he joined the air cadets and three years later he was called up into the RAF.

> I went straight into an apprenticeship at the Wessex Electric Company. Newbury was on DC then. There was an old generator down at the mill at Greenham and it just supplied Northbrook Street – there was one cable up the street. At that time it was national grid work. All the villages out in the country were just being installed with a grid system; otherwise they were on paraffin lamps and candles. Everyone had bicycles. We used to work at West Ilsley, which was 15 miles away. We used to cycle and carry all our tool kit and cable. Fifty yards of lead cable weighs a lot. It was really hard going in those days.

> I belonged to the Air Training Corps in Newbury. The CO there was a flight lieutenant Tempest, VC, a really

nice chap. He was the first man to shoot a Zeppelin down in the First World War. I signed up when I was 18. I volunteered for the air crew and failed on colour blindness – fortunately, or I may not be here now! In the air cadets, I had had training in radio and communications, so I went into the RAF in signals and communications. I went to quite a few places – Western Europe, Africa – but I had severe eye trouble. I came out in 1947. I spent my last few months in a hospital at Cosford, near Wolverhampton, so I wasn't feeling too good about studying after that.

After he left the RAF, Alan's previous employer changed. 'The Wessex Electric was now the Southern Electric Company.' He could have gone back to his old job if he had wanted, but he decided to do something different.

Toomer used to have a shop on the bridge in Northbrook Street. I went and saw the boss and he said, 'Yes, start straightaway. I'll give you the full rate for an electrician.' I was earning between £5 and £6 a week. We had a radio technician, one other electrician and an apprentice, that's all. I did all sorts of things. Washing machines were popular. Toomer were selling these, I was fixing them. Televisions were just starting. We went round to houses, put a massive great wooden pole on the chimney and hoped that the signal was there – usually it wasn't.

This was what Alan was doing when he walked down the drive into Ormonde House one evening in September 1948. Recently married, he had moved into Newbury and was living only a few minutes away from the Institute. The apprentice he was working with at the House of Toomer was allowed a day off 'for school'; but Alan was not. If he wanted to study, he had to do it in his own time, pay the fees out of his own pocket, and buy whatever books he needed.

I lived just down the road in Oxford Street, right opposite a pub called the Rising Sun.[26] I was in there talking to a

---

[26] Rising Sun public house, 2 Oxford Road.

chap and he said, 'The College is opening up the road.' This was the first I'd heard about it. I was very interested so I came and enrolled.

I signed on for the National course, electrical. I just heard about it and decided. I came as a part-time student, just evenings, two hours, three evenings a week. I did three different subjects – engineering science was the first year, with maths and AC and DC theory. There were about 35 in my class when I started. We were all adults, ex-service people in our 20s. The students were City & Guilds and mechanical mixed together; a lot were mechanical people. In those days mechanical and electrical were combined – they were taught the same subjects. In the second year we separated.

Three girls always sat at the back. I don't know where they came from. They were quite young, 18 to 20. They were a bit of a menace, giggling and larking about. We couldn't study because of the distraction. The chappy who was teaching us, he didn't put his foot down. So I thought, 'Well, somebody will have to.' Eventually I told them to shut up, and I don't think they came any more. They left soon after I'd told them off quite early in the course.

The classes were seven to nine, with a few minutes break in the middle. There was no facility to get a drink. We just sat around, had a chat and then carried on. I was taught mainly in Ormonde House, the main building, downstairs. There were three classrooms in there. The drawing was in the chicken house round the back – we went out of the back door of the house. I am always telling my contemporaries today about it. It was an actual chicken house. There was a door, but the hatch was still in the corner. In the second and third years I was still taught in Ormonde House – always in there – and the chicken hut. We just had a blackboard. We didn't have any equipment. We did a few lab experiments on a bench, but there wasn't really any labs or anything. We were provided with drawing boards and T-squares; that was the old-fashioned way. We didn't have

CAD (computer-aided design) in those days. Log tables were in fashion, although we didn't use a slide rule much. I enjoyed using log tables – they were easy to get round. It's all quick and easy calculators now. Calculators weren't there because transistors hadn't been invented. There was lots of homework. I would go home at nine and do it while it was fresh in my mind. On Sunday mornings I used to do the drawing.

We saw the Principal, Mr Owthwaite, quite often. I can't remember much about the man. He wasn't a chap who would talk to anybody. He was rather remote and sat in his office most of the time. Mr Evans was teaching maths in the daytime at St Bart's Grammar School and coming up to Ormonde House in the evenings. He was a brilliant teacher. We had a really good system with him. When he got into the really heavy stuff, someone would say, 'Who's playing rugby this week?' And, you know, he would go straight off on to rugby. This would break the tension. Charlie Sully was taking AC and DC theory, and a few lab experiments – he took engineering and that. He was a really nice chap. He was willing to drop everything to teach you something. He was always a 100 per cent teacher. He was a character. He was quite a Labour supporter, but this didn't come through really, not unless you actually challenged him.

In 1951 I took the ONC exam and failed on drawing, partly because the drawing office in the shed wasn't very good. I didn't acquire the right speed to pass the exam. So I took the whole of the third year again. I wanted to get a good pass, so I took all three subjects a second time.

The extra year was well worth the effort. Alan got his good pass and finished with a distinction. 'My certificates were sent through the post. The only knowledge I got that I passed was by looking in the *Newbury Weekly News*. Nobody from the college told me.' By this time, Alan had left Toomer. He was on the threshold of a new career at the Atomic Weapons Establishment at Aldermaston.

'It was all part of the image of nationalisation –
people joined to get free training'

Graham Curtis was also in his mid-20s when he started night school while he was working for the Southern Electricity Board.

Graham was brought up in Grantham in Lincolnshire, a town later to become famous as the birthplace of Britain's first woman Prime Minister. 'If my parents hadn't decided to send me to a little private school, I would have been in the same school as Mrs Thatcher, and possibly the same class – there's not a year between us.' When he was a teenager, Graham's family moved south to Newbury. 'I went straight into the third year at St Bart's, in the days when you were told off for roller skating in the street in your school uniform – I was!' Graham left school hoping to join the RAF.

I never sat my School Certificate. I left St Bart's in December 1938 to become an apprentice in the air force. I went in front of the medical board and they took one look at me. I was wearing glasses. No one had picked me up in the preliminary test, but the small rule was you had to be six-six and have perfect eyesight without glasses. They rejected me.

I didn't want to go back to school and I went and got a job with the Wessex. That was in 1939. At the age of not quite 16, I *was* the Wessex Engineering Department administration. I was the only one because everyone else had got called up. I had been in the post six months and I had to teach everybody that came in all the administration. I got 7/6 (37 pence) a week. That would buy me 45 bars of chocolate. I work everything on bars of chocolate – bars of chocolate are now three to the pound. In fact, the 15-year-olds today are earning considerably more than I did. My stoppages were four pence insurance – that's two bars of chocolate, the equivalent of 60 pence – and I used to give my mother three shillings (15 pence).

Graham had been at the Wessex for three years when his call-up papers arrived and he was 'on a boat out to the Far East'. In January 1947 he was demobilised – 'they didn't get released until after the war had been over a long time' – and he returned to the Wessex. The industry was nationalised and Graham's employer was the SEB. By this time, he was no longer behind a desk but working outside, being trained on the job.

> The job was a trainee jointer, joining the heavy cables, the big stuff. It was rather unfortunate. The gentleman I was going to train with decided to go out to the Middle East to the oil foundries. So his mate had to go on a course to become a jointer. He had to go to Henley, so for the first three months I just pottered around. I did do a bit of jointing but nothing in Newbury. I did a job down at Bradford-on-Avon. We used to work all day and then we would pack up for dinner – that was our late meal. We were sleeping in the substation. We had about four hours on the concrete floor and then we'd do another day's work. I managed to get into double figures on two bob (10 pence) an hour. But nobody told me you've got to climb ladders. In those days, you climbed the ladders carrying a sealing end on your shoulder, which was a hundredweight and a quarter. You didn't have scaffolding. I am frightened of heights, I always have been. So I had to give it up. Then I went down to Riverside, to the generating station where the old Greenham mill is. Then I went to the meter department. I was going to be a trainee fitter to go and do switchgear.

Night school would be useful, but it was difficult. 'People didn't have time to do any studying – it's not that they weren't intelligent.' Yet in spite of the 'standard 48-hour week', there were 'a lot of employees of the SEB signing on for courses'. 'All the big companies were quite happy for their employees to go to the Institute.' The SEB encouraged Graham to do the ONC; so on three evenings a week, he cycled to Ormonde House from his home in Fifth Road. 'None of the engineers had cars.' The Institute was 'mainly engineering – the commercial side was very small. There were no nursery nurses, there was no teacher training. Computers had been invented, but nobody knew anything about them. Things like flower arranging were done by the WI, if anybody.'

I was a volunteer, but the SEB paid the fees. It was all part of the image of nationalisation – people joined to get free training. I did S1 (first-year ONC) in 1948/49, three evenings a week plus homework. It was always a two-hour session, seven to nine. You had to get 80 per cent attendance – otherwise you didn't get your certificate – and you had to sit the exams. We did drawing and electrical theory. It was a three-year course, and you had to pass each one, S1, S2, S3. Then you went on to HNC. You had to go to Reading to do that. I was 25. They were all that sort of age, my generation-ish. Most of the people that were doing the ONC were not elementary school people. They were the grammar school types that had become apprentices, the type that now would go on to take a degree in engineering. Nobody from St Bart's or the grammar school field goes into trade apprentices these days, but they did then.

We were down to Northbrook Street – later the building became the Westminster Bank. We used to go in the back. Basically, it was the workshops, the technical side. We had very little equipment, nobody did. People don't realise, looking back. We were the first entry. It had just started. It's not like it is today when you start a new department – somebody gives you £10,000 and you go out and buy the equipment. We didn't, but you could go along to the local army unit to see what you could scrounge.

Charlie Sully was a real stalwart of the school and also a stalwart of the local Labour Party. He was the longest serving at the college – he did 30-odd years. He was a really nice bloke, one of the old school. He belonged to the intelligent Labour people before the war. He wasn't a cloth cap man, but he wasn't an Oxford graduate either. He was one of the foreman-grade types, and they were the backbone of the Labour Party. In all fairness, they've got some brains. And then it wasn't ideology only. I may not have agreed with them politically, but they were fine people. I bumped into him years later on a political course run by the WEA. He just wouldn't agree with this lecturer from Reading – he wouldn't believe the statistics. In the end, they agreed to differ.

Graham's time on the ONC was brief. In 1949 he dropped out, left the SEB and decided to go back into office work.

> I only did one year of the ONC. I'm not sure whether I actually went to all the lectures. I didn't sit the exams. I was in the meter department with the SEB. I realised I wasn't going to make anything in the technical side, so I was going back into administration. I started trying to get clerical posts, which was hard. I was even willing to take a temporary clerical position. I was that desperate.

Planning for the future

Berkshire County Council agreed an education budget each year, for schools and further education, school meals and school transport, the youth service and youth employment; and further education was allocated its share. The Education Act of 1944, and the subsequent school reorganisation, provided the framework for many of the discussions over how the money was to be spent. The budget increased year on year, a lot of the revenue came from the ratepayers, and there were long and sometimes heated deliberations as to how it was to be allocated. There was competition between the different sections as they each fought their respective corners. The champions of further education had to argue strongly to secure their share of the cake.

To FE supporters, the discussions over the budget could easily be mistaken for a battleground. In some ways it was easier for the schools to argue their case. After all, the law of the land decreed that children had to go to school from the age of five to 15; so a minimum of buildings, teachers and resources had to be maintained. It was more difficult to argue the case for the pre-school sector. Children under five did not have to go to nursery school. Similarly, at the other end of the age range, further education was voluntary, for young people and adults. Furthermore, vocational training was costly. Craft skills were expensive to teach, not only because of the necessary equipment and materials, but also because of the wastage. Students learn by their mistakes and it was inevitable that some items ended up in the bin.

As educational spending continued to rise in the years after the war, it was the discussions about FE which led to the liveliest debates in the council chamber. Its opponents were happy to exploit its recreational Achilles heel. When cuts had to be made, it was never too long before non-vocational courses were made the sacrificial lamb. After all, cried the critics, such courses are neither useful nor necessary as they are aimed simply at giving people something to do in their leisure time.

In 1948 there was a lot going on in education in Berkshire. Pupil numbers were increasing. An intake of 1,000 more children was expected in the coming year, so more teachers were required and extra staff was also needed because of the raising of the school-leaving age. There was an urgent need for accommodation and pre-fabricated huts became a familiar sight in the school playground. Buildings had been neglected during the war and the cost of their upkeep, as well as that of furniture and equipment, was rising at a time when more classrooms were needed. Provision for school dinners was up and transport costs increased as schools were reorganised. Yet significantly, the largest increase in the budget was for further education. Eva Jarvis, a leading member of the Education Committee, spoke enthusiastically about the 'great demand' for classes at the institutes at Maidenhead, Newbury and Windsor, but members, she cautioned, needed to look carefully at the budget because FE was a 'comparatively new' service and its spending 'could grow to very large amounts'.[27]

Inevitably the budget was to be increased for 1949-50 and the rates were to go up to help pay for it. 'An increase of 5½d (2 pence) in the pound in the county education rate, with the likelihood of further additions in the next few years, is the prospect confronting ratepayers in the coming financial year.'

The budget was agreed, and in the summer of 1949, the Newbury Institute was given £2,900 for its engineering and building courses. There was 'a real and enthusiastic demand' for engineering which was 'expensive' but the results were 'promising'. Most importantly,

---

[27] *NWN* 3 February 1949. Eva Jarvis was BEC vice-chairman 1946-51, chairman 1951-55.

employers were co-operating and this was good for the national as well as the local economy. 'Further education is building up a body of technicians who are going to be valuable in the productive effort of the whole country.'[28] Typewriters were also needed but at £40 each, they were a lot cheaper than engineering machines.

There would be more students in Ormonde House in 1949/50. With 'adequate workshops and equipment' it was intended to provide the second year of the ONC followed by the third year in 1950/51. Many of the pioneers of '48 would return and new students would enrol for the first time. The future was bright, but the anxiety about accommodation persisted. The three prefabs were eagerly awaited, but Dick Greet thought the situation in the immediate future was 'desperate'. One way forward was to use the schools, and there were discussions with the Newbury Division about using Speenhamland for evening classes. This was, however, thought 'unsuitable' and nothing happened.[29]

Staff salaries were the most expensive item in LEA budgets and the summer of 1949 ended with a flurry of appointments at Ormonde House. The complement of full-time staff was to be more than doubled with lecturers to be appointed in electrical and mechanical engineering, mathematics and science. This would improve the Institute's 'efficiency' but would 'not increase the expenditure envisaged on salaries in the current year's estimates'. The jobs were advertised in July. The one in science – degree essential – was the most important. Designated a post of special responsibility, this was the highest paid of the three. The person appointed was to teach mainly chemistry but also engineering science and mathematics. The second post – degree or professional qualification essential – was in physics and mathematics. The teaching here was to include ONC engineering science and/or technical drawing. The third appointment was for electrical and engineering subjects, preferably electrical installations and electro-technology, with the ability to teach mathematics, science or technical drawing. In all three jobs 'some help with English might be required during the first year'.[30]

---

[28] Lucian Oldershaw, BEC chairman, in *NWN* 4 August 1949.

[29] *NWN* 23 June 1949; Newbury Divisional Executive 20 June 1949.

[30] FESC 25 March 1949; Education Finance Subcommittee 8 April 1949; *NWN* 7 July 1949.

There was also the usual demand for part-time instructors.

BERKSHIRE
EDUCATION COMMITTEE

Applications are invited from
qualified persons for inclusion on
the panel of Part-time Instructors in
the following subjects:–
Institute of Further Education,
Newbury:
Economics
Secretarial Subjects
Commerce and Accountancy
Mercantile Law
Electrical Engineering
Painting and Decorating (Theory and Practice)
Leatherwork, Weaving
Radio Technology
Shorthand
Advertising and Display
Commercial Art, Lettering and Design
Evening Institute, Hungerford:
Keep Fit (Women)
French, German
Women's Crafts
Applications, in writing, stating
age, qualifications, experience and
subject(s) offered to The Superinten-
dent, Institute of Further Education,
Newbury, as soon as possible.

NWN 23 June 1949

INSTITUTE OF FURTHER
EDUCATION, NEWBURY

Applications are invited for the following posts:
PART-TIME LECTURERS
Interior Decorating (Prac.)
Wednesdays 7 - 9 pm
Handloom Weaving
Tuesdays 7 - 9 pm
Repairs in the Home
Tuesdays 7 - 9 pm
Drama and Play Reading
Fridays 7 - 9 pm
NWN 4 August 1949

The Superintendent was also keen to employ a full-time laboratory and workshop technician. 'The person appointed would work closely with the lecturers and needed a knowledge of science and electrical engineering with experience in one or more of these aspects: maintenance of scientific and electrical apparatus, general mechanical engineering practice (fitting, welding), or storekeeping. For an appropriately qualified man, there could be some part-time teaching.' The salary was £300-£360.[31]

A clerical post – good typist, preferably with shorthand – was also needed for general clerical duties and help with the library. The job was part time, two shillings (10 pence) an hour, for between 7½ and 12½ hours a week. The hours were to be split, preferably into two half-days and three evenings.[32]

A good start

The first year at Ormonde House ended on a high note. Early in the summer, Newbury residents were invited to an Exhibition of Work to see what had been accomplished over the previous ten months. There were many visitors and the success of the occasion meant that similar celebrations were to be held in subsequent years. The college open day became an annual event.

---

[31] *NWN* 4 August 1949.

[32] *Ibid..*

Albert Owthwaite and his staff had good reason to be proud of their achievements; so did the students. Many of them had taken examinations and their work made an 'impressive show'. There were exhibits in the house, in the chicken hut, in the garage and in the Northbrook Street annex. The creative displays were popular and attracted the attention of the visitors.

> The engineering classes (instructors, Mr C Sully and Mr G I Hughson) have an average attendance of 20, and there were many evidences of their skill and draughtsmanship in the annex. Building (apprentices come regularly to these classes) is under the instruction of Mr A H Owen; plumbing, Mr E Newport.

> The dressmaking and tailoring section had some striking dresses and suits on show, so well set out that one could imagine them in a Northbrook Street shop. Here Mrs K Turnbull and Miss J Fitchew reign supreme. The exquisite examples of embroidery were by the students of Mrs F L Green. Art and drawing are provided for by Mrs G Bissell and Miss P Helyas.

T D W Whitfield, the Deputy Director of Education, opened the exhibition. In his address, he spoke of the

> future of technical education all over the country, and felt that Ormonde House was satisfying one of the real needs. Facilities for similar work were available all over England, and Newbury had made a good start. He felt that the Education Committee were in the debt of the people of Newbury, who had responded so well to all appeals for help and interest.[33]

---

[33] *Ibid.*, 30 June 1949.

6

NEWBURY INSTITUTE OF FURTHER EDUCATION TO 1951

Taking the engineering and building courses are 250 boys apprenticed to local firms, and the final examination coincides with the end of their apprenticeships, so that successful students pass out as skilled men in their respective trades.

NWN 31 May 1951

Twelve months after the inaugural Exhibition of Work in 1949, the people of Newbury were again invited into Ormonde House.

1,250 Student Institute Has Two Show Days

Ormonde House Visitors

Visitors to the exhibition of students' work at the Institute of Further Education, Ormonde House, Oxford Road, Newbury on Friday and Saturday were impressed by the high quality of handicrafts and by the variety of subjects taught, though items on show represented only a few of the subjects tackled by day and evening students.

One room displayed a selection of the work done by the dressmaking and tailoring classes, and the garments on view would do credit to any professional dressmaker. All branches of the work are taught, and interest is so keen that 12 classes were needed last term, and have to be added to for the next session. A bridal gown, tailored suits, sundresses and children's frocks, beautifully embroidered and smocked, were all shown.

Fathers Liked This Section

Mechanical and electrical engineering exhibits and equipment interested the male visitors. Fathers with small sons vied with each other to switch on lights and make wheels go round. Scientific experiments held visitors' interest and examples from the woodwork section and art classes were of a high standard.

The building and 'allied trades' section was laid out so that visitors could see at a glance how the full course for the City & Guilds examinations are taught. These students are all local apprentices, who spent one day and two evenings at classes by arrangement with their employers who encourage them to attend. The five years' course coincides with their apprenticeship, so that students who pass their final trade examination complete their apprenticeship as skilled men.

NWN 15 June 1950

The Institute opened its doors again in the spring of 1951.

Where Apprentices Become Craftsmen

CRECHE FOR TODDLERS WHILE MOTHERS TAKE CHILD-DRESSMAKING COURSE

Over 1,600 students now attend day and evening classes of the South Berks College of Further Education in Newbury, and at the third annual exhibition held at Ormonde House, Oxford Road, on Friday and Saturday, employers and parents were invited to see examples of the students' work.

It was difficult to believe that most of the engineering and building exhibits had been executed by apprentices between 15 and 18, such was their high standard. Skilled examples of bricklaying, as needed for the City & Guilds examinations standard to which the boys work, were on view together with scale model and full size exhibits of carpentry, joinery, plumbing, wood graining and painting.

Employers Impressed

Taking the engineering and building courses are 250 boys apprenticed to local firms, and the final examination coincides with the end of their apprenticeships, so that successful students pass out as skilled men in their respective trades. Employers and experienced craftsmen who visited the exhibition were full of praise for the remarkable standard achieved.

Dressmaking and tailoring are two extremely popular sections at Ormonde House, and three rooms at the exhibition were devoted to first- and second-year students' work. Among the perfectly made garments on show were several model dresses and suits, evening dresses, day dresses, jackets, coats and man's trousers. One dress in navy blue linen had been made by a woman of 84 who does not even wear spectacles for her needlework.

A Two Shilling Dress

A child's dress that cost 2s. (10 pence), one made from another garment, as well as several exquisitely smocked children's frocks were among those most admired. In all, 11 separate dressmaking classes are run, including a special Wednesday afternoon class for mothers of young children. To make this possible, a free crèche was opened at the beginning of the school year, where babies and toddlers are left in charge of a trained nursery teacher for two hours, while their mothers are taught to make and embroider baby clothes.

In the woodwork and carving section, which has women's as well as men's classes, the furniture displayed had a uniform excellence of design and workmanship. Weaving was another new section which attracted attention, and the exhibition of drawing and painting was particularly good.

Wide Range of Instruction

In addition to the classes with work on view, the South Berks College teaches general and commercial subjects to students of all ages, at day and evening classes ...

NWN 31 May 1951

In three years, Albert Owthwaite was starting to achieve what the LEA had wanted. 'Once the college got going in the early days a lot of people had a lot to do with it.' By 1951, the Superintendent, now Principal, was assisted by a Vice-Principal and nine full-time lecturers. Their conditions of service, such as those relating to sick pay and holidays, were similar to those of schoolteachers.[1]

---

[1] Not long after the Institutes opened, the Superintendents asked the LEA to change their title to that of 'Principal'. On HMI advice, the LEA postponed a decision until the 'full details of the first year's work' were available. The new title was adopted in the autumn of 1949 and the salary scale of £700-£850 represented a significant increase. FESC 10 December 1948, 15 July 1949, 12 May 1950, 6 October 1950.

The number of students had continued to grow. There were new students as more companies took on apprentices with day release, and many of the pioneers of '48 stayed on for the second and third years of their courses. Engineering ONC students, however, had to complete their final year at Reading College because the regional inspector, 'without whose approval one dare not move', deemed the resources at Newbury inadequate. The Institute did not have an electrical machines laboratory with 'full-size' electrical equipment.

All the students were members of the Students' Association and teachers and support staff were 'honorary members without voting powers'. There were clubs for boxing and tennis. Ray Hammond from the SEB was one of the first student presidents. 'We raised money to resurface the tennis court.'[2]

The story of the Newbury Institute and South Berks College is a testimony to what can be achieved with inadequate accommodation. By 1951, there were seven classrooms in Ormonde House, five on the ground floor, G1-G5, and two upstairs, F1-F2. G5 was the conservatory, used exclusively for dressmaking. Outside amongst the wooden sheds, a Nissen hut was a useful addition. Altogether there were ten outbuildings, A1-A10, used as classrooms. A1 was the wooden hut next to the conservatory, A4 was the chicken hut. Away from Oxford Road, there were three rooms upstairs in the Technical Institute – NS 1, 2 and 3 – used for science and workshop practice. 'There we developed our first machine shop with nothing larger than Myford Super Lathes.'[3] Rooms in the County Girls' School, Shaw House and the Community Centre were used and an outbuilding at Donnington Lodge became the Institute's third brickwork shop.

Donnington Lodge was about half a mile to the north along the Oxford Road from Ormonde House. Berkshire County Council bought it in 1948 for £20,000 and developed it as a residential school for deaf children between two and seven years old. In the spring of 1949, staff and students of the new teacher-training college at Easthampstead Park stayed there

---

[2] *Newbury Advertiser* 17 September 2002.

[3] SBCFE 25 Years.

while waiting for their accommodation at Wokingham to be finished. The school opened in September 1949 with 20 children in residence.[4]

Between 1948/49 and 1950/51, the Institute's evening classes almost doubled, enrolment increased by nearly 40 per cent. There was an almost seven-fold increase in enrolment between 1947/48, the final year of the Technical Institute, and 1950/51.

Table 17 Newbury Institute: Evening Enrolment
1947/48 to 1950/51[5]

Session	Enrolment	Evening Classes
1947/48	200	–
1948/49	970	63
1949/50	1,250	90
1950/51	1,350	120

SBCFE Prospectus 1951-52

Engineering and building classes were held in the evening: automobile, electrical and mechanical engineering; telecommunications; and building construction, building crafts and builders' quantities. So were commercial subjects including accountancy, bookkeeping, law, secretarial practice, shorthand and typewriting. There were also classes in agriculture and horticulture, art and crafts, cookery, dressmaking and woodwork; and there were courses for handicraft teachers and grocers.[6]

Pat Harte took shorthand and typewriting in 1950.

It was two evenings a week, 7 to 9. Students today expect everything to be supplied but we were pleased to be there. We had shorthand with Mrs Sugg; she was a grand lady. My typing was in a room on the ground

---

[4] BEC 30 April 1948, 25 June 1948, 18 November 1949.

[5] The total of evening enrolments in 1948/49 is smaller than that in Table 16 on p.160. This table shows the number of students; the earlier table shows the number of enrolments – and those students who enrolled for two classes are counted twice.

[6] *NWN* 24 August 1950.

floor of Ormonde House – I never got in the chicken huts. The first time I turned up for typing I nearly went home again. There were 20 of us in the class: 18 girls, another chap and me. When we got in and sat down, the woman came in and she would say, by the blackboard, 'Right, you will do as I say. I am the boss. I won't stand any nonsense.' She gave us a whole lecture on that. She lay down a lot of ground rules. I thought, there's something to cope with here. This other chap looked at me. It was touch-and-go whether we were going to walk out or not. Anyway the teacher turned out to be one of the nicest people. She was asserting her authority straightaway, but she wasn't strict.

Dressmaking was one of the few non-vocational subjects available during the day as well as the evening. In 1950, a crèche was organised where mothers could leave their children while they went to class and made baby clothes. The two classes held at Thatcham in 1950/51 were both in dressmaking.

The Institute wanted to offer cookery classes 'as soon as a centre can be arranged as there is a great demand for them'.[7] They were eventually started in the domestic science room at the County Girls' School in 1950/51. In the same session, a second class of woodwork for women began on Thursday afternoons.

An evening class in 'small livestock' was started around the same time. The new Berkshire College of Agriculture was the county's centre for agricultural education, but the FE institutes were still involved and at Newbury there were classes in horticulture, poultry-keeping and agriculture. Agriculture was very popular and 46 people enrolled in the autumn of 1950.[8] Poultry-keeping and horticulture classes were smaller. Less formal, but much in demand, were the weekly meetings for gardeners at the Community Centre.

---

[7] *Ibid.*, 15 June 1950.

[8] The syllabus included the rationing of dairy cows, home-grown feeding stuffs, herd losses and their prevention, selection of dairy cattle and the use of records, supplementary stocking of dairy farms, crops for the dairy farm, cultivations, grassland development and management, pests and diseases of crops, and weed control. FESC 11 May 1951.

Recreational classes were important, but engineering had become the most significant part of the curriculum by 1951. At one point, the LEA was going to change the name 'Newbury Institute of Further Education' to 'Newbury Technical College' – until the Ministry of Education intervened. 'Further Education' encompassed vocational and non-vocational work and, in the eyes of the public, it was broader than 'Technical'.[9] Yet most of the full-time lecturers taught engineering and science, most of the budget was spent on vocational courses, and workshops and laboratories were the priority in the building of the new college.

'Employers were very co-operative'

The number of day-release students grew from 158 in 1948/49 to 250 in 1950/51. Most of the building firms supported the programme, encouraged by the LEA. In one case, young men from Wantage and Lambourn came into Newbury on a coach paid for by the education authority. In 1949, a building course was started at Wantage but in the second year the students needed 'more facilities for practical work'. So they were bussed into Newbury. The new first-year students travelled with them so there was no longer any need to run a course at Wantage. Moreover, the coach travelled via Lambourn, and picked up more apprentices, which thereby saved the costs of providing an evening class there.[10]

Between 1948 and 1951, apprenticeship training in the Newbury district was unobtrusively being reformed. Young workers benefited from the opportunities to achieve national qualifications locally and the *Newbury Weekly News* was pleased to publicise their successes. Employers benefited as well, as county councillor Eva Jarvis was always eager to point out:

> She could not help feeling that today education was doing what had been done in the past by industry, and these

---

[9] *Ibid.*, 12 May 1950, 1 December 1950. Kelly's Directory 1950 refers to the FE Institute as 'Newbury Technical College'.

[10] The coach was for two days a week for 35 weeks, and cost £280. BEC 22 September 1950.

classes at Ormonde House seemed to be taking the place of the old apprenticeships. Employers were very co-operative and provided a certain amount of equipment, but she felt they were getting considerable return. 'They pay wages while their men attend classes, but that is more profitable than paying craftsmen's time in teaching them.'[11]

Equipment was always needed at Ormonde House. Some was purchased new, some second-hand, and some was inherited from the Technical Institute. Occasionally employers offered to help out but these acts of generosity could not always be accepted. **Bill Yates** was working as a fitter with Marchant's Garages.

> It must have been late 1948 or early '49. Mr Marchant got a Churchill tank engine and transmission for the college. We took this tank engine round the back somewhere. It must have been a wooden floor. It wouldn't take the weight. We couldn't do anything about it, so we had to scrap it.

Most of the time, the education authority had to buy the engineering equipment. In the spring of 1949, £3,000 was required for 'equipment and furniture' and £1,700 for engineering items and the 'additional wiring' needed for the new course in Workshop Practice.[12]

For practical instruction, space was a priority. To run the third year in motor engineering in 1951, a new workshop was needed. The Institute was interested in 'certain outbuildings' at The Lawn, an attractive Georgian house on the Bath Road. Reasonably close to Ormonde House, the mechanics could easily walk to it. There was a possibility of a three-year lease for £100 p.a. but hopes were dashed when the owner changed his mind and withdrew the offer.[13] Space was also needed for practical brickwork, an area big enough to allow for the building – and demolition – of walls, columns and arches. The first classes

---

[11] *NWN* 18 January 1951.

[12] FESC 31 May 1949, 15 July 1949; BEC 23 September 1949.

[13] FESC 30 March 1951, 11 May 1951; BEC 25 June 1951.

were held in the garage. The Nissen hut cost £395 in 1950. The students put it together and then moved into it. It was their new brickwork shop. In 1951 the outhouse at Donnington Lodge was acquired – 'there happened to be a space there'– and £100 was spent to make it suitable.[14] This enabled the motor mechanics to move into the Nissen hut; but they were not there for long as it was declared electrically unsafe.[15] Donnington Lodge was used for two years until the greenhouse at Oxford Road was adapted to become the fourth brickwork shop in five years.

'He lived in a caravan near the tennis court'

In the summer of 1949, the three full-time lecturers were appointed. John Whitham was a 'big, tall fellow with a club foot which went down plonk. Flat-footed? Absolutely!' Like Charles Sully, he lived on site, but 'in a caravan near the tennis court, near the dog kennels (iron-railed pig sties)'. He taught electrical engineering, but only for a year. R T Ritchie replaced him and he stayed for four years.

The other recruits were both science graduates. W Atkinson (BSc) was a trained teacher (Dip Ed) who had worked at the Council School. 'He was quite a lad when he was young – I used to see him about town in this little red MG.' He was called up during the war and once hostilities were over, he resumed his teaching, first at Shaw and then at Park House where he was the 'number two'. 'He was a teacher out and out, and a good one.' He was not at the boys' school for very long. 'I don't know whether this was from Shire Hall or whether it was from the local division, but we all had to sign some paper to say that we would give two terms notice if we wanted to leave. Tommy Atkinson, who obviously had some idea of moving on, refused to sign. I can remember Turnbull being pretty annoyed about it because he honestly didn't want to lose him.'[16]

Tommy – 'it's the nickname for a soldier' – did move on and joined the Institute on 1 October 1949. He taught science

---

[14] FESC 20 July 1951, 5 October 1951.

[15] SBCFE 25 Years.

[16] Interview with Francis Titcomb.

and mathematics and for an extra £75 a year was given special responsibility: the 'number two' in Ormonde House, Vice-Principal and Supervisor of Evening Studies. A few months after he had started, the LEA was asked to upgrade him and increase his salary because of the 'number of part-time students now taking advanced courses'. This was rejected, but his responsibility allowance was increased to £100 a year.[17]

The first Vice-Principal worked at Ormonde House for three years. 'He used it as a jumping-off place to become Principal somewhere. If you were prepared to take any post at all in further education, you could find a Principal's job. So many colleges were opening.'[18] In 1952 Tommy Atkinson became Principal of the Technical & Art School at Hyde in Cheshire.

Enter Roy Pocock

With hindsight, we can see that the third newcomer was the most important. **Roy Pocock** was destined to play a central role in the early years of the college's history. He was appointed to teach science and mathematics, a young lecturer on the nursery slopes of a career in FE; but he was soon taking on other responsibilities. Within a year or two, he was in charge of the Science Department and when Tommy Atkinson left, he became Vice-Principal and Supervisor of Evening Studies. A few years later, while remaining Vice-Principal, he was made Head of the Engineering Department.

Roy Pocock (b.1918) came from farming stock with roots deep in the countryside of west Berkshire. His life began in Boxford, where both his father and his grandfather lie buried in the village churchyard. Newbury Council School was followed by a scholarship to the Grammar School as a day student 'although they had a few boarders in those days'. A few years later, a second scholarship took Roy away, to Sussex and Christ's Hospital School.

---

[17] FESC 5 January 1950, 27 January 1950, 1 December 1950.

[18] Interview with Roy Pocock.

Then at the age of 16 I left. I had just won the middle school science prize. Jobs were hard to get and my people decided that they had better find out what I was going to do. They went down there and the housemaster said, 'Young Pocock is very good at rugby and he's very good at cricket. He would do very well to stay on at school and be captain of the house in a year's time.' That didn't go down well with the farming community, let me tell you! They expected young Pocock to be good at science and good at maths and be off to do something else.

So in 1934 Roy went off, to London and work in engine research for British Petroleum and a first taste of night school. For five years he studied for a BSc at the Battersea Polytechnic College. With the onset of war, Roy spent a lot of time in Persia (Iran) working for BP and later, in RAF Education.

I was in charge of the blending of 100-octane fuel. The ambition was to produce a million gallons a day. In fact, we didn't do it until 1944. We had to meet two sets of conditions, the ordinary flying conditions, and take-off, when you had all the supercharging going to take off with a big bomb load. It was those two sets of conditions that were critical, to get them both right and produce the maximum. Being the youngest member of the BP engine research branch in 1934, I was steeped in it all the way. I just got left in Persia to look after it; and then, having done it, I started lecturing about it in RAF Education.

This was Roy's first experience of teaching, which was soon to encompass English lessons for Persians. 'They thought that I was a good bloke to teach them English. I wasn't a good bloke at all to teach them English, but that didn't matter.' Yet the experience in the classroom was not wasted. After nearly ten years overseas, family reasons brought him back to Berkshire. His father was unwell and Roy came home. He decided to stay and applied for a job advertised at the Institute. The application from a science graduate, with a background in engine research and lecturing, was the beginning of a new career. 'I started in

September 1949, taken on to teach engineering science. The HMI insisted that everything you had was to be real size. We had a big engine for doing our engine testing – that was the side I was doing. I loved it, mind, but it wasn't really necessary.' Roy also taught mathematics, 'which came secondary really', and whatever else came up. 'You had your own timetable, but if anyone was away, you filled in. You just opened the page in the book. You came in one morning, the person taking brickwork was away, and you found yourself doing a brickwork practical.'

The lecturers were flexible; so was the use made of the house. 'All the rooms downstairs, except the kitchen, were the office at one stage.' One of them was the library 'although there wasn't much in it'. Another was the common room where the students 'could get a cup of tea'. A lot of Roy's engineering science was taught in the carpenter's shop in the chicken hut. 'It was bloody cold in there because it was off the floor. It had the old wire netting over the windows. It had been a gym with St Gabriel's, but it had been something else previous to that. It had once been an old First World War army hut – there were several around Newbury.' Sometimes Roy taught in the annex in Northbrook Street – 'the lab was down there' – and when the brickwork instructor was away, he drove up to Donnington Lodge and taught there.

John Whitham started on the same day as Roy Pocock. 'He also taught engineering science, the lower end, the City & Guilds if you like, and I had the higher end.' John Whitham did not stay long. Neither did D W Mothersell, an engineer who started in March 1950 but left at the end of the year due to his wife's illness. J Forster (building) only stayed for twelve months. Changes at Maidenhead and Windsor also had repercussions on the staffing at Newbury. F W Tweddell, the Principal at Maidenhead, left in 1950, and J Martin at Windsor was put in charge of Maidenhead as well. In January 1951, Tweddell was given temporary work in Newbury to replace Mothersell. He left eight months later.

By the summer of 1951, four of Newbury's nine full-time lecturers were engineers: Cecil Cox, R T Ritchie, Charles Sully and John Trodden. Arthur Owen and C Taylor taught building, Roy Pocock was responsible for science, P C Garlick taught English and general subjects, and Jessie Searle was in charge of Women's

Subjects. Of the full-time academic staff, four were graduates (Owthwaite, Atkinson, Pocock, Garlick), and two were trained teachers (Atkinson, Garlick).

Dressmaking and embroidery were so popular that in the spring of 1951, the Principal suggested to the LEA the appointment of a full-time instructress in needlecraft subjects. The full-timer, to be paid on the women's scale, £338 to £504, could take over a lot of the teaching currently being done by part-timers. The FESC agreed and Thatcham dressmaker Jessie Searle started her new career. She was soon put in charge of Women's Subjects.[19]

> She used to live along the Bath Road. She had her premises close to Henwick Lane. She did dressmaking up there and she had her own business in her house. We used to go into her front room. She used to make things for me. She was into music and in a choir that my mother belonged to, the Thatcham Choral Society. We used to keep rabbits when I was a little girl – that was during the war years – and we used to breed them. I can remember her making me a pair of fur-backed rabbit-skin gloves out of some of the skins of our own rabbits. My mother must have had them cleaned. She also made a pair of gloves – they were grey in colour – for my sister. But she used to make other things as well.[20]

A series of advertisements was drawn up in the summer of 1950 for part-time assistants for the coming session.[21] A list of subjects was published in early July: commercial subjects, English for foreigners, secretarial practice, commercial English, company and mercantile law, accountancy, economics, land surveying, hand embroidery, bakery science. By the end of the month, there was a timetable:

---

[19] FESC 11 May 1951, 18 July 1952. Miss E J Searle, dressmaker, lived at 133 Bath Road, Thatcham.

[20] Interview with Iris Matthews.

[21] See *NWN* 6 July 1950, 27 July 1950, 31 August 1950.

Dressmaking	Wednesday	2.15 - 4.15
English, First Year	Monday	5.30 - 7.00
English, Second Year	Monday	7.15 - 9.15
Building Calculations I	Monday	6.45 - 8.15
Building English I	Monday	8.15 - 9.15
General Commercial Knowledge	Friday	7.00 - 9.00
Land Surveying	Wednesday	7.00 - 9.00
Secretarial Practice	Tuesday	7.15 - 9.15

At the end of August, with term about to start, assistants were still required:

Building Calcs. and English I	Monday	6.45 - 9.15
Secretarial Practice	Tuesday	7.15 - 9.15
Org. of Retail Distribution	Tuesday	5.30 - 7.00
English for Foreigners	Wednesday	7.00 - 9.00
English I	Friday	5.30 - 7.00
English II	Friday	7.15 - 9.15
General Commercial Knowledge	Friday	7.00 - 9.00
Principles of Law	Friday	7.00 - 9.00
Shorthand	Tuesday	1.30 - 3.00 and 5.00 - 6.00
Typewriting	Tuesday	3.00 - 4.30
Geography	Tuesday	9.00 - 10.00 and 2.30 - 3.30
Arithmetic and Accounts	Tuesday	3.30 - 5.00
Commodities (Retail Distribution)	Friday	7.00 - 9.00

The 60 or so part-timers shared an abundance of industrial and commercial experience and their contributions enabled such a substantial range of courses to be provided. More than one third of them were women, in contrast to the full-timers, where Jessie Searle stood alone. Valuable part-time work was done by schoolteachers and without them, developments at Ormonde House would have proceeded at a much slower pace.

Francis Titcomb was teaching the boys at Shaw House in 1948. 'Owthwaite rang me up one day wanting me to do one or two evening woodwork classes – that's how it worked in those days.' Francis politely declined, but one of his colleagues, G Hughson, obliged.[22] University graduate Gwyn Alderman was another of Francis' colleagues who came to Ormonde House. He had started at the Council School and taught at the Technical Institute (English and shorthand) in the 1930s. He returned from the war to teach French at Shaw and then Park House. Later, in the mid-'50s, having gone to Boxford School as headmaster, he organised the FE evening classes in the Hungerford and Lambourn area. Don Mott (M of E Cert) was another Park House teacher 'doing mainly horticulture work, which we did in those days'. At the Institute he taught building calculations to carpenters and painters, and mathematics to accountants, mechanics and engineers. In 1956 he became head of Compton School. Gladys Sugg (shorthand and typewriting) was married to Bill Sugg (MA), who 'started out' at Lambourn School and then went to Shaw and Park House. He was also involved with the Community Centre and was a college governor.

R L Evans (MA Cantab) was at Newbury Grammar School and he taught mathematics at the Institute. Freddie Hards (BA) taught physical education at the Grammar School; in Ormonde House, it was the less physically demanding English and mathematics. His wife Bobby taught dressmaking and needlework, with Kay Turnbull (M of E Cert). Mrs Sewter (M of E Cert), who taught embroidery and handloom weaving at Ormonde House, was the wife of the classics master at the Grammar School. W L Seaborne (MA Cantab) was another master from the Grammar School; he taught geography at the Institute.

A lot of the part-time assistants, then, were schoolteachers. Mrs Dolan (typewriting) and Mrs Stratton were at Shaw House. G Evans taught at St Nicolas'; Sid Norwood (woodwork) was at

---

[22] For this and the information on part-time assistants at the Newbury Institute, I am indebted to Francis Titcomb who taught first at Shaw House and then at Park House School.

Thatcham Council School; V C H Taylor and Miss Day were at Lambourn School.

There were also teachers like Iris Brooks (dancing) and Arthur Stubbington and Philip Levi (music). Southwood Lodge in Newbury was the home of the Iris Brooks School of Dancing, 'private lessons any time by appointment'. In FE she taught ballroom dancing. 'She was the dancing expert, really pukka. When I was at St Bart's we used to have these Greek plays and whatnot with dancing, and she'd come and coach us for that. Oh, she was good – there was no two ways about that!'[23] Arthur Stubbington was a singer (tenor) who performed at the Plaza Theatre during the 1948 Civic Week celebrations. Philip Levi was a former professor at the Royal Academy of Music and BBC broadcaster who gave piano lessons in his home at Elmore House in Speen.

Like plumber Ernie Newport, many of the instructors came out of the workplace. Stanley Creed (accounting) was at the SEB, Pat Wyatt (building) was at Camp Hopson, C H Stanley (art) was a probation officer and E R Broadbent worked as a youth officer. An HMI report of 1949 made the point that many FE teachers were 'engaged in industry and commerce' and 'not ordinarily experienced in teaching method'. The FESC wanted training to be provided, which would also keep the Principals 'acquainted with any desirable changes in the content of courses, textbooks, apparatus and equipment'. In response, the LEA organised short courses on how to teach.[24]

Nearly all the part-time staff was local and lived close to Newbury. Painting and decorating instructors seem to have travelled the furthest, with one coming from Southampton and one from Oxford, as we have seen. Another painter, Mr Daniels, made a round trip of 40 miles by car from Abingdon. The LEA's maximum allowance for travel was five shillings (25 pence), but the governors intervened on Mr Daniels' behalf, an exception was made and he was allowed 10 shillings (50 pence).[25]

Arthur Owen and Charles Sully were the first people to teach at the college and acquire qualifications there. Many others

---

[23] *Ibid..*

[24] FESC 1 December 1950; BEC 12 January 1951.

[25] FESC 19 January 1951.

followed. Pat Wyatt completed a certificate for handicraft teachers (1952) and metalwork (1953); Jessie Searle, cookery (1953) and ladies' tailoring (1954); Bobby Hards, dressmaking (1953); Mrs Runham, dressmaking (1953); Mrs Potter, dressmaking (1953), advanced dressmaking (1955); R C J Ireson, electrical engineering (1950-54); Miss Barnes, domestic cookery (1958).[26]

On the non-teaching side, there were three full-timers at the Institute by 1951. With caretaker Harry Whiting was laboratory technician C R White, who started in September 1949 on a salary of £330. He left in August 1951. The post was advertised for a workshop technician with practical engineering or laboratory experience. A technical qualification of ONC standard was 'desirable'. The vacancy proved difficult to fill. It took eight months, with S E Jeffery – usually known as Jeff Jeffery – not starting until the spring of 1952. He went on to become senior technician, 'set the standard for good service', and worked at the college for many years.

The third full-time post was in the office. All the clerical work was initially in the hands of women employed part time. From September 1949, the LEA allowed each of the three FE institutes 32½ hours assistance a week. Elsie Owthwaite worked for 20 hours at three shillings (15 pence) an hour with Mrs E W Hasker.[27] The hours were not enough and the Principals were soon asking for more. In 1950 the situation was reviewed, it was decided that the workload justified full-time appointments, and on 1 May 1951 Miss Mabel Lord arrived in Ormonde House. For four years she had been working for the Newbury Division at Weighbridge House on the Wharf.[28] Elsie Owthwaite continued part time, as personal assistant to her husband.

'It was a City & Guilds course, Electrical Installations'

---

[26] R C J Ireson was appointed FT lecturer in 1952 and Mrs Potter in 1959. Miss Barnes was PT tutor from 1951, appointed FT in 1956. Mrs Runham was PT tutor in 1956.

[27] FESC 15 July 1949, 21 October 1949; BEC 23 September 1949.

[28] Co-ordination Subcommittee 6 November 1947; FESC 30 March 1951.

One of the SEB's first major undertakings in the Newbury district was to supply those houses still reliant on paraffin lamps, 'which you carried from room to room', with electricity. Candida Lycett Green remembers the excitement when electric power finally reached her village. While the electricity line marched its way triumphantly across the fields, and men were seen sliding poles off low-loaders, the villagers were busy organising a switching-on ceremony. It was early in 1950 and folk from Farnborough, East and West Ilsley and Brightwalton gathered in Farnborough village hall for the Electricity Party. 'The vicar cleared his throat and said thunderously, "And let there be light." He pulled down the dolly on the switch. The three white-shaded light bulbs hanging from the apex of the roof flashed on.'[29] Modern technology had arrived on the remote and windswept downland of north Berkshire.

Pete Hutchins was one of the first of the SEB apprentices to come to Ormonde House. A photograph shows a group of young men in open-necked shirts, sports jackets and grey flannel trousers. Pete's father had worked for the Wessex and was one of those who had marked its passing with a meal in the Tudor Café in Northbrook Street, 'right on the corner of Northbrook Lane where the shoe shop is now'. Pete followed in his father's footsteps. His first pay packet was 16 shillings and six pence (82 pence), and his first job was at the Dower House on the London Road. On 1 April 1948 he transferred to the SEB.

> I was born in Thatcham down on the A4 by the garden centre. My parents lived in a bungalow just off where the new roundabout is now. I went to what is now the Francis Baily School; in my day it was known as the Council School. Mr Dominy was the headmaster. I did all my schooling there, left at 14 and went to the Wessex Electricity Company. I wanted to do electrical work. My father worked for the Wessex on the engineering side. He got me a job on what was termed the commercial side, doing internal wiring and repairs and that sort of thing, whereas the main business of the company was the distribution of supply with overhead and

---

[29] Lycett Green, *op.cit.*, p.312.

underground cables. I started there on August 6th 1946 as an electrician's mate. At that time there was not anything of an apprenticeship.

The Wessex office was at the rear of the shop which went into Park Way. Mr Lyford was my boss and he sent me down to the Dower House. Wessex had a radio and television section and they did a lot of speakers for shows, like tower systems for horse shows. 'Go down the Dower House – Mr Atkins is down there. They're getting ready for a show, a horse gymkhana.' The Dower House had huge great big grounds with chestnut trees – there was no Shaw estate or Western Avenue. Then I reported to Mr Atkins, who was our radio man. 'Right boy,' he said, 'Pull the cable!' And I was climbing trees, stringing it round for the tannoy system.

Another of the projects that I got involved with was out at the village of Brightwalton. They didn't have electricity laid on, so the Wessex were there putting the services round and feeding the houses and we were installing the wiring, lighting and power points. Brightwalton was just one village of several out there that were going on power.

Then the industry was nationalised and became the Southern Electricity Board. We were a large organisation, one of the biggest employers in Newbury. I worked at the district office, as the set-up was called, 39 Northbrook Street. That had been the Wessex Electricity Company's district office. We had a shop with offices above and an entrance in the rear in Park Way. At Oxford Road was the sub-area office. The area office was at Reading, so Reading was much bigger than Newbury staff-wise. The head office was at Maidenhead. From an administrative point of view, the staff worked in two halves, north and south, and the river was the dividing line. They covered a large area, right out to Hannington where the radio mast is, up to Lockinge near Wantage. I was on the north side.

I went from home by bike. I would cycle with the electrician out to Compton for an eight o'clock start, and he would send me back to the depot to get something. So I would go back on my bike, and then back out to Compton, eleven miles each way. There were no cars, but there were a lot more buses in those days. And there were trains. One of the electricians I was with was train-mad, and if we were working near a railway line he would say, 'That's the eleven o'clock to so-and-so.' And if we were going out in the morning, to work at Compton or Lambourn for instance, he would always go on the train.

The company introduced an apprenticeship scheme for trainees. I did a four-year apprenticeship. You were with an electrician, but the electricians in those days were taught on site. The electricians I served my apprenticeship with didn't do apprenticeships as we knew them. They got their training on the job, on half-days from seniors. We first went at the Liberal Club opposite our shop in Northbrook Street; that was day release using the SEB's own trainers. It was classroom stuff, theory. We didn't do very long at the Liberal Club. It was only a matter of months before we transferred to the college. I used to go one day a week to college, to Ormonde House as it was known in those days. Obviously when the college opened, there was a purpose-made facility to use. There were six of us – from Newbury, Reading, Hungerford and Pangbourne. They came from far and wide, from outlying districts, to go to the college. The SEB had depots at Hungerford, Marlborough, Pewsey and Reading. If you were in a depot, the SEB would get you to Newbury. They were very good in those days if you had further education. If you were based in Newbury, then it was your responsibility to get yourself to college

It was a City & Guilds course, Electrical Installations. You didn't do a lot of practical; it was all theory, classroom work. The Southern Electricity Board relied on your job the other four days of the week – or four and a half 'cos we worked Saturday mornings – for the practical side of it.

We started at nine, nine till one, and then two till six. You'd have a break at midday and take a sandwich with you. When we were at work, the finishing time was 5.30. My mother always used to say when I went to college that I'd be late for dinner.

All of my training was in Ormonde House, in one of the front rooms. The site was a lot quieter than the area is now, with the traffic. There was a long drive to the back of the house; the driveway went round to the left. There was a chicken hut, a big wooden building, in the back garden of the main house. They even had pupils in there – obviously it was done out. And there were cottages there as well. It was like a lot of properties in those days, they were really large weren't they, the big houses? I remember working at one further down the Oxford Road in Donnington Square. There's a big house, and they had a television, probably the only one in the area. That was where I saw my very first television picture.

'It was surprising how many cars there were about'

In 1948 Newbury's roads were busy and redevelopment was planned, 'arterial highways for fast long distance traffic, relief roads for local and cross traffic'. The age of the bypass, however, was a little time away and the cars and lorries still came through the town centre. Many of the larger garages were on these main thoroughfares. There were petrol pumps by the side of the road, and showrooms full of cars adorned with wood and leather trim and the emblem on the bonnet proudly displaying Morris and Wolseley, Humber and Triumph, and other long gone British marques.

The traffic approaching the town from the south would come down the Newtown Road and pass by Murray & Whittaker's Garage, and a little further on, as the houses turned into shops, Nias in Bartholomew Street. Across the bridge into Northbrook Street, and there was Stradling's. 'From Marsh Lane, where Jack of Newbury's house overhangs, you would have looked straight across to the vehicle entrance to Stradling's. Their petrol pumps were there as well – you just pulled in on the pavement.'

Next was Pass & Company. 'They were the main Ford dealers in the area. They went from Northbrook Street right back through into West Street, which was quite a depth.' At the northern end was the Broadway and here was Wheeler's Garage 'which had been in Newbury ever since the year dot'. Like many garages, its origins were in the bicycle trade. Close by on the opposite corner was Martin & Chillingworth. In West Street was Green & Whincup, owned by Marchant's Garages whose own business was on the Greenham Road.

Before the war, car mechanics were usually trained on the job. In 1944, however, a few started going to evening classes at the Technical Institute and when Ormonde House opened, some garages started to give day release. A handful of apprentices started there in January 1949, more arrived nine months later. Some of the older ones went to night school. This began the long and fruitful connection between the college and the motor vehicle industry in south and west Berkshire.

Nias was one of the first garages to use the Institute. Nias (1935) Ltd. was based at Herborough House on Bartholomew Street by the junction with Market Street. 'There was a big old house there – the garage was out the back of it.' It was here, many years before, that Miss Pollard had run her girls' school. The entrance to the house was in Bartholomew Street, access to the petrol pumps and the workshops was from Market Street. Close by were shops, a row of cottages and Plenty's factory.

Mick Terry lived 'out in the sticks', in Wickham. He went to school there until he was 11, when he had to move either to the all-age school at Lambourn or the secondary school in Newbury. 'The headmaster thought I should go to Newbury, so I went into Shaw House, boys downstairs and girls upstairs.' Mick was 14 in 1948 and ready to start work. 'I'd already secured a job with the SEB. Then the government said no, you must go on another year. It's funny how things happen, isn't it? I would happily have gone into the SEB, but it wasn't to be.' For his extra year he was moved again, this time to Park House, 'a lovely old house, and all the grounds, a lovely setting'. Twelve months later he was able to leave but he had changed his mind about the SEB. Instead he would look for a job in 'something more mechanical'. This interest in 'things mechanical' was kindled the day his father had given him a second-hand bicycle. 'When I looked at it, it was a tatty old thing; but I thought, I'm going to take that to bits and do it up, which I did.' Mick was used to tinkering with his hands – 'I had a natural leaning towards mechanical things' – but it was his father who directed him towards vehicles. He worked as a chauffeur for a gentleman at Wickham whose cars were looked after by Nias.

> My father said, 'Look, there's a job for you at Nias if you want it.' So I went along and had an interview. I left school and within two weeks I was at work. In those days they didn't have you hanging about. Newbury was a thriving market town. There was a market opposite Nias, the old cattle market, where the council offices and the bus station is now. That was the big cattle market on a Thursday, when all the farmers came to town. There was a real character about the place. It was lovely. The farmers used to love a drink – they would get pie-eyed as well as doing their business – and they all brought their cars in. Nias had a prime spot. They had a big piece of ground where the farmers would come and park their cars when they went to the market, and any jobs they wanted done, it was easy to do them.
>
> The ordinary working guy used to have his cheap Morris Minor and that sort of thing, but there's not many ordinary working people had cars. You had to be like a publican or a businessman, moneyed people, farmers for instance.

'The college gave me a voucher for books'

Ray Claridge (b.1933) also started at Nias around this time. He had been at school with Mick Terry and they knew each other well. Ray was born in the tiny village of Christchurch, near Inkpen. He was not there for long as the family moved, first into Inkpen, then to Kintbury and then, in 1939, to West Woodhay. Ray went to school in West Woodhay, then Hungerford and a few years after that he was at Shaw House. 'Then we moved to Park House. That was just the house. There were no other buildings there at all. We had to take plimsolls with us. There were polished boards in the house and you had to change your shoes before you went in the class.' Ray's father was a bricklayer, but Ray set out, somewhat cautiously, in a different direction.

> I don't know why I went into motor vehicles. I can't say that I was ever taken by motor cars. I just went along to Nias and started there straight from school. I worked there all the time I was an apprentice. For the first two or three years you worked with a senior man, a mechanic, doing all the jobs he told you to do. Then you'd be working on your own but under his supervision. A job would be given to him and he would say, 'Get on with that.' He would keep an eye on you. Then the last year, you were given jobs on your own.

> There wasn't the pressure then as there is now, like bonus schemes and that, to get jobs out quickly. It's all rush and tear today. You're given the hours by the manufacturer for how long you've got to do jobs. It was not like that then.

For three years the Nias apprentices were given day release. 'Suddenly it was thrust upon us. The college? You had never heard of it.' Once they were 18 they were expected to go to evening classes. By this time Ray was living in East Woodhay, cycling six miles each day into Newbury.

> There were a lot of garages about and it must have been a condition of your apprenticeship to come to college. However, there were occasions when Nias might ring up and say you can be excused college because of work. They did that sort of thing sometimes. I would rather have been at work, and I would rather have been at home than in night classes. We used to go to Somerscales down London Road, not far from the Clock Tower.[30] You always used to go in there from work for your fish-and-chip tea and then do your evening class. When I passed my City & Guilds, the college gave me a voucher

[30] Somerscales, fishmongers, 3 London Road.

for books. I had to say what I wanted and I had motor vehicle books. It's no good looking at them now; they are completely out of date.

When Mick Terry started work he earned 15 shillings (75 pence) a week. He gave his mother 7/6 (37 pence) and kept the other half of his pay packet for himself. As he worked on the vehicles, he became particularly interested in the electrics.

> There were two car electricians and I was put with the younger one of the two. I was with this guy all the time. It wasn't just stand there and watch me. It was hands-on. He helped with the jobs but he was a bit of a lad and wasn't too keen on teaching people things. He liked a laugh. I didn't learn too much about car electrics like I should have done.

'The practical was down the bottom in this old shed'

Mick Terry remembers 'about a dozen' apprenticed mechanics who started at the Institute in 1949. 'We were required to attend. It was no ifs and buts. They said this is part of your apprenticeship.' The course was demanding, with lessons in auto technology, calculations and practical mathematics, drawing, engineering science and garage practice. Charles Sully was the teacher.

> It was a full day. It went right through from nine to quarter past seven, with a lunch break, to try and cram everything into one day. At lunchtimes we wandered around the town, getting packets of crisps and whatnot. I don't remember eating too much during the day. It was a bit heavy going at times, because as the course went on, you did quite a bit. They covered everything – engineering science, maths, mechanical engineering – all in the one day. But they didn't care for car electrics as such, so I was at a bit of a disadvantage with trying to pursue my line of work. But because I had stripped my bike down and done it up, I had a leaning towards mechanical. It was a bit silly, but that's the way it went. I didn't mind.

It was hard to switch from one subject to the other. I'm not dumb, but I'm not a high-flyer. A high-flyer might have grasped all of it, but I found it a bit much. We had written theory as well. They used to give us the exercise books. There was more theory than practical. We had to take our overalls to college, but I can't remember safety boots. Safety wasn't important in those days. The practical was down the bottom in this old shed. Charlie Sully's house was along a bit from the shed. He used to try and do a bit of practical engineering. An old engine arrived, but it wasn't a lot. I don't remember a workshop with tools and different bits and pieces. It was pretty basic but I'm not knocking it. The place was just starting up. They didn't have proper facilities. It was the beginning, and oak trees grow from acorns. But really we were doing our practical in our other four days. All the stuff that the garage wanted, they had to teach you, and although the garage was teaching you, they wanted some work out of you as well.

Charlie Sully was organising all the things for our day. He used to come in and say, 'We're doing this today.' He used to have his day set out. He was an exceptional bloke, a very knowledgeable chap without a doubt. He knew about motor cars and whatnot, and he used to take us for the maths side of it and everything for a couple of years. He knew his job. He was a brilliant guy. I found it hard to grasp everything he was putting across. I imagine he was under a fair bit of pressure. He was taking four or five lessons and that takes some doing if you are going to get some content into it. I could never understand how he did it. He worked jolly hard. There were homework assignments. He liked to test our knowledge on what we'd been taught. It developed as you went through the course. He used to give us tests, but no exams as such. It was all the final bash at the end, the City & Guilds. Roy Pocock had been working abroad on the oilfields, and he used to like to tell us about his epics abroad as well as the science. We used to laugh! Funnily enough, I used to see him at cricket occasionally. I used to play cricket with my father at Speen, and Roy played for Speen. He played cricket very well.

Mick Terry and the others who started in 1949 left Ormonde House in 1953. By this time Mick was earning £3 or £4 a week. 'It wasn't a lot of money. You survived but you wouldn't run a car or buy a house or anything, that's for sure.' His apprenticeship completed, National Service could no longer be delayed. He joined REME, the Royal Electrical and Mechanical Engineers.

> The basic training at college stood me in good stead – it was well worth going. Some of it must have gone in because I would not have passed my second class trade test in the army, which was pretty rigorous. When people do things, it may not appear beneficial at the time, but it comes out later on in life. It's like anything you do: if you have a good base, you build on it. It's like the foundation of a house: if the foundation is good, the building will stand up. I've said this to youngsters who have worked for me, get a good basic knowledge. It's like going up a ladder. You won't get on the ladder halfway up. You've got to get on to the bottom rung and then go up. So, get as much stuff under your belt as you can. I've said this to many a youngster, 'If somebody is trying to tell you something, don't say, I know. You listen and say, thank you. If you don't agree with it, you keep your mouth shut, but you listen.'

'Charlie was the main man – he must have taken us for most of it'

The mechanics came from Newbury, Thatcham, Woolhampton and 'Reading way' to the east; and Kintbury and Hungerford over to the west. Another of the young men who started at this time worked in Lambourn. **Ron Pontin** (b.1932) came from a family of ironworkers.

> My ancestors were blacksmiths at Wilton, near Pewsey. Great-grandfather moved to Chisleden, and then my grandfather's family lived in Wroughton, where my dad

was born in 1896. They both worked in Swindon iron works for a time. The Pontins went from Wroughton to Upper Lambourn about the turn of the century. Then they went to Lambourn and then to Eastbury, and that is where I was born.

Ron and the other boys and girls went to school in Eastbury and celebrated the coronation of George VI (1937) 'with straw bales to sit on, a fancy dress parade and a bun fight'. He took the eleven-plus examination, and failed. 'I don't think I was ready really. I did better when I came to the college than I did when I was at school.' For the next four years he was at school in Lambourn, where Miss Day, part-time FE assistant, was the headmistress. 'When they opened the Forth Road Bridge – her family lived up there – she came down to mum and dad's to watch it on television.'

> She lived at Laburnum Cottage, the last house on the right going out of Eastbury. She was hard because she had to be. Lambourn was a bit rough and ready. There was a girl up the road from us and Miss Day used to take us both to school and bring us back if she had the car, but normally we would go on the bus. The first term I was at Lambourn, there was a diphtheria epidemic. I spent fourteen weeks in Alexander Isolation Hospital. The Americans at Membury airfield always used to give the kiddies at Lambourn School a Christmas treat. A Christmas treat during the war – you had ice cream! Anyway, I was in hospital so I didn't get any.

Ron could have left school in 1946, but his father made him stay on because he had been ill. When he left the following summer, he found a job on a farm; but his father had other ideas.

> 'You, working on the farm, boy? No you're not! You're working for Wally Stagg!' Dad and Wally Stagg came from Wroughton. Wally was foreman at Lambourn Garages. He was a bloke and a half. So I went to Lambourn.

COACHBUILDING

ALL VEHICLE, Building, Repairs,
Renovations, Conversions.
CHASSIS Modifications, Gas and
Arc Welding.
TRIMMING DEPT. for Seat and
Hood Repairs and Renewals, etc.

MOBILE SHOPS : TRAILERS : VANS :
PANTECHNICONS : COACHES :
HORSE BOXES, etc.

The LAMBOURN *Garages*
Coachbuilding Dept.

Lambourn Garages was in the heart of horseracing country.
The garage was owned by the Nugent family. Trainer Sir Hugh
Nugent arrived in the village in the 1930s. His grandfather
had trained horses there earlier in the century and when Hugh
took over the Windsor Cottage stables, he soon realised the
area's potential. He bought a farm and 500 acres, laid out the
Mandown Gallops, and encouraged others to take over derelict
farmhouses and turn them into racing yards. The Nugents also
started Lambourn Racehorse Transport. Hugh's son eventually
took over responsibility for the gallops while his brother took over
the garage and the transport business.[31] It was in the garage that
Ron started, 'just as a boy', becoming apprenticed two years later.

> Frank Thatcher was workshop manager. His father – we
> always called him grandad Thatcher – was the manager.
> We didn't start at the college until September 1949. Seeing
> as my birthday was about four days after I started, grandad
> Thatcher said, 'We'll start you on 25 shillings (£1.25).'
> A pound to mother, five bob (25 pence) to myself, that's
> how it was in those days. And if you had a good report,

---

[31] Oakley, *op.cit.*, pp.55-59.

you got an extra penny an hour. There was a big panic. We were taken on just as boys, then, all of a sudden, we were going to be apprentices and they were saying we had to go to college. I suppose they must have got some money. I'd been left school two years then. It was a bit of a worry that you were going back to school again. But it was a good thing, a five-year apprenticeship. When you were 18, you were due to go in the forces. I didn't want to go. I had a girlfriend and things were going well.

Lambourn had the garage side, the coachbuilding side, the trim side for horse-boxes, the agricultural side, and the hire vehicles. They also had a furnishing section. It was owned by Sir Hugh Nugent, who lived in Ireland. His son, John, still does. He's now Sir John, but he will always be John as far as I'm concerned. Lambourn was an agricultural district. We used to do tractors, cars, lorries, horseboxes. Four tons was the heaviest sort of lorry we ever had. We had two horseboxes with engines in the rear, low-loaders. We also had a low-loader with the engine in the front, which was a front-wheel drive. The trainers brought their Jag or whatever, and of course, tractors and combines were in. We had a more varied apprenticeship at Lambourn than people at Nias or Marchant's.

Ron's first report from 30 September to 16 December 1949 shows a total of 72 class hours in the daytime, 12 hours of drawing in the evenings. 'The first year we used to do the engineering drawing in Lambourn School. We got shoved into this class in the evenings in the old woodwork room.' During the day it was practical mathematics (24 hours), garage practice (24 hours), auto technology (12 hours) and engineering science (12 hours), with a test in each subject at the end of the term. Mathematics, 'an intelligent and studious lad'; garage practice and auto technology, 'has worked well and shows a very good result'; engineering science, 'should do well later'. Overall, 'very good lad who will do well later.' Ron's future looked bright.

Roy Pocock taught mathematics and engineering science. Tommy Atkinson also took mathematics and coming from Park

House, 'the Newbury lads knew him'. He was the 'only really schoolmasterish type we had – he used to walk in and he was always straight.' Charles Sully was in charge of the course and he did most of the teaching.

> Charlie was the main man – he must have taken us for most of it. During class, if you could get Charlie talking about his reminiscences, you wouldn't do anything else. Having said that, he didn't shirk the job he had to do. A lot of the stuff he had was in Nias' yard by Herborough House.

> He used to teach engineering drawing, garage technology and workshop practice – which was mostly hacksawing, filing, that sort of thing. I shall never forget John from the garage at Woolhampton because we were in class one day and we had a hacksaw. John was fiddling about. And Charlie Sully said to him, 'Steady'. 'It's alright sir.' And bang went the blade! We used to have a little workshop where we used to do welding and things like that, gas welding and soldering. It was like a blacksmith's shop really. In the second and third years, in the summer months, we did do the odd lecturer's car, de-coke and things like that. There was also a small workshop down Albert Road. Roy Pocock taught us engineering science there in the machine shop. There was a bigger milling machine than I'd seen before because, let's face it, you don't get big milling machines at Lambourn. There was also a couple of lathes and a surface grinder. What we did do, it must have been second or third year, we started to build a Stewart Turner engine. I can always remember being on this surface grinder doing the base plate. We never finished it – it was only about one hour a week.

> The tutors didn't go into the electrical side very deeply, which was most unfortunate. We did touch on it – plugs and points and what the dynamo did – but it was mainly the mechanical side. We did the theory, the timing of the engine, firing and all the rest of it. We also did gear ratios on the mechanics side, and the layout, where the engine is, and all the way through.

They didn't do meals for us in the first year, but in our second year they used to do us a little meal in the evening – bacon, beans, fried bread. It was something – you didn't used to finish classes till seven. You used to go into Ormonde House. There was a kitchen in there. Harry Whiting, being caretaker, used to help.

In the first two years, the apprentices took UEI examinations. In the third year, it was City & Guilds and Ron sat next to his tutor. 'We were in the chicken house with the electricians. It was one of the hottest days. Charlie Sully hadn't got that certificate, so he sat in the desk in front of me. I got a first class pass. I just had to look over his shoulder!' The examinations over, the mechanics enjoyed a day out. 'The electricians, the SEB-type blokes, used to have a trip out after exams and we went with them to Earley power station.'

Ron went to college for one more year, this time to night school.

We did the practical course for the National Craftsman, which was in a tin Nissen hut. There was no theory for that. I had to come in on the Newbury wagon, a flatbed with a tilt on it. It used to bring the chaps in from Newbury to Lambourn to work on the coachbuilding; there weren't enough carpenters out at Lambourn. We used to come back on the train to Hungerford at 9.35 – it was an evening stopper. I used to borrow June's bike to go home to Eastbury. Then to bring it back over, I used to ride my bike with one hand and steer hers with the other.

June, who lived in Hungerford, was Ron's girlfriend. Things went well and they were married a few years later.

'We studied in difficult conditions, all over the place, in odd rooms'

The Plenty company has the longest connection with further education in Newbury. From the time of the First World War it encouraged its engineers into the Institute in Northbrook Street. After the Second World War the apprentices went to Ormonde

House while the older workers were directed towards night school. Some of the company's senior staff was directly involved in FE as governors and committee members.

Once Sheila Smith had left school at Christmas 1948, she soon got over her disappointment of not being able to train as an architect. She was pleased to start work in Plenty's drawing office. 'Today everybody is always talking about the shortage of skilled people, but we used to have all the old apprentices, didn't we?' Yet the old apprenticeships could be difficult to get, especially for women. 'It was only because my parents knew somebody who knew somebody who said, "Oh yes, we'll take her on." ' Sheila was taken on, at 15 shillings (75 pence) a week in 1949. One of the first things she did was to buy a bicycle, complete with saddlebag and 'big dropped handlebars'. She used it to go to work from her home in Shaw, and to go from the drawing office in Cheap Street to the pattern shop in King's Road.

> Mine was a strange apprenticeship because I didn't actually go into the workshops. When I went there first of all, I was in charge of the printing of the blue prints – and they were blue prints in those days – and the distributing of them to all the departments. I used to whizz around the town on this bicycle with my prints. I was always nipping between Plenty and the pattern shop. I spent many an hour riding my bike between the two. It was funny, quite a landmark in Newbury. I also had to deal with any queries and things like that. I spent a lot of time in the workshops and obviously chatted to the foremen. I gained a tremendous amount of knowledge by doing that; but I did my main practical engineering at the college.

Sheila was given day release for the ONC in Mechanical Engineering, and this involved night school twice a week. Homework was set and everybody did it. 'You were there for a purpose. You just got your head down – everybody was very motivated. It was what you wanted to do and you were happy to get on and do it. There was no alternative.' Sheila passed her UEI examinations and completed the first two years of the ONC. Then she went to Reading to 'finish off'.

Sheila started in Newbury in a class which had been running for some time. 'I don't know how long it had been going when I went into it. It seemed to be established and they all seemed to know what they were doing.' Although she had been in Ormonde House a few months before, she still felt 'like the new girl who hadn't a clue'. Fortunately there were other apprentices from Plenty with her – 'there must have been at least ten' – and there were 'lots of lads' from the SEB. They all did technical drawing together. Sometimes the class was in the chicken hut. 'This was notorious. It was a wooden hut, always called the chicken hut. They put tables and chairs in it and at one end in the middle was this old cast iron stove with a pipe going up.' At other times the class would meet in the wooden hut outside the conservatory. When they were taught in the house itself, there could be some welcome distraction from the ladies next door.

> They seemed to have taken the conservatory over. There were two doors that went out into the conservatory and you could see through from our drawing class. All the boys used to be looking through at the women in there doing their sewing. There was always great merriment looking through to see what they were doing, especially when they were trying on the dresses.

One of the drawing instructors came from Theale, where he ran The Lamb public house. 'He was an ex-RAF type with a great big handlebar moustache, a great character. We all used to draw and he used to tell his stories and whatnot and we used to be in fits.' Sheila only saw Albert Owthwaite once, 'when I first went there', but she saw a lot of Roy Pocock for mathematics, and Charles Sully and Tommy Atkinson for practical work.

> We used to go to a place down by the Methodist Church. There was an old building behind the shop on the corner.[32] The Boys' Club butted on to Northbrook Street and there was a place behind where we had our workshop. There were lathes, drilling machines, things like that in there

---

[32] Burton & Hobbs Electrical Co., 58a Northbrook Street.

where we did our workshop technology. Mr Sully taught us down there. It had a lab in there as well, with the real old lab benches. The lab had quite a bit of stuff in it, Bunsen burners, and typical sort of lab stuff. We used to do our engineering science down there. Mr Atkinson did all the engineering science. He really was a brilliant lecturer.

At lunchtime, Sheila would get on her bicycle and go home to Chestnut Crescent, although sometimes she took sandwiches 'and ate them in the classroom or outside'.

The majority of us had bicycles. There were no sheds. You parked your bike wherever you could, outside the door of your hut or classroom. It was always there when you came out, lights and everything. You left it outside down in Albert Road as well, leaning against a wall. There was nowhere else to put them. Cars were not a prominent feature. There were so few you could park them on the gravel. There was no car park.

There was nowhere to have any social life at all. There was no hall or anywhere where you could do anything. It was just going there to do your course and that was it. You tended to belong to youth clubs in the town in those days, the tennis club and things like that. There was nothing else to do. We had a very good club called St Nicolas' Youth Guild. It was a youth club with Saturday night socials. It was a church thing – they kept an eye on it – but we had a committee and we ran it ourselves. It was progressive in that respect. It was brilliant. That was the social life. There wasn't really anything else much; you just did your own thing. There wasn't an awful lot of time for socialising. You were working from nine 'til half-past five and you were doing three evenings a week at night school. You had Saturdays and Sundays, but you had your homework to do.

'If you were absent, tough, you had to make it up yourself'

When Sheila Smith cycled over to the foundry in King's Road, clutching her blue prints, she would be meeting with Ron Mead and Pete Tidbury. These two young pattern makers were not given day release as there was no tailor-made course for them, but the company encouraged them to go and study.

Ron Mead (b.1934) did evening classes between 1950 and 1953. 'You weren't conscripted. You went of your own free will to help yourself. You did it in your own time.' Ron was born in Newbury and from Speenhamland School, although he passed the eleven-plus, he chose not to go to the Grammar School. 'Like an idiot, I jibbed and said I wouldn't go. The biggest thing was, you could not play football there. It was rugby. You were not even allowed to play football for anybody else out of school on Saturdays.' Ron was passionate about his football, and he ended up at Park House.

> There was one class which moved up there first from Shaw. I was the first pupil ever to step foot into Park House. We all had to wear carpet slippers or socks. You weren't allowed to wear shoes because of the parquet flooring. The headmaster lived over. He used to go fishing and he used to have a fair few pike and put them in a pond at the back. We used to go out there at lunchtimes and watch these pike going round this pond. It wasn't his pond originally; it was to do with Park House. We had gardens and we used to do a bit of horticultural stuff – you always used to have your growing a bit of whatever. There was a chap there who took woodwork classes in the evenings. He was a joiner. I got into woodwork and I won two or three certificates for the Boys' Club. My sister has still got the coffee table I made.

Edmonds was a furniture shop in Northbrook Street.[33] Ron enjoyed working in wood, and when he left school he thought about going there to train as a cabinet maker. However, there was a rumour going round the town that it was about to close down and while Ron hesitated, his uncle Charlie suggested Plenty's

---

[33] Edmonds & Son (established 1800), house furnishers, 40 and 41 Northbrook Street.

pattern shop. 'That's all woodwork.' In April 1949 Ron began his five-year apprenticeship on 19/6 (97 pence) a week. G T Shoosmith was Plenty's owner and managing director. Mark Wakeley was the works manager, 'a delightful ex-marine engineer with great energy and enthusiasm' and a Singer saloon car.[34] Ron remembers Wakeley well. 'He was there when I was, and he was there a few years before that during the war.' He was involved in the work of the Institute and was on the governing body. His brother was also at Plenty, 'on the shop floor as a fitter'. Gyles was another of the managing directors, also involved at Ormonde House in mechanical engineering. He retired from the company in the mid-'60s having worked there for virtually all his life. Les Jones was in the works and Mellor was in charge of finance. These were the 'three or four people' who had cars.

> My uncle was at Plenty for fifty years. My grandfather was there for goodness knows how many years in the foundry. He lost his legs with gangrene, kneeling in the wet sand and stuff. My father was a landscape gardener. He went into Plenty during the war on a drill. Uncle Charlie was a foundry man, working hand-in-glove with the pattern shop because the patterns went into the foundry. Everything in metal you make in wood first, to make a mould, whether it's a zinc tap or a car engine or a propeller. You've got the inside as well as the outside to make; otherwise you'd have a solid casting. Uncle Charlie knew all the pattern makers and it was through him that I got a job there.

> When I started work, it was bikes by the score. They used to sling the bikes in the main front entrance – there was about 100. Some chap that worked with me had a smallholding at Greenham Common. He used to come to work in a horse and cart and tie the horse up outside with a nosebag. They used to bring eggs in from there. Me and a mate of mine, we were apprenticed pattern makers but

---

[34] Only two of Plenty's employees owned cars when Shoosmith – whose father had been appointed chairman in 1934 – joined the company at the end of 1951. Shoosmith, *op.cit.*, p.8.

we used to do all sorts of odds and ends and maintenance in the works. We were out cleaning the works front once, scraping it down and re-varnishing it – this was a job that two apprentices had to do – and some chap comes along and says, 'I see you're scraping for a living!'

There was no course for pattern making, so what you used to have to do was a general engineering City & Guilds, which is good knowledge, good experience, but useless for a pattern maker as such. I did maths, engineering and tech drawing. It was voluntary, just evenings, two evenings a week. If you didn't go, there'd be no report back. Nobody got a grip of you at Plenty. They just said, 'You ought to go', and that was about it. There was no personnel department as such. It was just that the night school was there. You could go; it was your own choice. It was two evenings you were giving up, and when you're young, you don't want to give up evenings.

There were lots of people in the mathematics class that were office people. It wasn't maths for pattern makers, or engineers, or accounting. It was just general mathematics. A chap from Thatcham School came over in the evenings. I know it's only simple maths, to add up or subtract, but he taught me how to add up by missing out numbers. It's always stuck with me. Say you had 6, 3, 4 and 9. You would go, 6 and 4 is 10. You'd pick out the ones that made 10 and go back and pick up the 3 and the 9. Then you'd pick up another 10; simple, but it is important.

For technical drawing, I was sat on this boarded floor in the chicken shed. You didn't have posh drawing boards. It was just a basic drawing board and a T-square on your desk top, and you had your set squares and protractors – plastic, wood or whatever – and your pencils. That was about it. All your drawings were in pencil; we didn't do any printing there. At Plenty they used to do the original blueprint on a linen-based material, like a film of emulsion. One of the old things people used to do was to soak out the blueprint drawing and make themselves handkerchiefs. It was first class linen. If you washed the print out, you would have a nice hanky.

Ron lived in West Street, 'dead opposite one of the old garages in the town, Green & Whincup'. One evening a week he went across town to the 'old school by the Blackboys Bridge'.

> The school was bombed and all that was left was the building tight to Station Road. This one long building was still okay. Outside they had a metal stairway, like a fire escape. It went up one end, and you had a long walkway about four or five foot wide right the way along the top floor. You had classes underneath, but the night school bit was upstairs. You used to go up this iron staircase and walk along into your different classrooms. That was the engineering place up there, the mechanical bit, a bit of filing and all the usual. They had car engines on stands on these tripods. They turned round so that you could work on various sides, sumps and tops of the engine. I'm not saying you were doing massive strip-downs or anything, but you could learn how the engine worked and how to do general servicing, brakes and those types of things.

'Ormonde House was like an ordinary house, that's all it was'

Pete Tidbury started at Plenty in 1948. He lived on Benham Hill, between Newbury and Thatcham, and was educated at Thatcham Council School. He left in the summer of 1948, but he did not go into the pattern shop straightaway. He had another job to do first. 'I always used to help on the farm at Henwick after school and at holiday times, so I went to Plenty after the harvest time.' Six months on and Ron Mead joined him at King's Road, the start of a working relationship which was to last for 50 years.

> My father worked at Plenty. He did 51 years there altogether. He was machine shop foreman, ever since he was 24. His father before that was blacksmith, as was his father before that. Father said, 'Well, what are you going to do?' We had

woodwork at school and he knew I was happy with wood and all that sort of thing. He said, 'I'll get you a job in the pattern shop. I'll see Mr Cox.' He was the pattern shop manager. And I came to work in my little blue schoolboy's hat, a special peaked cap. I soon discarded that! There was an old pattern maker, Billy Farmer. He comes up and says to me, 'Well, the worst day's job you've ever done is to start work!' I always remember that.

For my first job, I was put on to work with Alec Tofield, who's departed from us now. The number of the engine was 2874, and that was the largest engine they had made. It was for the South African government, and the name of the tug, an ocean-going tug, was *J D White*. That sort of thing sticks in your mind. Plenty did a lot of ships' fittings – that's all pipe work. We call them T-pieces, and you used the same block of patterns. Very often they're identical, so you made them so you could add pieces on and take pieces off and change the flanges, whatever the ship required.

There was always strong competition between Ron and me, friendly competition you know, which is good isn't it? When you are boys you want to make the best. You polish them up as much as you can.

Pete had been at work for a couple of years when he decided to go to Ormonde House. 'Maths and technical drawing, evenings only, from seven o'clock till nine o'clock.' He was there for two years.

We weren't sent – we went all voluntary on our own accord. You went there and you paid your fee. I just thought, well, you wanted some better maths, you wanted some technical drawing for pattern making – you needed that to be able to read the drawings, all the blueprints.

Ormonde House was like an ordinary house, that's all it was, just an ordinary house. You went through the front door, and technical drawing used to be in the right hand side room. You brought your own drawing instruments, the dividers and compasses and scale rule, what have you. T-squares were supplied. At the back of the house you had these sheds. Maths was in the chicken house, but it did vary. You did have homework, some set things to do, but I never took any exams so I never passed anything. I always seemed to go away on holiday at that time.

'The tutor taught by torchlight and brought his own oil stove'

Mary Harte (b.1925) went to Speenhamland and then Newbury Council School which she left in 1940. She could have finished sooner but 'stayed on a bit at the discretion of the headmistress'. She started work, and in 1949 went to her first evening class. More classes followed, in shorthand, typewriting, bookkeeping and elocution.

Classroom space was very sparse, and classes were held in odd venues, in schools and halls scattered round the town. We attended shorthand classes in some very dilapidated chicken houses complete with wire netting. It was necessary to climb up some wooden steps to enter, and the tutor, a Mr Jones, taught by torchlight and brought his own oil stove. It wouldn't be allowed now because of regulations. In those early days, safety regulations were barely thought of, and due to some new and apparently heavy equipment being installed, the electricity system frequently failed under the strain. They built something to do with engineering, so every now and again the lights went out altogether. We brought our torches. If we had no light, Mr Jones said, 'Look, I've got a torch and I'm going to dictate. Just copy it down on any bit of paper. It won't make any sense but you can still get it into your head.' So we did it. We had no option. If we went there, we were going to learn. We carried on regardless and most of us enjoyed the lessons. It couldn't happen now – you would have to have sufficient power.

The chicken hut was crowded, about a dozen students. There were a lot of women students in 1949. You would see other people around, but you didn't get to know many people unless they had a direct link with you. We just had trestle tables, no desks. There were no roosts. They had taken those down. There was no blackboard. It was just the teacher and the book. It depended whether you were doing theory – in theory there were books, but not in speed. I had done shorthand at school and it was my speed I was getting up. Nowadays you would buy or borrow tapes. We accepted what we had and thought we were lucky to get it. We bought our own notebooks from W H Smith. There was a girl who couldn't afford to buy a book, so the teacher gave her money to go and buy one. Mr Jones was a very fatherly figure. He worked for Great Western, based at Paddington. He worked in London during the war, teaching shorthand in the evening.

Anxious to do well, Mary wanted extra help before the examination; and she knew Bill and Gladys Sugg.

There was a shorthand exam coming up. There were three of us were doing a higher speed than the others, and we were a bit worried. I said to these two girls, 'I wonder if we can get any private tuition from Mrs Sugg, because she lives in Newbury.'

So we asked her, and she said, 'How many of you want to come?'

I said, 'Three.'

She said, 'Alright, come up, come up.'

I said, 'We are going to pay you.'

'Oh,' she said, 'We'll see about that.'

These two girls and I went to her house and stayed there for the best part of three hours. All the time she was dictating to us and telling us what to do. She wouldn't take anything from us, so between us we bought her a big box of chocolates and took that to the house.

A mix-up over examination entries has stayed in Mary's memory.

One year there was some confusion in one class when it came to completing entry forms for Pitman typing examinations. Seven students arrived only to find that they had been entered to take the exam the previous evening. Nobody knew how this tragedy had come about. To avert World War Three, the tutor personally paid for the seven in question to be entered for another session.

'There must be no going back on reforms already started'

Further education in post-war Britain had as much to do with training as with education in the broader sense. Craftsmen and technicians were needed to increase productivity and to make Britain more competitive in world markets. This was the strongest argument for spending money on the Newbury Institute: investment in vocational training was vital for the country's economic success.

In the autumn of 1949, Berkshire's Scheme of FE was submitted to the Ministry of Education. The five-year programme, if it was fully implemented, could cost over £1-million. A lot of this expense was for county colleges, and the government would have to decide whether or not the country could afford them.[35]

While the future of the county colleges was being discussed in London, Berkshire's LEA was busy drawing up its annual budget. The estimated spending for 1950-51 was over £1,750,000, a significant increase from the previous year. Many factors contributed to this. The raising of the school-leaving age meant more pupils, more teachers, and more classrooms. The LEA was expecting 1,200 more schoolchildren and 25 extra teachers were needed. New buildings were planned and schools were reorganised. The revenue to come from the rates was around £630,000, an increase of £72,000 over the previous year. The county rate would have to be increased, again, to pay for this. A large share of the increase was for further education.

The County Council discussed the budget early in 1950. Eva Jarvis wanted it to be considered in the light of the country's economic situation. In the past 12 months, wages had gone up,

---

[35] *NWN* 27 October 1949.

the cost of living had increased, and the pound had been devalued. 'The time had come, as they knew it must come, for a curtailment of expenditure both national and local.' The Ministry had given some direction as to spending, and the council's subcommittees had discussed the 'possibility of economies which might be affected'. Yet the Ministry stipulated that 'there must be no going back on reforms already started'. Instead, 'they should look to see that they were getting better value for their money.'

> The policy of the Berkshire Education Committee was formed on the passing of the Education Act of 1944, and it was a long term policy. They were not looking for immediate benefits. They had to decide whether they should now scrap the schemes they had started or not. To her it would seem most unwise and uneconomical to abandon a scheme before it reached maturity, for that would result in the money already expended being wasted.

> To affect economies, she suggested they should not cut out schemes already begun, but watch carefully the administration of those schemes to see that they were run as economically as possible.

At the same time 'it is just as well to see some of the advantages, so that we can see where the money is going.' During the last four or five years, she pointed out, 'they had obtained on the credit side a training college, a farm institute, a special school for deaf children, primary and nursery schools, new classrooms and two institutes for further education.' 'It is not expenditure so much as an investment', she affirmed, 'for the young people of this country are our hope for the future.'[36]

Dick Greet could always be relied on to defend the further education adventure:

> The crying need in industry and every branch of commerce was for their placement of craftsmen, whom it was almost impossible to find. Key jobs were being performed by men

---

[36] *Ibid.*, 26 January 1950.

of 75 because younger men could not be found to replace them. The object of further education institutes was to try to provide for that.

Estimates for further education had been cut to the marrow bone, and if further cuts were made the effect would be that courses already in existence, to which young men had devoted two or three years study, would be left high and dry. These young men would lose the chance of getting their diplomas and qualifications.[37]

Harry Metcalf from Ormonde House emphasised that unless the county were prepared to pay for FE courses, then youngsters would be deprived of that type of education. 'If the country could not afford them they would have to go without them.'

Watching the 'frills'

Twelve months later, education spending was to be increased again. The proposed budget for 1951-52 was over £2-million, an increase of almost £350,000. 'Rising salaries, rising wages and the increases in prices make it impossible for us to keep our expenditure at a steady level, and we view with some concern the fact that for the coming year, the gross expenditure exceeds two million pounds, involving an increase of no less than a halfpenny in the county rate.' Again the ratepayers would be asked to pay more. As Eva Jarvis pointed out, 'on the one hand was the urgent need for economy, and on the other the inevitable spending of more money.'

The growth of further education was rapid and spending on it for 1951-52 was to be increased by £31,700. Between 1948 and 1950 the number of FE students in Berkshire had gone up by 125 per cent, from 3,560 to over 8,000, and there were 800 day release classes. Discretionary day release was emerging as the substitute for county colleges and compulsory part-time education for those young people in work.

However, many of the thousands of FE students were neither being trained for a particular trade nor developing skills to

---

[37] *Ibid.*.

improve the country's economic performance. Non-vocational classes did not benefit the economy in the same way as the vocational courses. Autumn arrived, imaginations were fired and people came to enrol. Some came to learn for fun, wanting to learn for learning's sake. Night school was an escape for a couple of hours from cheerless post-war Britain. Here there were opportunities to learn a foreign language or start a keep fit routine. What started as an interest could grow into a much loved hobby. Here were people who wanted to learn, in classes which gave them both confidence and enjoyment.

Yet the funding of such courses remained the weakest link in the FE armoury. Should the education authority pay for recreational courses? The use of money from the public purse rightly provokes debate and argument. Further education was growing, but where was the growth to be? Should a class in country dancing be publicly financed? Such questions can still be heard today. Is a course in scuba-diving simply a leisure pursuit or can it be justified as leading to jobs for industrial divers? When money was in short supply, and economies had to be made, non-vocational education was where the critics would focus their attack.

The attack came in 1951 from Sir George Mowbray, chairman of the Finance Committee. He criticised FE spending and his sentiments were no doubt echoed in council chambers round the country.

> Speaking on the broadest of lines, it seemed that the commitments as affecting basic education, which was primary and secondary, were more or less, untouchable. But what might, perhaps, be termed the 'frills' would need to be looked at carefully. He mentioned such things listed under further education as classes for glove-making, radio for amateurs, fencing, judo and modern dancing.

> 'One wonders whether there are not methods by which the young people at any rate, can get instruction in modern dancing other than through the Education Committee,' he said.

Eva Jarvis, much to her credit, retaliated with the kind of response that was often used when the so-called 'frills' were under attack. This was the committed stance of the liberal educationalist. The Education Committee, she said, 'tried to view education from a wide sense and the classes Sir George Mowbray had mentioned were truly educational. People looked at it differently but she would be very sorry if Berkshire were so narrow in its outlook that it did not include the arts as well as learning.'[38]

---

[38] *Ibid.*, 18 January 1951.

7

THREE DEVELOPMENTS

I n 1951 three developments took place which shaped the future of further education in Berkshire.

In the spring of 1949, an HMI inspection took place followed by a report on FE in Berkshire. As a result of this, in 1951, the responsibilities of the institutes were reorganised. The Newbury Institute was given responsibility for courses not just in Newbury but in the surrounding district as well. Its new name was the South Berks College of Further Education, with its headquarters in Ormonde House and Albert Owthwaite its Principal. The Institutes at Maidenhead and Windsor became the East Berks College of Further Education, responsible for FE in the two towns and in the surrounding area. John Martin, the Principal at Windsor and Acting Principal at Maidenhead became the Principal of the new college.[1]

The second development in 1951 was the arrival of full-time students at Ormonde House. Full-time numbers increased in the years that followed and the FE student community became increasingly diverse. School leavers came to study programmes with a vocational focus and continue their general education as well.

The third development was the most exciting one. The Ministry of Education and the LEA agreed to build a new college in the grounds of Ormonde House. It was to be constructed in instalments, the first to include workshops and laboratories, the

---

[1] FESC 11 May 1951.

second to include a library, a refectory and a large multi-purpose hall. By 1960 the two instalments were built and the physical environment of post-school education in the Newbury district had been radically changed.

New responsibilities

> An Area College is to be established, to be known as the South Berks College of Further Education, from the beginning of the session 1951-1952.
>
> *BEC 23 February 1951*

In 1948 the Education Committee had not defined the area of responsibility of the Newbury Institute; rather it was to develop by first of all meeting the needs of its immediate vicinity. Albert Owthwaite could help organise classes beyond the town if appropriate. The biggest FE centre outside of Newbury was at Hungerford, and in 1949, Owthwaite was given responsibility for the work there. During the next two years, English, French, German and shorthand were organised at the school in Hungerford, as well as choral music, dressmaking, home furnishing, keep fit and woodwork.[2] In 1950, Miss Moses and her German class completed a radio broadcast to Germany on the British General Election of that year.

Elsewhere in the Newbury district, classes continued to be arranged as they had been in previous years. At Kintbury for instance, the part-time Superintendent organised folk dancing. There were problems as the rooms in the school were too small and the floors were uneven. Consequently the class was moved to the village's Coronation Hall. This cost 15/- (75 pence) an evening, a special concession to the folk dancers as the maximum hire charge normally paid by the authority was 7/6 (37 pence).[3] At Lambourn there were courses in animal husbandry, cookery, dressmaking, mathematics, shorthand and woodwork. In St Mary's School at Thatcham in 1949/50, there was dressmaking, English

---

[2] NWN 8 September 1949, 31 August 1950.

[3] BEC 18 November 1949.

and shorthand. The following year, it was only dressmaking. Mrs Shaw was the instructor and 200 visitors came to an exhibition to admire the dresses, skirts, blouses, lingerie, two-piece suits and children's clothes made by her students. The visitors included Albert and Elsie Owthwaite and Miss Trickett, the county's organiser of domestic subjects.[4]

By 1951, three years after its opening, the work of the Newbury Institute was established. It had become apparent 'that it would be much more economical and sounder educationally to affiliate to the Institute classes in outlying areas, which, during the last two years, have been organised by the Principal and are now looking towards Ormonde House for certain senior courses.'[5] Consequently the institutes at Compton, Hungerford, Lambourn and Thatcham were affiliated to Ormonde House. Each centre was to have an advisory committee. This much expanded area of responsibility of South Berks College was the same as that of the Newbury Division which looked after the schools. The college was open to students who lived outside the catchment area if the class they wanted was not available in their neighbourhood.

SOUTH BERKS COLLEGE OF FURTHER EDUCATION
AREA EVENING INSTITUTES
OPENING DATES:
HUNGERFORD, LAMBOURN, COMPTON:
MONDAY, 24 SEPTEMBER, 1951
THATCHAM:
MONDAY, 17 SEPTEMBER, 1951
Full particulars from Local Posters or from the
Secretary, South Berks College of Further
Education, Oxford Road, Newbury.[6]

So in 1951/52, the college organised classes at Aldermaston, Boxford, Bucklebury, Compton, Hamstead Marshall, Hungerford, Inkpen, Kintbury, Lambourn, Stockcross, Thatcham and Wickham. It was also responsible for staffing, advertising for instructors at

[4] *NWN* 31 May 1951.
[5] BEC 23 February 1951.
[6] *NWN* 30 August 1951.

Bucklebury (cookery, drama, old time and ballroom dancing), Compton (English, mathematics, needlework and dressmaking, science, shorthand, technical drawing, women's crafts), Hungerford (cookery, drama) and Lambourn (choral music, cookery, English and mathematics, renovations and alterations, technical drawing).

This organisation of further education by area had been recommended by the HMI's report. Moreover, the FESC felt that many of the students taking technical courses at Maidenhead, Newbury and Windsor needed a preliminary programme, provided ideally in their local centre. They would then proceed to the main establishment for the senior work. 'By the gradual extension of an area organisation in the County, in which all FE will be directly supervised by one or other of the Full Time organisers, it will be possible to co-ordinate the work of the Evening Institutes and that carried on in the major establishments.'[7] This way of organising the work would be 'more economical and sounder educationally' than the separate overlapping providers which had existed since 1948. It would be easier for a student to move on from an evening institute to an FE College. Indeed, by 1951, some local institute organisers were looking to Ormonde House to put on more advanced courses for their students.[8] In sum, with this county-wide reorganisation, a student's journey along the FE highway would be easier to negotiate.

With these new responsibilities the LEA drew up a new constitution for the governing body. South Berks College had up to 30 governors, a lot more than had been allocated to the Newbury Institute. Most of them were in place by the start of the academic year in September 1951. Twenty-five were representative governors, five were to be co-opted. Their first term of office ended on 30 April 1952 and the body was reappointed for a further three years from 1 May 1952. A new governing body was to be appointed for the period 1955 to 1958.

---

[7] FESC 1 December 1950.

[8] BEC 23 February 1951.

South Berks College: Governors 1951

Representing Berkshire Education Committee:
    Revd Bertram Russell
    Alderman H R Metcalf, JP
    Councillor O S Brown, JP
Representing Newbury Divisional Executive Committee:
    Mr R H Greet
    Mr W G W Mitchell, BSc, JP
    Mrs M P Showers, BA
Representing Newbury Borough Council:
    Mr M Paine
Representing South-West Berks Youth Employment
    Committee:
    One member
Representing Newbury Community Association:
    Mr W T Sugg, MA
Representing Newbury Youth Advisory Committee:
    Alderman C A Hawker, JP
Representing Employers' Associations:
    Building: Mr R H Radcliffe
    Electrical Engineering: One member
    Mechanical Engineering: Mr M Wakeley
    Motor Engineering: Mr A R Marchant, MIMI
Representing Employees' Associations:
    Mr W Winter
    Mr D McMahon
Representing Newbury Chamber of Commerce:
    Mr G P Hopson, JP
Representing Workers' Educational Association:
    Mr G Suggett
Representing Churches:
    Church of England: Revd K C Joyce
    Free Churches: Revd C I Ward, MA
    Roman Catholic Church: Revd F Phillips
Chairmen of Local Evening Institute Advisory Committee:
    Compton: One member
    Hungerford: Mr C Audsley
    Lambourn: Revd E J Rumens
    Thatcham: Mrs C Hobbs

Representing Women's Interests:
   Two members
Co-opted Members:
   Up to three

Many of the governors were to serve for more than one term. People of local and civic distinction – five were magistrates – they gave the governing body a weight of authoritative opinion. Less than half were connected with the County Council. The Education Committee and the Newbury Division each had three representatives. The Youth Employment Service would have a particular contribution to make on the development of the full-time courses. Encouraging the college to respond to local economic needs, there were representatives from Employers' Associations and the Chamber of Commerce. The Community Association and the WEA ran FE classes with LEA support and were each represented. The inclusion of the Church of England (the Oxford Diocesan Council of Education), the Catholic Church (the Roman Catholic Diocese of Portsmouth) and the Free Churches (the Berks, Bucks and Oxon Free Church Federation) serve as a reminder of the important part played by organised religion in the history of education in this country. The area evening institutes were represented as these were now affiliated to the college. Two of the five co-opted governors were to be 'especially concerned with the interests of women', underlining the popularity of the cookery, crafts and dressmaking curriculum. The National Union of Townswomen's Guilds and the Berkshire Federation of Women's Institutes, both involved in adult education, were invited to suggest names of interested persons.

The new governors were appointed in the summer of 1951. Some of them – Oliver Brown, Dick Greet, Harry Metcalf, Maurice Paine, Bertram Russell – had been involved in the previous three years. Their re-engagement gave continuity, and nowhere was this more valuable than in the appointment of Dick Greet. At the first meeting, he was elected chairman and he remained a governor until 1954.

Dick Greet represented the Newbury Division, along with William Mitchell and Marjorie Showers.

Schoolmaster William Mitchell retired from St Bartholomew's in 1948 after 32 years. He had joined the school during the

First World War as senior science master and finished as second master. 'He was deeply interested in the welfare of the boys, and many Old Newburians and their parents have cause for gratitude for the advice and guidance which he gave when they were planning their future.' His interests included the groundbreaking communications technology of the wireless and the television. In 1922 he broadcast a series of talks for the BBC from a transmitter in Bournemouth and he played a leading part in the founding of the Television Society, editing publications and giving lectures to the Royal Society of Arts in London. On his retirement from the school he was given a television set. 'Youth movements of all kinds claimed his interest.' He was involved with the Air Training Corps and the Boys' Club and was assistant commissioner of the boy scouts.[9] He became one of the first members of the Newbury Division and was its vice-chairman in 1953-54.

Marjorie Showers (b.1895) devoted much of her life to the community, in the Women's Institutes, in local government and in education. From parish to rural district to county council, the University of London graduate served the people of Berkshire unselfishly for 30 years. One of her first contributions was to set up the WI at Padworth, holding the first meetings in her house. Within a few years she was on the executive of the Berkshire Federation. Her local government work soon extended beyond the boundaries of Padworth Parish Council and during the war she was elected to Bradfield Rural District Council which she served for many years. Her particular interests were council housing and education. She was a founder member of the Newbury Division, became its chairman and worked for it until she retired in 1967. For 16 years, she was a governor at South Berks College; and she also sat on the governing bodies of Park House and Shaw House, Newbury Grammar and the County Girls' School. In the '60s, she was elected to the County Council and was vice-chairman of the Education Committee 1961-63.[10]

Four of the college governors represented employers. Their contributions were vital, for the day-release courses in particular

---

[9] *NWN* 11 June 1942; *The Newburian* July 1948. *The Newburian* is the magazine of the Old Newburians Association.

[10] *NWN* 5 March 1971.

and the vocational curriculum in general. Those appointed in 1951 had already been associated with Ormonde House. Russell Radcliffe represented the builders, Mark Wakeley the mechanical engineers and Didge Marchant the motor industry.

Albert 'Didge' Marchant (b.1908) was Newbury's most important garage owner. He owned Marchant's Garages on the Greenham Road and Green and Whincup in West Street. A pioneer in the motor industry, he had set up his business – cycle and motorcycle agent and repairer – as early as 1924. He foresaw that mechanical transport was the 'mode of travel for the future', and was determined to 'extend his activities into car hire and repairs'. Within a year he was using the yard of the Queen's Hotel in the Market Place for his work. His business grew rapidly, causing 'traffic congestion' in the town centre, and he moved out to the Greenham Road where his premises included a cottage, a coach house and stabling previously rented by the Anglo-American Oil Company. This became the home of Marchant's Garages.

In the 1930s, the motor car was still a luxury and Didge Marchant took pride in the fact that 'he was able to meet all his customers individually, talk to them about their problems and remember them by name'. His business flourished and his garage became one of the most modern in the district. Neighbouring houses were purchased, the forecourt extended and fitted with electrical petrol pumps, and the town's first hydraulic car lift was installed. During the war, Marchant's was allocated government contracts and was responsible for the local distribution of 'pool' petrol. Didge Marchant trained his apprentices, giving them 'practical and theoretical instruction and examinations'. His mechanics were the first to study at Ormonde House, and his appointment as governor came as no surprise as he was 'particularly interested in the training of students for engineering and the motor industry'.[11]

Paul Hopson (b.1895) represented the Chamber of Commerce. He was a leading figure in the community, so much so that when he died in 1980, it seemed, to the writer of his obituary at least, that a chapter in the history of the town had come to a close. 'It is apparent that any full appreciation of the life and work of Paul Hopson would become the story of a town, and we who

---

[11] *Ibid.*, 28 April 1977, 11 June 1987.

continue to live in his town of Newbury, realise that his times will not recur, and we are thankful for the share he took in laying its present day foundations.'

Paul Hopson lived in Newbury all his life. He was educated at the Grammar School, trained as a surveyor with Newbury Council and after service in the Royal Army Service Corps, he joined the family firm and was put in charge of its building department. It was Paul Hopson who married the daughter of Alfred Camp and he became a director of Camp Hopson. He kept control of the building department and its work of 'high class alteration, renovation and extension'. He was a leader of the business community, one of the youngest-ever presidents of the Chamber of Commerce, and a director of the Newbury Building Society for more than 40 years. As a magistrate he was particularly interested in the juvenile bench. By the time he became a college governor, he was chairman and joint managing director of the family firm. His company was one of the biggest builders in the town, and had been one of the first to send their apprentices to Ormonde House in 1948.[12]

Governor George Suggett represented the WEA. A Liberal in politics and secretary of the South Berks Liberal Association, he worked as a dental technician in Cheap Street. Schoolteacher Bill Sugg represented the Community Association. Governor Revd Joyce was the vicar of St Mary's Church in Speen.

The work of the college was organised in departments. Their number and their names changed over the years, but the structure remained intact until the 1990s. Most of the departments were managed by a 'head' but in the smaller ones, a 'responsible lecturer' was in charge. The intention in 1951 was for the college to have six departments: Arts & Crafts, Building, Commerce (including General Education & Languages), Engineering, Science, and Women's Subjects.[13] Only five, however, were developed; a separate Arts & Crafts Department never materialised. In 1956, each department had a head, except Building, which had a tutor in charge. In 1960, the structure was the same, Building now managed by an 'acting head'.

---

[12] *Ibid.*, 27 November 1980.

[13] BEC 23 February 1951.

The structure and staffing at South Berks was typical of a 1950s FE college. It was hierarchical and departmental. At the top was the Principal, responsible to the governors and the education authority. From 1 September 1951, Albert Owthwaite's annual salary was increased to £900-£1000.[14] Tommy Atkinson was Vice-Principal and Senior Lecturer, responsible for the evening work in Newbury and the affiliated institutes. Below the Vice-Principal came the heads of department. Each department was graded according to the level of the courses it organised and its size. This produced a hierarchy of departments. Each full-time lecturer belonged to a department. The lecturers were grouped into those who taught (Grade A), and those who taught but also had other responsibilities (Grade B). The Grade A salary in 1951 was £375-£630, Grade B £450-£725.[15] The number, and grades, of lecturers in each department depended on the number of students and on the level of the work taught. Those departments with more advanced work were allowed more Grade B lecturers. In addition, each department had its part-time assistants, paid by the hour according to the level of the work they taught.

In 1951 the college had 11 full-time academic staff, including the Principal.

South Berks College: FT Academic Staff 1951-52
Area Principal: A H Owthwaite, MA, MA(Ed), MCollH
Vice Principal and Supervisor of Evening Studies:
　　　　　　　　　W Atkinson, BSc(Hons), DipEd
Lecturers:
Head of Engineering Department:
C L Cox, AMIEE, AIMechE, CGLI Electrical Engineering

Lecturer in Charge, Building Department:
A H Owen, ARIPHH, Ass Inst Clerk of Works

Lecturer in Charge, Science Department:
W B R Pocock, BSc(Hons), AFRAeS

Lecturer in Charge, Women's Subjects:
Miss E J Searle, CGLI 1st class

---

[14] *Ibid.*, 4 May 1951.

[15] *Ibid.*.

Assistant Lecturers:

Engineering:	J Trodden, AMCT, HNC(Mech), CGLI Engineering 1st class
	R T Ritchie, AMIEE, AMEME;
	C Sully, AMIBritE
Building:	C Taylor, HNC, CGLI Full Tech 1st class
Commerce:	P C Garlick, MA, DipEd

A year later there were 15, of whom five were Grade B Lecturers. These were Roy Pocock, Vice-Principal and Supervisor of Evening Studies; Cecil Cox, Senior Engineering Lecturer; Eric Carr, Senior Science Lecturer; Jessie Searle, Lecturer in Charge of Women's Subjects; and Arthur Owen, Senior Lecturer in Building.[16] By the mid-'50s, the majority of the teachers were in engineering and science.

---

[16] FESC 18 July 1952, 3 October 1952.

Table 18 South Berks College: Staffing Levels 1956

Department	FT	PT	Total
Engineering Head, Grade 2 W B R Pocock	6	11	17
Science Head, Grade 1 W E Carr	3	12	15
Women's Subjects Head, Grade 1 Miss A M B McGee	3	7	10
Commerce and General Education Grade B Assistant Acting Head, The Principal	2	7	9
Building Grade B Assistant Tutor in Charge, A H Owen	2	3	5
Total	**16**	**40**	**56**

'Largest in numbers is the Engineering Department'

In 1956, 37 per cent of the full-time lecturers and 30 per cent of all teaching staff worked in the Engineering Department. South Berks College had developed as a centre for engineering. Within a year of the 1951 reorganisation, approval had been given for the three years of the ONCs in Electrical and Mechanical Engineering; so students no longer had to go to Reading for their final year. Moreover, in 1954, South Berks and East Berks Colleges were confirmed as the two centres for courses in Electrical Installations in both Reading borough and Berkshire county areas.[17]

The Science Department had 19 per cent of the full-time lecturers, 27 per cent of total teaching staff. Women's Subjects had the same number of full-timers but fewer part-time assistants. The smallest departments were those of Commerce and Building. They each had two full-time lecturers, although Commerce had almost

---

[17] *Ibid.*, 17 September 1954.

twice as many part-time staff. Building had been most important in the early years but staffing levels had not increased significantly.

In the prize-giving evening held at Speenhamland School in 1956, Roy Pocock gave his 'rough analysis' of the college's work as follows: 49 per cent was in engineering, 14 per cent in commercial and general subjects, 11 per cent in building, 10 per cent in science, 9 per cent in women's subjects and 7 per cent in the area institutes.[18] Engineering was dominant and remained so, accounting for half of the college's work.

A more detailed description of this department was given to a *Newbury Weekly News* reporter in the autumn of 1957. The newly built workshops and laboratories had opened at the beginning of the year and the next phase of building was soon to start.

> Largest in numbers is the Engineering Department. Many of the mechanical engineering students come from the two atomic research establishments at Harwell and Aldermaston. The remainder are sent by Plenty, Vickers Armstrong and other local firms.[19] The five-year apprentice scheme is intended for boys between the ages of 16 and 21, but there is a full-time Pre-Apprentice course for the 15-year-olds ...

> The larger local firms have special apprentice supervisors, who organise schedules of work on which the youngsters may build a sound foundation of experience. The boys, who come for at least one full day each week, study for the City & Guilds examinations or the National Certificate. As an indication of the standard, a General Certificate of Education in mathematics, physics and chemistry gives exemption only from the first year of the course ...

> The 120 electrical engineering students are principally SEB employees. A three-year electrical installations course provides instruction in wiring, and September saw the

---

[18] *NWN* 23 February 1956.

[19] Many of the engineering apprentices at Vickers Armstrong studied at South Berks College until the company left Newbury in 1963.

beginning of a special course for electrical technicians. This gives practical and theoretical teaching in electronics, including the make-up of a television set.

The motor vehicle section, the smallest on the engineering side, is intended primarily for garage hands. It provides valuable experience in welding, turning and the ability to locate faults. 'In all these sections we depend a great deal on the co-operation of local industries' said Mr. Pocock. 'Much of our holiday period is spent going round the different firms, reporting on students' progress and exchanging views with apprentice supervisors. The general standard of work has improved immensely in recent years. At first the boys thought of it as just a day off work, but past examination successes have proved an excellent spur ...'

Equipment is a problem of major importance. Staff members have had to design or select benches, cupboards and machines throughout the workshops and laboratories. Practical work groups are restricted in number to 15, but even this means the provision of seven or eight sets of equipment wherever possible. Sometimes this is neither necessary nor practicable. One machine – for measuring and illustrating metal strains – cost £1,400! Although the College is instructed always to accept the lowest tender, this does not always turn out to be the cheapest ...

The drawing office was described as 'the best in the County for teaching purposes', giving the students an exact foretaste of what they can expect in industry. The main workshop is equipped with miller, grinder and lathes – a complete range of processes. Local industries often assist by providing second-hand machinery and instruments which are adequate for practical and experimental work.[20]

---

[20] *Ibid.*, 24 October 1957.

New students

> In September two full-time courses will be open to boys
> and girls of 15, to study either commercial subjects or a
> Pre-Apprenticeship course of engineering and building.
>
> **NWN 31 May 1951**

The first full-time students gathered at the front of Ormonde
House at the start of the Autumn Term in 1951. This move
into full-time provision was, indirectly at least, to do with the
Education Act of 1944. Of the three different sorts of secondary
schools identified in the Butler Act – grammar, technical and
modern – the second option was not available in Newbury. There
was no secondary technical school (STS) in the area. The college
was to fill this gap and provide technical education for 15- and
16-year-old boys and girls.

There had been some discussion about the lack of technical
education opportunities in the district. One way forward, favoured
by the Newbury Division, was to build an STS to complement the
work of the grammar and modern schools. Another option was
to provide technical courses at Shaw and Park House. In 1949 the
LEA instructed Newbury's Education Officer 'to make enquiries
of heads of local and rural industries to find out what educational
preparation they desired entrants to their employment should
have.' He was also asked to consult secondary heads to find out
what technical courses they could provide. The Newbury Division
wanted schoolchildren to have some contact with the workplace,
and it encouraged 'visits by senior children to all types of industrial
concerns'.[21] The FESC suggested a third option: full-time technical
courses at the Newbury Institute.[22]

Dick Greet was in the middle of these discussions, as chairman
of the governors and member of the Newbury Division and the
FESC. In October 1949, he informed the Division of the Institute's
plans for starting technical courses for school leavers. He suggested
that as there was little likelihood of a technical school in Newbury
in the near future, then four classes, each of 20 students, should

---

[21] Co-ordination Subcommittee 11 February 1949.

[22] FESC 25 March 1949.

be organised at Ormonde House – one for commerce for girls, one for building, and the other two for more practical instruction.

His colleague Oliver Brown had doubts about the proposal. He wondered whether parents were 'prepared to allow their children to stay on an extra year'. The 'trend today', he thought, was for the 'average parent to send his son out to earn money as soon as he left school.' William Mitchell, however, supported the idea; for the 80 young people involved 'it would help them decide on their career'.[23]

The Institute wanted to start the courses in 1950. However, there was some uncertainty as to whether a curriculum for 15-year-olds was the responsibility of secondary or further education. The FESC referred the issue to the Minister of Education, who decided that such courses could be part of further education. As a result the programme was planned to start in September 1951.

By this time, it was looking increasingly unlikely that an STS would be built in the Newbury area. The location for such a school was discussed by the Division, and in the spring of 1951, a 22-acre site in Thatcham was considered. However, the economic climate was not favourable and the government was restricting new building. Moreover, the national priority was the elimination of the remaining all-age schools and the development of the secondary modern school. This held back the building of technical schools thereby restricting 'secondary technical education to limited numbers of children in separate streams in other types of secondary schools'.[24]

Those responsible for schooling in the Newbury district found this procrastination 'disappointing'. However, Dick Greet and Albert Owthwaite went ahead and implemented their proposal. In the first instance, the college would offer two courses. The Pre-Apprenticeship programme was for boys, preparing them, as the name implies, for an indentured apprenticeship:

> The Course, which is of one year's duration, will prepare boys for entry to Mechanical, Electrical or Motor Vehicle Engineering and Building Apprenticeships, and will include in addition to General Subjects, Practical Mathematics;

---

[23] *NWN* 20 October 1949.

[24] Schools Management Subcommittee 13 July 1951.

Technical Science; Practical Geometry and Trade Drawing;
Sketching and Design; Woodwork; Workshop Practice and
Workshop Technology.

The Commercial course was to prepare school leavers for
employment. It led to jobs rather than apprenticeships, to
clerical and administrative office work. The syllabus included,
'in addition to General Subjects, Shorthand, Typewriting,
Commercial Arithmetic, Bookkeeping, Commerce and Handicraft
(Dressmaking or Woodwork).'[25]

Neither course was exclusively vocational. General education
– English, geography and history – was common to both. However
most of the timetable was given over to vocational education and
workplace visits were to be arranged. Each course finished with
external examinations. At the end of the Pre-Apprenticeship,
the boys would choose between building and engineering and
the lecturers would help them find suitable training. Many of
them would then return to Ormonde House on day release. On
completion of the Commercial course, the college would help the
young people find jobs and some would return to night school.
Both courses were free. The LEA's travel passes meant that students
did not have to pay bus or train fares and there were maintenance
grants for those families in particular need.

The courses were advertised, the schools kept up to date at
meetings of the Newbury Division, and the Youth Employment
Service was kept informed so as to be able to advise potential
students and their parents. Those young people who applied were
selected through an entrance test and an interview which took
place in the summer of 1951. A few weeks later 26 boys and girls
reported to Ormonde House.

This was a significant development in the history of FE in
Newbury; but the issue of providing a discrete technical school
did not go away. There were further discussions in 1952,
but a suitable site could not be identified.[26] By the end of the
following year, the Division wanted a meeting with the Director
of Education 'to discuss technical education needs in Newbury'

---

[25] SBCFE Prospectus 1951-52, pp.22, 32.

[26] Newbury Borough Council 30 December 1952.

and to settle 'the question of a site as soon as possible'.[27] Nothing happened, but a few years later, the Division was still talking about possible locations in the Bath Road/Turnpike Road area in Thatcham.

It was not just the education authority in Berkshire which failed to develop the STS; so did most of the LEAs in England and Wales. This meant that the Education Act of 1944 was not universally implemented with a genuine tripartite structure of secondary education. The Act did not require every LEA to provide the three different sorts of schools, but the Ministry's guidelines assumed that the tripartite structure would be followed. It was not, and the STS for those children with a mechanical aptitude was never allowed to develop. Indeed, in the 1950s, fewer than 5 per cent of children went to technical schools and the number of such schools declined.[28] Some commentators have suggested that this held back the development of an effective labour force in Britain and Michael Sanderson has argued that the 'deliberate neglect and demise of the STS was one of the most harmful educational developments of the post-war years'.

There were many reasons for this neglect. Technical education was expensive. For example, in 1953, the LEA allowed South Berks College £2,256 for equipment for science, electrical and motor engineering; in 1954, £683 for chemistry, applied physics, carpentry and joinery and heat treatment; in 1955, £618 for the ONC in Mechanical Engineering.[29] Like FE colleges, technical schools needed workshops and machinery and reinforced structures capable of supporting bulk and weight. Even commercially orientated schools needed rooms large enough for typewriters and business equipment. Such schools were more expensive to maintain than their grammar and modern counterparts. It was cheaper to teach a child an arts or pure science subject than invest in the equipment to train an engineer or technologist. Perhaps it was not surprising that most education authorities and their ratepayers preferred not to have them.

---

[27] *NWN* 19 November 1953.

[28] Michael Sanderson, *Education and Economic Decline in Britain, 1870 to the 1990s*, (Cambridge: Cambridge University Press, 1999), pp.79-80.

[29] BEC 19 June 1953, 17 September 1954, 7 January 1955.

There were also doubts about the validity of selection for such schools. Many psychologists believed that it was not possible to determine at the age of 11 whether a child had technical and mechanical aptitude, although interestingly, those same people thought it was possible to measure general intelligence. Technical schools were seen as 'aptitude' schools which did not sit easily alongside grammar and modern schools, entry to which was determined by 'ability'.

There were also political and social factors at work. Very few MPs had first-hand experience of technical schooling as part of their own education. The Labour leaders of 1945-51 saw the grammar school as the ladder of advancement for the children of their working-class supporters. Conservative local authorities, such as Berkshire, also preferred grammar schools as the pathway to university and the middle-class professions which their supporters desired for their own children. To Conservative supporters, technical education was inferior to the arts and sciences taught at the public and grammar schools attended by their own children. Moreover, amongst Labour supporters, there remained some suspicion that technical education from the age of 11 directed working-class children too early into manual, though skilled, working-class jobs.

There was also some confusion about the purpose of the secondary modern school. As many as 70 per cent of the children of England and Wales went to such schools, but little thought had been given to the curriculum. Accordingly, modern schools tended to justify themselves by moving into craft and technical teaching, such as typing and cookery for girls, woodwork and technical drawing for boys. This suggested that there was no need for a specific stream of technical schooling if the secondary modern could provide technical subjects cheaply. It also served to strengthen the idea that technical subjects were inferior and only appropriate for academic failures.

There were other ways, too, in which the outlines of the tripartite idea were becoming blurred. Commercial and craft subjects were introduced into the grammar school curriculum; and there was an increase in the volume of GCE work in secondary modern schools, with more children staying on up to and beyond the age of sixteen. In Newbury,

GCE O-levels were taught at Park House, but not at Shaw House, by the mid-'50s.

The future of the STS was finally wrecked by two factors. The Conservatives were in power, and in 1955 their policy was not to sanction the development of any more technical schools. The Minister of Education affirmed that a child's technical aptitude was undetectable at the age of 11. In any case, those academically able boys and girls who began to manifest such abilities should develop them in grammar schools in conjunction with scientific studies. Those with less ability could be catered for in modern schools where craft subjects were available. This was the beginning of the end of the tripartite structure and the existing technical schools were allowed to whither on the vine. A few years later, Labour Governments of the 1960s and 1970s completed the destruction and the tripartite framework was swept away by their policy in favour of comprehensive schools for all.[30]

From 1945, then, the technical school sector in England and Wales was at first neglected and then destroyed. No STS was built in the Newbury district. The eleven-plus examination enabled some children to gain entry to the boys' grammar and the girls' high school, but the majority in west Berkshire went to the secondary modern. Most importantly, however, at the age of 15, the teenager with technical or mechanical aptitude could apply for a full-time course at the South Berks College.

A new college

£250,000 To Be Spent on South Berks College

To cater for the growing demand for further education, particularly in view of the local demand for skilled scientific and electrical workers, £80,000 is to be spent in the near future on new buildings at South Berks College of Further Education, Ormonde House, consisting of a laboratory block, in nine sections with an area of 5,850 square feet, and a workshop block of 8,100 square feet.

---

[30] Sanderson, *op.cit.*, pp.79-81.

As soon as these buildings are completed and the necessary equipment installed, the College will be able to accept full-time students for scientific courses. Eventually other new buildings to cost £150,000 will be added for general subjects, embracing cookery, crafts, drawing offices, metal work and a county college. The existing buildings will become administrative offices, and the whole site will cover about 60,000 square feet.

NWN 31 May 1951

The most encouraging development of 1951 was the decision to build a new college. It was to be built in two stages and the work was to start within a year.

The first instalment was to be constructed along the eastern boundary of the site and the houses of the Shaw estate. There was to be a single-storey line of workshops with a two-storey laboratory block at its southern end. The second instalment was to be much bigger, and more costly. Buildings were to be constructed at the back of the house and run adjacent to the southern boundary. At the south-east corner, they would join up with the workshops of the first instalment. The accommodation would provide for a variety of subjects – cookery, crafts, technical drawing and metalwork – and, intriguingly, the provision of a county college. Communal facilities would include a refectory, hall and library. The rooms in Ormonde House would no longer be needed for teaching and would be used exclusively as offices.

With 60,000 square feet of floor space at a cost of £250,000, further education in Newbury had come a long way since 1948. It was anticipated that over half of the cost (60 per cent) would come from the government, with the LEA responsible for the remainder. As it turned out, the excitement was put on hold when building did not start in 1952. Repeated delays followed and the work did not begin until 1955. By this time, two prefabricated workshops had been erected. The horsa huts had arrived.

Horsa huts

The decision to put prefabricated huts in the grounds of Ormonde House was made before the announcement of the building of a new college. It was decided early in 1949 to erect three huts to be used as workshops. That summer Albert Owthwaite expected their construction during the next twelve months. Nothing was done and it was not until 1953 that the huts were erected. They became known as the horsa huts.

HORSA is an acronym for 'Hutting Operation for the Raising of the School-leaving Age'. Ellen Wilkinson was Labour's Minister of Education overseeing the raising of the school-leaving age, a reorganisation which required thousands of extra classrooms. The solution was the mass production of standard concrete huts, often referred to as 'horsa huts'. This became Ellen Wilkinson's legacy, an enterprise which had as great an impact on the landscape as the pillbox had earlier in the decade.[31] The name 'horsa', somewhat inaccurately, was attached to the new prefabs at Ormonde House, and it stuck.

There were to be three huts: two laboratories – one each for science and electrical engineering – and a mechanics workshop. Tenders were invited and in the summer of 1950 the work was given to H F Green of Thatcham. The cost was over £7,000.[32]

Before the work started, however, came the announcement about the new college and the plans were changed. Only two huts were to be erected but H F Green was still keen to do the work. Plans for the new buildings also meant that the prefabs had to be re-sited. There was some delay, however, before the work could start. In 1952 the Ministry instructed the LEA to revise its building programme. There was a need for 'financial economy' because of the shortage of steel and the 'temporary overloading' of the building industry.[33]

---

[31] Peter Hennessy, *Never Again, Britain 1945-1951*, (London: Vintage, 1993), p.160.

[32] The cost of the hut components was £850, and their erection cost £6,333. See *NWN* 9 March 1950; BEC 5 May 1950, 4 May 1951. The final cost of the two huts was over £9,000. Education Finance Subcommittee 27 August 1954.

[33] Co-ordination Subcommittee 21 March 1952.

The college's need for laboratories was urgent. The first apprentices from Aldermaston and Harwell arrived in the autumn of 1952, most of them to study science and electrical engineering. It was with some relief, then, that the horsa huts were finally completed in the spring of 1953.

£12,500 laboratories opened at South Berks College AERE apprentices study there

Open Day at the South Berks College of Further Education Oxford-road, Newbury, included the official opening by Mr W F Herbert, Berks Director of Education, of the new science and electrical engineering laboratories, built and equipped recently at a cost of £12,500. With 300 students attending day-release, full time and apprenticeship courses in science, electrical and mechanical engineering and allied subjects, these two new laboratories were needed to provide facilities for students taking Inter BSc and National Certificate courses in scientific subjects.

Among those who attended the official opening ceremony were several Ministry of Supply officials and apprentice training officers from Harwell and Aldermaston; apprentices from these two establishments are among the students already taking examination courses at the College.

Following the opening ceremony, there was an exhibition of students' work, and visitors were invited to make a tour of classrooms and workshops. A presentation of a turned bowl, and a water colour, two examples of students' work, was made to Mr W F Herbert by Mr R V C Wing, a student at evening classes since 1948. At that time there were 150 students. During the current session there are 50 full-time students, 495 part-time, and 1,700 evening students, some of whom travel to Newbury from distances up to 20 miles to take advantage of the College's up to date facilities.

From Accountancy to Plumbing

Classes open for inspection in the main building included women's woodwork and dressmaking, and general classes for physics, engineering, garage and workshop practice. Outside, in workshops and outbuildings in the grounds, subjects as varied as plumbing, accountancy, carpentry and science were being taught. Comprehensive as they appeared to be, these classes gave visitors only a brief indication of the full range of activities available to students, for in other parts of Newbury, members of the staff instruct classes in building, domestic science and commercial subjects.

An exhibition of students' work, including an excellent display of tailoring, dressmaking and needlework, crafts, cookery and art, as well as handicraft, woodwork, building, drawing and engineering was on view during the afternoon, and in the evening parents and friends of students were invited to see classes in progress.

NWN 7 May 1953

The huts were erected one behind the other in the north-east corner of the site. They were heated by gas until 1956, when, for £1,200, a boiler house was built between them – the students used this as a cloakroom – and a hot water system installed.[34] Both laboratories were used extensively until the new buildings were finished. In the early '60s one of the huts was demolished, but the other was used until 2002, the oldest building on the site after Ormonde House.

'The most important thing was getting the flame correct for the right weld'

Bill Yates (b.1926) arrived in Newbury during the war as a young soldier. Once his training as a vehicle mechanic was completed, he was transferred from the Royal Engineers to Signals and was sent out to Burma in the Far East. Once the war was over and he was

---

[34] BEC 4 January 1957.

finally demobbed, Bill went back to his home town in Lancashire, but not for long. He came back to Newbury in 1948, got a job at Marchant's Garages and married the local girl whom he had met in his lodgings a few years before. Five years later he went to work for Reliance Coaches and signed on at night school to learn how to weld.

> I left school in Warrington in 1941 and I did three-and-a-half years apprenticeship as an agricultural engineer. I went to evening classes at college. In the first year I did a commercial course – geography, maths and English – but after that I did two years engineering. I tried to go in the navy at 17 but I couldn't because I was apprenticed. So I thought, this is no good, have a go for the army. I said I was a shop assistant and I got in the next week. They sent me down to Newbury, to Wheeler's Garage in the Broadway. On both sides of the Broadway was an army school – 32 technical training group, War Office.[35] We were all billeted with civilians and I was billeted with my future wife's parents. It was a 14-week course, army mechanics. I went from there to Paddington Tech in London for a workshop fitting course and from there to Allard cars – at that time they were overhauling Canadian Ford army trucks. From there out to Burma. I started with REME and then when I finished training I was transferred to Signals. There were a lot of mechanics in Signals but not a lot of vehicle mechanics.

> I came back to Warrington in early 1948 and went back to the same firm I had worked for. I was only there a week as I got another job with a haulage contractor who had a garage business as well. I stayed there for six months then came down to Newbury. I came back to my future wife's parents and got married.

> I worked for Marchant's Garages as a commercial fitter. There was a body shop and welding separate. There were

---

[35] From 1940 to 1950, Wheeler's Garage was designated by the War Office as a training school for army mechanics, during which time some 20,000 military personnel were trained.

about five or six mechanics. We were Vauxhall agents. From the beginning the college did a mechanics' course and our apprentices went there on day release. I was selected for the Institute of Road Transport Engineers in 1950. I was sponsored by Road Transport Services in Thatcham – in the early '50s they were BRS.[36] All their heavy breakdown was usually passed on to me at Marchant's. I was well in with their engineer. He got me into the IRT originally and I eventually got up to full member.

I was working for Marchant's until 1953 and then I went to Reliance Motor Services. We were at Brightwalton and Newbury and when I started we had 14 buses and coaches. There were only two of us. I worked in the garage all day. It was a 12-hour day, 6.15 to 6.15, and then coaching at weekends. It was a similar sort of job to Marchant's. But before I went to Reliance we always had separate welders – welding didn't come into my job at all. But at Reliance we did everything. We had both gas and electric welding so I thought I would do a course to learn the right way to do it.

I saw this welding course advertised, one evening a week, and thought, we'll have a go. It was the first welding course at the college, one term, 6.30 to 9.00. I paid for it – it wasn't much in those days. It was oxyacetylene welding. We only had gas. The power supply was insufficient for arc welding.

The instructor was Bert Hill. He showed us his certificates. He had a book full of different ones for welding. He was a clever old boy. He used to tell us all his experiences with the welding. He was a well known character. He kept the gas works going during the war years – the big tower in King's Road. It's an industrial estate now. He was manager of Marsh Engineering in King's Road. He used to tell us

---

[36] Thatcham Road Transport Services was set up in 1921. In 1924 it moved to a depot at Colthrop and built up a fleet of 100 lorries. Taken over by the government in 1942, TRS was nationalised in 1949, denationalised in 1954, and later sold to Colthrop Board Mills.

about what he did during the war to keep things going 'cos that was the town's only gas supply. In 1953 he was the maintenance engineer with Elliott's. He did all the brackets and bits and pieces for the gliders as well as maintaining the factory machinery. Sadly he lost his sight in later years. It must have been due to the welding.

The clothes we wore were nothing special, no leather aprons or anything like that. We took our own boiler suits. In those days mechanics washed their own or took them to the laundry. Now everything is supplied. The college provided goggles and the materials. Bert brought all the bits and pieces, bits of metal and all sorts. All the equipment was new. It was good – six plants, two to a plant. There were two bottles on a trolley. And the proper lighter, a little flame on the side of the trunk, just a bypass from the main supply. You could put the torch on a hook and it cut the flame down to just a little one. The most important thing was getting the flame correct for the right weld.

There was no homework. We had this practical test at the end, a tube welded to a plate in aluminium which was pressed in a vice to test penetration. I came top, 95 out of 100. I got it a bit too hot; otherwise it would have been 100. There was no certificate. I was awarded a BOC welding manual. I was given this prize in the classroom at the last lecture. I had it for years. It was quite a thing.

'You can imagine what five to seven was like. Horrendous!

It was one Friday morning in September 1951 that **Robin Morris** made his way along the Oxford Road. He had recently started as an apprentice at the Colthrop Board Mills.

There had been a mill on the marshland by the River Kennet at Colthrop since medieval times. First it was used for grinding corn, and then making cloth, but by the 18th century, it was a paper mill. By the time of the First World War, Colthrop Mills were producing brown paper, paper bags and sugar bags. After the war, Cropper of London bought the business, produced folding cardboard cases and built the South Board Mill. Significant development occurred and a growing number of Thatcham folk were employed. The Board Mills sent a steady stream of apprentices to Ormonde House once it opened; and the first course to be taught in the workplace rather than the college, a City & Guilds in Paper Manufacture, was started at Colthrop in 1950.

Robin was born a few years before the Second World War. He grew up in Thatcham, going to school in the village, joining the cub scouts and singing in the church choir. As a teenager, he used to walk home from Newbury after a night out – 'it never caused any problem' – and sometimes on a Saturday he found himself walking back from Reading. 'You may have got picked up by a police car coming along – "Get in the back you old boys, we'll take you home" – just to make sure you didn't get up to mischief.'

In 1938, a tobacco store was built in the village for W D & H O Wills. War broke out, the warehouse was requisitioned and became an ordnance depot. Then the Americans arrived, the depot was taken over and General Depot 45 became one of the largest in the country. Supplies for the army and the air force, including transport vehicles, were housed in a multitude of sheds. Thirty-five miles of railway track were laid down, extending across the moors as far as Newbury Racecourse. There were around 7,000 people working in the depot around the time of the Allied D-Day landings and the invasion of Europe in 1944. Once the war was over, the property was handed back to the British army and it remained an ordnance depot until its closure some years ago.

> People can't understand when I say you walked through Thatcham as a child, when there was a war on, pitch dark, and you never had a problem with anybody. All the girls would walk home from brownies, eight o'clock at night, pitch black, no street lights, nothing. The place was full of American troops. You never had any problems.

> Jobs were no problem at all when I was coming out of school: Plenty, Opperman, Colthrop, and one that's not there now, Newbury Diesel. Coming on a bit behind, Mastergear. There was plenty of work on. There was a tendency at that time, your dad worked at Plenty, you

went to Plenty; your dad was at Opperman, you went to Opperman. It was like that. My dad worked at Colthrop Board Mills. Colthrop took apprentices every year. We did everything – pipe, steam pipe, machines, welding. In my first year I got paid 32 bob (£1.50) a week. A little bit of that was what we call tonnage. When they reached a certain production figure on the board machines, anything above that you were paid a bonus. But the sting in the tail was that the apprentices got half. So if the tonnage was 10 bob (50 pence), you got five bob (25 pence).

On his first day at South Berks, Robin was given his timetable. Mathematics took up the whole of the morning.

9.00 to 12.15 Mr Taylor	Practical Mathematics Room G3, ground floor of Ormonde House
1.30 to 2.30 Mr Garlick	English Room G4, ground floor of Ormonde House
2.30 to 4.30 Mr Trodden	Engineering Science Room 3, former Technical Institute in Albert Road
5.00 to 7.00 Mr Sully	Engineering Drawing Room A5, outbuilding

Charles Sully had now been at the college for nearly three years. Trodden and Garlick had recently arrived as full-time lecturers. John Trodden was there for three years, but P C Garlick only stayed for one. Mr Taylor was part time. In Robin's classes there were '15, possibly more'. They were all boys. 'There were no girls, good heavens, no! They were doing dressmaking.'

> The college was very much smaller to what it is today and everybody knew more or less everybody. I was day release – that was one day a week, nine till seven. Bearing in mind you usually started work at 7.30, you had the benefit of an hour and a half in the mornings. But you can imagine what five to seven was like. Horrendous! God forbid! It was like nothing on earth to do that last period! It was either engineering or maths. You imagine doing maths. That was inhuman!

The class was PS1, a preliminary course in engineering. It was general. You had a mixture in there: draughtsmen, basic engineers, boys of other trades. When you finished that year you went on to the S1 through to whenever you finished your apprenticeship or whatever exams you took. The main subscribers to the classes were certainly the Board Mills, but the students weren't all from Colthrop. Plenty was most supportive, and Opperman Gears, and we had them coming in from Lambourn, Hungerford, the Wallingford area and from a company in Compton which has now gone. There were very, very few from the grammar schools. One of the things you very rarely got in the college were grammar school boys. They had done the eleven-plus and passed, and even if they were technically failures and left school at 15, they were directed to offices as wages clerks, while us yobbos from the other schools, we went to college, a 'bit-of-dirt-under-the-fingernail' brigade.

The apprentices from Harwell and Aldermaston were certainly the top blokes, but I wouldn't say they were better than us. They were the top of the tree, the privileged, because they had all their books found for them, piles of books, text books, engineering theory, and all their instruments, everything provided. It was always a source of envy. You would sit in engineering drawing. You had two instruments, a compass and a square, and they had the full stuff which was supplied to them by the Ministry. We had to buy our own. We used to get salesmen come round to the works to sell books; that's where I bought some of the engineering books. I've still got them. They are pre-war, but everything's the same, isn't it – the threads, spars, stresses and strains, RSJ's, pipes and flanges. Everything's the same except for these bloody foreign measurements that have crept in. We paid for our own exams. The only time the company would pay was if you passed, so I'm not sure how often I got paid. You paid for your travelling expenses. If you came in on the bus, you had to pay.

The maths teacher wasn't much more than early 20s, ex-services. We were all sat in his classroom one day, and there was the girls dressmaking. The dressmaking class was right by the side of Ormonde House. They used to have these wooden partitions on the windows, and we'd open them up a little bit. All the wags used to sit in this area so they could keep peeping through. Those who were devoted to study and education tended not to look. The old boys were looking through there, and the teacher patted me on the shoulder and said, 'Which one are you looking at?'
I said, 'She's alright!'
And he said, 'She is nice, isn't she? I think you had better go and join them.' So I was unceremoniously dumped out. I presented myself to the lady teacher, a woman called Miss Searle. She was a cub mistress at Thatcham, so I knew her when I was a seven-year-old in the cubs. I had to sit with all these 16-, 17- year-old girls while they were dressmaking. We came out for the morning break, and I went back into maths. 'Oh no,' he said, 'that's your class in there.' And I was kicked back in there again.

The morning break was a cup of tea and a biscuit from the kitchen. At 12.15 it was time for lunch, after which it was back to the house for an hour of English and then down to Albert Road for engineering science.

For dinner you used to wander down the town. There was nothing else. There weren't any canteen facilities. You used to go to a café up Northbrook Street, or to the Silver Lantern or, of all places, the Empire Café, which was right at the far end of the town. A lot of us used to get up there. The staple diet was cottage pie and chips.

We made our own way to the classrooms in Albert Road. You would go off down and get a cup of coffee and a bread roll. You can imagine the old boys drifting in at all times. One classroom was a machine shop. There was lathes and all the gubbinses that go with it, and on the side was a classroom where you did engineering science. We all went into the classroom down there. We all sat down and in walked this new teacher and said, 'Good afternoon. My name is John Trodden. I shall get to know you.'

And some idiot called Morris sat at the back said, 'And who trod on you then?'

He looked and he said, 'I get that wherever I go. I'm glad that's out of the way. I shall remember you.'

He had a sense of humour, but he was good. I had one or two lectures from him because he felt I was wasting my abilities. He felt I should be trying to go on to better things, but what can you tell an eighteen-year-old?

'All we wanted was an argument with him, but he would discuss politics'

The last class of the day, in the first year at least, was back up the Oxford Road and into one of the outbuildings with Charles Sully. Robin was at the college for four years, and Charles Sully taught him a lot, mainly engineering drawing but also engineering science and, occasionally, mathematics.

The top of the list of people who taught me has got to be Charlie, or Spike to his friends. We called him Spike. He was absolutely brilliant. You could not fool Charlie. You would sit there from five to seven doing engineering drawing. You had your drawing boards, not like the big fancy ones they got now, but portable ones. You would set your drawing out. You had to put a line all the way round for it to be a square. You didn't have pins, you had to have clips. It was five minutes to seven. We old boys started to remove everything, and the crafty old so-and-so would get you to put everything back on and square it all up before he'd release you. He knew what you were up to, and he would say, 'Now you can put everything back as it should be.' It was only later that you realised he was a good teacher. At the time he was just an awkward old so-and-so. You'd look down, we've got Sully, oh God! But, you know, with the fullness of time ...

He took his time with you, and we had all abilities. I couldn't do maths. I couldn't add up to save my life. I still can't work a calculator. He always took time and he would spend time with everybody. Just because some were brighter than others, he didn't push the others to one side. He accepted that they probably had some other abilities which they didn't know about.

The only way you could ever draw Charlie away from tutoring was politics. Argue the political case with him, argue conservatism, and he was away. You could get him off on whatever subject. He would really go to town; he would really get involved. He was absolutely dedicated. Whether you call him labour or socialist, he was a man of high principles in this respect. All we wanted was an argument with him, but he would discuss politics. I disagreed with Charlie because it was an argument, but if we'd sat round the table to chat, just him and me, we'd have hit it off. But that was just me being bloody awkward. Charlie had two daughters a few years older than us boys. They were rather dishy. We used to sit in the class and look out. They used to walk by. We were looking out the window. You can imagine the comment that was going on, but they wouldn't look at us of course.

We had a chap, I'm sure he'd been a fighter pilot during the war. He had a moustache, which is what you'd expect. He took us down the chicken hut, and we could divert him. Somebody would say to him about the relative merits of the Spitfire and the ME019, and that was it, he was off. He had a dogfight on the blackboard. A quarter of an hour later, he would stop and say, 'You lot have done it again!'

J S Theodorson came to the college in the summer of 1953, and worked there for two years.

He was tall, bad on his feet for some reason. Today you would probably think he was an old farm boy. He did eject me from the classroom once for falling asleep –

that was in the chicken house. I'd been cycling on the Sunday, done about 140 miles. The sun was coming through the windows, and I sat there. All of a sudden he said, 'I think you had better go out.' And I can remember where I went. I walked up the road to the stream at Donnington and sat on the bridge. But at least they didn't report me to the firm.

I liked him because he didn't mind a bit of fun. We was sat in there one day. You had a copper wire going round all these wheels and various things, looking to see the stretch and this type of thing. We used to work it out in theory and practice. He'd turn his back. Some idiot put a bloody great weight on. Of course everything went bang! You can imagine it, 16-, 17-, 18-year-olds, and it all went bang! But he took it in good heart. I can remember sitting right at the back, and he was on the blackboard. It was all wooden floors. And again it was one of those big round weights. And I can remember leaning across, rolling it along the floor, and it rumbled all the way up, and we all sat and watched, and it hit his desk with an almighty thump – and he just looked and shook his head.

Robin took the City & Guilds examinations, the intermediate and the final. 'You presented yourself in the classroom and you just sat there and done it, to the best of your ability.' The 'real smarty boys' went on to the National Certificate, but Robin did not. He left South Berks College in the summer of 1955.

8

A TWILIGHT WORLD

> Dealing with the less spectacular part of the College work,
> Mr Owthwaite said classes were provided over a wide area
> roughly encircled by Hungerford, Lambourn, Compton,
> Bucklebury, Woolhampton and Aldermaston. Within this
> area classes were held in 30 villages and attended by 500
> students. Subjects ranged from shorthand and typewriting
> to women's handicrafts, music and drama.
>
> **NWN 5 May 1955**

N ight-school students were the heirs to a rich tradition of adult education going back to the 19th century. Once Ormonde House had opened there were more classes and more students. Around 200 people had enrolled in the final year of the Technical Institute in 1947/48. The following year, there were 970 students in 63 evening classes. In 1949/50, there were around 1,250 men and women in 90 classes; and in 1950/51, 1,350 students and 120 classes.[1] With the area organisation and affiliated institutes from 1951, evening classes became more numerous.

The idea of an evening class conjures up for many people a twilight world somewhere between learning and pleasure. It will be improving but not unduly taxing, and its participants may not need to concern themselves with marks, tests and essays. The students attend enthusiastically and often make many friends in

---

[1] SBCFE Prospectus 1951-52, p.7.

the process. Throughout the 1950s, the majority of the students at South Berks College went to night school, and a lot of them studied recreational courses.

The pattern of the evening scene was a mosaic, with its overlapping and interlocking parts impossible to reduce to order and neatness. 'For the outsider entering it for the first time it is in fact not so much a field as a jungle.'[2] J F C Harrison, historian of adult education, wrote these words 50 years ago and they remain true today. The undergrowth in south and west Berkshire was 'lush and tangled' with plenty of non-vocational subjects providing fun and colour for the participants. The courses were organised in a democratic spirit, with the college eager to listen to the voice of the people.

Evening classes were open to anybody over 15, although boys or girls in their final year of compulsory schooling could join with the permission of the school and their parents. The classes were free to three groups of people: those under 19 at the start of the academic year (1 September); those apprentices under 21 who went to classes related to their apprenticeship; and those who were serving in the army, navy or air force. Everybody else had to pay a tuition fee, which varied according to the type of class. Classes were graded, I, II and III. In 1951 the fees were ten shillings (50 pence) a session for any number of grade I classes, and £1 for one or more grade II or III classes. This fee structure was generous, encouraging people to take more than one class if they had the time. If a student chose to attend classes of different grades, enrolling in both grade I and II classes, the fee was that of the highest grade. Those evening courses which only lasted a term had reduced fees: a grade I short course, 6/- (30 pence), grades II and III, 12/- (60 pence).

A few years later the fees were increased. In 1956, a grade III class cost £1/10/- (£1.50), and by this time there were grade IV classes for £2.00. From 1958 fees were no longer based on the grade of the course. Instead, those students under 21 paid 10/- (50 pence) for one or more courses and those over 21 were charged according to the number of courses and their duration.

---

[2] Harrison, *op.cit.*, p.313.

Number of Subjects	Two Terms	Three Terms
1	20/- (£1.00)	30/- (£1.50)
2	30/- (£1.50)	40/- (£2.00)
3 or 4	40/- (£2.00)	60/- (£3.00)
5 or 6	60/- (£3.00)	80/- (£4.00)

SBCFE Prospectus 1958-59

'This course is becoming popular among women'

In 1951, the rooms of Ormonde House bustled with activity until late in the evening. In dressmaking and needlework, if there were more than 16 students in a class, an assistant was taken on 'at two thirds the normal fee' to help the instructor.[3] Jessie Searle and Kay Turnbull were in the conservatory four evenings each week – and another eight classes were held in the daytime. In the outbuildings there were nine more classes, in dressmaking, hand embroidery, handloom weaving, needlework, tailoring and women's handicrafts. The demand for some craft subjects was so great that they were organised as 'graded and progressive courses necessitating certain conditions of entry'. When cookery started in 1951, the first level was for people 'with little or no previous knowledge'.

Woodwork vied with dressmaking in popularity. There were five classes in 1951, three for men and two for women.

WOODWORK AND CABINET MAKING

For Women
This course is becoming popular among women. The use of tools – saws, planes, chisels – and woodwork processes are taught, so that within a few weeks useful pieces of furniture can be made. The student decides what she will make.

---

[3] FESC 20 July 1951.

For Men
A course for the handyman who wishes to make more
ambitious pieces of furniture, and also for the novice
who will be taught all the woodworking processes,
and who, from small pieces, will eventually be able
to make larger pieces of furniture.

Such craft courses were at the heart of the non-vocational curriculum,
with over 40 on offer in Newbury in 1951. They included art,
'drawing and painting in water colours and oils'; household repairs
and maintenance, 'of immense value to householders who need tips
and advice'; millinery, 'a new course which has been very successful
at other centres'; and metalwork and model engineering, 'for the
adult engineer who wishes to supplement his knowledge of workshop
practice and for the model engineer desirous of full workshop
equipment'. There were also classes in basketwork, leatherwork
and textile renovations and alterations.

A list of the 'Miscellaneous Classes' in the college prospectus
for 1951-52 provides us with a series of snapshots of this twilight
world. There was elocution – 'voice production, prose and poetry-
reading' – English for foreigners and the history of architecture
with 'illustrated lectures'. Charles Sully – who else? – taught motor
vehicle maintenance. 'A well equipped motor engineering shop is
now available and the owner driver will find this course extremely
useful.' Public speaking was 'for those aspiring for public office',
and those who are 'diffident about voicing their opinion in open
debate'. At the County Girls' School, there was 'keep fit and
dancing for women', agriculture, and horticulture for the 'serious
student of gardening subjects and for the professional gardener'.
There were 11 people in horticulture, not many, but their 'keen
interest' warranted 'continuance of the classes'. Many wanted
to take Royal Horticultural Society (RHS) examinations.[4] For
the enthusiastic amateur there was the less demanding 'starting
your garden' at the Community Centre, where an average of nine
people met every fortnight during the spring and summer months
of 1952, with occasional visits to local gardens of interest.[5] This

---

[4] Agricultural Education Subcommittee 30 May 1952.

[5] *Ibid.*, 17 October 1952.

course targeted the residents of the Shaw estate, 'occupants of new houses who are faced with the problem of creating a garden from barren ground'; but it was also for those with older 'cultivated gardens'. The practical work was on the neighbouring allotments and Mr Spackman was the instructor.

The college organised the work at the Community Centre. Eight courses, including the Friday evening gardeners' class, were available in 1951. The week began with drama, 'the presentation of a good drama or comedy'. Mary Wingfield taught the same course in Boxford village hall. Tuesday night was music night. 'The pleasure to be obtained from singing together is one of those things to be experienced before really appreciating its full significance.' Arthur Stubbington was the teacher. At six o'clock he began his class at Hungerford; by eight o'clock he had to be ready to start in Newbury. On Wednesdays the Centre was given over to ballroom dancing. 'There are two ways to dance; one is the right way and the other the wrong way. How much greater is the enjoyment when you learn to dance the right way.'

Mary Harte remembers earlier dancing classes in 'what was the Social Club over Marks & Spencer – initially intended for war workers' recreation.' The classes continued after the war 'in the Community Centre on the Blackboys Bridge under Iris Brooks, Fellow of the Imperial Society of Teachers of Dancing. From the outset this activity was financed by the Berkshire County Council, latterly under the umbrella of Ormonde House.' While the dancers were practising their steps downstairs, Mary was learning to type in one of the rooms above.

> Miss Brooks was downstairs in the big room. She was there for a long time and we did a lot of her secretarial work. She would say, 'Can you come and help me? I've got all these figurations and I don't know what to do with them.' We used to mark the registers. We shouldn't have done it because of the college, but she couldn't get on with all this. She liked to do her own thing.

Miss Barnes taught women's handicrafts at the Centre on Thursdays, 'for the lady who wishes to learn the art of making things'. There was also lip-reading, useful for people working with the [deaf] children at Donnington Lodge and Mary Hare. The afternoon class was for 'residents in country districts', as those women relying on the train or the bus might not be able to get back home in the evenings.

Around 60 courses were held at the affiliated institutes in 1951/52. Hungerford was the biggest centre, where Roy Pocock organised 19 courses. There were eight classes in the school and others in the village halls at Hamstead Marshall and Kintbury. Twice a week, a brass band practised in the Wesleyan Sunday School at Inkpen. New centres opened in the village halls at Boxford, Stockcross and Wickham. There were five classes in women's handicrafts and four in dressmaking, some of them in the afternoons. We have seen that this expansion of opportunities for women was a characteristic of adult education in the post-war years, with crafts such as basketwork, glove-making, leatherwork, rug-making and making lampshades. The following year, cookery was taught in the Hungerford Handicraft Centre and there were new classes in English, soil fertility and animal husbandry. Dressmaking was held in the Parish Room at Kintbury and at Great Shefford School.

The Thatcham Institute organised work in Thatcham, Bucklebury and Aldermaston, all villages where there were classes before 1951. Of the six classes at Thatcham's St Mary's School, four were in dressmaking and there was one in women's crafts. A brass band used the Iron Room in Green Lane in the village. This tin hut had been erected years before as a place of worship for the Plymouth Brethren, but they had long gone.[6] In the hall at Bucklebury, dressmaking and women's crafts were taught in the afternoon, dancing and choral music in the evening. The courses at Aldermaston Court – French (Scientific), German, shorthand, typewriting, woodwork – were for the employees of Associated Electrical Industries in the village. In 1952 there was a new class in woodwork at Thatcham and one in soft furnishings – cushions, covers, curtains and eiderdowns – at Bucklebury.

---

[6] The Plymouth Brethren had a new church built in the 1930s at the top of Green Lane. The tin hut was demolished in 1986 and a house built on the site. Peter Allen, *A Popular History of Thatcham*, (Oxford: Foxhole Publishing, 1999), p.70.

R G Carter was Superintendent at Lambourn, the village tucked away in the downs where the 'time of classes may be changed as necessary to meet bus times'. All 16 classes in 1951 were in the school. Four of them – English, mathematics, technical drawing, woodwork – made up what was called a 'Preliminary Technical Course' for apprentices who lived locally. The other classes were all recreational.[7] Cookery was held on an afternoon when the domestic science facilities were not being used by the schoolchildren, but all the others were held in the evening. Philip Levi took choral music, as he did at Bucklebury, while the vicar of Lambourn and college governor, the Revd Rumens, took another music class. The energetic Miss Barnes taught women's handicrafts, as she did at Boxford, Bucklebury, Hungerford, Kintbury, Stockcross, Thatcham and Wickham. In 1952 there were classes in typewriting, animal husbandry and soil fertility.

Compton was a new FE centre, the smallest of the institutes with eight courses held in the school in 1951. As at Lambourn, four of these – building construction, English, mathematics, technical drawing – made up a preliminary course for apprentices. Of the others, shorthand was vocational but the rest were recreational: choral music, drama, needlework and dressmaking. Bobby Hards taught dressmaking, as she did at Boxford. In 1952 woodwork was organised at the school in Hermitage.

'Many were surprised to see how many classes are now in being'

Visitors to the Community Centre for an open day in the spring of 1952 were impressed by the variety of work on display. 'In addition to the dressmaking and tailoring classes which have always been so popular, women students are now learning pottery, weaving, needlework and embroidery, cookery, basketwork, leather craft and woodwork.' There were also classes for hobbies 'such as physical culture, art subjects and music'.

---

[7] The courses were appreciation of music, art, athletics training, cabinetmaking, cookery, choral music (theory), choral music (practice), dressmaking, French, keep fit and dancing (women), renovations and alterations, and women's handicrafts (embroidery).

During the past year, centres have been opened in several villages outside Newbury, and it is now possible for classes to be arranged through Women's Institutes and other rural organisations, in any subject for which there is a regular demand by eight or more students. Cold Ash, where basketwork has been taught by a highly trained teacher, sent a display to the exhibition which aroused a lot of interest ... Instruction in most subjects continues right through the summer, and already plans are being made to include extra subjects and more village centres in the autumn where there is a demand.[8]

By 1956 there had been some administrative reorganisation. Lambourn was merged with the Hungerford Institute, its centre was Boxford School and the Superintendent was Gwyn Alderman, who had worked as a college instructor for some years. Similarly Compton was joined with the Thatcham Institute under one superintendent. Women's Institutes and Townswomen's Guilds continued to bring together groups of enthusiasts in the outlying villages.

'People taking advantage of the scheme are from all walks of life and of all ages, from the university graduate to the errand boy, from the lad just leaving school to the old-age pensioner.' Some of the students at Hungerford came from Wiltshire. In 1956 there were classes in dressmaking (6), drama (4), crafts (3), brass band (2), woodwork (2), ballroom dancing (1), choral music (1), cookery (1), country dancing (1), German (1) and shorthand (1). The venues were schools, at Great Shefford, Hungerford, and Kintbury; village halls, at Boxford, Inkpen, Kintbury, Stockcross and Wickham; the Handicraft Centre and Church House at Hungerford; and the White House at Chaddleworth. The following year, classes were also organised in Lambourn (cookery, woodwork), East Garston (drama), Chieveley and Shefford Woodlands (old time dancing) and Speen (drama, dressmaking).

In 1948 Berkshire LEA had appointed its first county drama organiser. Although the work was mainly with the schools, eight years on, there had been some impact on further education and drama was taught at Boxford, Great Shefford and Kintbury.

---

[8] *NWN* 15 May 1952.

Amongst adults an attempt is made to meet the needs of the amateur actor by holding drama classes in Evening Institutes and Colleges of Further Education. The object of such classes is to provide basic training in acting with the emphasis on public performance, and incidentally to encourage and develop an interest in dramatic literature. Tutors who are sufficiently well qualified in all departments of dramatic art are not easily available in all parts of the County but in the larger further education centres it has been possible to establish regular classes ...

Unlike in other counties, the drama organiser in Berkshire works mainly with the schools. There is, however, a valuable link between school work and dramatic work amongst adults in that a large number of teachers are keen to take part in amateur acting. One particular movement which has developed in recent years is the annual open air production of a Shakespeare play by a group of amateurs. This has attracted many teachers and the production is visited by many school parties.[9]

The Thatcham Institute grew faster than the one at Hungerford. In 1956, all its advertised classes, with the exception of shorthand and typewriting, were non-vocational. They included dressmaking (8), woodwork (4), cookery (3), brass band (2), millinery (2), soft furnishing (2), choral music (1), embroidery (1), fabric printing (1), glove-making (1), lampshades (1) and soft toys (1). There were more than 30 classes across ten villages held in a variety of premises: Aldermaston (Aldermaston Court), Burnham Copse (Chiver's Coffee Lounge), Bucklebury (Memorial Hall), Cold Ash (Acland Hall), Compton (school), Curridge (Women's Institute Hall), East Ilsley (village hall), Hermitage (school), Thatcham (Band Room, parish hall, schools) and Woolhampton (King George Hall, Gill Campbell Hall). In 1957 the newly built secondary modern school opened in Thatcham. This was the Kennet School and its first headmaster, T G B Howe, became the Institute's Superintendent.

---

[9] Since 1945, *op.cit.*, pp.56-58.

Some issues

At the monthly FESC meetings in Reading, matters arose which were of particular concern to non-vocational tutors. One such concern in the early 1950s was the tuition fee for physical education and dancing classes; and discussions over this could lead into the larger question about the extent to which public money should be used to support adult/community education.

Before the end of the 1950-51 financial year, Berkshire's LEA was worried about an overspending on teachers' salaries of £3,000. Economy became the watchword and the FESC discussed ways of saving money. One option was to close all evening classes for a week, 'except those taken by full-time staff as part of their normal working week', possibly to coincide with the schools' half-term in February. Other suggestions included combining classes, reducing their duration, closing classes immediately the attendance fell below the minimum requirements, and not starting any new classes in the Spring Term.[10]

The crisis passed without any emergency action being taken, but the steady increase in both day and evening work across the county had obvious financial implications. In any economy drive, non-vocational classes were vulnerable, and physical education and dancing were the most vulnerable of all. In 1951/52, over 1,000 students were enrolled in such classes, more than half of them in physical education. The cost to the LEA was £1,128.[11] To save money, the Education Committee took a radical step: there were to be no classes in either of the subjects in the coming year.

This decision was criticised by instructors and students alike. It also led to intervention by the Ministry of Education who wanted to keep the classes going, convinced that such activities helped to strengthen the social life of FE centres. Such classes were to continue, declared the Ministry, but they were to be 'self-supporting' with the charging of 'adequate fees' and the strict monitoring of student attendance. Under this pressure from London, the Education Committee relented and agreed to run the

---

[10] FESC 18 January 1952.

[11] *Ibid.*, 21 November 1952.

classes in 1952/53 as long as they were self-supporting. This meant that the fees paid by the students had to cover all the costs of a class, and every student, irrespective of age, had to pay.[12]

This change in policy put folk dancing at Hamstead Marshall, which had been held 'for some years past', at risk. The fees covered the costs of the instructor and the pianist, but the LEA still had to pay for the hire of the hall. This it now refused to do. Country dancing at the Coronation Hall in neighbouring Kintbury was also under threat. The villagers were unhappy and letters of protest were fired off to the County Council. The advisory committees at Hungerford and Lambourn put forward alternatives, lobbied the college governors and urged the LEA 'to continue to bear the cost of accommodation either in schools or village halls in small centres where physical recreation has been the major activity in Further Education'. The protests were to no avail. The LEA stuck to its decision to incur no expense on such classes. The result, predictable perhaps, was that there were few enquiries for such courses, and so none were organised in 1952/53.

Physical education and dancing had collapsed, the stringent policy remained in force, but the argument would not go away. In 1954 the committee for North-West Berkshire expressed concern about the lack of support for physical education, suggesting, without success, that this should be treated differently from dancing and the constraint of self-financing. For 1955/56, the FESC wanted the LEA to support two classes in physical training in each of the colleges and evening institute areas. At a County Council meeting, Dr Watson, thinking of National Service, thought it 'essential to run PT classes for teenagers before they joined the Forces'. Sir George Mowbray, Finance Committee chairman, agreed that a 'good many' people were in favour of physical training and boxing, 'but many thought these things should be self-supporting and not be provided by county ratepayers'.[13]

However, the Education Committee amended its policy and agreed to cover half the costs of classes in physical recreation; consequently the fees were reduced by half. The change, however, did not apply to dancing. In 1956 country dancing was organised

---

[12] BEC 20 June 1952, 19 September 1952; FESC 18 July 1952.

[13] *NWN* 3 March 1955.

at Kintbury and ballroom dancing at Wickham, but the classes had to be financially self-supporting.

'We try to help people to live full and interesting lives'

In the spring of 1953, 500 people gathered in the Plaza Theatre in Newbury for an 'Any Questions on Education?' evening organised by the Teachers' Association, the WEA and the Townswomen's Guild. A panel of educationalists was chaired by BBC Radio's Freddie Grisewood. One of the questions from the audience was: What ought to be the function of non-vocational adult education? The headmaster of Bradfield College saw two purposes: the 'encouragement of and help with a pastime or hobby' and the 'encouragement of the aesthetic appreciation of the arts'. The chairman put in a plea for nature study, something of 'unbounded interest' which 'remained with them all their lives'. Berkshire's Director of Education took the opportunity to defend further education:

> Mr Herbert said persons who were beginning to become critical of money spent on education were inclined to suggest adult education should be the first part of the service to suffer. That would be a great mistake. He took the view that education proper did not begin until you were an adult. The fundamental function of adult education was to make people first class members of the community and give them a chance to refresh, re-equip and reorientate their background.[14]

A few months later, the Rotary Club organised a similar evening, a Careers Question Time with a panel this time of educationalists and employers. There were three headteachers: J A Ballantyne from Newbury Grammar School, Derek Turnbull and Albert Owthwaite. The president of the Chamber of Commerce was in the chair. Again, predictably, one of the questions was to do with adult education; and this time it led to a heated exchange of views.

---

[14] *Ibid.*, 14 May 1953.

A question which produced a 'duel' between Mr Ballantyne as headmaster of Newbury Grammar School and Mr Owthwaite as Principal of the South Berks College of Further Education was: How is it possible for our children to receive adequate education when so much of the money available is squandered on teaching elderly ladies and others how to make pottery, baskets, hats, clothing and other articles, which no one could either wear or use?

Mr Ballantyne assumed the question meant: Is it right and proper that a proportion of the funds available for education should be spent on providing what were purely recreational facilities for adults? He said everyone was aware, to one's personal cost, that the education rate was extremely high and likely to get higher. It therefore often came to people as a shock to learn of the shortage of equipment in schools. It was impossible at his school, for the moment, to purchase enough paper for the pupils to write on, and he said that morning he saw an exercise book which had been written across horizontally and now was being written across vertically. Boys preparing for an examination in science were unable to do certain work because of the high cost of chemicals. He thought it entirely wrong that recreational classes for adults should not be entirely self-supporting. He was all in favour of providing such facilities but the people who wanted them should be prepared to pay the full cost of providing them.

Mr Owthwaite Displeased
Mr Owthwaite said he was of the opinion the question was not put seriously in which case it was 'irresponsible and highly slanderous'. He took exception to the final words in the question 'which no one could either wear or use', claiming that this was entirely proved to be false from press reports which referred to 'perfectly made garments' on show at the College exhibition and which, he said, to his knowledge, had since been worn and worn out.[15]

---

[15] *Ibid.*, 3 December 1953.

Such comments about the finance of voluntary non-vocational courses were heard at education meetings and Berkshire's arguments continued at Shire Hall. As the budget for 1954-55 rose to almost £3-million, the chairman of the Finance Committee returned to his concept of the frills of adult education, and introduced a new one, that of the semi-frill:

> Referring to Further Education, Sir George (Mowbray) thought rather more money than was absolutely necessary was being required for classes dealing with less vital topics, particularly where the numbers attending the classes could hardly be said to justify their continuance.

> In the main he would say that the frills of which he had been somewhat critical in the past had been cut out, but possibly there were semi-frills which would bear examination.[16]

The following year, for the first time, the budget exceeded £3-million. This time it was Major-General Beak (Finance Committee) who thought that there were 'trimmings' which could be 'jettisoned'; and such excesses were to be found in adult education. 'Were they spending more than was required on further education, especially having regard to sparsely attended classes? He did not see why they should advertise for students. Why press them to take classes?'[17]

There seemed to be plenty of critics of recreational education. Yet such classes played only a small part in FE spending. At Newbury in 1956, only a little over three per cent of the college's time was devoted to such courses, according to Roy Pocock. Moreover, education departments were urging their colleagues to carry out a 'more liberal education' and they should not be criticised for doing so.[18] Principal Eric Lansley put it this way: 'We deal here with education in its broadest sense. Education does not mean merely learning to earn your living. We try to help people to live full and interesting lives.' College governors did not seem

---

[16] *Ibid.*, 4 March 1954.

[17] *Ibid.*, 13 January 1955.

[18] *Ibid.*, 23 February 1956.

to have any doubts about the value of non-vocational education as several of them enrolled as students.[19]

Another issue close to part-time assistants was the remuneration for the work they had to do outside the classroom. They were paid for the time they spent teaching, but their work could entail other obligations. For some of these they were paid, such as attendance at staff meetings and enrolment evenings, but not for others, such as helping with exhibitions and open days. This was an issue for some of them. Exhibitions were usually held at the end of the academic year. Lots of visitors came and there was much preparation required. Assistants wanted to be paid for their work on the day and in 1955 the advisory committee for Central Berks asked for part-time staff to be remunerated for two hours work at 10/- (50 pence) an hour with travelling expenses. The FESC rejected this; but the issue came up again 12 months later. Nothing changed. In 1957 an exhibition of students' work – dressmaking, lampshades and woodwork – was held at the Corn Exchange in Hungerford, starting at three o'clock in the afternoon and going on until ten o'clock in the evening. There were craft demonstrations, dramatic presentations, country dancing and music courtesy of Kintbury's brass band. The part-timers had a busy day but in spite of a request from the college governors, the FESC decided against any change of policy. Part-time staff was not to be paid for their work at open days.

The cost of journeying to work was another issue for some part-timers. Those who lived a certain distance from where they taught were entitled to travel expenses, but the amount was limited, and occasionally a teacher would ask to be paid above the maximum. This happened in 1952 with the shorthand teacher at Lambourn. He was travelling from his home in Thatcham, but his request to be paid more than the 5/- (25 pence) maximum was rejected. However, the pianist at Hungerford lived near Kintbury and at the end of the dancing class for which she provided the musical accompaniment, she had to take a taxi home for which she was allowed 7/6 (37 pence).[20] In certain circumstances, then, the LEA was prepared to bend the rules.

[19] *Ibid.*, 24 October 1957.

[20] FESC 18 January 1952.

This sometimes happened when it was difficult to find a teacher who lived locally. As we have seen, a painting instructor in 1952 travelled by train to Newbury from Southampton. On his behalf, the governors asked for the return fare of 11/6 (57 pence), and this was agreed. A few years later, and another successful request was made. The embroidery teacher at Mortimer was a full-time lecturer at the college who lived at Padworth. She was allowed the return taxi fare from Padworth to Mortimer on a Monday afternoon.[21]

'Are you Edwards? Thank God you speak English!'

Dick Edwards taught woodwork and metal work at South Berks College for over forty years. When he started, he was one of only three full-time lecturers – Eric Carr and Vera Garlick were the others – who were trained teachers. As qualified teachers, this trio enjoyed a special relationship with the Principal. 'Owthwaite left us alone, but the others he used to chase unmercifully.' When Dick was appointed in the summer of 1952, he was teaching in a school in Leigh in Lancashire. He had to work out his notice and did not arrive in Newbury until the following year, moving into lodgings on the Andover Road while his wife Connie stayed with her parents. A few months went by, Connie joined him and they moved into their house in Chandos Road. With his bicycle in storage, Dick spent his first term making his way round the town on foot.

'I came to organise craft classes and also to do maths and engineering drawing; and I did business arithmetic and machine shop maths.' His craft classes were at Oxford Road but the arithmetic was down at Station Road where he put in 'quite a few hours'.

Welshman Dick Edwards has a vivid recollection of his first day at the Community Centre. The first person he met was the formidable Vera Garlick. They were to become good friends.

> The first morning that I came, I landed up at the college and Owthwaite said, 'Well, you're down at the Community

---

[21] *Ibid.*, 21 November 1952, 18 September 1959.

Centre.' He told me how to get there and whatnot and said, 'Go down there and find Miss Garlick.' So I wandered down and I found the Community Centre. I went upstairs and coming along the corridor was a real caricature of a woman teacher – tall, tweed suit, brown stockings, straight hair.

I said, 'Are you Miss Garlick?'

'Yes', she said, 'Are you Edwards?'

And I said, 'Yes.'

'Thank God you speak English!'

'Cos they had somebody in before I came doing my job part time, and he was a broad Berkshire lad and Garlick couldn't stand it. She was great was Garlick – oh, she was good. She was a marvellous teacher. She was a Grade A when I came. She and Owthwaite used to swear at each other every day, literally. But it was more than a normal swearing match on one occasion. She chucked it in and went as headmistress at Highclere School for a couple of years. And then she came back, still as a Lecturer One, but she soon went up and became Head of Commerce – Business Studies – and a very good head she was too.

Garlick spent a lot of time in the Community Centre. Gladys Sugg spent all her time there. Bill Sugg taught at Park House. He was the local agent for the British & Foreign Bible Society. They were very involved with the B & F and they had both been missionaries. He used to take services in St Nicolas' quite frequently.

In 1953, the full-time Commercial course was taught at the Centre alongside women's crafts, cookery and domestic science. Miss Barnes taught crafts, Kay Turnbull the dressmaking and needlework. Mrs Sylvester, a full-timer appointed in 1952, took cookery and dressmaking. She was a domestic science teacher from Lambourn School. 'She lived down in the Community Centre because the cookery centre as such was there.' They all worked closely with their head Jessie Searle, 'a formidable lady – she used to do ever such a lot'.

Dick spent a lot of time making his way round the town to his various classes. He taught a lot of drawing in the rooms in

Northbrook Street.[22] 'Call them workshops! They were three classrooms – they weren't very big.' One was used as a science laboratory. 'It was the only lab, both physics and chemistry, before the prefabs were opened.' 'We used to go across the road to the Devonia Café – they treated us very well because they knew we were regulars.' Dick spent the rest of his time at Oxford Road. He taught mathematics in the wooden shed, the former chapel, but most of his time was spent in the chicken hut teaching his favourite subject.

> The main chapel was a fairly long room and it had a step in the ceiling. If you got in one place there, your voice echoed all over. There was another little room, what had been a vestry; you could only get a small class in there, eight or ten people.

> I taught in the chicken hut for years and years. It was a First World War 60-foot army hut, divided into two rooms. In the very early days, half was a classroom, the other half was the carpenter's shop. Arthur Owen and I shared it – I spent hours in there. Those benches, if you started chopping up a decent mortise, putting a bit of weight behind it, you could feel the floor bouncing away. I have one very funny memory of seeing a kid down at the far end of the room, and he was messing. And I said, 'Come here!' And he started walking up to me, and all of a sudden he was only half-height. The floor had given way and he had gone through. He was on his knees!

> In those days we ran twilight classes, five to seven. It was still light at five o'clock. There was an occasion when one brainy kid went in there, took an electric bulb out, put a halfpenny in, and then put the bulb back. It blew all the fuses in Ormonde House. It was a long time before they found the cause. The fuses were going every time they were put in.

---

[22] 'The roof leaked, the ceiling fell in, the stove boiled the central heating water, the boys from the Boys' Club raided and walking time was allowed back to Ormonde House.' SBCFE 25 Years.

When Dick arrived in Newbury in 1953, some of the rooms in Ormonde House were classrooms; others were used as the library, the canteen, the Principal's office and the staff room. Downstairs was the general office and the telephone switchboard – Newbury 1384 – with its two extensions. 'Owthwaite had one and Roy as Vice-Principal had the other.' The library – 'a few shelves, 40 or 50 books' – was in the same room. Its French windows opened on to the rose garden, with the orchard beyond. This part of the garden was used for archery practice.

> There was a staff archery club and the Newbury Bowmen was a successor to it. There were a few of us interested, a few part-time people and one or two friends as well. A number of outsiders joined. We shot from the steps at the back of the house, and we shot down the length, the canteen as it became. When they started building the first instalment, the machine shop, we lost the range. So these friends, and a couple of part-timers, went up to the Blue Boar at Chieveley.

Mrs Whiting made the tea for the staff. 'You went in, got your cup of tea, and took it upstairs. The kids could have some as long as it lasted.' The staff room was upstairs, on the other side of the landing from the Principal's office. It was in here that Dick and his colleagues relaxed, ate their lunch and, if they could find any space, kept their books and paperwork.

> The accommodation was pretty basic. There was a box about two feet wide, with six shelves down, each about three inches. On one side were all the registers, with sections on the other. You were lucky if you had one of those sections – I didn't have one for about a twelvemonth. There was also one cupboard five foot high and six feet long, which was divided into shelves. If you were lucky you had a section in it. And that was it. That was all the staff accommodation for books and whatnot, half a shelf and one cupboard.

Some time later, Vera Garlick had a gas point installed so they could boil a kettle and make their own drinks. Dick usually had his lunch up there. 'We used to get school meals from the county's schools' canteen. They were delivered to college – Mrs. Whiting used to dish these out.' If he wanted a change of scenery, he went down to the Community Centre, where technician Jeff Jeffery sometimes joined him.

A year or two after Dick had started at the college, the staff celebrated Christmas together in a local pub. 'It was a dinner. We sat down in the lounge afterwards and nattered. It was the first social occasion that the college had had.'

'I must have been going to woodwork for at least six years – it was a recreational something to do'

Marjorie Fisher's father was a boilermaker in the Wiltshire town of Swindon and when a young man he had got a job abroad with the East Indian Railway. 'My mother went out to India and they were married in the Baptist Church in Calcutta.' Marjorie was born in India (1915) and lived there as a child. A few years passed and the family returned to Swindon. Marjorie won a scholarship to grammar school after which she took a secretarial course. 'The bookkeeping was a nightmare – I was never any good at sums.' A variety of jobs followed and with war imminent, she learnt first aid and became an ambulance driver. 'I was drafted in full time, around 1942 to 1944. In my spare time I used to go to this wartime nursery for mothers who went into munitions factories.' The war over, Marjorie embarked on a new career. She got a place on the emergency training scheme for teachers, went to college in Hertfordshire – 'a beautiful place, a huge mansion with gorgeous cedars of Lebanon' – and in 1947 started teaching in Kent, a class of 49 five-year-olds. A few years later, she decided she wanted to be in a school nearer her family in Swindon. 'My mother had had the flu badly and had been very ill.' There was a vacancy at Speenhamland School in Newbury. Marjorie applied and was interviewed by the headmaster.

> It was the first day of term. I got the twelve o'clock train from Paddington for an interview at Speenhamland at two. There were two others. One was out of college from Wales, and one was teaching at a country school around Newbury.

I was called in. There were three there besides Mr Watts. Mr Watts said, 'First of all, Miss Fisher, how many in your class?'

And I said, 'Forty-nine.'

So he said, 'When can you start?'

He couldn't believe it. 'Now we know somebody who knows about teaching numbers.'

They were ever so good to me, the Watts family, when I moved. He put an advert in the *Newbury Weekly News* about digs, and he vetted the replies and sent them to me with a note, where it was and what type of house it was. I decided on Fifth Road. My friend from Kent came for a weekend, and we went to Newbury Show which was at Elcot Park. I started with six-year-olds. Then when Winchcombe School was built, three teachers went there and I moved across to the old building at Speenhamland to take the five-year-olds. I had the whole building to myself. There was a piano in there, and I could play sufficiently for the children to move around and play, nursery rhymes and things. I would tell a story and we would have music and movement and things like that. And then we had music and movement on the radio. At teacher-training college we did lots of murals, lots of sticking on paper. It was always big work; you didn't do pokey little things. And it was the Queen's coronation. The whole of the big wall in my classroom was a gorgeous stagecoach with horses, and it was all with tissue paper stuck on. I did lots of big things like that. Mr Watts gave me a free rein. We kept record books and he had them in on Monday morning to know what we were going to do every day, all the way through the week.

I came to Newbury in January '51 and went to my first college class in September, in the Girls' School on Andover Road. I knew I would enjoy it. I would meet people, and I wanted to go somewhere, because I didn't know many people in Newbury. I hadn't done very much cooking other than at home with my mother. The teacher was ever so good. She went to a lot of trouble to get things for us. I finished that class and went on to the next grade. It was at the Community Centre, in the double-storey building. They did meals there and that is why we were able to have the cookery. The children used to eat there in the daytime, those who stayed for school dinners. They used to be marched down from St Nicolas' School in Enborne Road, and we went into their kitchen in the evening.

We had six or seven of us in the class. I did two terms but I just couldn't fit it in with my school work. In those days, infant teachers had to make all their equipment. We spent hours making things, and I found I couldn't do all the reading. The practical work was a dolly, but the theory – you had to know everything about nutrition and vitamins. It was a terrific amount we had to learn, it really was. It was very, very tough. It was a tough exam, which is only right, isn't it, if you are going to take an exam at an advanced level. Somebody stepped in at the last minute and took my place. She wanted to take the exam because she was assistant cook at Mary Hare and if she got this qualification she could get that much more money and take over being cook. One day, after we did our City & Guilds, the person who was in charge of cookery in Ormonde House came into my class in Speenhamland and said they were wanting a cookery teacher and would I go. And I said, no.

At the same time I went to woodwork evening classes. I must have been going to woodwork for at least six years if not more – it was a recreational something to do. It wasn't mental – it was completely different – and I wasn't any good at sewing. It was in a shed by Ormonde House, but we were fine. Dick Edwards took us all the time, all the way through. He did ever such a lot. There was a group of Shaw House teachers and we used to have a whale of a time, 'cos we used to have a break for coffee. With Dick it was a social evening more than anything, but I must have made five tables. The first one was a little table that had drop ends, and you swivelled it round to make it one table. Then I did a nest of tables, and then I did one large one. So you see I must have been going to woodwork for years. Those tables would have taken us two sessions, two whole winters, I mean, at the speed we worked and the chat that we did.

'I made my husband buy me a sewing machine so that I could do my homework'

Another Speenhamland teacher also started at night school around this time. **Audrey Lewendon** had begun teaching at the school in 1949. Straight out of college, this was Audrey's first job. Her family came from South Wales, but in 1939 they moved to England. 'My dad was ill and had to leave work and the doctor suggested that my mother went to Weymouth and open a guest house, and that's what she did.' They had not been there long when war broke out. 'That put paid to any visitors.' Once the war was over, and Audrey had left school, she trained to become a teacher.

That's why I came to Newbury, to teach. I was at Speenhamland six years, then I got married. I was there a year after I was married, and then I left. It was the era of the New Look. We all went round in long skirts and long coats. I had a lovely smart mackintosh down to my ankle. On my 21st birthday I was given a bicycle, a green Raleigh. It was my pride and joy; I've even got a photograph of it. It was a present from my parents and it meant I was more mobile. I was in digs with my aunt in Bartlemy Road on the south side of Newbury, so it meant I could go on my bike to the cookery class which was in Shaw House. I cycled through the City Playground and up through Northbrook Street. I remember cycling up this dark avenue of trees which led right up to Shaw House.

It was a beginners' class. I couldn't cook. I never even boiled an egg or anything. Not that I never wanted to – I wasn't allowed to cook. I was an only child and I decided it was time I learned, so off I went. It was really basic cookery, no exam. It was all practical. The tutor would demonstrate quickly and then we would get on and do it and she would come round and make sure we were doing it right. Very enjoyable it was. I like cooking and it did help. There was about 12 of us because we had to share two to an oven and that sort of thing. They were all females and all fairly young. I went to college cookery classes much later on and I was surprised to see older people at them, whereas when I went first of all it was mostly young people. We're doing different skills now, vegetarian cookery and things like that, which we had never heard of then.

We had to take the ingredients because we did still have ration books. They weren't able to supply us. The first thing I made up was a crumble. You always made the crumble first, 'cos you rub in fat and flour but you don't put water with it. You only put it on top of the fruit, so that's always the first step. The next step is, you put water with it and make pastry. That was the second lesson. Then a sponge cake and different sorts of cakes and icing. And then at the end of the term I made a Christmas cake. You couldn't cook it in the time you were at the lesson so you had to take it home. I was lodging with my aunt and I had to cook it in her oven and then take it back the next week and decorate it. It wasn't so good taking the stuff home on a bike, the cake tins and things, but we seemed to manage it alright. I took the cake to Weymouth for Christmas because my parents lived there.

I did go to a class at the Community Centre, '53, '54, for something to do, just as an interest. It was all practical. I was still in digs, so it was to get out and do something. That's why I did it. It was not to meet people in my case, but I certainly enjoyed going. In the leather class I made a purse, a very simple purse, making holes in the leather and then using a leather strip to join it together. But there were people in there making beautiful gloves and things like that. It was in the same class that I made a stool out of seagrass. You bought the legs and knocked it together and then you made a seat and did all the work with this material called seagrass. It was very popular. It was thick, like rope, and you wove it. It was green and cream. It made a very hard-wearing stool. I had it for a long, long time.

In the late '50s – I'd left Speenhamland by then – I did a dressmaking class. Why, I can't think, 'cos I hate dressmaking. We had this class in a chapel building which was knocked down for Waterside Youth Club. You went down Toomer's yard – there was a big yard right down – and there was a house there. It was part of the original chapel. It was all practical, no exam. I made myself a skirt and a dress which I was pleased with, but I didn't take to it very much, and I still don't. I only went because I thought I ought to be able to do it, not because I wanted to. I wasn't enjoying it really, so I never got on very well. We bought the material and the pattern and took it to the class, and she showed us how to cut it out and get cracking on it. You had to do some sewing at home. You were supposed to finish the garments you had started. You did this at home and took the hard bits back, like putting a zip in or something, and let the lecturer show you how to do it. I made my husband buy me a sewing machine so that I could do my homework. I was quite keen to get a machine. There was a Singer sewing shop in Northbrook Street.

Dressmaking classes were very popular. It was so much cheaper to make your own clothes then. People weren't so well off and couldn't afford to buy them. And it had been the sort of thing your mother did. She always sewed, so you wanted to copy her and do the same.

'Students turn mannequins at South Berks College exhibition'

Audrey's dressmaking was in the college's new annex, the Waterside Chapel on the north bank of the River Kennet behind the House of Toomer. This 'early nonconformist chapel of distinction' had been built at the end of the 17th century, an attractive building with walls of red brick and a tiled roof with gables. The chapel was no longer used for worship, the box pews had gone but the carved gallery remained. Outside, the graveyard had fallen into disuse. The property belonged to the County Council and was used as a youth club by the Newbury YWCA. For five years, from 1954 to 1959, the chapel was the venue for the college's women's subjects, the Women's Craft Centre.

Negotiations for the use of the building had started in the summer of 1953. The town's primary schools needed more room and wanted to use the Community Centre. The full-time Commercial course in the Centre could be moved back to Ormonde House while most of the other classes could be transferred to the Waterside building except cookery as the chapel was without kitchen facilities. Agreement was reached, the lease was signed and FE activities started at the Waterside in the autumn of 1954. Lighting had to be improved because of the intricacies involved in needlework and embroidery and, a few years later, the budget was overspent by £351 because of the purchase of dress stands, a desk and a set of chairs to replace those on loan from the youth club.[23] The college used the building until 1959.

Jessie Searle's dressmaking classes were transferred from Ormonde House to the Waterside and the conservatory became a science laboratory. 'The number of courses which require chemistry laboratory facilities is greater than can adequately be dealt with in the one existing science laboratory' in the horsa hut.[24] The conservatory was used until the laboratory in the first instalment was ready.

By 1959 there were two more annexes in use. The college was already using a property on two floors at 94a Northbrook Street, above E Hill & Sons, the leather shop. Here there were four large rooms, three smaller ones and two cloakrooms. A six-year lease was signed in 1956. The rent was £160 p.a. In 1959 accommodation was leased above the Trustee Savings Bank at 134 Bartholomew Street. 'We had a room over the top – Toc H was up there as well.' The previous tenants sold the water heater and nine light fittings to the college for £10.[25]

---

[23] FESC, 16 July 1954, 13 September 1957.

[24] *Ibid.*, 16 July 1954.

[25] BEC 14 September 1956; FESC 22 May 1959.

Miss McGee, Jessie Searle's successor responsible for women's subjects, looked forward to the second instalment of the new college. 'Our main difficulty at the moment', she said in 1957, 'is that our classes in Newbury are so scattered. When the new buildings are erected we should have ample accommodation and excellent kitchen facilities.'[26] In 1960, the buildings were finished and all the women's subjects were taught at Oxford Road. The chapel was demolished and the Waterside Youth & Community Centre was built on the site.

Miss McGee came to the college in September 1954. She was in charge of the Craft Centre although she was always keen to point out that her department was 'not reserved solely for the fair sex'. Men occasionally went to cookery and tailoring 'and made a very good job of it too'. Yet nearly all of her 800 or so students were women and at the end of each session, the fruit of their labour was proudly exhibited. There were models and paintings and items for the home; and the instructors had the opportunity to demonstrate their skills to the public. The mannequin parade was the exhibition's highlight. The students modelled their garments and children showed off the clothes which their mothers had made.

1955

Over 500 part-time students and 50 full-time are taking advantage of the facilities available at the college, where the syllabus in dressmaking enables a student to obtain examination qualifications as high as the City & Guilds (Advanced) for those wishing to make teaching, dress designing or modelling their careers.

One student's work for this included a history of costume (1846-1954) with some beautiful old French prints showing original designs. She had made miniature models to support her study which were beautifully worked and embroidered. Two complete miniatures to half-scale were of evening frocks, one in white net and the other in dark red silk with a petal design skirt embroidered with beads and sequins.

---

[26] *NWN* 24 October 1957.

By Easy Stages

First-, second- and third-year work was among that on display showing how a student's knowledge and skill increases in easy stages and logical sequence so that by the end of the third year quite professional results are achieved.

Among clothes modelled in the mannequin parade was an afternoon dress in soft glazed cotton on caramel ground with black design, the H-line accentuated by a hip band of black tricoline. This was made to the student's own drafted pattern. An oatmeal wool bouclé suit with yoke effect formed by darts radiating from the neckline had low slung hip pockets fastened with cream pearl buttons. A coffee needle run lace over deeper shade of taffeta had a slim fitting skirt and off the shoulder neckline.

What Mother Made

Children modelled clothes made by their mothers and a two-year-old boy was proud to display shorts and blouse in red check on his birthday. Two young sisters wore dark red corduroy dresses over vilene petticoats. Vilene was also used to give support and shape to a strapless bodice in a blue and white stripe cotton dress with soft unpressed pleated skirt and low hip-line.

The many uses of vilene were shown on a display unit. This new material is likely to revolutionise dressmaking and take the place of canvas. It looks and feels like blotting paper and is used for interlinings being supple and light. Another new material was rayon shantung, uncrushable, washable and in a large range of shades.

Exhibition's Wide Range

Although the main exhibition was of needlework, dressmaking and tailoring, and also of materials now available, there were also art, soft furnishings, lampshades, basketry, rug-making, leatherwork and weaving. Rugs included some incorporating the Berkshire stitch, a firm hardwearing uncut weave forming a herring bone pattern in four movements.

Women have joined men in woodwork classes and examples of their skill in carpentry were displayed in sewing cabinets and tables.

Advanced work by men students in this section included a three-foot Bermuda rig boat which is going into a model yacht club and a bedside cabinet with oak facing.

Food and Wines
Dishes suitable for a children's party, a buffet supper and an exhibition of wines and preserves were on view in the cookery section. This also included crystallised flowers for cake decoration. Some of the full-time students take cookery as one of their subjects for the General Certificate of Education. Many students come in to classes from country districts and they are also well supported by members of Women's Institutes and Townswomen's Guilds. Where it is difficult for people to get in to Newbury from outlying districts, staff at the college go out and conduct weekly classes where the demand is sufficient. Some of the most enthusiastic classes are among those taken in the villages.[27]

In 1955 there was a new group of students in the Craft Centre, American women from the airbase on Greenham Common. At the end of the war the airfield had been vacated and the 101st Airborne Division had gone home, but a few years later the US air force was back. Greenham Common became a base for heavy bombers and Newbury's American connection was resumed. Servicemen moved in and their wives found their way down to the Waterside Chapel.

1956

There was special applause for American students, wives of servicemen at Greenham, who have joined classes this year. Several have plunged into tailoring with quite professional results. Girls studying for the UEI on full-time courses displayed blouses and skirts made for their exam this term.

---

[27] *Ibid.*, 2 June 1955.

Tailoring has been given prominence in the syllabus this year because of an increased demand. There was a display showing the progress of tailoring and although the jump from dressmaking is difficult many students appeared to have mastered it.

A man's blazer made by Mrs J Lambourne for her husband has won third prize in a recent competition in which Mrs Watts' boy's suit was highly commended. Mrs Roberts not only made her small son's legginette outfit but also her husband's flannels, so professionally that they might have come straight from a tailor's shop. Miss Adey was ambitious enough to make an astrakhan fur coat.

Millinery has been another popular hobby, beginning with one class it has now increased to two and there are four planned for the autumn. Several hats were admired, including a red velvet boater, a chic little model trimmed with black velvet appliquéd with red hearts.

In the handicraft section students are encouraged to work with local materials and have gathered reeds to make baskets and mats. Honeysuckle and dogweed have been picked for their cane work. Weaving cloth and mats has been popular and there was a fine display of lampshades. One of the prettiest was made from an old Honiton lace collar mounted on a fluted buckram base.

Fleece-lined quilts from original designs were exquisitely made and there were examples of many other crafts – block printing, slipper and glove making. These students even have their own spinning wheel. They seem to tackle any job and are encouraged to bring their individual craft ambitions to the class.

Younger students showed versatility and enthusiasm in their displays of fine needlework, illustrating examples of the standard of work required in their GCE examinations. As a renovation test, a girl made a pretty smocked frock from a boy's shirt bought at a jumble sale for 1/6d (7 pence). Another contrived a scarf and gloves from her father's old white flannels and appliquéd them with red animal motifs. Advanced work by City & Guilds students was an example of the high standard achieved in these classes.

Full-time domestic science students displayed upholstery – a sugar box lined and padded as an ottoman, an old chair re-upholstered and the woodwork scraped and stained, curtains and smocking. Smocking is still enjoyed by those taking needlework and one adult student had smocked a dress for her daughter using the effective pleated new method.

Cookery prepared for examination work was also on display, together with a selection of exhibits from class work including special sections for egg dishes and preserves.

A colourful arrangement of pictures in all mediums was contributed from the art classes. They attracted a good deal of attention and there were several landscape pictures which anyone would have been proud to possess.

Over 800 part-time students have taken courses this year, an increase of 300 on the previous year. There are only about 25 young people taking a full-time examination course. Four evening classes are held in Newbury every night and the same number in the villages. Needlework crafts and cookery classes appear to be filling a need in the locality and it is an encouragement to staff as well as pupils that such satisfying results are being achieved as those displayed in the exhibition.[28]

1957

Many Try Tailoring
A new type of polished cotton seemed popular this year and an attractive summer dress and coatee in this fabric made by Mrs Billington received special applause. Tailoring classes seem as popular as ever and several students made ambitious attempts at suits and coats during the year.

Young Artists
Art students working with Mr C Stanley have made amazing progress since last year and some of the still life in oils was excellent work.

---

[28] *Ibid.*, 24 May 1956.

In the soft furnishing classes under the direction of Miss D A Barnes, students made a beautiful quilt filled with raw fleece, washed and carded, a contemporary lampshade from pleated cartridge paper and a waste-paper 'basket' from a tin quilted with remnants.

Basketmaking, too, showed improved skill and there were exhibits in willow as well as cane, including attractive picnic baskets on square bases with lids. In the weaving processes raw wool was shown on the spindle, later to be dyed in shades of yellow, brown and rust by fustic, weld and walnut.

Demonstrations began after the mannequin parade and continued until 7 pm. They included millinery, embroidery, bookcrafts, basketry, dressmaking, spinning and weaving, tailoring, cookery and light upholstery and were given by the college lecturers, Miss A M B McGee, Principal, Miss E J Searle, Miss D A Barnes, Miss E Elsom and Mrs Jones.[29]

SBCFE Prospectus 1959-60

Classes are available in a wide range of women's subjects

New students to the College will not be eligible for advanced work unless they show sufficient background to justify their admission. Most students will therefore work through the grades which will simplify the work and speed their progress.

Provision is made for students to take the City & Guilds Examinations in Cookery, Dressmaking, Tailoring, Embroidery, GCE Needlework and UEI Embroidery.

---

[29] *Ibid.*, 4 June 1957.

Grade	Subject	Day	Time	Place
I	General Domestic Cookery 1st year	Wed	7.00-9.30	CC
I	2nd year	Thurs	7.00-9.30	CC
II	Cookery - City & Guilds 243	Tues	6.30-9.30	CC
II	Cookery - C & G Adv. 244	Tues	5.30-9.30	CC
I	Christmas Cookery Sh/C. Sept/Dec	Tues	2.00-4.30	CC
I	Cookery - Cakes, Pastry and Yeast Mixtures Sh/C. Sept/Dec	Fri	9.45-12.15	CC
I	Cookery - Continental Sh/C. Jan/Apr	Tues	2.00-4.30	CC
I	Cookery - Continental Sh/C. Jan/Apr	Fri	9.45-12.15	CC
I	Cookery - Wines, Preserves & Cold Sweets Sh/C. May/June	Tues	2.00-4.30	CC
I	Basketry Sh/C. Sept/Dec	Tues	2.00-4.30	94a
I	Basketry Sh/C. Jan/Apr	Tues	2.00-4.30	94a
I	Basketry Sh/C. Sept/Dec	Fri	7.00-9.30	94a
I	Basketry Sh/C. Jan/Apr	Fri	7.00-9.30	94a
I	Leatherwork Sh/C. Sept/Dec	Wed	2.00-4.30	94a
I	Leatherwork Sh/C. Jan/Apr	Wed	2.00-4.30	94a
I	Fabric Printing Sh/C. Sept/Dec	Tues	9.30-12 noon	94a
I	Soft Furnishings Sh/C. Sept/Dec	Tues	7.00-9.30	94a
I	Soft Furnishings Sh/C. Jan/Apr	Tues	7.00-9.30	94a
I	Soft Furnishings Sh/C. Sept/Dec	Wed	9.30-12 noon	94a
I	Soft Furnishings Sh/C. Jan/Apr	Wed	9.30-12 noon	94a
I	Small Upholstery Sh/C. Sept/Dec	Thurs	9.30-12 noon	94a
I	Small Upholstery Sh/C. Jan/Apr	Thurs	9.30-12 noon	94a
I	Weaving	Mon	7.00-9.30	94a
II	Embroidery Adv. City & Guilds	Thurs	9.15-12.15	134
I	Embroidery	Wed	7.00-9.30	94a
I	Millinery Sh/C. Sept/Dec	Mon	2.30-4.30	94a
I	Millinery Sh/C. Sept/Dec	Thurs	7.00-9.00	94a
I	Tailoring	Wed	7.00-9.30	134
I	Tailoring	Thurs	2.00-4.30	134
I	Dressmaking II	Mon	2.00-4.30	134
II	Dressmaking City & Guilds 233, 234	Mon	5.00-9.00	134
I	Dressmaking I	Tues	2.00-4.30	134
I	Dressmaking II	Tues	7.00-9.30	134
I	Dressmaking I	Wed	2.00-4.30	134
I	Dressmaking I	Thurs	7.00-9.30	134
I	Dressmaking - Advanced	Fri	2.00-4.30	134

Sh/C. - Short Courses

All other courses are sessional (3 terms).

Key to location of Classes –

94a = Women's Craft Centre (over E Hill & Sons, Northbrook Street).

CC = Community Centre

134 = 134 Bartholomew Street (over Trustee Savings Bank).

9

FULL-TIME STUDENTS ARRIVE

Twenty-six school leavers arrived at South Berks College in September 1951. They came to study one of two full-time programmes, the Pre-Apprenticeship course for building and engineering or the Commercial course in shorthand and typewriting. Twelve months later, a course in domestic subjects was started, for girls interested in dressmaking and domestic science. It included GCEs (O-level) in cookery and needlework, human biology and hygiene, art and English. It could take up to three years, and the GCEs were useful for entry into nursing and teacher-training colleges. A separate GCE programme was also available and in 1953, a secretarial course was started. More advanced than the commercial programme, it was for students who had already achieved three O-levels, including English.

In the 1950s then, full-time courses became an integral part of the college curriculum. 26 young people in 1951, 55 in 1956 – in five years the numbers had doubled. By the early '60s there were 115 full-time students at the college.[1] This had a significant effect on the student hours' total.

---

[1] FESC 4 June 1965.

Table 19 South Berks College:
Student Enrolment 1951/52; 55/56; 56/57; 63/64

Session	FT	PT Day	Evening	Total
1951/52	26	351	2,069	2,446
1955/56	48	545	1,016	1,609
1956/57	55	631	901	1,587
1963/64	115	1,016	1,900	3,031

Table 20 South Berks College:
Student Hours 1948/49; 52/53; 55/56; 58/59; 60/61

Session	Hours
1948/49	48,522
1952/53	214,286
1955/56	250,000
1958/59	274,910
1960/61	334,555

The full-time courses were 'intended primarily to meet the needs of boys and girls at all-age schools or secondary modern schools which were not equipped or staffed to provide a satisfactory fifth-year course'.[2] They were popular and there were usually more applicants than there were places available. Students came from both LEA and private schools.[3]

We have seen that there was no technical school in the Newbury district for those young people who wanted that special type of learning with a specific vocational reference. However, when the college's full-time programmes started, enough concern was shown by Newbury parents to hold a public meeting at Speenhamland School. Anxiety was voiced – the Commercial course was too narrow and limited to shorthand and typewriting. Only by staying on at a secondary modern school until 16 could a girl receive a 'more general education'.

Lecturers Roy Pocock and Cecil Cox were not at the meeting but felt that a response was necessary. They wrote a letter to the

---

[2] *Ibid.*, 9 November 1962.

[3] *Ibid.*.

Newbury Weekly News, pointing out that the course included an RSA Certificate in eight subjects: English, history, geography, arithmetic, shorthand, typewriting, bookkeeping and commerce. So, contrary to what some people were suggesting, the students' 'general education' was not neglected. Some parents had also claimed that boys who stayed on at school until 16 would 'derive greater benefit' than by attending the Pre-Apprenticeship course at 15. Here the college spokesmen pointed out that those boys who left school at 16 were not automatically eligible for the college's engineering courses. Consequently 'after leaving the secondary modern school, they are obliged to take an additional examination at the age of 17 to qualify for entry to senior courses.' Those boys who completed the Pre-Apprenticeship, on the other hand, were eligible for such courses at 16. The lecturers concluded:

1. That the technical equipment of the College gives an opportunity for a wider range of studies than is possible in a secondary school, and

2. That it would be to the students' advantage to start and continue any further education course at the College specifically provided for further education.

    We feel that parents should be aware that courses in further education at the College are individually approved by the Ministry of Education and by Berkshire Education Committee, and that this is not so for pre-apprenticeship courses in secondary modern schools.[4]

The public concern did not affect interest in the courses; and the successful recruitment of full-time students had many implications for the college. In particular, it meant a stronger relationship with the schools. Many of the girls on the commercial/secretarial programmes came from Shaw House while Park House, with over 500 boys by 1955, provided many of the pre-apprenticeship students.

---

[4] *NWN* 8 May 1952.

There were also opportunities for students from Mary Hare School and in 1951, 20 of their older pupils joined in classes at Ormonde House for a few hours each week. 'There, studying side by side with other students from Newbury, apart from the valuable training they received, they began to realise that they could join in perfectly normal activities and be treated as responsible, intelligent people.' This FE experience made an 'invaluable contribution in developing their independence and self-confidence.'[5] In the college's history, this was the first example of a group of students spending some time in college classes whilst still at school.

The beginnings of a network of support for students can be seen with the developing liaison with the Youth Employment Service. In 1950 Berkshire Education Committee took over responsibility for the employment and training of young people up to the age of 18. The Youth Employment Service reported to the FESC. The county was divided into four areas, each with a youth employment officer and an area committee. The employment officers gave schoolchildren information and advice on college courses, training opportunities and jobs. The south-west Berkshire area covered Newbury, Thatcham, Hungerford, Lambourn and Compton. Its Youth Employment Committee was represented on the college's governing body. In 1950/51, the Youth Employment Service dealt with 2,579 school leavers; in 1959/60, there were 4,090 on its books, its busiest year of the decade. This was partly because of the increase in the number of leavers and partly because of the growing interest in the service not only by the young people themselves but also by their parents, the schools and employers.[6]

From 1951, the mix of college students became more diverse, teenage girls giving a softer touch to the more masculine profile of the pioneer years. The new students were together all week and they got to know each other very well. They chatted to each other on the bus and in the railway carriage and socialising continued in their breaks and through the lunch hour as they wandered round the town. At Christmas the girls in the Community Centre gathered round the piano and sang carols. The lecturers got to

---

[5] *Ibid.*, 23 October 1952.

[6] Education in the Royal County of Berkshire 1959-60, Report by the Director of Education, pp.42-43.

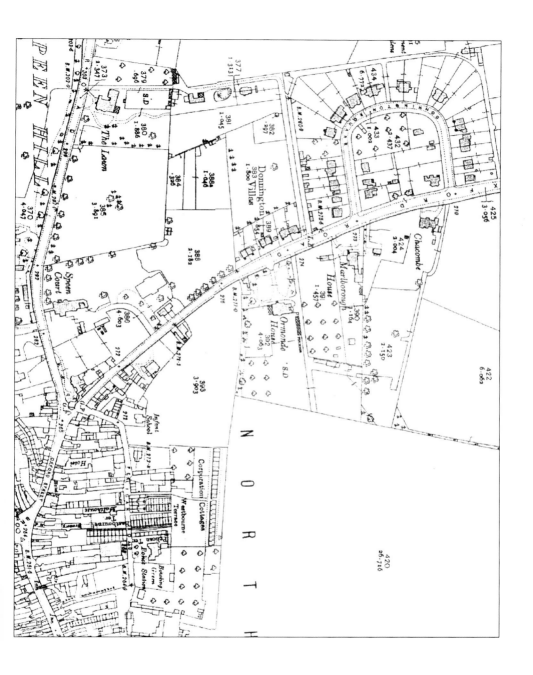

A walk along the Oxford Road

NEWBURY, BERKS.

IN THIS FAVOURITE SOCIAL AND SPORTING DISTRICT.

One Mile from Newbury Station with excellent Train Service to all parts.

Particulars and Conditions of Sale

OF THE VERY ATTRACTIVE FREEHOLD

Residential Property

KNOWN AS

"ORMONDE HOUSE,"

NEWBURY,————————BERKS.

COMPRISING A

Well-appointed, comfortable, and medium-sized Residence.

ELECTRIC LIGHTING.   ::   CENTRAL HEATING.

::   COMPANY'S WATER.   MAIN DRAINAGE.   ::

GROOM'S COTTAGE. STABLING, COACHHOUSE. GARAGE.

Extensive Grounds, in all

About 4 Acres.

WITH POSSESSION.

which will be Sold by Auction (unless previously disposed of) by

MESSRS.

A. W. NEATE & SONS

In their Sale Room, 8, St. Mary's Hill, Newbury,

On *MONDAY, 12th FEBRUARY, 1923,*

AT 3 O'CLOCK P.M.,

by direction of the Exor. of the late MR. JOHN PORTER.

Solicitors :—Messrs. GUSH, PHILLIPS, WALTERS & WILLIAMS, 5, Throgmorton Avenue, London, E.C. 2.

Auctioneers :—

Messrs. A. W. NEATE & SONS, St. Mary's Hill, Newbury.

Ormonde House sales brochure 1923

PLAN OF CORN EXCHANGE EXHIBITION

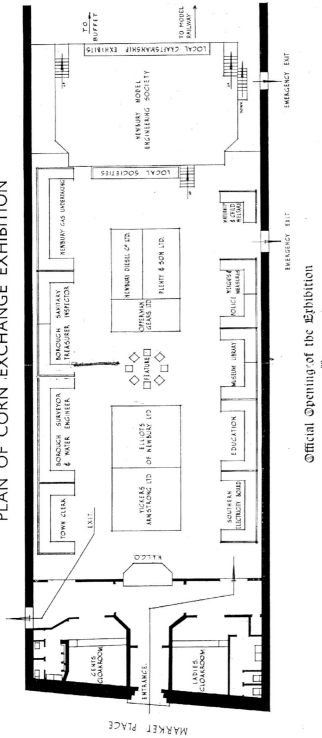

Official Opening of the Exhibition

BY

L. JOHN EDWARDS, O.B.E., M.P.

Parliamentary Secretary, Ministry of Health, on

TUESDAY, OCTOBER 26TH, at 3.15 p.m.

supported by the MAYOR AND CORPORATION.

The Exhibition will afterwards be open daily from 2 p.m. to 8 p.m.

Civic Week, October 1948

Len Hoyland in the drawing office

Typewriting in Ormonde House

Folk dancing at Kintbury

Eric Lansley, Principal from 1956 to 1970

Dressmaking in the conservatory

Roy Pocock, from lecturer (1949) to Principal (1970 to 1979)

Arthur Owen, in charge of courses in building from 1948

Oliver Brown, governor at Ormonde House from 1948 to 1958

An artist's impression of the chicken hut

Students on the Commercial course, 1953

*Gladys Sugg, Miss Sylvester and Vera Garlick
at the Community Centre, 1953*

*Plenty's apprentice
Sheila Smith, 1949*

*Dick Edwards at the
Community Centre, 1953*

The brickwork shop in the Nissen hut

South Berks College in the 1960s

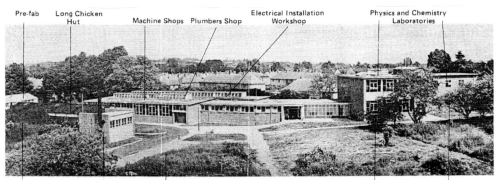

Pre-fab   Long Chicken   Electrical Installation   Physics and Chemistry
           Hut   Machine Shops Plumbers Shop   Workshop   Laboratories

Stables (Old   Boiler House   Staff Car Park   Applied Mechanics   Building
Plumbers Shop)   Science

ORMONDE HOUSE GARDEN
The first instalment

*Ormonde House, the conservatory with the
second instalment coming into view*

know them better than they did the part-timers as they spent more time with them. Commercial students were taught English, geography and history with a recreational afternoon of woodwork or dressmaking. The pre-apprenticeship boys had lessons in English and history and, on one afternoon a week, they played football in the winter and in the summer went swimming in the outdoor pool at Northcroft.

On a more practical level, the canteen service in Ormonde House had to be developed. In 1951 the refectory was open for mid-morning snacks, and, if there was sufficient demand, for tea in the afternoon. The LEA subsidised it, but county policy was that the money was to be progressively reduced so that from 1954, the service was to be self-supporting.[7] From 1952, meals were available at lunchtime from the School Meals Service. Orders had to be placed before 10 am for the food to be prepared at the depot in Thatcham and delivered to the house in time for lunch.

Another practical implication of full-time students was that the LEA needed to clarify its policy on books and stationery. In the schools, students were loaned their texts and provided with exercise books. In the new college policy from 1952, it was decided to treat the new FE students, and some of the part-timers, in the same way. Full-timers were to be loaned their texts and given exercise books and stationery. So were day-release students, and those under 19 in night school. All other students were to buy their books – unless there were copies in stock cupboards which were not being used – and provide their own stationery. The college would provide drawing boards and T-squares to use in class, but these would remain on the premises. Students, including those on day release, were expected to provide their own drawing instruments, 'including pencil, ruler, compass, protractor, set square 45, set square 60 and Armstrong Scale Rule'.[8]

---

[7] FESC 23 May 1952. For the refectory accounts see FESC 23 January 1953, 13 July 1956, 13 September 1957, 4 July 1958, 18 September 1959.

[8] SBCFE Prospectus 1951-52, p.13.

BERKSHIRE EDUCATION COMMITTEE
SOUTH BERKS COLLEGE OF
FURTHER EDUCATION,
NEWBURY.

Full-time Courses 1953-54

The following full-time Courses for boys and girls from Secondary, Grammar, Secondary Modern and All-Age Schools, will commence in September 1953. Entry to all Courses will be by Selection Examination. For admission to the Secretarial Course, candidates should have had full-time education in a Secondary Grammar or Secondary Modern School up to the age of 16 years. Preference will be given to candidates holding a General Certificate of Education. For admission to all other courses applicants should be 15 years of age on or before 31 December 1953, and should be eligible to leave school not later than December 1953.

1. One-year Secretarial Course (Mixed)
2. One-year General Commercial Course (Mixed)
3. One-year Pre-Apprenticeship Course (Boys)
4. One or two-year Domestic Subjects Course (Girls)
5. Two or three-year General Certificate of Education Course (Mixed)

No fees will be charged and travelling and maintenance allowances may be granted in accordance with the Authority's regulations to Berkshire students. For other students the fee is £30 per annum for which the appropriate Education Authority may accept responsibility. Further particulars, and application forms obtainable from the Director of Education (FE) Shire Hall, Reading or from the College, should be returned to the Principal, South Berks College of Further Education, Newbury, not later than 31 May. The Entrance Examination will be held in June.

'It was such a small place – we all got together'

Shirley Woodage was among the first group of full-timers to come to Ormonde House. She had taken the eleven-plus examination at Hampstead Norreys where she lived. 'The children of all the posh people in the village used to go to St Gabriel's. If you didn't pass to go to grammar school, you paid to go there if your parents could afford it.' Shirley did not pass, so she stayed at the village school for two more years and then went to Compton a few miles away. Here she made new friends, from Aldworth and Ashampstead, Chaddleworth and Farnborough. In her new surroundings she enjoyed art and learned to draw with charcoal and Indian ink; and Wednesday afternoons were great fun, playing netball and rounders against girls from Hungerford, Lambourn and Thatcham. With lots of good memories, Shirley made sure that before she left, her teachers were recorded for posterity in her treasured autograph book.

Shirley's ambition was to join the police force, but she could not do this until she was 21 years old. In the meantime, she decided to go to college and was accepted onto the Commercial course in January 1952, even though it had already been running for a term.

> We were taught in Ormonde House and in the wooden classrooms at the bottom. We did all the typing and shorthand in the classroom next to the conservatory, and for geography and history and that, we all went down to the wooden huts. You walked down the side of Ormonde House. I can remember seeing a vine in the greenhouse. There was the orchard and the gardens, and as you walked down you turned and there were two wooden huts.

For one afternoon a week, the 'three or four boys' on the course did woodwork and the girls did dressmaking. 'We had treadle machines in the conservatory. The tutor was Miss Sibley. We used to have to design our own patterns, all on graph paper. We couldn't go out and buy one.' The refectory was 'a small room where we had our sandwiches. We used to have cooked lunches. I don't say they were full-blown courses but it saved going into town.' It was in the refectory that Shirley heard that King George

VI had died. At lunchtime she occasionally played tennis on the court at the bottom of the garden. Miss Garlick took the class to the Bath Road 'to see the Queen go through', and to Speen to see the Lady Well. More ambitiously she took them to Fleet Street in London, the home of the British newspaper industry. On the way the coach stopped at Reading to pick up a student who lived at the YWCA in the town.

As Shirley had started the course a term late, she was not surprised to find that she was not ready for the examinations; so she decided to take the course again. However, before she finished, she managed to add to her cherished autograph collection. She still has the book as a keepsake. Arthur Owen is in there, so are Charles Sully and John Trodden. 'It was such a small place – we all must have got together.'

Second time round, and all Shirley's classes had been relocated to the Community Centre. On Monday, 15 September 1952, Shirley caught the train into Newbury and walked the short distance along Station Road. Starting with her were **Jill Delaney, Vi Chandler** and **Rosemary Lambourn.**

'So that's how I came to the college, with a bit of a push from my parents'

Jill Delaney lived in Lambourn where she spent all her schooldays. Her friend Vi Chandler joined her there when she was 11. Rosemary Lambourn, like Jill, also went to an all-age school, staying at Hungerford until she was 15. All three girls had taken the eleven-plus, but none of them had passed. Rosemary's disappointment was far from unusual, an unfortunate consequence of the 1944 Education Act.

> I was expected to pass but I didn't, so I stayed at Hungerford Council School. I was very upset and I went home and cried my eyes out. My three friends had passed. If I'd passed I would have gone to high school where I'd set my heart on going. It was the end of my dreams for what I wanted to do, to teach domestic science. When I didn't pass the eleven-plus, I remember going with my

parents to the school and it was said that I couldn't go on to college, university or whatever. So that was the end of that. I should have loved to have gone to university, but you can't put the clock back. All that stemmed from one day, when I didn't put my back into the examination. It was a very unhappy period in my life.

Like a lot of people today, I didn't know what I wanted to do when I left school. I remember my mother encouraging me and saying the college is a very fine place for me to go to for a bit more education, which she thought I needed. I didn't want to do office work, but my parents encouraged me into doing something like that. You had to get a career, as it were. So that's how I came to the college, with a bit of a push from my parents. People these days have got so many options, but in those days there weren't. Basically it was college or work.

If Rosemary was unsure about her future, Vi Chandler was just the opposite. She knew what she wanted to do.

I wanted to be a nurse. In those days you could not start training until you were 17 and a half. We had a youth employment officer who came to the school and said, 'Go into a factory or something until you are 17 and a half.' I didn't really want that. The alternative was to do one of the courses at the college. So that's how I came. It was drummed into us by our parents. 'You are very lucky. At your age we were out working. You are staying on until you are 16.' I thought I was very privileged in not having to go into a factory.

The entrance examination was taken early in the summer. The two school friends, Jill and Vi, journeyed into Newbury together. The day was warm and sunny, but Jill in particular was in for something of a shock.

We had to be at Ormonde House at nine o'clock. We came in thinking we were coming for an interview, but when we arrived we were suddenly confronted with an entrance exam. We did the exam in the huts at the back, two hours maths and a couple of hours English, and then we were allowed out. It was such a shock to the system, to think you were going for an interview and having to sit all morning doing exams. They didn't tell us that. In the afternoon, we had an interview with the Principal. He had his office upstairs. He had his back to the window and you stood in front of him. He told me that I had no worries that I would get in because I had passed well enough on my maths; he hadn't got the English result. That was the only time I ever saw Mr Owthwaite.

Vi passed as well, although she remembers being 'as nervous as anything'. Rosemary had an anxious wait. 'I had to go to the headmaster at Hungerford and ask him if I had a place at South Berks College. He couldn't understand how anxious I was about what was going to become of me at that stage.' Rosemary passed, and the disappointment of the eleven-plus was forgotten.

'It was such a drab building'

There were around 15 students selected for the course in the summer of 1952. They came from Newbury, Didcot, Hampstead Norreys, Highclere, Hungerford, Lambourn and Wickham. One of them travelled from Reading. Many were girls, a few were boys, 'but there weren't many boys left at the end of the course'. Hardly any had been to grammar school although two girls from Didcot 'were better educated than we were'. They had been to a convent school. 'They knew it all when it came to geography, maths and things like that so they could spend all their time on their bookkeeping, shorthand and typing. They were top of the class and we were holding the bottom up. Put another way, they were just revising and we were learning.'

Many of the students travelled by 'good old steam train', with the LEA paying for their season tickets. Rosemary Lambourn boarded the train at Hungerford, Shirley Woodage at Hampstead Norreys. 'I had a good half-mile walk to get to the station. We used to have a shoe repairer and he always used to set his watch by me.'

The Didcot girls were already on the train. Jill Delaney came in on the Lambourn Valley line with 'all the high school and grammar school lot – and they all had their uniforms'. The only time she was late for college was when they were 'loading racehorses' on the train at Lambourn station. When classes finished at the end of the day, Jill remembers the 'mad dash' to the station. 'Once Vi fell downstairs. We were rushing and I'd gone down first and I suddenly heard all this noise. I looked round and there was Vi bouncing down there. And then we both burst out laughing! I felt very guilty. She could have broken her leg.' Vi Chandler often went home by car. 'I lived at Wickham, down the old Ermine Street. Mr Pocock came from the same village and he offered to give me a lift in every morning and take me home at night.' So at the end of the afternoon, Vi would walk through the town along Northbrook Street and up to Ormonde House. The car was parked in the front drive and she would get in and wait until Mr Pocock was ready to leave.

Rosemary's memory is of a world of navy blue. 'It was coats, macs, navy blue was the accepted colour.' Shirley: 'At College you could wear what you want.' Jill: 'Basically we went in what we had been to school in. We didn't have uniform at school, only the Grammar School did. We had nothing to show we were at college. It would have been lovely just to have a scarf. We had left school. We were semi-adults. In those days you weren't too adult too early. We didn't have the fashion or the money that the children have today.' Rosemary: 'We weren't supposed to be adults at 16. What you think of as adult now at 15 or 16 is nothing like what we were supposed to be. We still had the ideas that they have today but we weren't allowed to carry them out. You kept them quiet.'

The entrance to the Community Centre was through a pair of iron gates on Bartholomew Street, opposite the junction with Pound Street. The gates opened onto a yard, and running along the north side, parallel with Station Road, was the two-storey building. Downstairs was the kitchen and a snack counter. 'It wasn't a canteen. It was like a tuck shop, a little place where we could buy crisps or whatever. We used to sit down there and eat our sandwiches and packed lunches.' 'We used to have a break halfway through the morning for ten minutes, for our bars of chocolate and that. You went to a little hatch and someone served you.' 'You could get anything cold, crisps and things like that, nothing cooked. It was very basic, not like a canteen. It was a hole in the wall.' The downstairs room was large enough for a stage and a piano. 'At weekends they used to have country dancing and hold a youth club.' A 'wide staircase' of 'horrible concrete stairs' led to the two classrooms above. Rosemary evocatively remembers the smell. 'When I walk into a highly polished room now, the smell of the polish takes me straight back to that Community Centre. That room we used to go in, it always smelled very highly of polish.' Outside was the 'old fire escape'.

Jill Delaney's introduction to the world of FE was 'one big disappointment'.

> We thought we were going to college at Ormonde House. It was only towards getting near to starting that we were told to report to the Community Centre. It was an awful shock when we were told, 'This is where you're going to have your lessons.' It was such a drab building. The windows all had wire mesh in them and you couldn't have them open because it was too noisy. It really was depressing. At lunchtime we had to go down the town just to get out of the building.

> The accommodation was occasionally used by day-release chaps. They weren't in our course – they were doing engineering or something like that. We only ever saw them once or twice a week.

'I couldn't get the hang of this shorthand lark – it was absolutely dreadful'

The learning environment was uninspiring, and the course was hard. Jill: 'The work was totally different from the sort of education you'd had at school.' The 'secretarial bits' were taught alongside the general subjects, and 'it was very much like what we call a sixth form now'. Shirley struggled, even though she had done some of the course before. 'We learned things that we had never learned at our secondary schools. That is why we found it hard.'

Gladys Sugg taught the commercial subjects. She was an active Christian, as was Rosemary Lambourn, who belonged to a youth group in Hungerford known as the Christian Endeavour. 'I was telling Mrs Sugg about it. I don't know whether she suggested or I suggested that she came down and had a look. I had to go and meet her off the train and I took her down to where we met in Hungerford. I remember walking back with her to catch the train after.'

The 'secretarial bits' were new to many of the girls. Pens dipped in bottles of coloured ink were used for the figures in bookkeeping. 'The credits were blue and the debits were red.' Vi had not done anything like this before – 'we started that sort of thing from scratch' – but she soon found she loved shorthand. Rosemary, in contrast, found the typewriting, and especially the shorthand, difficult. She learned to type on a machine fixed to the desk and she was not allowed to look at the keys.

> We had desks, the ones that the typewriter went down in the well. When it was your time, you put your typewriter up. They were fixed to the top as such, but when you put them down they made another top for you. I sat at the back, as far away from Mrs Sugg as I possibly could, and she'd say, 'You're looking at the keys. You will have a cover on your typewriter.' They used to put on covers if you looked at the keys because we had to touch type. I never actually got mine covered.

> I guess the way we were taught was very good; to do the things we did on the manual typewriter, an old Remington or something. But when I first started, for quite a while I didn't enjoy the shorthand and the typing at all. I hated it. I couldn't get the hang of this shorthand lark – it was absolutely dreadful. On many occasions I went out at lunchtime and thought, should I go back? I used to go home at night and cry because I couldn't do it and I was absolutely hopeless at everything. And my mother said to me one day, 'Well look, if you really don't like it, you can give it up.'

That very week we had some test or other – like we were always having with Mrs Sugg – that I dreaded and went hot and cold about before I started. We were in class, getting the results, and I was thinking, I will be last or bottom or whatever. And Mrs Sugg stood up and said, 'I don't know whether you'll actually believe who has come top.' Nobody moved. I knew it wasn't me – but it was me as it happened. And she said, 'I can't really believe this!' She didn't know how I'd managed it – neither did I at that stage. There was one symbol which I hadn't got right, the symbol for a dash. After that, it wasn't so bad. From then on, this shorthand lark actually clicked.

'It wasn't like being at school – it was a more adult line of teaching'

Vi Chandler: Miss Garlick was a great favourite, very strict, very manly-looking, always wore tweeds, and hair cut straight. She was lovely.

Shirley Woodage: Miss Garlick was a trained teacher; she had been to college. She was absolutely lovely, really old-fashioned with thick horn-rimmed glasses and great thick stockings. She took us for the academic subjects. She made an impression 'cos she was lovely.

Jill Delaney: I used to look forward to going into Miss Garlick's class. She was very tall. We all thought when we saw her she was ever so strict. She would speak her mind, very much so, but she was lovely. We all adored her, we really did.

Rosemary Lambourn: Miss Garlick was lovely. I can picture her. She was a very kindly lady; she was a very amusing lady. One thing I remember is that she never said, like we'd always been taught to say, 'Trafalgar'. It was always 'Trafflegaar'. The first time she stood up and said something about 'Trafflegaar' I thought, what is she talking about?

Caught in this drift of memory, Vera Garlick is seen as vividly as if she is still in the room with us. One of the old school of Newburians, born and bred in the town, educated under Jane Luker at the County Girls' School, away to study at the University of London and then returning to Newbury to teach at Shaw House. 'She took us for English,' remembers Mick Terry. 'She was good. I always remember her telling us that she much preferred to teach boys than girls. And we thought, lovely, very interesting.' Vera Garlick joined the college in 1952, an 'all-rounder', teaching English, literature, geography and history. Not seeing eye-to-eye with Albert Owthwaite, she left in 1954, only to return two years later with a new Principal at the helm.

'Goody-two-shoes I am not, but I was always very keen and I enjoyed my time there.' Vi loved books and English was her favourite subject. 'I had a grandmother who was a schoolteacher, and when I was a child, you always had a book you ought to read. My cousin used to say, not another book from Grandma!' Vi still has her exercise books with the work she did with Vera Garlick on John Buchan's *Prester John* and William Thackeray's *Vanity Fair*. She read essays by Hilaire Belloc, G K Chesterton and J B Priestley, and there was a 'little bit' of poetry, Lord Tennyson and Robert Graves. There was language work as well and for her first piece of written work, an essay on 'Courage', she was given a disappointing one out of ten. 'It was very hard.' There followed essays on a variety of topics: 'The Happiest Person I Know', 'Cats', 'Valentines', 'Pancakes', and 'Uncles'. She got nine out of ten for a description of Northbrook Street. In history, she learnt about the agricultural and industrial revolutions, the British Empire and the American War of Independence. In geography there was a lot of tracing, colouring in maps with red and blue ink and sticking them into her exercise book.

'There was one male teacher at one point.' This was Dick Edwards, who taught arithmetic, a subject many of the girls found difficult.

> I wonder if he can remember us – 'They were the most hopeless class I ever had in all my life!' I remember a group of us being taken into a room and being told that our maths weren't good enough. It was virtually half the

class. I can't remember who actually gave us a bit of a
dressing-down, someone a bit higher than the teacher, but
I remember being told off.

One day each week the pressure was off; it was the 'relaxation
afternoon'. The girls made their way to Ormonde House and the
conservatory. 'We had dressmaking on a regular basis, but it was
not really part of the course. We had this awful old treadle sewing
machine.' Jill: 'It wasn't serious dressmaking – it was just a break
from lessons. We designed our own patterns. I made a dirndl
skirt, just a circular skirt.' Shirley: 'You went to Camp Hopson
and looked in a book. I saw a picture of a dress I liked and I had
to design it on graph paper. It was black. I was proud of that.'

'We had homework every night –
you didn't have a night off'

Evenings meant homework, and it had to be done. 'People
like Miss Garlick, and certainly Mrs Sugg, were disciplinarian,
probably a lot more than lecturers are now.' 'Mrs Sugg wouldn't
let you get away with you not doing your homework in the
bookkeeping; you had to hand your books in the next day. You
did it because you'd been brought up to. You did what you
were told to do.' Vi Chandler used to think she was given more
homework than her brother who was at Newbury Grammar
School. 'We were trying to cram everything into one year.' Her
brother worked while listening to Dick Barton on the wireless; Vi
did her homework with 'no noise at all'. Jill used to finish hers
on the 20-minute train journey in the morning; Shirley sometimes
got help from her brother.

> While the grammar school girls could cope, it came hard to
> us. It was so difficult going from secondary school to this
> and having homework. We had homework every night.
> You didn't have a night off. You had your essays to write,
> reading up an English thing and having to put it in your
> own words. You had your arithmetic to do, bookkeeping,
> geography, history. At weekends, we seemed to have an
> immense amount. I can't remember anyone not doing it.

There was no getting away from it. At that time we were getting into dances but you had to have your homework done before you were allowed out.

There were tests at the end of the first term and 'if you didn't do too well, I don't think you were invited back the next term'. The examinations were in the summer. The students worked hard and Rosemary's sentiments were felt by all of them. 'I would have hated not to have passed at the end of it all.' The examinations were held in Ormonde House, which won Jill Delaney's approval. 'Just think we could have been down there for a year instead of up in that horrible building!'

At the end of your year you did your RSA in each subject. We had exams in every subject, English language, literature, history, geography, bookkeeping, shorthand, typing, commerce, arithmetic. Some were in the afternoon, some were in the morning. We had some time off which we thought was great – we don't have to go in until the exam starts. We were treated more like adults than when we were going to school, which is what we had been used to.

The end of the course and Mrs Sugg took them to Cooper's jam factory in Oxford. 'We had little pots of sample jam given to us.' Some of the girls brought their cameras to college to take photographs of their teachers: an individual one of Dick Edwards, a group picture of Gladys Sugg, Vera Garlick and Miss Sylvester. There was also a photograph of all the girls on the course, wearing full skirts, cardigans with the sleeves pushed up and white ankle socks. They are not wearing make-up. In Shirley's case, her father would not allow it.

The summer examinations were not quite the end as a few months later there was a prize-giving evening. This was held in the Plaza Theatre. Built nearly 30 years before by a local entrepreneur, the Plaza was planned as a multi-purpose entertainment centre with an arcade of shops. It became the venue for a variety of events in the town and was hired by the college for its prize-giving evening in 1953. The director of AWE Aldermaston presented the certificates and it was a big occasion for Rosemary and the others. 'I remember sitting in there waiting for my turn to come, thinking I was going to get up there and fall flat on my face. We shook hands with William Penney, and I remember going up and getting my certificates in fear and trepidation of this huge man. My parents were there, quite proud of me 'cos it's the only thing I'd ever done.'

'I don't know why I went to the college – I expect it was my dad'

From the autumn of 1953, with the rooms at the Community Centre needed 'to ease the overcrowding of Speenhamland School', the governors suggested that the Commercial course could be moved back to Ormonde House if alterations were carried out on the second floor to make 'one large classroom from two smaller rooms'.[9] Some time before, Albert and Elsie Owthwaite had vacated their flat, thereby freeing more rooms for teaching purposes. The proposal was adopted, the alterations were made and the course returned to Oxford Road. 'The introduction of Business Studies into Ormonde House meant the need for female students' toilets and we lost our precious store rooms.'[10]

Val Walters from Shaw House was one of those who enrolled in 1953. 'I only lived down the road', in Rowan Drive on the Shaw estate. She had done typewriting at school, so she had a head start over many of the other students. 'That's how I met my friend – we sat together because we were the only two in the class that could already do shorthand and typing.'

> When I went to Shaw House, all my friends except a couple went into the A-stream. I went into the B-stream. I didn't like that and I worked myself right up to going into the A-stream in the fourth year. When I left I was the top student, and Mrs Mott said, 'I've written in one of the reports – I'm not going to say who it is – that this person works hard and plays hard and thoroughly enjoys both.'[11] And that was me. I was pleased.

---

[9] BEC 18 September 1953.

[10] SBCFE 25 Years.

[11] Mrs Mott taught at Shaw House School from 1948 to 1970.

You could leave Shaw at 15. A lot of people just got jobs. There weren't that many people who did further education in those days and I don't know why I went to the college – I expect it was my dad. At college you could wear what you want. There were no restrictions, no uniform or anything like that. They expected you to be adult and to think for yourself – that's how it came over. I felt quite grown-up although they didn't push you as hard as school, 'cos they expected you to be a bit more adult, which was a good thing really.

Miss Garlick was a character. She was at Shaw House before she came to the college, and I followed her on sort of thing. She knew her stuff. She really knew her history and I went and bought the book about Newbury when she did it. She signed it for me.

You were in a position where if you really worked hard, you could get pretty good exams. We had hundreds of certificates! But the commercial side of things wasn't as it is now. As long as you could read, write and add up, you were alright. It's a bit different now.

Twelve months later, armed with her certificates in shorthand, typewriting, commerce, bookkeeping, English and history, it was time for Val to start work. 'There was no anxiety about getting jobs, and we would have been told about some jobs that were available just before we left college.' She got a job in the National Provincial Bank, by the bridge over the River Kennet 'in that building where Britannia is now'. She was pleased, especially as 'there were two of us from the college that went for it'. She was paid £3/10/- (£3.50) a week.

'With the progression to modern technology I often reflect on the days when I first learned to type on the old Remington and Underwood machines in the wooden well desks at Ormonde House'

Iris Matthews was another of the full-time students in the '50s. Iris was from Thatcham, and when I interviewed her she was still living in the house in Northfield Road where she was born. From Thatcham she went to Shaw House and then on to Ormonde House in 1953. This is her story.

I went to Thatcham School, which is now Francis Baily, but I didn't pass my eleven-plus. So my mother had a word with the headmaster and he recommended me to go to Shaw. Thatcham was an all-age school when I left. They had some girls coming from Brimpton on the bus, and they had one or two temporary classrooms put in the grounds. Youngsters I used to go to school with, their fathers worked at Colthrop. They employed a lot of people. They used to have big parties at Christmas. My father didn't work for Colthrop – he worked for the County Council.

I went to Shaw in '49. My birthday's at Christmas so I would have been nearly 12 when I went. I left when I was 15 and I went to the college in '53. I would have been nearly 16. I went from Thatcham to Shaw on the bus and walked up the long avenue, from the A4 right through to Shaw House. There were gates on the A4 and there was a lodge, the entrance to what was the private parkland. Shaw House was a private house up until the war, and then the family moved out. Some of the houses of Shaw were built then, and there were some girls came to Shaw House from there. We used to go through these park gates and up the avenue. The houses were over to our left and then there were green fields. We had quite a trek.

Shaw House was beautiful when I was there, it really was. It breaks my heart to think it's gone like it's gone. You had all the marble fireplaces and this long gallery along the back of the house, and that was all panelled. There was a door like you see in these stately homes, all concealed in the wood panelling, and there were wooden seats in the windows. It really was lovely. There were boys on the ground floor, but the girls had the majority of the floors. My first form was right on the top floor. They used to bring busloads of youngsters in from all the villages. Miss Garlick was my third-year teacher – she moved on to Ormonde House where I eventually met up with her again. I did a little bit of typing in the fourth year on a very part-time basis and got a little baby certificate for that, 19 words a minute, signed by Mrs Dolan, 28th July 1953. That was just before I left.

In those days, when girls left school, typing was one of the things to do because there weren't the opportunities then. Newbury hadn't got the commerce or the business that it's got now. The town was much smaller, so unless you went into office work or shops or banks – banks were always a good place to work – there wasn't really a lot to do. My parents thought that secretarial work was the right direction for me to go. My sister was already at work at the Electricity Board, having done a secretarial course at Mrs Spackman's, the private school at the other end of town in The Litten on the corner of Pound Street.[12] My sister went there during the war years, on a part-time basis.

We had to have an entrance exam and interview to get into the college, to see if we were suitable – they didn't take all and sundry. It was English and maths; we didn't do anything for typing. I went for the Commercial course, but because of the results of my exam I was put into the Secretarial which was slightly different, a higher standard. This was a two-year course, and you were expected to do more. It included shorthand and typewriting, English language and maths, and bookkeeping and commerce. It was like a full-time education, with homework, which was always a bit of a pain.

I know that if I hadn't gone to Shaw House – and I said this to my parents many times – I wouldn't have coped with the course. Going from Thatcham, an all-age school, I don't

---

[12] Newbury Commercial School, (Mrs H J Spackman, Principal),
   1 Newtown Road.

think I would have been of the right standard. There would have been too big a gap. Going into Newbury made you more independent – it was part of growing up. I had a free bus pass and getting to school on your own, that was a big step. There weren't many of us, eight or nine. There was the Commercial course running alongside it as well. I enjoyed it, and it was a nice little crowd we were with.

All the classes were in Ormonde House. We had a refectory and a common room. We took sandwiches and we could get a drink. The typing was upstairs and I can visualise the big staircase that came down. All the typewriters were in those big wooden well desks, which we used to pull out every morning and bring them up on a level, 'cos the lid went over it. You pulled this up, and that made your desk. They were the old Remington and Underwood machines, those funny old typewriters with the ribbons sitting on the top and the big basket in the middle. They used to have funny margin things – you had to manually move them on.

I can well remember typing to music and, being musical, this made the lessons more interesting and also fun. They were very particular. You had to learn like learning to play the piano, not like people today poking about on a keyboard. You had to learn the basics and place your fingers on the central row of keys and type rhythmically and with the same amount of pressure, 'cos the little fingers can be a bit weak. They put this music on and we used to sit down and type in rhythm. You would go along and then it would say 'carriage return', and we all had to do it. It was an exercise and you'd get this voice in between. I'd been taught to play the piano anyway. I started to play when I was seven or eight years old, so I enjoyed going along with this music. It was all touch typing. You were expected to look ahead or look at what you were typing, very useful training.

There used to be a weekly typewriting magazine which you bought from W H Smith or wherever, and there were exercises in there for you to do, manuscript work and things like that. On the front page you had a speed accuracy test paper, because that was the big thing, to be accurate in what you type. And the speed, you were timed on that to see if you could type it with the least mistakes. The magazine was recommended and we used it along with our course.

The manuscript work I used to enjoy, all the crossings out and the circlings round and that. And then you had set patterns. All these accuracy tests had the little figures down the side so you knew how many strokes you'd done. You deleted for any mistake, but they were all done in double spacing. You had a certain amount of tabulation work to do as well, like an account, bookkeeping. That was a pain. I couldn't stand bookkeeping. I struggled with it, but I did get a certificate. You had a mapping pen and red ink and this ruler, and you had to hope it didn't smudge. And there was a piece in your typing to do, tabulation work, your articles, your amounts of money and your total. The exam used to frighten you to death – the ink's sure to smudge.

Mrs Sugg was one of the teachers. She used to take the typing in my last year at Shaw. You always used pencil for shorthand so you got your thick and thin outlines. You could use a fountain pen, but pencils were recommended for speed. We had English and shorthand homework. You had to practice your outlines and learn the short form of things ready for the next class. You had Pitman's textbook to work to and you were set different exercises to present the next day. When we did English, we joined with the O-level class. There was a small group who did GCE, so we came together for that. Mr Edwards used to teach maths. Miss Garlick was a great historian. I treasure that book, her history of Newbury, 'cos I liked her. I was frightened to death of her when I first went to Shaw. She used to say she didn't like girls very much. She'd been in a boys' boarding school so she was used to boys. A very clever lady, but a great disciplinarian. She always wore the pinstripe suits. She left Shaw and went to the college and we met up again.

We worked hard with exams at the end of the course. The main ones were for shorthand and typewriting. We did an exam in the morning and then we had the afternoon off and we used to go down to the swimming pool. Then it was time to look for a job. The course set us in good stead to go on to employment, as a qualified typist and secretary.

I could find work. The first interview I went for was at Elliott's but I obtained a post as junior shorthand typist with New Brothers, the seed merchants in Bartholomew Street, on £4/10/- (£4.50) a week. I got it from the Newbury paper, as we were advised to do. By the time you'd been at college for two years, you were expected to stand on your own feet and find yourself a job. You were an adult and you had to look out for yourself. Also we were advised at the college to go to a job and stay there for a twelvemonth or so, because it didn't look good to have lots of different jobs on your application forms – you know, go there for a few months and then leave and go somewhere else, like they do today as if it doesn't matter.

I started work in August '55. I was nearly 18. New Brothers was a family business, big premises with a huge yard at the back for all their lorries and everything. It was interesting 'cos we had a lot of dealings with farmers and the farming community. My mother had come from a farming background and I had always lived in Thatcham, which was a village, so I was used to the countryside. I had a new typewriter and it had what they call the magic margin. You could take it along to wherever you wanted it, set it, press a key and it set the margin automatically.

'In those days it was considered a great honour to gain a place at the South Berks College'

Jennifer Foster lived in Maple Crescent in Shaw and went from Shaw House School to South Berks College in 1957.

At Shaw House they didn't do external examinations of any sort. There were no O-levels taken. They just didn't do it, because we had been graded at eleven, the eleven-plus, and considered wanting. They didn't bother with people after that. I didn't pass the eleven-plus but most of my friends did, so it was a bit of a wrench. They went to the Girls' High School and the rest of us went to Shaw. When I was thirteen I could have gone to the High School – the top three in the top class were asked if they would like to go – but my parents couldn't afford all the uniform and everything, so I didn't go. It was quite simple: if you wanted to teach or to nurse, you had to have gone to high school in those days.

When I was 14 we had to make a choice, typing or cooking, and I hated cooking, so it was decided for me really. Mrs Spackman from The Litten came to teach us. The typing was on manual typewriters. We were up in the attics in Shaw House. You used to type away in these attics and you were thumping away at the keyboards, doing the carriage return, and the floor would be going up and down. I had a year with her at Shaw, shorthand and typing. I left at 15. The headmistress was not happy. She wanted me to stay on, calling me into her study to tell me I was being very silly leaving school and would I reconsider. I would have done a commercial course – you could do that if you wanted – but I was glad I didn't. I never regretted the move. Val Walters went to college three years or so before I did. We knew her and my parents thought it wonderful that she had got to college. 'Why don't you do something like that?' It went on from there.

There were only 12 places on the course. You had to sit this entrance exam to get in. That was a bit of a trial because we had never done anything like that. I took the exam at the Waterside Chapel. I remember the large room with all these individual desks – 30 maybe – being so far apart, as they are for exams. It was a new experience for me, quite demanding. It was English in the morning and maths in the afternoon. The English was fine and I enjoyed doing that. We had to write an essay. We had four choices and I chose to write about a favourite television programme which I was watching at the time, *Emergency Ward Ten*. The maths in the afternoon was like maths always is for me, a bit of a disaster. I remember staggering home afterwards, feeling very drained.

We were then called for an interview at the college with Mr Lansley. His room was on the first floor of Ormonde House. At the top of the stairs was a wide landing where there were chairs on which we sat and waited. I remember him saying, 'Your maths wasn't much, but your English was so good we'd like to take you anyway.' I have fond memories of Eric Lansley. He was a lovely man, what we would now call a real old-fashioned gentleman. He used to live at the end of Donnington Square, on the corner with the Oxford Road. He was a really nice person.

Monday morning, 16 September 1957, and Jennifer and the other students assembled in Ormonde House. There were 11 girls, and at least two of them were from Shaw House. Making up the 12 was a young man who was not old enough to join the police force. 'He would fill his year in by going to college. He thought the shorthand would help him with court notes and things.' By 1957 the Commercial course had changed. It still included English, shorthand, typewriting, bookkeeping and arithmetic, but history and geography had gone, and so had the recreational afternoon. Instead it was office practice, 'filing, telephone, that sort of thing', and some work experience.

Part of our course was to do some time working in the general office, a day here and there, each term. It wasn't much we were allowed; it was just to say we'd been there and had a go. There was no work placement outside college. The course wasn't very sophisticated. Nowadays it's really thorough, this and that and everything else. Things have moved on so. We covered the same things, but it wasn't so specialised. Mr Jakins was our form teacher, in overall charge of us. He was a biggish chap, black hair – he used to wear it oiled down. He took us for bookkeeping, at which I was no earthly good whatsoever. We were right up on the top floor with him. We had a little classroom at the back. There was a fire escape, a metal thing, right outside the window.

Miss Garlick was an incredible person. She had a very dry sense of humour. She could wither any thoughts of messing about with a single glance. She used to say, 'If you don't do it, you don't do it. I don't care. You will be the one who will suffer.' Oh, she was great! She could destroy anyone, just with a comment. She spoke her mind, but she was jolly good, she really was. She was a real character. I liked her – we used to get on well. I gained my only O-level, in English Language, under Vera Garlick's supervision.

Homework was a bit of a shock. At Shaw, no one had really bothered with homework – it was something we weren't used to. I don't remember anyone being in trouble for not doing it. We all did it, we all wanted to do it, and we all wanted to be there. That was the difference with school. It was very friendly in those early days. There weren't very many of us. It was all very cosy, a very nice atmosphere. One or two of us were friendly, but I don't remember any social life at all. Although there were mechanics, we didn't see much of them. It was simply there as a school: you went there, you did what you had to, and you came home and did your homework. The strongest impression I have of the early days is of being treated as an adult and not a schoolgirl. We were treated so differently from school, it was amazing. The way the teachers approached you, 'How do you feel if we do so-and-so today?' There was no 'Sit down and do that!' It was a different attitude altogether. I respected that, and we responded to it. It was so different to what you had been used to, being ordered around.

In the spring of 1958, building contractors moved on to the site. From their classroom at the top of the house, the business students had a bird's eye view of what was going on. 'The foundations were laid down for the new buildings to be erected at the rear of Ormonde House, and from our vantage point in a top floor room we could keep watch on the developments.' A few weeks later and it was time for examinations, 'Pitman, RSA, that sort of thing', and in Jennifer's case, the O-level in English Language. Then it was out into the world of work, to a shop which provided guns for Newbury's farmers, gamekeepers and country gentlemen.

> The college used to try and find jobs for everyone – they tried very hard. I went to Turner the gunsmiths, in Northbrook Street.[13] The college got me that. It was Mr Lansley who said to me about it. 'How would you feel about working at so-and-so? Would you like to go along and see them and see what you think?' And it went on from there. I started more or less straight after the course, general office work, £5 a week.

> I thoroughly enjoyed the year at college. What I'd learnt was useful. It was a good starting point as it got you into working life, used to the way things happen.

'It was an all-round course – we did everything'

While the young women were busy with their typewriters and shorthand notebooks in Ormonde House, the pre-apprentices were 'round the back' and **Derek Loosen** was one of them.

Derek was born in London just before the war. An engineer in a 'protected trade', his father was not called up for military service; but when the aerial bombing of the capital started, Derek was sent to live with his grandmother in Wales. His father stayed in London, but reporting for work one morning, he found his factory had suffered a direct hit. 'All that was standing was one wall.' His employer, however, had another factory in Newbury, and Derek's father went to work there. The family 'finally got

---

[13] Thomas Turner & Sons, sports outfitters and gunsmiths, 86 Northbrook Street.

together again' in Hermitage. Not long afterwards they moved to
Thatcham. Derek went to the Council School when Mr Dominy
was the headmaster. 'I was one of your B-pass eleven-plus people
and I didn't pass the interview, so I stayed on until I was 15 and
then went to college for a year.' Following his father's advice – 'he
was one of the old school and you had to have a trade' – Derek
signed up for the Pre-Apprenticeship course. It was 1954.

> I came to college by bus. There were plenty of buses
> running in those days. They used to come from all the
> villages – Bucklebury, Cold Ash, Brimpton, Tadley and all
> those places. At the bottom of Henwick Lane there used
> to be 20 people at a time to wait for the bus.

> There were 16 in the class, all boys, and all school leavers.
> A couple came from Didcot and went to Harwell after the
> course. We did everything. It was quite unusual; they don't
> do anything like it now. It was regimented, like being at
> school. It was an all-round course. It brought us up to the
> standard that we'd have been at Park House. By the '60s,
> the education system had changed. All the schools had
> been upgraded as secondary schools, like Kennet. Thatcham
> Council School ceased to be a school for 11 to 15 – it was
> just a primary school. Other schools did the same, so there
> wasn't the need to bring us up to a certain level of education.
> The course was tailored to bring our level of education
> up to a standard so that we could cope with being an
> apprentice. We had electrotechnology, which was electrical
> not electronics; chemistry; workshop practice, which was
> workshop technology; garage practice, or autotechnology;
> woodwork; technical drawing and design; science; algebra,
> geometry, arithmetic, trigonometry; and history and English.
> At the end we did UEI exams, written exams.

> My most vivid remembrance was the chicken house out
> the back. We went into this long building, all wood, off
> the ground. They still had the little trap at the back. The
> heating wasn't very good. We had English in there, with
> a reverend in his dog collar. He'd been a paratrooper in

the paras or the war. The class was a mixture of literature and language. We even had to submit essays. History was my strong subject. It wasn't kings and queens – it was the industrial revolution from the beginning through to the modern day.

Charlie Sully was the guy who used to do garage practice. We used to do it in a building on the side of a house at the back – viscosities, oil, and all those sorts of things. The bit I didn't like was taking the engines apart and putting them back together. We had quite a few engines. There was nothing that worked properly. We had to get an engine, strip it down, rebuild it and get it going. We ground and re-ground sinks and valves, that sort of thing. It was primarily for whoever was going to go into garage fitting – mechanics – to give them an idea of what was involved. But it didn't matter what you were going to do eventually or what line you were going to go into – we all did it. I didn't do very well in that – it wasn't my forte. As I ended up as a mechanical engineer, that was stupid, wasn't it? If a car goes wrong, I don't even bother, and I did that course!

We used to do science down behind what was the old Boys' Club in Northbrook Street. There was a big building with a white façade that had a green door – Frankie Vaughan's song *The Green Door* was out at the time. We went in a little side door in Albert Road, and it backed on to what was the Boys' Club. We used to go in there and have mechanicals. We were shown a lathe and the lecturer did all the work on it. We didn't actually work at one. We were shown by the lecturer what you did and what happened and then he used whatever he told us in some bits of theory. We did chemistry as well in there.

We also used to go to the old chapel down by the Waterside. It was a dull-looking building, a bit austere, a horrible place it was, really old with ivy growing all over it. And in the grounds there was this old wartime pillbox overrun with creepers and everything else. When we were down there, at lunchtimes we used to go Victoria Park and there were girls from the college there. On other days we used to either take sandwiches or, at the end of Park Street, there used to be a coffee bar. There was a record shop at the top of Park Street, called Alphonse Cary, and they sold musical instruments, sheet music and records.[14] We used to spend our lunchtimes in there listening to records, and go down the road to the coffee bar.

At the end of the course everybody went their own different ways. I went to Aldermaston on a five-year apprenticeship and I wouldn't have gone there if I hadn't done that course as I would not have passed the entrance test The education that we got at the Council School was basic 'cos in those days if you didn't pass your eleven-plus, you were forgotten. At Aldermaston they had a strenuous selection, a test and two interviews. When you got to the second one you were more or less in – it was to check your security rating more than anything else. I joined Aldermaston in September 1955, and my indentures state that I was going to be trained as an instrument maker. I came back to college on day release, mechanical engineering. I was doing City & Guilds Machine Shop Engineering to start with; then you could transfer into the Ordinary National. City & Guilds was for the ones that hadn't got GCEs. It was practical.

---

[14] Alphonse Cary, musical instrument manufacturers, 47 and 48 Northbrook Street.

10

PLAYING THE ATOMIC CARD

The Ministry of Education agree that there is a need for the rapid development of FE in this area, particularly in view of the establishment of atomic energy research stations at Harwell and Aldermaston, and of the great demand for day and evening technical and professional courses in the neighbourhood.

Co-ordination Subcommittee 25 May 1951

We have agreed that because of the special requirements in the Newbury area due to pressure created by the Ministry of Supply, provision should be treated as exceptional and approved on projects additional to what might be regarded as the normal major building programme allowed to the County.

Minister of Education 1952

The largest single employer of young people requiring Technical Education is the Atomic Energy Research Establishment.

FESC 12 July 1957

I n 1952 Britain exploded its first atomic bomb. The message to the world was clear: Britain had moved into the nuclear age, the third member, with America and Russia, of the world's most exclusive club. The 1950s was the time of the Cold War when the armed camps of the USA and the USSR faced each other with a military arsenal far more destructive than any weapons ever known to man. These were the years of NATO and the Warsaw Pact, the division of Germany and the Berlin Airlift, the Korean War and the Soviet invasion of Hungary. Russian communism in the East was the big bad wolf of the collective imagination of the West. It was the Cold War which brought the American GIs back to Newbury and it was widely believed that the planes at Greenham Common were armed with atomic bombs. Towards the end of the decade, the Campaign for Nuclear Disarmament (CND) was launched. With its thousands of supporters, it became the most celebrated pressure group of the day, arguing that there was a peaceful alternative to nuclear weapons.

These were also years of espionage. In the summer of 1946, German-born scientist Klaus Fuchs took up his post at AERE Harwell. During the war he had been recruited into the West's secret atom bomb project and while working in Britain and later in the USA, he gave Soviet agents valuable information about his work. This spurred on the USSR to develop its own bomb and helped the Soviet project come to fruition. Fuchs came to Harwell as head of theoretical physics. Few people knew as much about atomic bombs as he did, and he continued to betray Britain's nuclear secrets to the USSR – until 1950 when he was arrested and sentenced to 14 years imprisonment. Fuchs was not the only betrayer of Harwell secrets. In 1951, Bruno Pontecorvo, another AERE scientist, defected to Moscow where he was rewarded with a job in nuclear research.[1]

Britain's decision to develop its own atomic bomb was taken in early 1947 by Prime Minister Attlee and a small group of ministers. From the beginning the work was shrouded in secrecy, and even Parliament was not told of the programme initially. Yet few people doubted that Britain should have the weapons that the two superpowers possessed. The development of a nuclear deterrent – 'the bomb with a bloody Union Jack on it' – went forward independently of the United States. In 1957 Britain exploded its first hydrogen bomb on Christmas Island in the Indian Ocean. Then, the following year, the USA became a partner in the project and Britain's independent nuclear tests were halted.

---

[1] N Moss, *Klaus Fuchs, The Man Who Stole the Atom Bomb*, (London: Grafton Books, 1987), p.183.

Much of the research and development for Britain's nuclear arsenal was carried out in the countryside not far from South Berks College.

The Ministry of Supply was responsible for Britain's atomic energy programme. Early in 1946 the Ministry took possession of an area of land in Harwell on the north Berkshire downs. This former RAF airfield was where the government decided to build its Atomic Energy Research Establishment. Nuclear physicist John Cockcroft was appointed Director. Quiet-spoken, modest and retiring, he was the scientist who had been the first to split the atom. Now, in the late '40s and '50s, he recruited staff from all over the country to work in the atomic industry and involved himself in every aspect of Harwell life. He loved gardens and hired a landscape gardener who had been in the royal family's employ to lay out AERE's lawns and flower beds.[2]

At first most of the scientists and their families lived in the house on the site which had been RAF officers' quarters. Soon rows of prefabricated houses were put up and families moved into these as they were finished. As the numbers of people grew, houses were built in Newbury and Wantage and at Abingdon, where, thought John Betjeman, there was a 'really decent modern estate for the Atomics.'[3]

Harwell came to have two roles. It was a major academic research centre, its scientists producing work for publication in the field of atomic physics, sometimes in co-operation with universities. It also provided the scientific backup for the creation of atomic weapons and atomic power. The laboratories were built in the RAF hangars, as was Britain's first nuclear reactor and Harwell rapidly developed into one of the most important centres of atomic energy research in Europe.

---

[2] John Cockcroft (1897-1967) and E T S Walton were the first scientists to split the atom in 1932, an achievement for which they were awarded the Nobel Prize 19 years later. Cockcroft was Professor of Physics at Cambridge 1939-46 and Director of Air Defence Research during the Second World War. He was appointed Director of the Atomic Energy Establishment at Harwell in 1946, was knighted in 1948, and in 1959 became Master of Churchill College, Cambridge.

[3] John Betjeman to Lionel Brett, 25 January 1957, in Candida Lycett Green, ed., *John Betjeman, Letters, Vol. Two, 1951 to 1984*, (London: Minerva, 1996), p.120.

Recruitment of staff was not difficult as a lot of people wanted to work there. The work was exciting. Everything was a new area of investigation: the design of an atomic reactor, the dangers of radiation and how to protect against them, the production and use of radioactive materials. Scientists were offered greater resources for research at AERE than in a university or industrial laboratory. Some of those who had worked on the bomb were positively attracted by the prospect of developing atomic energy to help mankind. 'Harwell shared with the rest of Britain a sense of optimism, a feeling that a new and better world was coming now that the long war was over.'[4]

'The great attraction of Harwell in the '50s for young men was, they would offer day release as well as a house – it was the two things together'

The Ministry of Supply was committed to apprentice training. Each of its establishments had an apprenticeship board responsible for the 'selection, training and vocational guidance of apprentices'. There were training workshops on site complemented by day release to the local college. The 'dominant feature' of the Ministry's scheme was the provision of a workshop where for one year the young apprentice could be given practical training in the basic hand and machine skills by an instructor whose sole duty this was. Few apprentices nationally had the advantage of being trained in a centre set apart for basic instruction. In the world of education and training in the austerity of the post-war years, these were 'revolutionary features'.[5]

At Harwell an apprenticeship board was established, a training workshop set up in Hangar 9 and on 7 September 1948, 13 young men were signed on, seven craft and six engineering apprentices. The craftsmen were local boys living at home with their parents; the engineers were recruited from all over the country. Many of them were housed in a hostel, Portway House, which a few years

---

[4] Moss, *op.cit.*, p.95.

[5] The Ministry's establishments included Radar Research at Malvern, Royal Aircraft at Farnborough and the Royal Ordnance factories such as Woolwich Arsenal in London.

earlier had been an NCO's mess. The apprenticeship was for five years. The craft boys were to be trained for the workshops, the engineering apprentices hoped to become professional engineers. Their instructor was John Wallace.[6] 'I found myself in charge of a small training shop and 13 budding engineers.'

Harwell's apprenticeship scheme was born, coincidentally, a week before Ormonde House opened its doors in Newbury. Maurice Marchbanks was chairman of the apprenticeship board from 1948 to 1957. He worked with South Berks College and sat on both the electrical and the mechanical advisory committees in the 1950s.

'Harwell established a national reputation which brought visitors from near and far to study the training methods'

The apprentices spent their first year in the workshop learning the basic hand and machine skills. The trades for which they could be trained included tool and gauge maker, turner, miller, moulder and coremaker. The centre was equipped for mechanical engineering, with four lathes, two milling machines, two drilling machines, a shaper, a surface grinder, a band saw and a brazing hearth. Each apprentice made a selection of small tools which would embody in their design most of the essential lessons. Yet the training was not limited to the development of technical skills. It was seen as 'equally important to develop character and produce the type of employee that any employer would be proud to have on his staff.' John Wallace and his colleagues were interested in the development of the whole person. 1949 saw Harwell's first prize-giving ceremony, from 1952 the Apprentice Association organised sports and social events, and the first Apprentice Newsletter appeared in 1956.

It soon became apparent that an annual intake of seven craft apprentices was not going to meet the needs of the rapidly expanding industry. Moreover, there was also a wish to provide opportunities for the many local boys who wished to train for engineering. Consequently a second training workshop was

---

[6] John Wallace was Harwell's Chief Instructor 1948-55, Apprentice Supervisor 1955-58 and Apprentice Training Manager 1958-78.

opened, another instructor was appointed and in September 1951, 15 craft and six engineering apprentices were taken on as well as the first graduate apprentice. This brought the total number to almost 100. By 1952, across the country, there were 31 Ministry of Supply apprentice schools with more than 500 first-year apprentices.[7]

In the '50s, the training developed to include both mechanical and electrical trades, in instrument making, electronics, instrumentation and control. The craft apprentices were the most numerous.

UNITED KINGDOM ATOMIC ENERGY AUTHORITY
HARWELL
CRAFT APPRENTICESHIP SCHEME

Applications are invited for a limited number of Craft Apprenticeships in the following engineering trades:-

FITTER GENERAL	TOOL MAKER
TURNER	SHEET METAL WORKER
MILLER	ELECTRICIAN
MILLWRIGHT	ELECTRONICS MECHANIC
INSTRUMENT MAKER	WELDER
INSTRUMENT MECHANIC	

NWN 29 March 1956

From 1954, the engineering apprentices were known as student apprentices. In 1958 an advanced training school (mechanical) was set up for those in their third and fourth years. Two years later, developments in electronics, instrumentation and control engineering encouraged the establishment of an advanced electrical workshop.

The young men were trained on site and given day release to college, in some cases a generous one and a half days. Those adults who wanted to study, especially those who had been denied the opportunity during the war years, had to go to night school. Some of these came to the Newbury Institute. Harwell

---

[7] *The First Thirty Years of Apprentice Training at Harwell*, (Harwell: Education and Training Centre, 1978), pp.4.2, 5.

asked the LEA to arrange a course which would lead to the Intermediate BSc examination of the University of London. Before the introduction of A-levels, this was a main route to university. In 1948, however, the resources at Ormonde House were inadequate, and the students went to Oxford instead. Within a year, however, the demand on Oxford was so insistent that A-level science subjects, which were to replace the Intermediate BSc, were begun at Newbury.[8] The demand from Harwell, and later Aldermaston, for such a course enabled Newbury to become an important centre for science A-levels.

In the early years a lot of Harwell employees went to Oxford College where 'seven or eight' ONC courses in engineering were run each week.[9] Sheila Smith's future husband was one of them. He did mechanical engineering and Sheila knew a lot of people who were doing National Certificates. 'They all went to Oxford and they used to run buses in at night to the college.'

The atomic connection

September 22, 1952, is one of those important dates in the history of South Berks College. This was when the first group of Harwell apprentices came to Ormonde House on day release. They were accompanied by apprentices from AWE Aldermaston, 90 students altogether. Many of the Harwell students lived in Berkshire, in Challow, Compton, Faringdon, Hampstead Norreys; and the LEA was reluctant to pay out-county fees for boys on ONC and City & Guilds courses which were now available at Newbury. Dick Greet pointed out that if the 90 apprentices had gone to Oxford or Reading, it would have cost Berkshire £3,000 in fees[10] – although, of course, 90 additional students meant a significant increase in teaching hours to be paid for at Newbury.

The apprentices enrolled in science and engineering: A-levels in mathematics, physics and chemistry, ONCs in Electrical

---

[8] Education in the Royal County of Berkshire 1958-59, Report by the Director of Education, p.36.

[9] *The First Thirty Years of Apprentice Training at Harwell*, p.2.

[10] NWN 15 January 1953.

and Mechanical Engineering, City & Guilds in Machine Shop Engineering. Some were school leavers, others transferred to Newbury from Oxford. Many came to night school and for those who lived in Harwell and Didcot, public transport was difficult. The education authority, however, was in no doubt that the numbers justified 'special arrangements' and a coach was hired to take the students home each weekday evening.[11] The Harwell coach became a familiar sight on the Oxford Road, at first in the evenings and then in the mornings as well.

This influx from AERE established the atomic connection at the South Berks College. Harwell continued to use Oxford, but hundreds of young people chose, or were directed by the Ministry of Supply, to study at Newbury instead.

For the first three years of the apprenticeship, the programme for both craft students and the engineers was similar.

> They spend a year in a training shop specially equipped to teach them the basic crafts of the machine and fitting shop; after this, they spend two years in the various shops learning by doing and helping. Throughout their training both craft and engineering apprentices attend courses at local technical schools, aiming at the different National Certificates as appropriate. At the end of their third year craft apprentices are asked which craft – turner, fitter, instrument maker, electrician, millwright and so on – they would like to follow and then they spend the remaining two years of their apprenticeship developing their specialist skill. The superintendent of apprentices plays an important part in advising boys on their choice if they are uncertain, since he watches their development closely and can form an accurate judgement of their abilities.

> Engineering apprentices go at the end of their third year to the drawing office or to a laboratory to continue training as professional engineers, their immediate goal being either a degree or associateship of the appropriate professional

---

[11] BEC 7 November 1952, 9 January 1953. The Reliance coach cost £8 a week in 1952/53.

institution. They may in certain circumstances be sent to a university. These boys are recruited from all over the country in an open competition organised by the Ministry of Supply; it is, however, by no means uncommon for craft apprentices to develop so well that they transfer to engineering apprenticeships at the end of their third year ...

Training concessions would be useless however unless there were schools offering suitable courses and the Establishment is fortunate in being near the excellent Technical College at Oxford and a new one that has been built in Newbury; close and cordial relationships are maintained with the advisory committees of both. These schools give courses that meet the needs of most part-time students from the Establishment over a wide range of subjects. Rather more than 250 students take examinations each year, most of them for National Certificates (Ordinary and Higher) and the General Certificate of Education (Advanced).[12]

Also at Newbury by the mid-'50s were the scientific assistants from Harwell's laboratories,

on a different footing from apprentices inasmuch as they are qualified to do a job, and are paid for doing it, from the start of their employment. On the other hand, the majority of them have not, on entering the Establishment, reached the educational limit of their intellectual capacities. It is therefore desirable not only in their own but also in their employer's interests to encourage them to take further technical training. The Establishment plays its part by allowing students time off with pay to attend courses and examinations, and by paying course and examination fees and extra travelling expenses. A student may be given some or all of these concessions depending on circumstances; the group leader under whom he works is responsible for making sure that the student's progress

---

[12] K E B Jay, *Atomic Energy Research at Harwell*, (London: Butterworths Scientific Publications, 1955), pp.71, 77.

satisfies the criterion upon which concessions are based, namely, that the additional training enables him to do more efficiently the job for which he is paid.[13]

'That strange, fluorescent kingdom'

In 1956 the Atomic Energy Authority, which had taken over responsibility for the industry from the Ministry of Supply, opened Harwell's security gates to invited guests and John Betjeman was one of them.

> Last week I passed through the concrete and chain-link fences which surround Harwell AERE (pronounced 'eerie' locally) for an Open Day, when the atomic piles were on view to specially selected members of the public. Perhaps I was not quite the person to ask, for though the scientists explained things to me as simply as they could and with the greatest courtesy, I could only pretend to understand what they were saying. I left with an impression that immense power was being generated somewhere, with no sparks, no explosions, no wheels and no noise. My idea of science is retorts, Bunsen burners and a stuffed crocodile hanging from the ceiling, and I must confess Harwell was a disappointment to one so behind the times as I am. Certainly the ladders, walls, and things containing uranium, plutonium and heavy water were painted in bright festival colours. All the other visitors seemed to understand what they were looking at and one of them made my flesh creep by telling me of what will shortly be revealed in a Government White Paper about the effects on health all over the world from the recent letting-off of hydrogen bombs. I was pleased to see the wind waving over the grass of the Berkshire Downs when I stepped out of that strange, fluorescent kingdom.[14]

---

[13] *Ibid.*.

[14] John Betjeman, *Coming Home – An Anthology of Prose*, Selected and Introduced by C Lycett Green, (London: Vintage, 1998), p.330.

Harwell's focus was research. The weapons to keep Soviet Communism at bay were assembled at Aldermaston. Here a wartime airfield was handed over to the Ministry of Supply on 1 April 1950 and the Atomic Weapons Establishment was developed on the site.

Sir William Penney, affectionately dubbed the 'atomic knight', was the Director. He was one of several British scientists who had worked in the USA on the development of the bombs dropped on Japan in 1945. He returned home with the details of the Nagasaki bomb in his head to become one of the leaders of Britain's nuclear weapons programme.[15]

Aldermaston's growth was as rapid as Harwell's and a community quickly developed in the village. Young married couples were provided with a home of their own and this influenced 'many newly-weds in their choice of employer'. Accommodation was built at a 'phenomenal rate' for the 'gigantic' influx of people. The initial scheme for over one hundred houses went ahead in 1951 and seven years later there were 1,100 on the AWE estate as well as shops, a library and a church. It was a youthful community and the average age of the 5,000 residents was 'fractionally over 30 years'. The welfare clinic was one of the largest around, with 450 children on its books and 100 mothers using it every week. The number of older children in the area put a 'considerable strain' on schooling and when the secondary school opened at Tadley in 1957, 85 per cent of the pupils came from the AWE estate.[16]

AWE employed almost 2,000 people within three years of its opening. Alan Gibbs went there in early 1952. 'There were a very small number of people there when I went. Then they had to produce the teams for going to Australia and Christmas

---

[15] Hennessy, *op.cit.*, p.267. William Penney (1909-91) was Professor of Mathematics at the Imperial College of Science in London. He worked at Los Alamos, New Mexico, on the atom bomb project 1944-45 and was an observer when the bomb was dropped on Nagasaki in Japan in 1945. He was Director of AWE Aldermaston 1953-59 and chairman of the UK Atomic Energy Authority 1964-67. He was the key figure in the UK's success in producing its own atomic (1952) and hydrogen (1957) bombs. Knighted in 1952, he was made a life peer in 1967 and Rector of London's Imperial College 1967-73.

[16] *NWN* 20 February 1958.

Island. They became massive and they were recruiting thousands of people.' The top secret work excited public controversy. At Easter 1958, several thousand CND supporters arrived outside the high perimeter fence, having marched the 50 or so miles from London. Their demand was for Britain's unilateral renunciation of nuclear weapons. There were more demonstrators the following year. Indeed, opinion polls showed that CND had the support of between one quarter and one third of the British public and in 1960, the Labour Party Conference adopted a resolution in favour of unilateral nuclear disarmament. Thereafter, however, the campaign seemed to lose some of its impetus although the annual Easter march to Aldermaston became a ritual in the history of peaceful protest in this country.[17]

AWE's five-year apprenticeship programme was started in 1952, and from the beginning, some of the apprentices went to South Berks College.

Newbury did not have a monopoly of the training. AWE also used the colleges at Reading and Basingstoke as AERE used Oxford; but Newbury had the highest number of atomic apprentices in the '50s. In the years of the Cold War, technical education at Ormonde House became a national and international priority. The college was 'rapidly expanding on the engineering side' and its location was ideal 'because there was a big overlap here in the Harwell and Aldermaston catchment areas'. Furthermore, as the needs of both establishments were similar, it became possible to run some classes 'almost entirely' for them.[18]

'One of the finest in the country'

There were 59 AWE apprentices in 1954, and Director William Penney was convinced that this 'would certainly increase in the near future.' It did, to 80 in 1955 and 120 in 1956, when the workshop for advanced training was opened. The aim was an annual intake of 30 apprentices until the total reached 150.[19] The target was reached, only to be surpassed. By the end of the decade

---

[17] Marwick, *op.cit.*, p.96.

[18] *The First Thirty Years of Apprentice Training at Harwell*, p.9.

[19] *NWN* 21 January 1954, 10 February 1955, 23 February 1956.

there were 170 with more anticipated with the bulge in school leavers in the early '60s.

A variety of trades were open to the craft apprentice: tool and gauge maker, fitter, turner, miller, planer, shaper and slotter, instrument maker, machine tool fitter. Training included mechanical, electrical and electronic subjects. The boys were carefully selected and expected

> to have attained a standard of education which will enable them to take full advantage of the technical instruction included in the craft apprenticeship course. All applicants are carefully tested and interviewed, with special attention paid to intelligence and mechanical aptitude. Experience has shown that it is unwise and contrary to the boy's interest to make any final decision concerning his ultimate trade until the general basic training has been completed. While boys are encouraged to express their preference for a particular trade, the early training period enables the apprentice training staff to assess a boy's abilities and aptitudes and to advise them accordingly.
>
> The first year of training is employed in teaching basic workshop techniques on the bench and on the machines. During the year, these techniques are utilised in the making of a tool kit which is made to a standard comparable to any in the country, and better than most. No distinction is made between mechanical crafts or electronic crafts at this stage because it is felt that these techniques have in common a skill useful to both sides. At the end of the first year of training, the apprentices divide into the two basic sides, namely mechanical or electronic. If an apprentice stops to follow the mechanical line, a further year will be spent in an advanced mechanical engineering workshop within the Apprentice School and then continue for approximately the next three years within a programmed scheme of study within the workshops and laboratories of the Establishment.
>
> An Electronic Craft apprentice after his first year divides into the Electronic course and follows a year's scheme

within the Apprentice School, during which time he is taught basic electronic techniques such as soldering, prototype chassis making, cable formation, wiring, testing faulty instruments. At the end of this year he now spends a further three years of programmed training within the workshops and laboratories appropriate to his craft.

Throughout the five years of training, the Craft Apprentices also follow courses of theoretical study at colleges in the vicinity of the Establishment. Most Craft Apprentices follow part-time day City & Guilds or National Certificate courses leading to the final certificate in Machine Shop Engineering or the final certificate of the Electrical Technicians' course. Occasionally Craft Apprentices also study for the National and Higher National Certificate in Mechanical and Electronic Engineering. One day per week is normally spent on these subjects.[20]

Apprentices for the drawing office were selected from the craft scheme. They had to have completed an Engineering ONC by the end of their third year and, if selected, they would continue their studies to HNC level.

Student apprentices were fewer in number, recruited by advertisement in the national press, followed by shortlisting and interviews in London. Slightly older than the craft apprentices, they came to AWE with A-levels. In the first year they were in the training workshops. 'On the practical side they undertake exactly the same course of practical training as a craft apprentice, and are expected to attain a very high standard of practical work even though their main interest may not lie in this direction.' There was also study at college, with release up to two days a week 'normally authorised'. The student apprentices usually took ONCs in Electrical and Mechanical Engineering, after which came higher education, to degree or HNC standard.[21]

The AWE apprenticeship – like that at Harwell – was one of the finest in the country, and competition for places was keen. In

---

[20] *AWRE News* January 1961.

[21] *Ibid.*.

1955, there were several hundred applications for the 22 craft and eight student places available, making selection 'extremely difficult'. In 1956 there were ten applicants for every place, while the following year it was anticipated that there would be 400 applications for 22 craft places.[22] The craft apprentices came from local secondary modern schools. 'As well as testing their intelligence and mechanical aptitude, we pay particular attention to the character of each of the candidates.'[23] The student apprentices – 'we like to feel they are capable of obtaining an honours degree at a university' – often came from a long way away. Of those first apprentices in 1952, 15 were taken on by AWE five years later, eight as draughtsmen, five as research and experimental mechanics and two as technical assistants. The majority of apprentices, once qualified, stayed at Aldermaston. In 1958, out of the 20 who completed their training, 16 stayed on. In 1961, 25 qualified, of whom 22 chose to remain at AWE.[24]

The recruits who were not local lived in the Blacknest hostel on Brimpton Common. Run by the YMCA with warden supervision, there were rooms for 60 people, a television lounge, a study and a room for hobbies. 'Midnight raids and all that sort of thing used to go on.'

> **Progress is Charted**
> Thoroughness is a keynote of training. 'The boys have to master each stage before passing on to the next', stressed Mr H E Fish, apprentice supervisor. Initial training is common to both craft and student apprentices for each boy has to know how to carry out filing, milling, grinding and lathe work. Individual progress is charted throughout, and parents are always kept in the picture. By the end of the first year, each apprentice will have made a set of tools, ranging from callipers to vices. These they are allowed to buy at scrap metal prices.

---

[22] *NWN* 14 February 1957.

[23] George Lindsay, chairman of AWE's apprentice board, in *NWN* 20 February 1958.

[24] *NWN* 27 February 1958; *AWRE News* January 1959, December 1961.

Accuracy and safety are points emphasised again and again. Much of the work is correct to less than a thousandth of an inch.

Safety First
All machine handles and levers are painted a warning red, while notices caution, 'Wear goggles – Your eyes cannot be replaced!' Working models of machines are made, and special equipment wanted on the site is frequently furnished by the apprentices.

To ensure they receive a broad engineering knowledge and liberal education, the apprentices visit industries varying from iron foundries to precision engineering works. Films and lectures are given in a well equipped hall. Once they have their basic grounding, craft apprentices can specialise in any branch of engineering for which they have shown particular talent or interest.[25]

Like at Harwell, the programme was more than technical training. AWE emphasised that it was 'not only looking after the young people during their working hours, but was catering also for their leisure activities.' It encouraged the boys in 'good citizenship' and how to 'work together'. There was concern for their social welfare, and there were lots of sporting activities and opportunities to go on Outward Bound courses. Recreational interests abounded: badminton, dramatics, archery, hockey, jazz, ballroom dancing, table tennis, angling, sailing, mountaineering, photography, motorcycling, soccer and boatbuilding. The Apprentice Association arranged dances, ran its own magazine, and invited prominent members of the Atomic Energy Authority to its annual dinner.

In particular for student and craft apprentices physical education is undertaken for at least one hour per week during the first and second years. After that, attendance is optional. A high standard of agility work is attained

---

[25] *NWN* 20 February 1958.

in a particularly short time and its aim is to develop a better co-ordination between hand and eye as well as to stimulate activity of thought through activity of body. Each year, selected apprentices are nominated for two other types of courses which are non-vocational, namely Outward Bound courses held in the Lake District, and weekend Keble College courses organised by the Industrial Welfare Society, or courses of a management nature. In each case, the aim of these courses is to develop skills and characteristics which are normally latent in craft and vocational study. Reinforcement and breadth is given to their training through the medium of films covering a wide range of topics, film strips, wall charts, and participating in trips to outside industry.[26]

Competition between the young men, and between the establishments, was encouraged. For the fortunate few, cups were awarded and the accolades flowed. There were glittering prizes to be won. The Harold Tongue Cup was open to all first-year Atomic Energy Authority apprentices in the country. It was won by Aldermaston in 1955 and again the following year. The Dolphin Cup was for AWE's top apprentice; the Craft Cup for the best set of tools made by a first-year craft apprentice; the Student Cup for the best tools made by a student apprentice; the Student College Cup for the best student apprentice at college; and the Craft College Cup for the best craft apprentice at college.[27]

There are a number of competitions both internal and external for cups, prizes and merit awards, and these are presented at the prize-giving day held each year to which parents, friends and distinguished guests are invited.

The prize-giving day includes an exhibition in the Apprentice School and an exhibition in the canteen. Emphasis in the school is usually placed on the type of work undertaken

---

[26] *AWRE News* January 1961.

[27] In 1961 both Craft and Dolphin Cups were won by young men who had completed the Pre-Apprenticeship at South Berks College.

by the apprentices still in the school, while the exhibition in the canteen includes work by apprentices who are in the various workshops and laboratories.

The prize-giving ceremony was an important occasion. With AWE staff, Roy Pocock was usually on the platform and lecturers from South Berks were on hand 'to demonstrate some of the electronics on display and answer questions'.[28] Parents were invited, shown round the Apprentice School – one of the few buildings on site which was not a security risk – and the hostel at Blacknest. The presentations were followed by 'fast-moving entertainment' by the boys themselves – dramatic sketches and skiffle music.

'The high number of university awards gained by part-time students was unusual in a college of this category'

The apprentice schemes were 'ideal', according to Roy Pocock, who personally managed the college's atomic connection. The Departments of Engineering and Science were dependent on Aldermaston and Harwell, whose students were 'in a better position than those from works tied to production'. There was more time for training, with less commercial pressure than in private manufacturing industry.

At the college Speech Day in 1955 the examination successes were proudly celebrated, with a record number of university scholarships for scientists and engineers. The Director of Education commented that 'the high number of state and university awards gained by part-time students was unusual in a college of this category.' South Berks was competing favourably with some of the biggest colleges in the country, with five technical state scholarships in 1956, and four in 1957 – when Reading College only had one.[29] These first university successes were Harwell and Aldermaston students.

---

[28] *AWRE News* December 1961.

[29] *NWN* 5 May 1955, 24 October 1957.

'This is the geographical and cultural centre for Harwell and Aldermaston'

The large numbers of atomic students at Newbury put great pressure on resources and supplementary finance from the LEA was regularly needed to pay for the extra teaching. We can speculate as to how the college might have developed without the atomic connection; but all we can say with confidence is that it would have been very different.

The implications were immediately felt. To pay for the teaching of the 'extra' students who started in the autumn of 1952, the college needed an additional £1,000. Three years later, vocational numbers were larger than anticipated and again, a supplementary £1,000 was needed. A similar increase in 1958 meant another supplement; and in the next two years, the college's teaching hours increased by 22 per cent.[30]

There was an urgent need for laboratories and workshops. In 1952 the only laboratory was in Albert Road and this was inadequate even before these new pressures. The prefabricated laboratories, the horsa huts, were ready by the spring of 1953. Yet in the next academic year, there were 'excessive difficulties' in accommodating technical courses, with staff and students working under 'exceptionally unpleasant and adverse conditions'; and it was 'necessary to improvise where two groups required the use of a single laboratory which had been fully occupied from 9 am to 9.30 pm for five days per week.'[31] The first instalment had to be completed as quickly as possible. Too much delay and the LEA would play the atomic card. Without the new facilities, the demands from the Atomic Energy Authority could not be met. It was with great relief, then, that the instalment was completed early in 1957 and the second one started 12 months later. As Newbury's MP succinctly put it: 'This is the geographical and cultural centre for Harwell and Aldermaston. Our position fully justifies the new building programme that this college is undertaking.'[32]

---

[30] Education Finance Subcommittee 17 October 1958; FESC 19 January 1962.

[31] *NWN* 5 May 1955.

[32] *Ibid.*, 27 February 1958.

'Some indication of the rate at which the demand for further education classes is growing is given by the history of the ONC in Applied Physics'

The atomic connection stimulated the curriculum at Ormonde House. In 1954 a new day release started, the ONC in Applied Physics, which quickly became the flagship course for the college.

Applied Physics was already taught at Reading College. However, in 1954, both Harwell and Aldermaston decided to recognise the ONC and HNC in Applied Physics as a basis for promotion. This led to such a demand for the ONC that an additional course was started at Newbury.

The three-year course included mathematics, physics, chemistry and workshop practice. Newbury, however, could not run the third year without the new laboratories, so final-year students might have to go to college at Oxford or Reading. The numbers were impressive and 80 students enrolled in 1954. Moreover, the third year was available from 1956 as the new buildings neared completion. By this time there were around 150 students on the programme, all from Aldermaston and Harwell.[33]

Many of those who completed the ONC went on to the HNC. This higher level certificate was not available at South Berks, but the governors were keen to establish it once the second instalment, which was to include specialist accommodation for Applied Physics, was completed. HNC work was new and the college's attempt to move into advanced further education – higher education – was not going to be easy. There were other players in the game. The HNC was well established at Oxford while Reading had already been given permission to offer it. Was there sufficient demand to run the HNC at Newbury as well?

The discussions that followed involved the Southern Regional Council, the three LEAs – Berkshire, Reading and Oxford – HMIs and the Ministry of Education. The Regional Council would make the final decision.

One of the arguments for running the HNC at Newbury was financial: if Berkshire provided the course 'locally', it would save on out-county fees. But the situation was complicated. Reading

---

[33] FESC 19 November 1954, 16 September 1955; BEC 4 November 1955.

College, already running the ONC, had been approved to provide the higher level course, whilst those students living in north Berkshire went to Oxford. Berkshire LEA argued that the HNC at Oxford would not be affected by developments at Newbury 'because there will probably always be a number of students from the Abingdon/Botley area who could not attend at Newbury.'

Neither Reading nor Oxford authorities wanted an HNC at Newbury, but Berkshire thought that some of their arguments were disingenuous. 'The Oxford and Reading Authorities claimed that they have planned their new Colleges on the basis of an agreement that having hitherto sent our advanced students to Oxford and Reading, we would continue to do so. While there is no record of such an agreement having been reached, it is true that we have relied considerably in the past on the facilities offered by the other two Authorities for courses in Applied Physics.' Berkshire also claimed that it had not been consulted about the proposed HNC at Reading.

The Ministry of Education had to approve all building programmes and it was impatient for agreement to be reached between the three authorities. The Ministry was concerned that 'the provision of facilities at Newbury may be redundant in view of the facilities which exist at Oxford and have been approved for Reading.'[34] So a meeting between HM Inspectors and the LEAs agreed that Berkshire should provide 'alternative uses for the specialist accommodation for Applied Physics' in the plans for South Berks College should the Regional Council not recommend the facilities in Newbury.

Decision-time came at the Southern Regional Council meeting on 30 November 1955. For those involved in further education in Newbury, this was the most important regional meeting to have taken place since 1948. In Ormonde House, the governors and lecturers waited anxiously for the outcome.

The meeting began with the representatives from Berkshire outlining their proposal. They emphasised the number of enrolments on the ONC in Applied Physics at Newbury, estimating those who would go on to the HNC when the accommodation was available. The numbers were healthy. Also, the proposed HNC at Newbury was to include electronics, giving the course a different

---

[34] FESC 16 September 1955.

slant from the one at Oxford and thereby avoiding duplication. Comments were invited from Oxford and Reading representatives, after which a vote was taken. Five were against the proposal, only one was in favour, and even that was 'subject to the safeguarding of the two existing centres'. The decision was taken: for the time being at least, there would be no HNC in Applied Physics at South Berks College.

Yet the matter did not end there. Berkshire LEA informed the Ministry that it was not abandoning its proposal and a few months later, Ormonde House governors returned to the issue. There were so many students on the Newbury ONC courses that they recommended that the college should offer HNCs not just in Applied Physics (with electronics), but also in Electrical and Mechanical Engineering. The facilities would be provided by an extension to the second instalment.[35] The LEA supported the governors and put the proposal to the Regional Council in the summer of 1957. Council approved the HNC in Mechanical Engineering, but deferred a decision on the others. The governors, however, wanted the three proposals considered together as they were 'interrelated in the matter of staff and accommodation'. They felt confident. When in early 1958 they reviewed their teaching requirements, it was done in the light of the 'increased volume of advanced work and the probable introduction of new work of university level' in the next session.[36]

At a meeting of the Education Committee in the summer of 1958, the Director of Education was asked to discuss with the HMIs the possibility of including two new laboratories at Newbury in the 1960-61 building programme. These were for the HNC in Mechanical Engineering, to be built for £15,000 on land adjacent to the college site. Governors' chairman Ron Spiller was keen on the project. 'It is an interesting development and I sincerely hope that it will be possible to get it through so that we can carry on with the course in this part of Berkshire.'[37]

To strengthen the college's argument for advanced work, the governors recommended a change in Newbury's admission

---

[35] *Ibid.*, 8 March 1957.

[36] *Ibid.*, 12 July 1957, 14 November 1958.

[37] *NWN* 26 June 1958.

procedures. Their ONC courses were 'protected' in the sense that all those students who lived in Berkshire but wanted to do an ONC in Oxford or Reading needed the LEA's permission. In other words, Berkshire students who could 'conveniently attend' at Newbury were expected to do so. One of the arguments against Newbury's HNC proposal was that the number of ONC students at Newbury was protected and therefore 'artificially high'. The governors felt that 'the liaison is now such between the College and the employers of the students concerned, a majority of whom come from the two Atomic Energy Establishments, that there would be little risk in relaxing the protection of the three courses.' For 1958/59, therefore, Berkshire ONC students were not required to get permission to go out-county if they so wished. This move, however, did not shift the majority opinion of the Regional Council. In September 1958 it again felt unable to support the proposal for an HNC in Applied Physics at Newbury. Interestingly, the change in admission procedures at Newbury did not affect enrolment.

In the end, no HNC in either Applied Physics or Engineering was introduced in the '50s or '60s. The third instalment of buildings, optimistically designed to house HNC programmes, had to be adapted for technician and craft-level work. For the time being at least, there was to be no higher education in further education in Newbury.

Yet the atomic connection extended the curriculum at South Berks College in other, non-advanced, ways. In 1956, the four-year City & Guilds Electrical Technicians' course was introduced as a day-release programme.[38] In 1957 an evening class for Medical Laboratory Technologists started at Harwell,[39] followed by a day-release City & Guilds for Laboratory Technicians. The Laboratory Technologists' course was also taught at the Agricultural Research Station at Compton, an establishment set up by the Agricultural

---

[38] The first year was taught on one day and one evening a week. It included electrical engineering principles, engineering materials and drawing, practical mathematics, technical reports and workshop practice. SBCFE Prospectus 1956-57, pp.21-22.

[39] This intermediate level course was for two years on two evenings a week, 5.15 to 7.15 pm. It included histology, bacteriology, haematology and bio-chemistry. SBCFE Prospectus 1957-58, p.20.

Research Council in 1937 for the study of infectious diseases of farm animals. This was the first time South Berks College had organised a course there.

AERE Harwell needed 'trained industrial-grade laboratory staff to provide the necessary support to those professional and scientific staff responsible for pushing forward the nuclear research programme.' One way to achieve this was to enhance contacts with the schools 'with a view to giving special training to those who showed an interest in scientific work'. The Harwell laboratory training scheme started in 1958. The training was for three years with work experience in a variety of on the job placements. The 'more formal, academic side' was at South Berks College, day release to the City & Guilds Laboratory Technicians' Certificate – mathematics, physics, chemistry, workshop practice and English. The programme began with an intake of 21 young people in 1958.[40]

An obvious source of teachers for the atomic apprentices was the establishments themselves. Engineer **Reg Hanks** started at AWE and his job soon involved him in liaison work with the college.

> I moved from Whitley Bay (Northumberland) to Newbury to take up an appointment as a professional engineer at AWE Aldermaston in 1952. At that time there was a committee of members of industry and research establishments to advise the education authority of the numbers of students they would be sending, and the subjects they needed. I was the AWE representative. At one of the meetings the college member said that one of the lecturers had left at short notice. He asked if two of us could help cover some of the evening class sessions. My services were accepted in respect of the second-year ONC Electrical course. One night a week was lecturing and the second laboratory work. I did this for the two terms after Christmas 1952 and then for the following year. I enjoyed the lecturing experience and also, with my wife, the staff party at The Bear in Hungerford. As a student I attended

---

[40] SBCFE Prospectus 1958-59, p.19; see 25th Anniversary of the Harwell Laboratory Trainee Scheme 1958-1983.

the evening woodwork class to complete a veneered item of furniture I had been making at Whitley Bay.

Reg was the first of many tutors from the two establishments. In the mid-'50s at least three of the college's part-time engineering lecturers worked at Aldermaston.[41]

It was around this time that South Berks College was facing a staffing crisis. Fears were expressed as early as March 1955 that there would not be enough tutors for the anticipated volume of work in the next session. Aldermaston and Harwell people were approached, the overtures were not successful, and so the FESC recommended the appointment of a full-time lecturer. The concern was justified when 'unexpectedly high' numbers enrolled for technical classes in the autumn of 1955.

The recruitment of full-time lecturers was difficult. Three Grade A posts – in mathematics and physics, and chemistry – were advertised in the summer of 1955, but nobody suitable applied. The new term started, and the governors were worried. 'At present the work of these lecturers is being done either by part-time staff or by the employment of other full-time staff beyond their normal working hours, and if this situation continues, it is likely that the teaching will suffer.'[42] The governors' response was to re-advertise the posts as Grade B lectureships with the correspondingly higher salary.

This put the education authority in a dilemma. The existing practice for the county's FE colleges was for the number of Grade B lecturers not to exceed one third of the total number of lecturers on the staff. Two additional Grade B posts would upset the formula at Newbury. However, because the situation was serious, the LEA agreed to re-advertise two of the posts at the higher grade.[43] Again there was disappointment. Nobody suitable applied and the extra teaching had to be continued with full-time staff working overtime, supported by part-timers. However, one consequence of this recruitment crisis was that the LEA relaxed its policy towards

---

[41] These were apprentice instructor Fred Stevenson, W J Garland and B C Hedge.

[42] BEC 4 November 1955.

[43] *Ibid.*, 6 January 1956.

staffing. No longer were Grade B lecturers to be restricted to one third of the total teaching staff. Instead, it was left to college governors 'to appoint such members of staff at Grade B salaries as the situation may from time to time require'.

The atomic card was dealt. The training needs of Aldermaston and Harwell were not to be restricted by a formula. Yet recruitment still remained difficult. In 1959 the Education Committee reported that it remained a problem in science and engineering in all of its FE institutions. 'Well qualified applicants are not coming forward for appointment to the lower graded posts.'[44]

'It was the largest centre for Applied Physics in the country'

In Berkshire FE, the range of courses in science was 'considerably less' than those in engineering. Yet South Berks College developed as a science centre, the only college in the county to have a separate Science Department in the '50s and early '60s.

Eric Carr came to Ormonde House as the lecturer in charge of Science because of the students from the atomic energy establishments. He remained Head of Science for fourteen years. In fact, he is the only departmental Head of Science in the history of the college and when he retired, his work was absorbed into the Engineering Department, and the provision of science courses never recovered its independent departmental status.

Eric Carr was at the centre of this exciting phase in the college's history. He developed the Science Department, brought in staff and initiated courses. By the mid-'50s, he was responsible for three full-time and 12 part-time lecturers. The full-timers were F S Barnes, who came in 1953, and J W Ballard and J H Scott, who both joined in 1956. Fred Barnes eventually left to become an FE Principal in Somerset. Eric Carr organised the ONC in Applied Physics and saw his college become the largest centre for this course in the country. He worked hard, but in vain, to introduce the HNC.

Born in Carlisle (1906), Eric graduated from the University of Manchester with an MSc in Physics and went into teaching.

---

[44] Education in the Royal County of Berkshire 1958-59, Report by the Director of Education, p.37.

When the Second World War broke out, the schoolteacher became a gliding instructor. 'We went to the Lakes quite a lot.' The war over, Eric returned to the classroom, in Wigton in Cumbria.

> It was a boarding school. I got extra money for being in charge of the labs. It was hard work; somebody had to be on duty all the time. There were three masters. The poor little boys used to wake up with toothache. We had to play games with them and take them to church on Sundays. There were not many boarders. When I started, there were about 20 but it dwindled and dwindled to only six. It was miserable up there. I wanted to move because the headmaster who appointed me was retiring. The new head was one of the pupils I had taught, and I didn't fancy it.

> I moved to Newbury in 1952. I was going for the Physics Department and was interviewed by Mr Owthwaite. At the same interview, Roy Pocock was going for the Vice-Principal job.

> We built up the physics. The students came from Harwell and Aldermaston. They had to have physics A-level and maths A-level, so it was easy teaching. All the boys took physics and maths. I was in charge of Applied Physics. It was the largest centre for Applied Physics in the country. I had 72 pupils. As soon as it got to 12, they started another class. I had six classes. You made your own examination, in February. All my physics students had to take workshop practice; Mr Jeffery did this at Albert Road. My daughter was in the Applied Physics. She was at AEI, Associated Electrical Industries, next door to Aldermaston. I went there for a few years. I used to go for a fortnight in the summer and they paid me. It's disbanded now. I had a number of students from there. My daughter went there as a research student. She was in the fifth form at the Girls' High School when we moved, and the next year she applied for a job in research. She was really good at physics. I taught maths as well. And I had the first computer course

going, in 1960.[45] It was upstairs in Bartholomew Street. A man from Harwell used to set the papers – I didn't do anything. Reading pinched it, so the course went there.

We were the only place in this part of the world to get any state scholarships. We got four scholarships a year to university, £300. I objected to one of them – he was hopeless – but it was no good. I started teaching physics in Albert Road, before the new building was built. There was not much equipment, but they spent any money I wanted. £2,000 a year they spent on equipment. The Grammar School didn't get anything, and we got a new building. I taught at the Grammar School as well. The teacher left suddenly, and Roy taught maths and I taught physics. It was only for a few months, to get them over the final part of their A-levels. The college made an allowance for it. I used to take the equipment from the college to the Grammar School 'cos they didn't have much. I taught my son there – he was in the sixth form.

We taught drawing in the chicken hut. One teacher put a thermometer on the bench and as soon as the temperature went below, I don't know what it was, 15 degrees or something, he cancelled the classes. He wouldn't teach under 15 degrees. The chemistry lab was the conservatory. There was a nice tiled floor, but all the stuff was spilled on it. They were starting the new college, and we soon got the new labs. I taught in the new physics lab and there was a new chemistry lab as well.

In 1952 the staff room was upstairs in Ormonde House, overlooking the front drive. You could get a drink in there, but the students couldn't. I can't remember much of a library in 1952. We had a new library with the new building

---

[45] This was a day-release course, 'Computations - Preliminary Course for entry into Northampton CAT Computation Course.' SBCFE Prospectus 1959-60, p.19. This was Northampton College of Advanced Technology in London. It became City University in 1966.

and Mr White was the librarian in charge. Betty Ward was my secretary. Roy Pocock was Head of Engineering, I was Head of Science, and Betty was secretary to both departments. Charlie Sully taught motor mechanics. He was trained at Rolls Royce. He lived in the gardens to the house and taught in a tin hut, very near to where he lived. He told his class not to strike a light near the fuel – of course somebody did and it went up. He was a Labour man, a marvellous man. Ron Spiller was strong Labour as well and he was chairman of the governors. Miss Searle did dressmaking and she would shout at various things Owthwaite did. She went to Leigh in Lancashire. Miss Garlick taught English. She was very strict and she used to tell everybody how to get on, always laying the law down. She left and went to teach in Basingstoke, but she didn't stick it for more than 12 months. She told them what she thought, and she came back to Newbury College.

'It was lovely looking down there in the spring with the apple blossom'

Betty Ward was Eric Carr's secretary. A local girl from Speen, Betty had been in the forces for five years before starting in the office on 1 April 1952. She was 26 years old.

I was employed originally as receptionist and secretary to Roy Pocock and the engineers. Eric Carr was Head of the Science Department and I used to do his work as well. When I started, there were two admin staff, Mabel Lord and myself. That's all there was. Mabel was the Principal's secretary. I wasn't there alone for very long. Another girl came in and it ended up with three of us in the end.

I was in charge of the general reception. You came through the front door of the house and went straight along to the office. This was reception. The students had to come there for the tickets for their tea and biscuits and then they would go next door, the old kitchen. Mrs Whiting was in there. She used to serve them up tea and biscuits.

The first prize-giving day that I attended must have been in 1952. It was held in the Corn Exchange – the only one I went to at the Corn Exchange. It was on a big scale. They used to get up on the stage and they were in this queue all the time. It was so big that half the time when the names were called out you did not know whether that was the person getting the certificate or not.

In my office the French windows opened on to some steps and then you had this gravel path in front of you. There were lawns each side with these round evergreen bushes. You went down just a bit and then you had this old-fashioned trellis, an archway with roses. And you went down a bit further and there were gardens with flowers. Then, when you got about three quarters of the way down, there was the orchard and all these daffodils. It was beautiful. It was lovely looking down there, especially in the spring with the apple blossom. If my door was open you could stand in the front door of Ormonde House and look straight through. Lovely, it really was. It was a pity when they put the first instalment up there.

'They were absolutely wonderful students'

Len Hoyland joined the staff in 1956, to take charge of the workshops and teach technical drawing. He had no doubt about the significance of the atomic connection in the college's history.

As to the reason why the college expanded dramatically, it was chiefly because we had very close links with both Harwell and Aldermaston. Mr Pocock gains the credit for this. He spent a lot of time personally making the contacts. Pocock was the man, no question about that. He got to know everybody who mattered in the training programme at the establishments, and he arranged for those people to come to the college to talk with the staff. The result was that we got all their students, the apprentices. Some of them were student apprentices, some were craft apprentices. Both Harwell and Aldermaston selected not only their student apprentices carefully; they selected their craft apprentices as well. There was a big demand to get a craft apprenticeship, a long waiting list, and they could only take, say, 40 or whatever. So they got the best, and the ones that they didn't want, Newbury could have, Plenty and places like that.

The student apprentice was a young man, aged about 17 or 18, who had taken his A-levels. He'd got A-level in mathematics, and he was interested in a career in engineering. The interesting thing about these student apprentices was that having got their A-levels, and then having decided that they were interested in engineering, they came to us and they attended for one year. And we arranged it so that they could sit two certificates, the ONC in Electrical and Mechanical. Now you might wonder what value was that when they wanted a degree. The value was it acted as a bridging course, a perfect bridge between grammar school, which is where they'd been, and their university. And by allowing them to study to ONC in Electrical and Mechanical, that was going to help them in their studies in electrical or mechanical engineering. It was helping them along the road. We were teaching them the technology from the engineering point of view, which they wouldn't have got at grammar school, which would have been more theoretical. I'm not saying it wouldn't have been good enough; it obviously was, because they had good A-levels.

I remember them with great pleasure. I used to look forward to taking the classes, and they all passed because they were bright. They were absolutely wonderful students. There was no chivvying. You didn't have to persuade them, or even ask them to be quiet. Having been to grammar school, they understood the importance of behaving themselves. They knew why they were attending, they wanted to learn and they didn't want to fool about. It made our job so much easier. We could take them up to the level of an ONC and they would all pass. They did very well. Some of them went to Cambridge – we got feedback on the sort of degrees they got. They were remarkable boys, they really were. I like to think we managed to give them a push over to the technology side a little bit more than they would have got at grammar school. That was the purpose of it and it worked very well.

Side by side with the student apprentices we had the ordinary craft apprentices who had not been to grammar school and certainly had not got any A-levels. Yet it was a wonderful training programme at both establishments. They got first-rate instruction in the workshops, they really did. I've been over there, I've seen them in action, and you couldn't fault them. They were very fortunate; they really were the chosen few. And they had confidence in themselves. A lot of the craft apprentices trained at Harwell and Aldermaston, once they'd passed their exams, their City & Guilds Technicians' Certificate – which they did at Newbury – and had passed their craft apprenticeships in the establishments, they couldn't wait to leave. And they were snapped up because they'd got the practical and the theory, the best obtainable.

I do believe if all these apprentices had gone, say, to Abingdon and to Swindon, instead of Newbury, we would have been struggling. The college was built round them; in the Engineering Department we were dependent on them. And of course, they were brought in by coach; they didn't even have to have transport. A coach would bring them from Harwell; deposit them at a quarter to nine; a coach from Aldermaston, quarter to nine. They were there, on the nail. A full group, lovely, the whole class was there. It worked a treat.

'People have always said to me, you had the best training in the country'

Derek Loosen was one of the craft apprentices. He had completed his Pre-Apprenticeship, navigated AWE's rigorous selection

354

procedure and signed his indentures to train as an instrument maker. This time at Ormonde House he studied mechanical engineering.

> In the first year at AWE there was the Apprentice School, a prefab building that was full up with lathes, milling machines and grinders. It was better equipment than at South Berks College. The year's course was intensive. The first thing you had to do was file a piece of metal and get it flat and square in all directions. There were exercises as well; I've still got some of them at home. One of them was a square piece of metal with a triangle in the middle. You had to be able to press the triangle in and out and fit it into all three different sides, and hold it up to the light without any light shining through it. The two surfaces on either side had to be so flat, you would rub it with this glove and it would stick to the table. That's the sort of thing they made you do. We made a tool kit. You couldn't progress until you'd finished the first set.

> Originally it was only just mechanical, but then they started an electrical one. After the first year you could go and do some of that. I didn't. I went straight into one of the workshops, and then you did all the basic things, knocking hell out of sheet metal. Normally what happened then is you were given an exercise to manufacture something. But Aldermaston in those days was not a profit-making organisation, so they didn't need an apprentice to be producing something, not all the time anyway. It wasn't until towards the end of my apprenticeship that I actually started producing parts that were going to be utilised in any of the equipment. Up until then, I was making things for myself, model bits and pieces. There wasn't the pressure there from the employer – 'I've got to get my five penn'orth out of this person.' What they were trying to do was train people so they had a skilled workforce all the time. When I went to English Electric and I told them I was at Aldermaston, they said, 'Why do you want to leave?'

People have always said to me, you had the best training in the country. We did, because of the mixture we had – if you made use of it – when you think of all the different things there were. There were eight different departments. There was the place where you worked on radioactive materials. I never went into that because what I was doing on the instrument side wasn't involved. I did watchmaking and watch repairing for a few months. There was electrical and electronics and although I was mechanical, I still did that for a time. And we did PE once a week. We were herded on to a coach, taken off out, and then had to run back. In the gymnasium there was the vaulting equipment and all that sort of thing. And there were squash courts; that was the first time I ever played squash.

The apprentices used to come from all over the UK and the world. In our year they were from up north and all over. I was a craft apprentice, and there were student apprentices with us as well, A-level students who went to university to become engineers or scientists. The apprentices had Blacknest hostel at Brimpton, a big old house for the people that didn't live locally. That was full up. Harwell had a hostel as well, and there was big rivalry between the two. The hostels had mascots. That was a game in those days; it was just like kids at university. We used to go in the middle of the night and raid each other's hostel to steal the mascot. Then the whole structure changed and they just went local on their intake.

'It was very much blackboard and standing up in front of the class instruction'

Colin Roberts was Aldermaston's apprentice of the year in 1957. 'It depended on two things, your college results and your training at work. I got a slide rule. That was the calculator of the day. You could only do very basic things with it.' Colin was 16. He had gone to Aldermaston straight from school and had just finished his first year.

I went to Park House in 1951. For two weeks I was at Shaw doing exams, and then some boys in the lower groups stayed at Shaw while the upper groups went to Park. Originally it was only the higher classes that were at Park House. Then it became split and there were just girls at Shaw and boys at Park. The first year or so I was in the classrooms in the house. We used to have to take our shoes off and have our slippers 'cos there was all polished floors. Park House had stables and garages with rooms above and in the gardens were big fir trees and a sunken lawn. The gym was an old hut with a tarpaulin roof. We used to have to walk along a path through the trees to get to it. While I was there the building of the new school was going on and later, while I was at college, that also was being built. They almost merge in my memory. They were both oldish houses with high ceilings with the building going on in the background.

I left school at 15 with just a UEI. That was four things – science, technical drawing, maths, English – a kind of leavers' exam. If you stayed on another year, you did GCEs.

My father was a driver of the coaches at Aldermaston and they did an awful lot of transporting of nuclear things to Shoeburyness or wherever. People used to ask him to drive and take the lorries. He said AWE would be a good apprenticeship to get into though it wasn't really my intention. I was always into cars and I thought I would work in a garage, but atomic energy sounded really exciting – that was an attraction. It was a bit of a status thing – it was the thing. When you were there, it was all secret, hush-hush.

I was surprised to have got in because it was difficult. It was a nationwide advertisement and there were people applying from all over the country. In any particular year there were 30 or so apprentices. Some would do electrical, some would do mechanical. Some would have come from a long way away and stayed at Blacknest hostel. Some of them only went home weekends and even not then if they were too far from home. I went for three series of interviews. They were long sessions and you had the medical checks as well. Part of the interview was bending a piece of wire. You had a straight piece of wire, and there was a pattern, and you used to bend this wire like a diamond, twist it square, twist it again, and at the end it was like a heart.

I was an apprentice mechanical instrument maker. The whole of my five years was associated with the mechanical side. I ended up with a City & Guilds in Mechanical Engineering. The end of the third year you would take the intermediate examination, the end of the fifth year you would take the final. I went on day release – it was one day with an evening – from nine till seven o'clock at night, which made a very long day. There was maths, technical drawing and the engineering. The evening was usually practical machine work. In the first year it was in the place in Northbrook Street. There was a machine shop down there with really, really old lathes and things. That was with Mr Bedford, before the new college was built. Soon afterwards it was in the brand new engineering workshop down the back. We used to have maths in an outbuilding outside of the conservatory – Mr Hoyland was in that little room as well, taking us for technical drawing. We were provided with drawing boards and T-squares, ordinary desk ones that you could pack away at the end of the class.

It was very much blackboard and standing up in front of the class instruction and writing. The subjects were all associated with one another – designing something, calculating it, drawing it so it could be produced in the workshop. One led on to the other. The homework was particularly science and maths. You had a week to do it. Reports went back to those people at Aldermaston in charge of the apprentices and if you didn't turn up, they wanted to know why. There were so many students and they were all going to college on different days. Henry Fish was the governor of the apprentices.

Harwell and Aldermaston would have been the main suppliers of people to go to the college, but in a class of 20 it wasn't just an Aldermaston group. There were some people I had been at school with who had ended up at places like Plenty and Opperman Gears and Colthrop. And there was a guy from a small engineering company. It wasn't just the big names; there were small companies represented as well.

There was a canteen in Ormonde House. You went to a hatch for a cup of tea and a couple of biscuits and then you walked into a room at the front. There was no students' room like there is today – it was really very restricted. At lunchtime I went into town or went home. I lived in Elizabeth Avenue, a new council house when we moved there. Valley Road, Henshaw Crescent and all those were known as Aldermaston houses. They're very similar to some of the houses at Aldermaston outside of the fence. It was a long day. We used to pack up at half past four, have half-an-hour break, and come back at five. We used to go down Northbrook Street and have a bun and a cup of tea in the Tea Bar. It was very narrow and went back a long way and all round was a ledge where you had your fixed bar stool. There was many a time you didn't want to go back to college after being there since nine o'clock in the morning. They didn't get the best out of us at that time. It would have been better if it had been over two days, or one and a half, rather than going back at five o'clock. It was an effort to get back into the swing of it after half-an-hour's break, thinking I'd really rather go home.

It was one day a week at college, and four days a week on site. There was a special bus from Newbury to Aldermaston. At one stage you had to pay for it, or for a proportion of it. The bus was seven o'clock in the morning and we clocked in at ten to eight, until five or half past.

First year was a workshop. You went very thoroughly through hand tools, filing, hacksaws, through lathe work and into milling work, and you did a little bit of welding. It was very much on machine tools, and then in the second year you went on and made specialist objects. I remember making a thing with a small thread one end, about four-inch diameter with a big thread on it, which was about one turn. These were show pieces. You used to make them, polish them and chromium plate them. They were just exercises in machining really.

After the second year you spent three years on the site in various proper workshops, in the real world, actually producing rather than being trained. But you were still under one person. He was your guide. You were responsible to him, and if you did anything wrong, he was to sort you out. He had to do written reports. It was very much one-to-one. There was grouping in the school, but not when working in the real workshops. You always had lots of equipment, the best tools and things, and you never wanted for anything. They had very large stores and if you wanted anything, you used to be able to get it there. All the lathes and the milling machines were very good, better than the college ones. We were privileged in that way.

I was in the instrument department and we used to make prototype instruments for measuring radioactivity. I also spent some time in a camera department, which was very, very interesting. We used to make lenses from glass, grind and polish them and then put them in and test the camera. They used single-shot cameras for taking the explosions as they happened. You could only take one picture, but it was a very crucial picture. We also had cameras with rotating mirrors. When the blast went off they sprayed about 20 or 30 images. The mirror rotated – it was an arc of lenses – with shots of these seconds of explosion. This was when they used to go to Christmas Island and Australia to carry out controlled explosions. We spent a bit of time in the welding workshop and we spent a month in the woodwork shop. I made this beautiful instrument maker's cabinet, with the lock at the top and the drawers dropped down. All the drawers were felt-lined and it was all French-polished on the outside. That was pretty good – I was pleased with that. The Apprentice School had a big classroom, a stage at one end, and a machine shop. It was within its own perimeter fence, so you could shut it off from the rest of the site and allow people to come. In the first year we had an Open Day.

Nothing that you did at college carried over into work; they were totally different. It wasn't that you designed something at college and then made it at work. At work you had particular things to do and a course of duties, whereas at college all the work was academic. It was the same target, but they weren't together. And we did homework for the college, but we didn't do homework for work. But the time at college was very helpful. It was putting the theory behind the practice we were doing every day at Aldermaston. It was a mixture between school and work. It was a bit like school, but you were treated more grown-up, and it was a stepping stone to what you were doing at work. Also, it was a day off, a different day, when you could look forward to not getting the bus at seven o'clock in the morning. It was a day when you were in Newbury and it broke the week up. It was very useful because it gave you a different insight into what you were trying to achieve. The aim was the same, but it was approaching it in a different way. At work, you were being trained, but it was more work. College was definitely still teaching and training.

The college today has more of an identity; before it just seemed to be an off-shoot of working. You only got to know the people in your class. Obviously to itself it was important, but it was there to support people going to work and training for work, whereas now it seems to have more of its own identity, a community where people go to learn typing or to play music or whatever. It certainly wasn't the community that it is today. It was there to serve a purpose, it served that purpose, and then it was goodbye to it

*'Calculus was my downfall –
I couldn't get a grip of it'*

Ken Hunt also went to Park House School. He worked hard, passed his examinations, stayed on for an extra year and developed an interest in woodwork. He left to join AWE in 1956.

> I started at Shaw House in 1951, where I spent a year. Mr Hughson taught me woodwork and technical drawing. Mr Turnbull was really good. I was always keen on fishing, and he was a keen fisherman.[46] All of us who liked fishing he used to have on the lawn at Park, casting up, plates, flies and that sort of thing. I stayed on the extra year. Normally you did four years and left at 15 but I stayed on until I was 16 to do GCEs. About 20 per cent stayed on. I got an O-level in English, maths, technical drawing, art and general science. The year before I did my GCEs, I did a UEI. This was in English and maths, and the practical subject was woodwork. I was always interested in crafts and practical things, and I particularly liked woodwork.
>
> When it came round to looking for a job, I wanted a practical job working in wood. My parents thought I should have an apprenticeship and I saw an advert in the *Newbury Weekly News* for Aldermaston. It was all the trades, and one of them said pattern maker. I thought, yes, that sounds good, rather than just be a chippy. So I applied for the apprenticeship. I didn't know at the time but there were 400 applicants each year, and they accepted 40. They came from all over and the policy was to spread the intake throughout the whole country. They were aware that a lot of these lads would go back home when they finished their apprenticeship – they wouldn't stay at AWE – and they wanted to spread their skills back round the country.

---

[46] At the Careers Question Time evening in 1953, organised by Newbury Rotary Club, the Park House headmaster said that if he could have his time again, he would be a professional angler 'of which there were only a couple in the country'. *NWN* 3 December 1953.

You had a one-in-ten chance of getting in to AWE, but I didn't apply anywhere else. There was a practical test, an IQ test and a general knowledge test. I did those, went back to Aldermaston for the interview, got through that, told them of my interest in woodwork and was offered a place. At the introductory chat when I started, I said what my interests were and which way I wanted to go, woodwork and pattern making. And they said, 'We don't do that. That's not part of the apprenticeship.'

So there I was, and because I had GCEs, they thought a draughtsman would be the thing to go for. In our year of 40 apprentices, there were 70 per cent craft, 30 per cent student, and we had three older graduates tacked on. I was a craft apprentice. We were the guys with one or two O-levels, or maybe no O-levels. The student apprentice had the potential for studying for a degree or HNC. They were destined to become engineers whereas we weren't. And then there were the graduate apprentices, who were definitely degree people.

I came to South Berks College to take the ONC in Mechanical Engineering – maths, technical drawing, and engineering science. I passed the first year, S1, got on to the second year, and failed the practical maths. In those days if you failed one subject, you failed the whole course. So I retook the course the following year, and failed maths again. Calculus was my downfall – I couldn't get a grip of it. When I failed on the S2, that put me out of a draughtsman trade – that wasn't possible without the HNC.

By then I'd moved on to the third year of my five-year apprenticeship, but the training we'd done up till then had been the same, whether we were going for a draughtsman or one of the skilled trades. So I chose instrument making, the manufacture of scientific instruments. It was interesting and I was happy to make the move. At the college, to be sure I was going to come out with a qualification, I moved over to City & Guilds Machine Shop Engineering, which was a more practical course. I went straight in at the second year. I passed that okay, and I finished with a final City & Guilds rather than an ONC or HNC which I'd hoped for.

College was one day a week and a different evening. We all used to go up on motorbikes. It was an open site and there was some sort of farming going on over on one side down the back. There were some lessons taught in the house. Half the class of, say, 25, were from Aldermaston and Harwell; the others were apprentices from Newbury Diesel, Plenty and Opperman Gears. In my first year there were three ladies from Aldermaston. They weren't apprentices; they were tracers from the drawing office hoping to upgrade to draughtsmen. Newbury Diesel did general engineering, machine castings. Plenty were very popular. Opperman made gearboxes and transducers. Newbury wasn't an industrial town in those days – it is more now with the electronics growth.

We had practical sessions, which were pretty well the same as lab work, but it was more in the machine shop. It was before the new workshops. The old workshops were in terrapins and not very well equipped, Boxford lathes and that sort of thing. Then they built the new facility and we moved into those. Arthur Bedford took us for machine shop practice, actual workshop practice using all the machines. Mr Sully took us for engineering science, a lot of theory, friction on inclined planes and all those sorts of things, the theory side of all the stuff you use in practice. He was very good indeed. He really taught us the basics, which was very important for the rest of our lives. He was a real stickler on basics and it's amazing as you go through your career in engineering how often you have to refer back to those basics. It's the most important bit we did, and Mr Sully was very good on that. He was very socialist, more than a Labour man. He really was very left-wing. Coming from AWE, we used to try and wind him up.

In the first year at Aldermaston you had to make a set of tools. I've still got some of mine. In the third year in the workshops, you were attached to a craftsman, and he was paid an allowance for training you. In each workshop there was a great community spirit and at lunch breaks there used to be darts and table tennis tables set up in the gangways. The apprentice scheme at AWE was a way of life. We had the Apprentice Association, a football team, floats in the carnivals and a skiffle group – that was a big thing at the time. We used to have a social club where you'd go out to various events and we did lots of activities together. They used to put on a show at Open Day, taking the mickey out of the management and the instructors. Harwell was the same. There was a lot of competition between us and Harwell in many ways, especially if you lived in the hostel – midnight raids and lots of that sort of thing used to go on.

Henry Fish was the manager of the Apprentice School and Mr Pocock would regularly be up there to visit. Lansley the Principal did come to Aldermaston, but Mr Pocock was the prominent figure. The chief engineer was Mr Dolphin, and he was very supportive of the apprentice scheme. Ron Spiller was on the planning side. He was involved in the union there and very active in the labour movement.

'It was a Harwell/Aldermaston driven course for ordinary mortals who do practical things'

CITY & GUILDS ELECTRICAL TECHNICIANS' COURSE

This is a new four year course introduced by the City & Guilds of London Institute to provide qualifications for technicians engaged in the design, manufacture, testing, erection, operation and maintenance of electrical plant and equipment in one of the following branches of electrical engineering: Power and Machinery, Power Generation and Supply, Industrial Electronics.

This new day-release course was launched in September 1956. The demand for it came from Harwell and Aldermaston. The subjects in the first year (T1) were electrical engineering principles, engineering materials and drawing, practical mathematics, and technical reports; and there was an evening class in workshop practice. The intermediate examination was at the end of the second year. Industrial electronics was introduced in the third year. The fourth year (T4) was electronics, testing methods and 'special technique', and the final City & Guilds examination. A new course meant new equipment, £1,500 allocated in 1958 to resource the third and fourth years. A fifth year was also available – electronics, semiconductors, mathematics – for those who wanted the full Technological Certificate.

Ian Walker was a craft apprentice at Harwell who lived in Headington outside Oxford and started his day-release training for an ONC at Oxford College. This did not work out and in 1956 the apprentice manager moved him to Newbury and the new course for electrical technicians.

> I left school a little early and it was decided that I ought to do some sort of training. My father hoiked me round various laboratories in Oxford where they would take you on as a test tube washer – it really didn't look very much of a thing to do. The alternative would have been quite different. My uncle was an organist and one of his friends in Oxford was an organ tuner and repairer. He offered me an apprenticeship but my father, who knew about such things, felt that he was a one-man band and thought there was no mileage in it. He didn't recommend it. Then my mother picked up that they were recruiting for craft apprentices at Harwell and I got put up for that. There was a written exam, an aptitude test and a short interview, and I got a placement there. That was a real switch. I was 15 or 16 and up to then, I had not got on well at school. School was academic and I didn't fit but once you put me in a workshop with machine tools and things I could hold and understand three-dimensionally, then I did much better.

The way that the Harwell transport system worked was that you could get a bus pass. I would go down into Oxford every day on my bike, and there was an old lady who kept the bicycles in her back yard. The buses were driven by Harwell employees, double-decker five cylinder ex-London transport buses that had been painted blue for Harwell.

It was the usual apprenticeship scheme where you spent the first year in the apprentice workshop being taught basic techniques, and then placement in the main workshop – electrical engineering, reactor maintenance, and instrument engineering and so on. I was there before they sent the lads down to the training school in Dorset – then you were away from home for your first year. I lived at home all the time. The apprentice training manager was Jock Wallace. It must have been one of the best apprenticeships in the country. It was very, very good, with modern equipment and modern teaching techniques. We were taught at Harwell, why there was this top break and this front break and so on, and why you had to put a breaker into it.

Throughout the '50s Harwell apprentices kept going to Oxford and I would have stayed at Oxford if I had done the National Certificate. We did liberal studies where a guy would take us through various books and read us a bit of poetry. I was the only one who was interested in that, having come from an   academic education. Everybody else thought it was absolutely dreadful.

But I did not manage to adapt to life in Oxford Tech. I didn't get on well enough and they decided it would be more appropriate for me to do the Electrical Technicians' course which was in Newbury. This had the excitement of getting from Oxford to Newbury for one day a week. That was either done by going down to Gloucester Green in Oxford and catching the bus – this took a very long time because it went to every village between Abingdon and Newbury – or the more popular way, which was to go down to Oxford Station. In those days you could leave your bike there without it getting stolen. You had to collect your rail warrant – it was free – and you took it to the ticket office and they stamped it. You would catch the train to Didcot and then wait for the train to Newbury on the line that is now defunct. I went back with one guy from Oxford. We would sometimes have to wait around in Didcot for an hour and he used to go off into the town and chat the girls up and come back telling stories that in retrospect one wonders if one should really believe. There are always ones for telling you about their great prowess and their conquests. Anything to the south of Newbury was a totally unknown land. The limit of my knowledge went as far as Newbury, 'cos that was where I went to college.

When I made the changeover from the ONC to the T3, T4, one of the guys at Harwell said, 'That's a course for junkies'. Quite what a junkie was I don't know. He meant it was for ordinary mortals who do practical things. It was a Harwell/Aldermaston-driven course, well attended, obviously popular.

The thing about Newbury Tech at that time is that it was very tacky and bitty. The students came for the day, one day a week, and they went away. It was really a transit camp, in in the morning and out in the evening and have nothing to do with it for the rest of the week. It was what you did on whatever day it was. There was a single line of concrete-type of building, the sort that is built out of a set of beams and you see the beams inside, very much old-type school buildings. There was a long building like that. The building was damp and there was a lot of white mould about. It was cold as well.

The electrical laboratory was where you went to learn about motors, generators and so on. There were these wonderful benches, with incredibly ancient pieces of electrical rotating equipment. On the back of the benches were these great big terminals. Some of these terminals went down to the kit below, and some made their way to a huge great box on the wall, which was driven by transformers, rectifier sets and possibly even a motor generator set. And when you had connected your watt meter and your voltmeter and your amp meter up to do whatever particular test it was, and you'd got the dynamo meter set up, this guy would come along and check your wiring. Then you would be allowed to switch on. Bench number three was powered up with 50 volts – you could hurt yourself – and you did the test and plotted the results.

There was an endorsement subject, electronic testing method, the 'special technique'. This was the pulse techniques which covered the use of electronic circuits specifically for generating and handling electrical pulses, very radar-related. This was advanced for the time. An awful lot of people from RE Malvern went to Harwell to support the nuclear programme bringing with them their knowledge of radar. This was very important because Harwell was very much into the use of pulse techniques in counters and things like that, as opposed to analogue techniques. These were electrical pulse techniques using delay lines and flip-flops, all valves. There was a simple electronics laboratory, the standard sort of lab with the bench and this test equipment and little boards with the odd valve on that you connected up to do various things. At home I built a similar set-up, a board with a whole lot of meters and terminals and HT and LT power supplies and so on.

We went in Ormonde House and had coffee, but in the main, the house was the business school. The typing classes were in a room with an old mechanical typewriter on each desk, and they were paced by the instructor playing a record. You heard the music accompanied by the regular thumping of 20 typewriters – quite an experience. The business people were full-time, the young ladies causing the young men great fascination.

We would arrive in Newbury a little early. The bus came straight down from Oxford past the college and we would get off at the Clock Tower and go and sit in a café. In Northbrook Street there was a pedestrian crossing controlled by traffic lights and we would sit in this café and watch the way it worked. As close observers of this for a number of years, we decided that they had got it wrong. A popular place for lunch was the Tudor Café down on the bridge, which we used to call the 'hot plate' because it was always very warm and the plates were absolutely red hot. Polly Peacham's was the bow-fronted building by the Clock Tower – a restaurant with pictures of the characters from the musical on the wall – and there was a milk bar in the Market Place opposite the Plaza.

I used to trog off and go to these various places, which in a way was rather nice because it got you out into the town. There was no bypass and so all the traffic was going straight through the middle of Newbury, and that was quite something when the larger lorries went through. Down on the Kennet there was a chap who hired out little aluminium rowing boats, painted green, obviously ex-military, and the sort of thing that would be carried on a landing craft. A pair of oars, and you could trundle up and down, up to the monkey bridge in one direction and Victoria Park in the other. I did this a few lunchtimes because I was a bit of a loner and I didn't always join in whatever was going on. I would go off, have a quick lunch and have a little row round.

Occasionally I did once or twice drive over to Newbury, which involved going through Ilsley which wasn't bypassed. The lorries going north came down the big hill and one or two of them didn't make it. There was a chap living there who was so fed up with the lorries that would plough into his cottage that he put a huge great block of concrete in front of it so they would stop before they got to the house.

11

ABOUT A 12-VOLT
CAR BATTERY

In 1955 there followed a series of rather unhappy events
which resulted in the resignation of a number of staff of
whom the Principal was the most senior.

SBCFE 25 Years

O n 20 June 1955, Albert Owthwaite was suspended
from duty as Principal of South Berks College.
A series of allegations about his conduct had been
made to the education authority; the governors investigated
and recommended the termination of his contract. The LEA
accepted the recommendation. However, to avoid the ignominy
of dismissal, Owthwaite was given the opportunity to resign. He
was allowed seven days to do this, but he declined. Consequently
in July, he was dismissed from office; but this was not the end of
the matter. The Association of Principals of Technical Institutions
intervened and held discussions with the Principal and the LEA.
As a result, Albert Owthwaite agreed to resign, with effect from
31 December 1955, and the previous decision to dismiss him
was rescinded.

Albert Owthwaite was allowed no contact with the college
from the day of his suspension. Vice-Principal Roy Pocock was
appointed Acting Principal and he was in charge for nine months.
A new Principal, Eric Lansley, took over in April 1956 and the
drama came to an end. A new era in the history of South Berks
College was about to begin.

Many stories have been told about the 'unhappy events' of the summer of 1955. This is not surprising. Any story about the dismissal of a Principal is major news in a college staff room. The allegations focused on the disappearance of particular items of property from Oxford Road and their subsequent reappearance in the garden of Bridge House on Red Shute Hill in Hermitage, where Albert and Elsie Owthwaite had lived since 1951. Hence comments from people I interviewed such as, 'it all seems a bit petty really'; and 'the caretaker used to know what was going on'; and 'it was to do with some equipment he had borrowed which belonged to the college, a lawnmower or something'. The greenhouse was the brickwork shop in 1955, and it features in many of the stories. One account has the Principal taking the doors off and transporting them to Hermitage to be used in a greenhouse which he was building in his garden. Another story has a lecturer arriving one Monday morning to find that most of the glass from the roof had been removed, only to be found later at Bridge House. A more imaginative version has the lecturer arriving at the brickwork shop early one morning to find that *all* the glass had been removed. Moreover, it had rained overnight and bags of cement and plaster lay ruined. New timber ordered by the Building Department was also disappearing before it could be used. All these items, and others, according to which stories are believed, were finding their way to Hermitage. The more stories that were told, the more items seemed to have been removed. 'Have you heard the one about the 12-volt car battery?' This was bought by the college to be used in the motor vehicle workshop. It went missing and was found under the bonnet of the Principal's car. Dramatically, we are told it was there on that Monday morning in June, the day he was suspended.

Other stories have circulated which try to explain Albert Owthwaite's conduct without ever quite justifying it. 'For three years he lived in the flat in Ormonde House and except for minimal holidays virtually never left the college.' Not surprisingly, he sometimes used college property for his own purposes. Living over the shop, the dividing line between what belonged to the Principal and what belonged to the County Council could become a little blurred. Lecturers would sometimes borrow an item, take it off the premises and use it at home; but, of course, it would be strictly on loan, to be eventually returned to Ormonde House. Albert Owthwaite was 'not really a rogue'; he used to borrow things and 'just went over the mark a bit'.

What we do know is that the specific allegations were made in a letter sent to the LEA. It was anonymous, signed by the ubiquitous 'ratepayer'. The implication was clear: Albert Owthwaite was using items paid for out of public money for his own private pursuits. It is likely that the letter was written by an insider as the detail could only have come from someone at the college, or at the very least, from somebody closely involved with Ormonde House. Stories have circulated as to the identity of the correspondent, but not surprisingly, the name has never been revealed. Such a letter, however, not only begs the question, 'Who?' but also, 'Why?'

As the college grew in size, Albert Owthwaite had disagreements with some of his staff. This is not unusual although perhaps not quite everyday life in an FE college. One of his engineering lecturers, for instance, was unhappy with his grading and salary. Heated arguments were overheard, with the engineer demanding to be upgraded and the Principal 'having none of it'. Their relationship was not good, and it deteriorated further when Owthwaite heard the lecturer address one of his students as a 'stupid bugger' for dropping a large spanner on one of the electrical motors which resulted in a short circuit and blew the fuses in the workshop. He reported the indiscretion to the governors. No doubt there were arguments with other staff as well. Jessie Searle used to 'shout at various things' that the Principal did; but she was not the angry ratepayer. Neither was it Roy Pocock, or Eric Carr or the formidable Vera Garlick who was not at the college as the drama unfolded, having resigned the previous year. And it was not Dick Edwards. 'Owthwaite was a bit of a devil. He scrapped with pretty well everyone and he used to drive them.'

The events of the summer of 1955 have generated the occasional conspiracy theory. Were the allegations a 'set-up?' Did Owthwaite have enemies amongst some staff who were anxious to be rid of him? There was a story about one lecturer 'ganging up' against him, and meeting unofficially with a couple of governors to report anything untoward about his behaviour. When Albert

Owthwaite drove in to the college on 20 June, two or three 'official people' were waiting for him – and they discovered the 12-volt battery in his car. Another theory was that the Principal did not get on with one of the college's inspectors, a difficult relationship which went back many years. Perhaps this had an influence on the course of events. It is possible that Albert Owthwaite was nurturing a grievance with his employers in Shire Hall. 'He was not able to negotiate personal holidays during term time, and this left him a little sour.'[1] This could have affected his relationship with the LEA.

Mabel Lord is one of the personalities in the story. She came to Ormonde House in 1951 to work in the office, when Elsie Owthwaite was the Principal's personal assistant. When the Owthwaites moved to Hermitage, Mrs Owthwaite gave up her work and Mabel Lord became the Principal's secretary. 'The Principal's secretary was very much the Principal's secretary and didn't really interfere with the office at all.'[2] Miss Lord left the college when the Principal was suspended, and over a quarter of the full-time lecturers resigned in the wake of Owthwaite's departure. Was this a coincidence or did it represent something more serious? The search for motive is a fascinating one, but in the end, it is fruitless. However, we do have the facts – albeit unexplained – recorded in the minute books of the FE Subcommittee.

These tell us that three lecturers left Newbury in the summer of 1955: R C Ireson, W J Ramshaw and J S Theodorson. Another, L T Basketeer, went at the end of the year and a few months later, A G Elgood and Cecil Cox handed in their resignations.[3] Cecil Cox was the most senior of these, having been appointed in 1951 to teach engineering and take charge of the electrical machines and engineering drawing.

'He was out straightaway – I was the last person to see him as Principal'

---

[1] SBCFE 25 Years.

[2] Interview with Roy Pocock.

[3] FESC 28 November 1955, 9 March 1956, 13 July 1956.

Dick Edwards reported for work as usual on the eventful Monday morning. His first lesson was in a ground floor room in the house. Roy Pocock was teaching next door. Little were either of them expecting the drama that was about to unfold.

> A kid asked me a question. I said, 'I don't know the answer but I've got it upstairs in the staff room – I'll go and get it.' I went up. This was between 9.30 and 9.45. Owthwaite was just coming in. 'Morning Dick,' he said, bright and breezy.

> At the end of the period I went up to the staff room again and he was coming down the stairs with a face like thunder. He did not know that waiting for him upstairs had been the Deputy Director of Education, the chairman of the governors and the county auditor.

> And that was the last time he was in college. He was out straightaway – I was the last person to see him as Principal.

The Deputy Director had told Albert Owthwaite that serious allegations had been made about his conduct. As a consequence, he was to be immediately suspended from duty, pending the results of a governors' investigation. As Owthwaite walked out of the house, Roy Pocock was summoned up the stairs and appointed Acting Principal.

> I happened to know Whitfield who was Deputy Director. He just called me up from downstairs where I was teaching and said, 'Will you take that chair over there? That's yours from now on.' We had a sort of sympathy, one with the other, and got on well. He was the army man, a tall, smart figure with what was called a 'territorial decoration'. Herbert, the Director at that time, was all for delegating anything which smelt a bit to Whitfield.

Vice-Principal Pocock was in charge of the college for nine months. His salary was increased by £160, to £1,165.[4] 'The full-time staff were marvellous and gave me good support' – but these

---

[4] *Ibid.*, 28 November 1955.

were difficult times. 'We were left with an Acting Principal, one member of the office staff, Betty Ward, and the junior girl on the telephone. That was it.' Betty Ward: 'Pocock was left Acting Principal and I was Acting Everybody. There were only two of us there. We did all the admin work between us.' Lecturers were resigning and had to be replaced, student numbers were increasing, and the building of the first instalment was under way.[5]

The details of Albert Owthwaite's departure can be put together from the FESC records where the allegations of misconduct are there for all to see. Unfortunately the Principal's defence of his behaviour is not recorded; neither are the interior thoughts and feelings of committee members and the other persons involved.

The dates of the alleged offences are not recorded but one assumes they must have occurred in the recent past. The identity of the 'ratepayer' is concealed from view, if known; so are the names of the witnesses of the misconduct, if there were any. Three of the allegations were to do with the theft of items of property; the other was about the use of the time of the college technician, a charge in which Mabel Lord was indirectly implicated.

- That material taken from the roof of the building material store and brickwork shop at the College was removed to his (the Principal's) private residence.

- That certain timber purchased from Messrs James of Newbury for the use of the College was removed by him to his private residence.

- That the time of the College workshop technician was improperly used on maintenance and other work on his private motor car, and maintenance of lawn mowers belonging to him and his Secretary.

- That he used for his private car a 12-volt battery belonging to the College.[6]

---

[5] 'From June 1955 until April 1956 the Vice-Principal acted as Principal while running a department, planning the new college and acting as registrar. Miss Ward was the only member of office staff except for a girl on the switchboard.' SBCFE 25 Years.

[6] FESC 10 August 1955.

Events moved quickly after the excitement of that morning on 20 June. An audit of college property was undertaken at short notice. 'All of a sudden somebody said that the Director was coming down. We had a full inspection. Everything was inspected. There was the gardening equipment – spades and all that – on the bank just outside Ormonde House where the steps are. It was amazing, it really was, all the things spread out on the grass bank.'[7] Behind the scenes, the governors proceeded with their investigations. They met with Albert Owthwaite on 11 July. No record of this meeting exists, but we know that the Principal was unaccompanied and was given the opportunity to defend himself.[8] After what must have been the most careful deliberation, the governors concluded that Owthwaite was not a 'suitable person' to continue in office. The LEA was to be asked to terminate his contract.[9]

Such a recommendation was one of the most important the governors of an FE college could make. Their constitution recognised this by stipulating that the decision had to be confirmed at a further meeting to be held within 14 days of the previous one. This would allow time for reflection, time to think carefully about what was best for the future of the college, a breathing space, time for emotions to settle, for reason and, above all, for justice to prevail.

The governors met again on 26 July with at least 15 of them present. Albert Owthwaite came, this time with a 'friend' and they were each given the opportunity to address the meeting. The identity of the 'friend' remains tantalisingly unknown, undisclosed in the minute books. Was it his secretary, who had been identified in one of the allegations? Was it Jeff Jeffery, the technician whose 'time' the Principal had been accused of using 'improperly'? Was it another member of staff who was anxious to speak for the defence? Was it one of the lecturers who left with Owthwaite? Whoever it was, the governors were unmoved. They resolved by 12 votes to three to confirm their previous decision. The education authority was to be asked to dismiss Albert Owthwaite from office.[10]

---

[7] Interview with Betty Ward.

[8] I have been unable to trace the records of the governors' meetings and can only assume that they have been destroyed.

[9] FESC 10 August 1955.

[10] *Ibid.*.

Two weeks later, on the morning of Wednesday 10 August, 16 members of the FESC met in Reading. Two were governors from Newbury, AWE's Ron Spiller and Father Zollo, the priest from St Joseph's Church. There was one item on the agenda, the administration of South Berks College. The meeting lasted for over two hours. Albert Owthwaite and his 'friend' were each given the opportunity to speak, after which they left the room while the committee considered its verdict. In the end, it was decided to accept the recommendation from Newbury. Albert Owthwaite was not to continue as Principal. However, rather than dismiss him, he was to be asked to resign. If he did not resign within seven days, he was to be dismissed. His salary was to be paid until the end of the year.[11] A week went by, and Albert Owthwaite had not submitted his resignation; consequently the LEA terminated his contract.

The matter did not end there. The Association of Principals took up the case and their representatives met with Owthwaite and the LEA. Although the seven-day deadline had passed, they diplomatically encouraged resignation as the best way to conclude the matter. Albert Owthwaite listened, changed his mind, and submitted his resignation with effect from 31 December 1955. This was accepted, but he had to agree 'to regard his contact with the college as having ceased when he last undertook duties there'.[12] When Albert Owthwaite walked out of Ormonde House in June 1955, he may have looked back, but he never returned. From an upstairs window, Dick Edwards watched him drive away.

'No one worked harder for the success of the College than did Albert Owthwaite'

Albert Owthwaite had been Principal for seven years, and the manner of his departure must not be allowed to detract from his achievements. He had overseen the transition from local institute to area college and under his management South Berks College had become one of the leading providers of further education in the county.

---

[11] *Ibid.*.

[12] *Ibid.*, 28 November 1955.

With the LEA in Reading, he had resolutely argued Newbury's case for staffing, accommodation and equipment. Closer to home, he had always been willing to defend the college's autonomy against interference by the Newbury Division. 'There was this fight between the county and the local authority. The local education officer at Peake House (Newbury) thought he was in charge of us here. There was always a fight between Owthwaite and him as to what should happen.'[13] When Owthwaite was appointed Superintendent, he was the only full-time member of staff. By the time he left, he was responsible for at least 20 full-time lecturers, two or three times as many part-time assistants, and a technical and administrative support staff. For seven years, he had overseen the development of an extensive curriculum – in building, commerce, engineering, science and women's subjects – with a rich and lively non-vocational programme. The range of courses was impressive, further education at its best. Moreover he had worked as a 'hands-on' Principal, so much so that he was capable of timetabling 'pretty well any range of subjects – he did it all himself, engineering, building, you name it, he'd got it all there'.

Albert Owthwaite's final Speech Day was in the spring of 1955. The academic year that was coming to a close had been one of 'record enrolment', with more students than ever before. At Newbury there were 66 full-time, 620 part-time day and 1,245 evening enrolments. 499 of the 620 part-time day students were doing engineering or science. In addition, there were 500 enrolments in the institutes. Here the increase was most marked in Thatcham. The total number of college enrolments was almost 2,500.[14] As the Director of Education put it, 'Further education at this end of Berkshire had a bright future.'

The college had grown 'more rapidly than the education authority could expand the buildings' and the ever increasing number of students had been accommodated with creative adaptations at Oxford Road and the hiring of venues across the town. Most importantly, the building of the new college had already started by the time Albert Owthwaite left; and he had made a personal contribution to its design. 'He had that very much

---

[13] Interview with Roy Pocock.

[14] *NWN* 5 May 1955.

under his control.'[15] The first instalment was a physical reminder in bricks and glass of his time as Principal.

Albert Owthwaite's most important legacy, however, was the day-release programme and the network of supportive employers which he initiated and encouraged. 'The war had just finished, everything was in chaos. Companies didn't send people to college in those days in 1948.' Owthwaite had developed a web of relations with employers and forged close links with industry and commerce during his years at the helm. The county college dream had faded. Employers were not legally obliged to release their young workers and successive post-war governments, first Labour and then Conservative, were reluctant to make it compulsory. There were no laws covering training – and no penalties either. Yet Owthwaite had encouraged a number of companies in the Newbury district to change their perception of training and apprenticeship. A few of them had worked with the Technical Institute in the interwar years, but by the mid-'50s the situation had been transformed.

Employers participated because of the quality of the training curriculum. The courses were relevant, meeting the needs of industry. Employers were involved as governors, and the advisory committees provided a series of conduits from the community into Ormonde House. There were no fewer than 10 of these by the mid-'50s, with 80 people involved.[16]

'If an individual lives in a community he should play his part in it'

Ron Spiller was a governor at the time of the 'unhappy events'. He was one of the most active on the board and served from the mid-fifties until the end of the sixties. He was appointed in 1953, representing Youth Employment, became vice-chairman in 1956 and chairman the following year when he took over from Russell

---

[15] Interview with Roy Pocock.

[16] There were four advisory committees by 1951: in building and in electrical, mechanical and motor engineering. The committee in women's subjects was active by 1952, those in agriculture, commerce and science by 1956. There were also committees for the institutes of Hungerford and Lambourn, and Thatcham and Compton.

Radcliffe. He led the governing body during the time when the new college was built and staff and student numbers increased beyond all expectations.

Ron Spiller was an engineer who had come to Newbury during the war to work for Vickers Armstrong. He joined AERE Harwell shortly after it opened and moved to AWE Aldermaston in 1953 as a technical officer. His work covered most aspects of the engineering trades up to workshop management. He was a man of broad horizons, with lots of energy and commitment, and he gave the college a 'constant link with local industry, with the trade union movement and with youth employment'. He believed that 'if any individual lives in a community he should play his part in it', and he certainly did.[17] In 1952 he was elected to the County Council representing one of the wards in Newbury. A Labour man, he was passionate about politics and had been involved with the labour movement 'since an early age'. He was chairman of Newbury Labour Party but as a Labour councillor, he was in a minority among rural Berkshire's ruling Conservatives. He sat on the County Council for 15 years, and was a keen member of the Education Committee and the Newbury Division. He was always arguing in favour of education spending, vehemently opposing cuts in the service whenever 'economies' were on the agenda. In 1956, when the budget was being discussed,

> Mr Spiller declared that the needs of education locally and nationally were greater now than they had ever been. 'At the moment we are losing the battle of education' he said. 'This country, to be strong economically in the future, must rely on the skill and ingenuity of its craftsmen. We can only do that by providing the same educational facilities as are given in every other major industrial power. I say we should not go to the County Council with tongues in cheeks. We should go and say that these are our minimum requirements.'[18]

---

[17] *NWN* 12 April 1973.

[18] *Ibid.*, 12 January 1956.

There was a need for increasing educational expenditure. Twelve months later, 'I certainly hope that people who have bees in their bonnets about education will continue to push these things. There is great need to push forward even further than at present in the improvement of our education services.'[19] In 1958 he appealed for extra provision for FE colleges to cope with the increase in school leavers expected over the next few years. He also argued strongly for the new laboratories at Newbury and the much hoped-for HNC work.

When John Rankin School opened in 1955, many of the children came from the Valley Road estate where a lot of AWE workers lived. Ron Spiller was chairman of the school's managers. A few years later, he became a governor of Reading College and the new Turnpike School between Newbury and Thatcham. He was chairman of the Youth Employment Committee for 20 years, an active trade unionist and an enthusiastic member of the Newbury and District Trades Council. In 1966 he stood as Newbury's Labour candidate in the General Election. His Conservative opponent was John Astor. Ron Spiller failed in his bid to get into Westminster, but it was a close contest.[20]

Ron Spiller's wife Aileen was also committed to community work. By the time of her appointment as magistrate in 1957, she was secretary of the local Labour Party, chairman of the local Family Planning Association and member of the Ministry of Insurance and Pensions Disablement Committee. Aileen was on the bench for 16 years. She also served as governor of the County Girls' School and worked for the Newbury and District Disablement Committee and the local Transport Users group.

Ron and Aileen Spiller died some years ago, leaving their sons Roger and Barry with an abundance of warm and cherished memories of a mum and dad who really did try to make a difference in people's lives. 'I wish they'd written all this down because their history would have been interesting.' This is **Barry Spiller's** voice.

---

[19] *Ibid.*, 24 October 1957.

[20] The result was Astor (Con) 25,908, Spiller (Lab) 21,762, Davies (Lib) 9,571. The Conservative and Labour candidates knew each other as John Astor had been a college governor since 1960.

Mother and father moved into Newbury in the mid-1940s. He was originally in Salisbury, where he was a union organiser and in the Socialist Youth. My grandmother was always very proud that when Oswald Mosley went to Salisbury to give a speech, she hit him over the head with her umbrella. In the early part of the war my father was a lorry driver and he used to travel down to the West Country a lot. He tried to get the union organised for the drivers, and he was drummed out of the town. He had three or four months even in the war of not being able to work. His political attitudes were against the overall consensus of opinion. They then transferred to Ipswich where my mum had relations. He went to Ransomes 'cos they were looking for engineers, and he was involved in the union there. Then he moved down to Newbury to work in the Vickers factory on Shaw Road, which is now Quantel.

After the war there was a shortage of engineers and trained people. When Harwell opened, they were looking for engineers and he transferred from Vickers. He went to college in Newbury on the engineering side, and was still carrying on his college work into the early '50s. He was at Harwell for a few years and then when Aldermaston opened and they were looking for people there, he transferred. He was still very much involved on the union side, ending up as local chairman of the Association of Professional Civil Servants. He was involved in union meetings all his working life. He ended up as a technical officer at Aldermaston. He went in as engineering foreman and then got transferred up to management. He was in charge of a workshop where they used to machine for bombs or whatever the research was at that time. He ended up in charge of the Apprentice School – so he was then involved with the supply of further education to the apprentices.

He became involved in the college because he was very interested in youth work and training people. He was chairman of the Youth Employment Committee in

Newbury. He was very much involved with the Stradling family, who were builders in the area; old man Stradling was a very keen apprentice man.[21] My father was involved with education all the way through his life. He was chairman of the governors at John Rankin School when that first opened, and he was very much involved in Reading College. He actually met the Queen when she went there – I don't know how well that went down!

There were two things which he was passionate about, health and education. He thought they should both be free. If you've got health and education, you've got a healthy society.

When he was on the County Council, he was involved in employment, education and planning. Things were always going on, people coming and going, 'phone calls from whoever. He did a lot of things, but he did it without any fuss. When he died I had a 'phone call from a woman completely out the blue. 'You won't know me but I've lived on the Shaw estate since it was built. When Western Avenue was built, your father was involved and I'd just like to say that his involvement was very much appreciated.' The underpass which goes between one part of the estate and the other, where Winchcombe School is, was never going to be an underpass – it was just going to be a pelican crossing. My dad fought and fought to get an underpass put in, and in the end it was. His argument was that there were children going to the school and they should never have to cross the road. It took a long time, but he did get it through, and for somebody to ring up out the blue to say she appreciated what he did – that meant a lot.

Dad was left-wing and was chairman of the local Labour Party for quite some time – mum was secretary. There were a lot of people within the party who were from a similar

---

[21] Thatcham builder H A Stradling became a college governor in 1959 and served throughout the 1960s.

background, going through the war, coming out the other end and being very much involved with people rather than profit. It was that era, the early stages of social awareness. He stood as parliamentary candidate in the '60s. At one of the counts there were piles of votes in certain districts where he was ahead of Astor. It was one of the closest votes that there had ever been in Newbury. Politically one of the proudest moments was seeing him on stage next to Harold Wilson at a meeting in Reading during one of the election campaigns.[22] He knew quite a few people in the Labour Government, people like Tony Benn for instance. They were Labour friends and they went out to meetings quite often. When Paul Robeson came to England, the Labour Party had a lot of involvement, looking after him. He used to come to Labour Party rallies and the story goes I actually sat on Paul Robeson's shoulders![23]

Political parties didn't seem to have the insular attitudes that they have now. Lots of dad's friends were Conservatives. They used to talk to each other on the 'phone, travel with each other in their cars to meetings, and there didn't seem to be the animosity that there is between people today. When dad died, we had quite a bit of correspondence from people of completely different political persuasions.

Charles Sully used to come on holiday with us. Today, he would be called socialist, but in those days he was just straight average Labour Party. He was teaching on the motor vehicle side. He knew his mechanics; he really knew what was going on. I can remember going up to his house on Boxing Day one year and going to spend the day with them, and him talking about tanks in the First World War, and saying how deadly they were, not for the enemy but for the drivers of the damn things because they could always

---

[22] Harold Wilson (1916-95), Labour politician and twice Prime Minister, 1964-70 and 1974-76.

[23] Paul Robeson (1898-1976), African-American singer, actor and civil rights advocate.

explode at any time. He was involved in car racing because we used to go down to Goodwood with him. He used to have a little Singer sports car. In the late '50s we used to go on camping holidays abroad, to France, Germany, and Switzerland. Late one evening, we went into this café in Cologne, and there was this chap sitting right down the other end. There was mum, dad, my brother and myself, and Charles. After about half an hour, this chap paid his bill and started to walk out when he turned round to Charles and said, 'Excuse me. Aren't you Charles Sully? I don't know whether you remember me, but you taught me motor vehicle mechanics in the early '50s.' He was in the army and stationed in Germany.

'We learnt the fancy stuff at college – it put me in good stead 'cos I've done a lot of it since '

The Abraham family were builders in Kintbury. Mr Abraham senior started the company with his brother in the mid-'30s. During the Second World War, the brother was killed. A few years later, the eldest son joined the business and was sent to Ormonde House to learn carpentry with Arthur Owen. The younger son also joined the firm and he, too, was apprenticed and sent for training into Newbury. 'The bricklaying side was only a small part of building, but it was a trade and you had to have a trade.' The bricklayer's name was **George Abraham.**

I was at school at Christchurch near Kintbury, then to Hungerford modern at the age of 11. I never thought of doing anything else than building and I worked for my father and became a partner when I was 18. I didn't go to the college before I was 16 or 17 because I had been at work for a year. I was apprenticed for four years and did all four years at Newbury. At the time it seemed better than going to work, but there wasn't much in it really. We never thought apprentices came into it, 'cos the idea was that fathers taught sons, like it or not; but once colleges started, we went away from that theory a little bit. It was the builders that made the college work because you were encouraged to have apprentices. There were a lot of big builders round our side of Newbury, such as Wooldridge at Hungerford.

In most cases the apprenticeships were pretty hard times 'cos you didn't get paid much. When I started I was paid about three pounds a week. Sometimes at the end of the day you had your work knocked down and you had to do it again tomorrow if you didn't get it right. The one thing which did encourage apprenticeship was that you didn't go in the army at 18. You didn't go until you were 21, National Service. That steered a lot of people into taking a trade. The army was not as well paid as the other side.

Father's firm was based at Kintbury but we used to go as far as Reading, Tilehurst, and Upper Basildon. We were covering a big area. We've always done private houses, never council. We've done a lot for the Catholic Colleges: Douai, St Cassian's De La Salle, and St John's, which is now Inglewood, at Kintbury.[24] They were our main customers because the Brothers bought cheap – over the years the buildings had got into a bad state – and spent a lot of money restoring. As a young apprentice, I was working on private housing or the colleges. I was building new bungalows, one at a time, for specialist people, as far out as Frilsham and Yattendon. Most of my customers would live in them and then sell them on. They were living comfortably doing that.

We were also doing bungalows in Kintbury when I started. Kintbury's mains drainage had been done, so we were involved in a lot of conversions. There were two or three houses which had had nothing done since the war. They were getting government grants to put them on mains drainage. When you look back now, it seems impossible, because you had no machines. You were digging 16 foot deep, mostly at night 'cos there was no traffic and nobody

---

[24] St Cassian's Centre, run by the De La Salle Brothers from 1946, was in a manor house outside Kintbury.

would take a bit of notice. Now you would have to have machines, lights and so on. In the 1950s we hadn't come into the mechanical age of building. All you had was a wheelbarrow. It was all physical work. We were better for it. There's a lot of the chaps who worked with me still alive in their 80s and one or two of them are still building now, so manual work didn't kill you.

I did four years at Newbury on day release, starting in 1953. It wasn't that bad, but we were in a situation where you had been working all day and then you had to go two evenings – it tended to make it a long day. In the end, to save splitting it up, we were doing from 9 am right through to 7 to 9 pm. We did a bit of science, and for technical drawing and that we came together. We went in with the plumbers as there weren't enough people to do it separately. We did some work with motor vehicle. In technical drawing you ended up doing a bit of maths. There was a marvellous old chappie who used to take us for maths who had a patch over one eye. He was one of the best men with figures that I've ever met – he was really good. The drawing was done in the house, and we used to use a building down Albert Road for science. We used to go there on the days. The evening stuff was all at the college.

The brickwork construction was in the lean-to greenhouse at the back of the house – that was where we actually did the work. Bill Parrott and Ken Morton took us. The greenhouse was big, and it was very, very cold in the winter. But normally we would be working outside, so to work in a greenhouse, which was covered, was a luxury. There were about a dozen students. You'd be building columns and piers in fancy work, so you didn't need a lot of space. Normally we would build something and knock it down the same day, or if we didn't, we would knock it down the next week. You didn't throw stuff away – you recycled it all.

We were also up at Donnington for a while at the beginning. The college had a place at the top of the hill and we used to go to Donnington Lodge, into a garden shed or something like that, big enough to house ten or 15. That was for the construction, the practical side. Tools were provided by the college. All you would need was a level, a trowel, a pair of lines, and a hammer and a bolster, scotches, you know, things basically for cutting and shaving bricks. There were no electrical cutters. I enjoyed it. We had a good game with the brickwork chaps and a lot of builders came out of that year.

While we were at college, they were building St John's Church. It was a big thing – Princess Margaret opened it. We were brought down two or three sessions to look at the brickwork. It was something that we wouldn't normally have seen as there wasn't much of that size of building going on. It's got terrible big joints, which had never been done before like that. That was a bit modern. As the building progressed, we saw different sections. They were doing all the barrel arches. It was very educational – we'd drawn arches but we hadn't seen how they were constructed.[25]

They treated us well at college 'cos you were encouraged. If you came first you got a prize but you also got a book if you did better than in the previous year. It was a good way to encourage a chap who'd come up a grade or two. The prize would be presented in the class at the end of the year.[26]

When we were in our third and fourth years, we used to go to competitions in Reading. That was a privilege, a day out. It was always a bit of fun, a sport really, challenge Reading! We would do exhibitions, with brickwork and all the trades competing and all judged at the end of the day.

---

[25] The foundation stone of St John's Church was laid by HRH Princess Margaret in 1955, and the building was consecrated in 1957. Designed by Dykes-Bower, much of the interior was unrendered brick and the quality of the brickwork and vaulting was much admired. In 1988, it was amongst the first of Britain's post-1939 buildings to be listed as being of architectural interest.

[26] George Abraham won the best first-year student prize in 1954.

Reading was much bigger, but Newbury always came out quite good. It encouraged you to be in competition. The trouble with being an apprentice, time was one thing but speed wasn't. You weren't taught to do things quickly, you were taught to do them well. But when you went on these – it was only a day or two days – you were in competition on time.[27]

A lot of the lecturers were craftsmen that turned to teaching. Arthur Owen was a chippie, Ernie Newport was a plumber. He had a plumbing business and he did a lot of lead work on some jobs we were working on.

I don't think we were looking for qualifications. We were looking for training to be able to do the job. Qualifications were something which sounded new. The time at college was to be trained in the more specialised brickwork, as against the more normal day to day. We looked at it as additional training. For lots of the lads it was the only thing they ever did except for the same basic sort of council house. It was good experience for them. We learnt the fancy stuff at college – that's what we thought it was about. It put me in good stead 'cos I've done a lot of it since, things like brick altars, ornate and nice to do. You look back and think that was good. My father worked on the statue at St Joseph's Church by the Robin Hood roundabout – that was always his mark as we drove by. 'You ought to aim for doing one of those.' Lots of the apprentices only ever built one type of council house. They weren't trained on site really. They had one plan and they just went on up the street. It was always the same. It was a sore point with

---

[27] The Regional Building Crafts Competition started in 1955. Organised by Reading LEA and the SRCFE, the competition was open to all FE Establishments in the Southern Region and held in one of the colleges. The competitions were well supported – five students represented SBCFE at Bournemouth in 1959 – and they did much to bring together the craft standards of the colleges. A student from SBCFE won second prize in the junior carpentry and joinery section in 1955. See SRCFE 21st Anniversary 1947-1968, p.5; FESC 8 July 1955, 6 March 1959.

them. All the training they had was at the college, so it was a good experience for them.

There were no discipline problems. You were privileged to be there. When you said you were 'apprenticed', it was something a bit special. To walk down the town from the college was something quite smart wasn't it? We used to come down the town for meals with a gang of 20. There used to be a café at the end of Park Way opposite the cinema. It was only a small place but it was cheap and alright. The chap in the café was doing a good trade. Later we did some work for him. It was the wrong time 'cos I probably could have got free meals if I had done it before.

Other than lunchtimes, there wasn't much of a social outlet. You were so tired; you didn't really want to do much else. It was a hard life, one day and evening, and one other evening. You didn't eat until you got back. It was a long day. College was an offshoot to going to work for a day. You didn't have a social evening on your day job, and you didn't expect social evenings going to college. It wasn't a social thing. There was nothing at all.

We were only there one day a week. There were other students in there every day, but you didn't see much of them. We kept ourselves to ourselves, or they kept us away. The women were in Ormonde House, bookkeeping and secretarial girls who had left secondary modern school. It was getting mixed when we left. Motorbikes were not common, but there were two or three of us from Inkpen. There was no bus at the time we needed at night, so in the end we got bikes. Hungerford lads were alright; they could train from Hungerford.

I got a certificate for the intermediate City & Guilds. The exams were done in the classroom and covered all the things we were doing, building construction, the technical side and the theory as well. In building, construction wasn't just bricklaying as such. We got involved with stresses and loadings and things like that, and they also came into technical drawing. We were not tested by the staff. Somebody else came in for that, somebody foreign.

After four years at the college, they had given me all I could take – I didn't have any room for any more.

Bill Parrott was one of George Abraham's teachers.

I was at the college in 1953 being appointed straight from my teacher training at Huddersfield College. I was in the Building Department to teach City & Guilds courses in brickwork and the associated subjects.

The brickwork shop consisted of an old greenhouse complete with growing vines and other plants together with a varied assortment of livestock including rats.[28] As can be imagined the temperature in winter was a bit low, but some very competent work was produced in very poor conditions under the glasshouse roof. I taught building science in an ordinary classroom – one sink, a bench and a blackboard. This led to a student at the time writing up his notes of an experiment: 'The experiment was a failure'. The theory subjects were taught in a wooden hut. On one occasion in midwinter, when it was snowing outside and so cold inside we all kept our overcoats on, I was obliged to require one student to leave since he was being a bigger pest than usual. After about one and a half hours the class ended and we left. Standing outside the door was this student with about four inches of snow on his head and shoulders. Why? It seems I had told him to 'Go outside!'

'I want to be a mechanic like my dad'

Mick Palmer arrived at the college while Roy Pocock was Acting Principal. Mick was from Kintbury, educated at the school close to the church in the village. His secondary education was in

---

[28] The rats were 'monsters, kept in check by the Sully cat'. SBCFE 25 Years.

Hungerford. Mick managed to leave school before he was 15 – 'nowadays it would never be allowed' – and he was taken on as a garage mechanic. He started his City & Guilds at Ormonde House in 1955. Fifty years on, and these are Mick's memories.

I took the eleven-plus and out of the whole school there was only two that went through in our year. There was the initial exam, another exam if you passed the first one, and then there was an oral. I passed the two exams and I went before the board, but didn't get any further. There was quite a kerfuffle. It was very selective as to where you lived and what your parents did. But I thoroughly enjoyed Hungerford, a wonderful school because it had marvellous playing fields. There was a big playground area and we had one enormous field for football and cricket. The girls had a separate one for netball and rounders. We had to go through their field to get to ours, so we always made sure that the girls were playing when we walked through.

I left school in December 1954. My 15th birthday fell the day before they started back in January. I went through a sketchy careers advice.
'What do you want to do?'
'I want to be a mechanic like my dad.'
'Fine. Where would you like to go?'
And I went down and had an interview with Mr Norman at Norman's Garage in Hungerford.[29] He was a severe-looking man, very strict, and I was frightened stiff when I sat in his office. He gave me a job with an indentured apprenticeship.

Dad used to work for the flour company in Kintbury – the headquarters were down Bristol way. The mill at Kintbury by The Dundas is where they used to grind

---

[29] In 1956 William Norman was on the motor engineering advisory committee. Didge Marchant was chairman and the other members were R C James, A E Smith, W H Sutherland, F W Thatcher (Lambourn) and A H Brown (Thatcham).

all the flour, bag it and transport it. Dad was in the workshop. He maintained the vehicles and I was always down there with him, weekends and evenings, and going out on breakdowns. I used to take a great delight in going out. We used to go all over the place and I would help on the spanners. One midwinter we had a breakdown at Guildford. I was only about 12 or 13. To journey to Guildford of an evening after school, repair this vehicle and change a lever spring by the side of the road and come back again – mum went mad! Again, going out in the winter, you'd see the drivers stop and take the vehicles apart in the cold weather because they had no additives to put into the diesel. Diesel freezes up. It won't go through the pipe and the vehicle stops. To overcome that you had to somehow thaw it out and light a fire underneath the fuel tank. Of course, the drivers were skilled in this. There was very little problem with it. There weren't enough of the AA or breakdown companies about on the road.

We had an old Austin Seven and we used to go to the Motor Show at Earls Court. It was a long day but it was a good day out. You'd start for London at five o'clock in the morning, on the A4, through Reading, Maidenhead, Slough, and Windsor. It was a horrendous journey.

I started at Norman's Garage in January '55. He'd been running for donkeys' years and had a very good client base. When I went there the franchise was with the Rootes Group: Sunbeam Rapier, Hillman Minx, Humber Hawk, Snipes. Later on it moved to Rover and British Leyland. The chap that trained me had been there since the year dot, but he was brilliant. Old Jack Ferguson was an engineer foremost. If he wanted anything, he would make it. The spares situation wasn't brilliant, and vehicles were actually repaired – there weren't new bits put on. I couldn't have asked for a better grounding, 'cos what he instilled in me from the word go was, if you are going to do a job, then you do it properly. If you made a botch-up, then he'd certainly let you know about it, but you went out of your way not to make a botch-up. He instilled discipline, which is what I needed. It was a brilliant introduction.

I was fortunate in that I spent a lot of time with him. He wouldn't rush. He'd walk round, pipe in mouth – he'd always have his pipe on, even underneath the vehicle – with his cap, pair of thin-rimmed spectacles, and his bicycle clips. I was the gofer, jumping up and down the pit and doing the graft. You would fetch and carry the spanners. For the first year it was just a case of 'Do this' and 'Do that,' but all the time if you were doing a job, he would stand and watch. That was permissible by Mr Norman. If he could see that you were being trained, then that was okay, but if he saw you dossing about, then he would wonder why you weren't moving a broom around and keeping things tidy. If he saw you walking round with your hands in your pockets in the middle of winter, he'd tear you off a strip.

The garage was damp and in winter it was very cold. The facilities were pretty bare. They had a little gas ring that we used to boil up for lunch and tea, but there was no heating and you had the river running underneath, where they'd concreted over to enlarge the showroom.

At the time it was a bit of, 'Don't want to do this' and 'Don't want to do that', but it was a grounding that's never left me. If a big end got wet on a vehicle, which was quite common, it would be re-metalled by a firm up at Reading or Theale. They would then bring the rods back to us, and we had to fit them. We had to physically scrape the bearings in, and that meant up and down, and fitting them on, putting them on the crank and making sure they fit. Nowadays you just get a set of shells, whack it in, torc it up, and that's it. But then you had to actually fit it. I spent a day with that chap just scraping bearings out, put the glue on, down the pit, bolt it up – and he would turn it round and make sure it was a perfect fit. I could never see, initially, why he was messing about like that when all he had to do was basically bolt it up and do it. If he did anything he instilled me with patience, and it was a good exercise in how to do the job and do it properly. You wouldn't do that now because it's not cost-effective, but it is a good grounding as a mechanic or a fitter.

When I said to Mr Norman about college, he said, 'If you go to college, I'll give you a day off, but you pay your own way.' I started in September, but I had to pay all the fees. It was quite steep 'cos my first wage was a guinea (£1.05). It went up after the first month or so to £1/10/- (£1.50), then it went up every year, and after four years you got the improvers' rate. At first, I was the only one from Norman's to go to college. There was another chap that started the same time as me, but he never attended college so he got no qualifications as such. As an indentured apprentice – the apprenticeship was for five years – Mr Norman's job was to provide you with employment and make sure you were trained. And there were certain things written into the document that you had to keep to, that you'd be a loyal servant and all the rest of it, real 'olde worlde' stuff. Your father had to sign the indentures as well.

I did three and a half years at college, day release, nine till nine. Initially I went by train. The station wasn't far from where I lived. Then I used to get a lift in on the back of a motorbike. There was 12 in the group, all the same age, all apprentices from local garages: Marchant's, Nias, Martin and Chillingworth, Wheeler's. A year after I started, another apprentice started at the college from Norman's, then another shortly after him in '57 and then another in '58. So we had a stream of first-, second-, and third-year apprentices. There were no girls though; you wouldn't get girls going into motor vehicle.

The motor trade was very much in its infancy. It's obviously mushroomed in the last 30-odd years. Then there were not the amount of cars on the road. Petrol was a lot cheaper, tax was a lot cheaper, but cars weren't so reliable.

For instance, because of the fuel that you were using and the type of engine, you had to strip the cylinder head down every 10,000 miles and do the valves and that. Nowadays you don't touch a cylinder head. Cars today are a big improvement; suspensions, engines, it's changed enormously.

My knowledge of cars and how they worked was very limited. I was only 15 and even though I did help my dad and did a lot of physical work with him – taking stuff off and putting it back on – I knew how things worked but not the intricate details. So being at college was a backup, what we now call the 'underpinning knowledge'. There was no practical exams. The only thing you had was theory exams. Motor vehicle was always considered part and parcel of engineering, and the syllabus was always written in engineering terms. The exams lent towards the engineering side and nowadays they would be regarded as very difficult.

We were taught maths, technical drawing and science as separate subjects, and we took separate exams with them. The day was split up into these subjects. Mr Pocock was doing general studies and some calculations and we did a bit of science with him and a bit of English. We had a science separate subject with an engineering science teacher. He was way up in the clouds for motor vehicle students. He knew his science, but he couldn't bring it down to the level that the students required. This was a failing of the course rather than the teacher. The course was designed as an engineering course, not motor vehicle. Consequently the group tended to fall apart at times – to say it got disruptive is putting it mildly.

The college wasn't really big 'cos we did our classroom work in the house. Then we had the chicken house at the back; that's where we used to have some theory lessons. It was just a shed. It was cold – it had one of those old tortoise stoves stuck in the corner – but we didn't think anything of it because the garage was a lot colder. We had

a few lessons down Albert Road, and for exams we used
to go down to what is now the Waterside.

Charlie Sully was our main teacher. The basic training
that I had with Charlie at the college and Jack Ferguson
at Norman's was the bedrock really. Charlie gave me the
knowledge. He used to take us for the functional stuff,
workshop practice. He would take us for all the practical,
plus the theory on vehicles. There was no practical in the
first year, but the second year there was a three-hour slot in
the afternoons. Charlie had a big garage next to his cottage
and we used to do our practical in there. We worked on
his car. It was the only one we had. It was an old Singer,
overhead cam. He made some camshaft bearings for it out
of brass. He used to have his engine stripped down every
year. He'd go on holiday, come back, start his college year,
and the first job we had to do was whip the engine out. It
served a purpose because it gave us training.

There were also odd bits and pieces that we would work
on, units and stuff like that. The amount of electrics
on a car was very small, the battery, lights and starting.
In some cases it was a starting handle. The lights were
very basic, headlamps, sidelamps. The indicators were
the side-type ones which came out. The early ones didn't
light up; they were electrically operated at the side. So
it was just treated as, oh well, we'll do a bit of electrics.
We'll show you how the charger system and the starter
and the lights work, you know, the line diagrams. You
flick a switch and make the contact and you've got a
complete circuit. Then you started having things added
on to the cars, such as heaters. We used to have to fit
them as an extra when I started in the garage. And
electric wipers came in. The majority up till the '50s
were vacuum-operated. Then came radios. They were all
extras, and they were electrically operated. Nowadays
everything is electrical or sensed by units. You've got
electronics all over the place.

Charlie had a way of getting things over to you. He could describe something – he could do it how we needed to be taught. I liked him because I could respect the chap because he'd done it and he knew how to teach. We had some good times with him. He was very strong Labour, a member of the Labour Party in Newbury. He didn't hide his politics. If something was said, and he didn't agree with it, he would soon let you know. He used to go to the continent every year and take slides and show them in class. Other than that, the teaching was all lecturing and chalk and talk, but I learned because they made it interesting, and I was interested in the subject.

We had a lot of homework, especially science and Charlie's lessons on 'fundamentals' as he called it. Everybody did it, 'cos it was all marked and went on to the report; and if you didn't do it, the reports went to the firms straightaway. There was no hanging around waiting till Christmas or whatever, saying no homework had been done during this period of time. If you didn't do it within a short space of time, everybody was notified. If I didn't do it, Mr Norman would have drawn me in.

You can't equate 'then' with 'now'. 'Then' there was discipline in society. You were expected to do it, you were told to do it, and you did it, a bit like Pavlov's dogs. One day I was feeling ill, so I went home at seven o'clock. The college sent an absence form and Mr Norman didn't go very kindly on this. He claimed I was wasting time going home, even though I was paying my own way. He said, 'I'm giving you a day off', and even though this was in the evening, he didn't go much on that.

Normally there was very little trouble in the classroom. If you were in class you kept quiet. This science chap did have a bit of a problem, but nothing to what I've seen some classes degenerate into since. We used to come in, do our thing in the classroom and then clear off until the next week. That was it.

12

RAYS OF SUNSHINE

> Eric Lansley's arrival as the new Principal caused rays
> of sunshine in all directions.
>
> ***SBCFE 25 Years***

Eric Lansley was appointed Principal of South Berks College in November 1955. He took up the post on 1 April 1956 and stayed until he retired in the summer of 1970. Fourteen years in charge, he remains to this day the longest-serving Principal of the college.

He took over in Ormonde House at a difficult time. The events of the previous 12 months were fresh in everyone's mind, rankling perhaps with some. The departure of six lecturers in the wake of Owthwaite's resignation was not calculated to improve staff morale. When Roy Pocock stood down as Acting Principal, the FESC were quick to put on record their appreciation of his work.[1] But Vice-Principal Pocock was not given the top job. 'We were all rather surprised when Lansley was appointed. Pocock was Acting Principal and everybody thought he would get the job. He was interviewed and all that, but he didn't get it.'[2] It is likely that the LEA and the governors wished to appoint someone from outside the county, a person unconnected with the recent sorry events. They were looking for someone to run the college

---

[1] FESC 9 March 1956.

[2] Interview with Betty Ward.

with 'tact', and their choice was a good one.

Eric Lansley was from London and he started his working life as a schoolteacher. At night school he studied economics and once he had graduated, he moved into further education as a lecturer in a college for the distributive trades. He stayed there until 1948, when he became Principal of a new FE college in Leek in Staffordshire. He was there for eight years. When he moved to Newbury, he chose to live close to Ormonde House, at 32 Donnington Square, five minutes' walk across the Oxford Road.

The father of the college

Governor Didge Marchant was involved in the Principal's appointment. Looking back years later, he was convinced that 'they had chosen the right man for the job'.[3] At some point during his time at Newbury, Eric Lansley acquired the title, albeit unofficial, of 'father' of the college. Important to him was the need to establish a feeling of unity amongst staff and students and the name 'father' emerged because of the 'excellent relationships' which he developed. The name caught on and captured the imagination and when he bid his final farewell, the newspaper headline was 'Retirement gifts to father of college'. More than 200 people gathered in the hall on a warm summer's evening to hear the president of the Students' Union affirm how Eric Lansley 'was looked upon as a father figure by all of us'. The chairman of the Staff Association thanked him for his 'fatherly' role. 'He always left his door open to all of us. He was always ready to listen to our problems and give advice.' The college's 25th anniversary publication acknowledged the 'very fatherly eye' Lansley had kept on the college departments, 'persuading and controlling in a very professional manner'.[4]

---

[3] *NWN* 25 June 1970.

[4] SBCFE 25 Years.

And a gentleman

Newbury's second Principal inspired great loyalty amongst his staff and was supported by the experience of Vice-Principal Roy Pocock and a constructive governing body led by Ron Spiller. He was – and is – remembered with warm affection by the people who worked with him. The county's Director of Education said of him in 1970: 'When you first started, further education was not always welcomed but you have won the respect of your colleagues throughout the area. You have become a leader among college principals, and I think they have looked to you as a source of wisdom. You are one of the architects of further education in Berkshire and I think it will be a long time before it has made strides as great as it has in the last 14 or 15 years.'[5] The word 'gentleman' kept coming up when I spoke to people about him. Betty Ward: 'He was a gentleman, a true gentleman, he really was. A very quiet individual, very pleasant; you hardly heard anyone say a bad word against him.' Dick Edwards: 'The governors appointed a man who, at first sight, as soon as you saw him you knew he was a gentleman. He was straight as a die, up and down. You couldn't fault him, he was a lovely bloke. He did a lot to clean the name of the place up.' Roy Pocock: 'He gave an air of stability not only to this college but to the whole of Berkshire.' Eric Carr: 'He was a nice man; you could talk to him.' Mary Harte: 'Although he was Principal, he wanted to know everybody. In the first two weeks of term, he would spend a lot of his time popping into classrooms to see who was who. You couldn't not know him. He was literally everybody's friend. People got quite fond of him. He would say if you have a problem, let's talk about it; come up to my room and sit down. By the time you left you didn't have a problem. He was that kind of person to both staff and students.'

During his time as Principal, the college continued to grow. Student numbers increased, student hours doubled. By the late '50s, some of these students could be seen sporting a college blazer, complete with badge, and a black and amber college tie. The 'father' had inherited about 20 full-time lecturers. When he left there were more than 40. The curriculum was developed,

---

[5] *NWN* 25 June 1970.

and Eric Lansley was particularly responsible for liberal studies. 'He felt there was a need among technical students for something more than just a period of English a week.' A quotation from the ancient classical writer Aeschylus was included in the prospectus in 1963 – 'Learning is ever in the freshness of its youth, even for the old' – followed the next year by verses from Rudyard Kipling. Black-and-white photographs appeared in the prospectus for the first time. In 1959-60 it was buildings: the main entrance, the workshops of the first instalment (completed), the second instalment (under construction), and a perspective from the (new) Oxford Road roundabout. Two years later it was images of students receiving awards at the AWE Prize-Giving.

The college became a venue for cultural activities and the Principal participated in them. He had a public profile. Within a year of his arrival, he was chairing a public meeting organised by the WEA on 'Egypt – Its People and Customs'. Beyond the college, he continued to strengthen the all-important links with the business community. 'One of the things I have found particularly gratifying is the wonderful association I have had with industry and its representatives.' At the same time he worked hard for the Youth Employment Service. 'It is important for youngsters to know what opportunities are available and what would be suitable for them.' In 1958, with his 'considerable experience in training staff for the distributive trades', he addressed the Chamber of Commerce on the subject of salesmanship.[6]

Eric Lansley's achievements go beyond the confines of this volume. One of his first responsibilities on his arrival was to oversee the building work although at his first Speech Day he reminded his audience: 'We have been given good news of new buildings, but fine buildings do not make fine colleges; it is the people in them who make fine colleges.'[7] Within four years of his coming to Newbury, most of the new college had been built.

---

[6] *Ibid.*, 27 March 1958.

[7] *Ibid.*, 23 February 1956.

The new college

> Since August 1954, the volume of work at all Berkshire FE Establishments has continued to increase although relatively few new courses have been approved during the period because of the lack of suitable accommodation.
>
> **BEC 2 November 1956**

Work on the new college started in 1955. It was well under way when Eric Lansley arrived and by the beginning of 1957, the workshops and laboratories were finished. The second – and larger – instalment was started in 1958 and was finished in 1960.

The first instalment

The LEA and the Ministry of Education decided on the building programmes for schools and colleges. Each year Berkshire submitted its proposals to the Ministry for its approval. Other authorities in England and Wales did the same. The decision to build a new college in Newbury, as we have seen, had been taken as long ago as 1951.

The timing depended on the government. The Ministry provisionally agreed the first instalment for 1952-53 at a cost of around £70,000 with another £22,000 for furniture and fittings.[8] The buildings would be a fine accompaniment to the area college; but the excitement was short-lived. The country was experiencing economic difficulties. The demands of post-war reconstruction meant that the building industry was overstretched, and there was a national shortage of steel. The Korean War (1950-53) aggravated the problems and the government reduced its public spending commitments. All over the country education building programmes were cut back and the new South Berks College was one of the casualties. The Ministry failed to include it in its starts list but it did make the LEA's reserve list, and this was approved by the government.[9]

It was expected that building would start during 1953-

---

[8] Co-ordination Subcommittee 12 October 1951.

[9] BEC 20 June 1952.

54. The LEA argued that Newbury's needs were 'exceptional'. The pack was shuffled and the atomic card was dealt. The relationship with Harwell and Aldermaston created 'special requirements'. Newbury's instalment was of high priority because of the 'urgent need for accommodation for technical classes in the area'.[10] The Ministry accepted the plea of the special case. Hopes in Ormonde House were high, only to be dashed when the project was again postponed.

There was an HMI inspection at Newbury early in 1954. The previous inspection (1949) had emphasised the importance of new buildings. Since then the two horsa huts had been erected, but they were not enough. This time, the report again highlighted the need for additional accommodation before there could be any further expansion. The pressure point was science facilities. There was a laboratory in one of the prefabs, but another one was needed. As a stopgap, in the summer of 1954, the Victorian conservatory was turned into a chemistry laboratory. There were also problems in motor engineering, in finding somewhere to teach 'heat treatment'. The outbuilding next to the garage was used as a plumber's shop. Now it was to be converted into a heat treatment room 'provided that all timber work within twelve inches of any heat is protected with Turnall asbestos insulation board blocked half-inch away from the timber'. The students were to do the work.[11]

The HMI's report and the appeals from the atomic establishments added to the pressure for the first instalment to go ahead. By the mid-'50s, the national economic climate was improving. Moreover, the post-school educational hinterland was changing and there were plans to expand further education. David Eccles, Minister of Education, was keen to promote technical education and training. The White Paper of 1956 which bears his name allowed for the creation of ten colleges of advanced technology. The Ministry underlined the 'great importance' of the 'expansion of facilities for technical education' with additional accommodation for a wider range of vocational courses. Part of this strategy was to reorganise colleges, to allow 'major' colleges to be able 'to shed their lower grade work and have more freedom

[10] Co-ordination Subcommittee 27 November 1953.
[11] BEC 18 June 1954.

to provide for advanced technology and research'.[12]

South Berks was not a 'major' college as it did not teach the higher level courses. However, the sentiments of 1944 were again being heard in the corridors of power. The country needed more technicians and craftsmen and the government wanted to double the number of day-release students.[13] Old colleges were to be expanded; new ones were to be built. At the beginning of 1955, the Minister let it be known that he was prepared to consider adding to the building programme which had already been agreed for the coming year. He would give further consideration to 'deferred projects' and 'instalments', as well as those proposals 'which will provide accommodation for courses of a type hitherto not allowed'. Moreover, the programme for 1956-57 was to be expanded. The future looked promising for local authority building.[14]

This was the climate in which Newbury's instalment got under way. The Ministry agreed for it to start during 1954-55. It was to be built along the eastern boundary at the back of Ormonde House. The line of one-storey buildings was to include workshops for engineering, electrical installations, building, carpentry, plumbing and welding. A corridor was to link the workshops to a two-storey building at the southern end of the site. Here, on the ground floor, there were to be laboratories for building science and electronics, a drawing office and a technicians' workshop. Above, there were to be laboratories for physics, chemistry and mechanics.[15] The accommodation did not include any general purpose classrooms.

The LEA employed private quantity surveyors so as to avoid any delay in getting the work started. Before building could commence, an access roadway was needed. The FESC wanted this to be 'put in hand' in the spring of 1954, but the road was

---

[12] *Ibid.*, 25 February 1955.

[13] *Ibid.*, 14 September 1956.

[14] *Ibid.*, 25 February 1955.

[15] *Ibid.*, 15 June 1956. The allocation of space was as follows: science laboratory, preparation room, balance room, physics room, dark room, physics store, drawing office, building science laboratory, building science store, electrical and radio laboratory, applied mechanics laboratory, laboratory technicians' room, machine tools shop, machine tools store, motor engineering shop, plumbing and welding shop, electrical installation shop, woodwork shop, gas welding and arc welding benches.

not constructed until the autumn.[16] Building only began on 28 March 1955. The cost was estimated at around £60,000, a little below the original estimate of a few years before. The project was expected to take 18 months and as long as it went according to schedule, it would be finished by August 1956, ready for the start of the Autumn Term.[17]

The contractor was E A Bance & Sons of East Woodhay. The firm knew of the 'considerable urgency' and wanted to do the 'bulk of the construction work' over the summer; but the steel was not delivered on time and the schedule slipped. Most of the building had to be delayed to the winter months and a foreman had to be maintained on site – 'an uneconomical procedure' – throughout the waiting period. The delay caused 'considerable losses' to be incurred because of the increase in the price of materials over the ensuing months. Furthermore, the contractor was 'obliged, as a result of the repeated delays, to take a succession of small jobs at cut prices to ensure that they did not lose their operatives'.[18] By the summer of 1956, the completion date had been pushed back to the end of the year.

Albert Owthwaite's work with the clerk of works and his contribution to the design of the workshops came to an abrupt end with his suspension. However, Roy Pocock welcomed the opportunity to get involved and this continued after Eric Lansley's appointment. The completion of the building required Roy's careful supervision and he got a lot of pleasure out of this part of his job, so much so that as soon as the project was finished he turned his attention to the next phase.

> I helped on the design of the first instalment. Owthwaite had had that very much under his control. Lansley had no idea of where to start. He didn't want to do it and he was only too happy to hand it to me to get on with. They asked me if I would continue doing the plans. I had a very sympathetic friend in Shire Hall and we worked on it

---

[16] Co-ordination Subcommittee 27 November 1953; BEC 5 November 1954.

[17] FESC 14 January 1955; BEC 25 February 1955, 29 April 1955, 16 September 1955, 24 February 1956; NWN 11 November 1954.

[18] Education Finance Subcommittee 21 October 1955.

together. Then it followed naturally that I did the second instalment. I enjoyed that side of the work. Everything was so new then – you could go down to Swindon or somewhere like that where they were building new colleges and find out what their plans were.

Berkshire County Council valued Roy's advice, so much so that when they decided to build colleges at Abingdon and Bracknell, they were only too pleased to employ him as consultant. His experience at Newbury was invaluable. He knew, for instance, that the regional inspector wanted 'huge motors and things like that', so the electrical machines laboratory at Abingdon 'had to be on the ground floor because no floor would take it'.

As the workshops and laboratories started to take shape, equipment, furniture and fittings costing thousands of pounds were ordered. Some items were brought up from Albert Road, but most of them were new. £22,000 of machinery and equipment was purchased, for building, engineering and science, and for the technicians' workshop.[19] From W H Ryder in Reading came items for electrical installations, motor engineering, plumbing and woodwork. Clocks came from Gent in London, blinds from Tidmarsh & Sons in London, chalkboards from a company in Stevenage. British Oxygen supplied the acetylene bottles for plumbing and welding and an external shelter was built for their storage.[20] Arthur Owen was delighted with his new carpenter's shop in which he could display his students' work, examples of panelling and door construction. He had waited for this for eight years. Moreover, to ensure a safe environment, master switches enabled him to cut off the electricity if he considered a machine was being used 'ill-advisedly'.[21]

The instalment was finished in December 1956. The final cost was £60,620.[22] The first classes were held on Monday, 21 January 1957. It was only ten months after Eric Lansley's arrival, a most encouraging start for the new Principal.

---

[19] BEC 1 November 1957.

[20] Education Finance Subcommittee 1 June 1956, 7 December 1956.

[21] *NWN* 24 October 1957.

[22] BEC 6 May 1960.

Monday was a big day for the South Berks College of Further Education in Oxford Road. It marked the completion of the first instalment of the new College buildings – a £60,000 job for which Messrs E A Bance, of Ball Hill, were main contractors. For some time past there have been difficulties in accommodating all who wanted to join the College, a considerable increase being experienced in day-release classes – chiefly in mechanical and electrical engineering, building, commerce and applied physics. Many would-be students had to be refused. Altogether, counting evening classes held in the villages, about 2,000 are taking courses in the College syllabus. The chemistry laboratory is typical of the modern facilities now provided. The extension contains new engineering and building trade workshops, a working office, and laboratories for electricity and radio classes, physics, chemistry and applied mechanics.

NWN 24 January 1957

The second instalment

Continuous Building Programme

At the beginning of this year new laboratories and workshops, erected at a cost of over £60,000, came into use for the first time. 'Now our greatest need is for more classrooms' said Mr W B R Pocock, Vice-Principal and Head of the Engineering Department. 'At the moment we even make use of what was at one time a chicken hut. The chicken's hatchway was closed only last year.'

NWN 24 October 1957

In 1955, Berkshire LEA asked the Ministry to start the second instalment in 1956-57, with phase two immediately following on from phase one. The second instalment was much bigger and more expensive than the first one. The schedule agreed with the HMIs in 1951 was for 21,000 square feet of floor space at a cost of around £120,000, excluding the cost of equipment and furniture. Five years later, however, and plans had to be changed. Part of the excitement of working in further education is that its demand is dynamic and unpredictable, and sometimes surprises. At Newbury, some courses had proved more popular than expected. Consequently, further discussions were held at which it was recommended that provision should be made for developments which had occurred since 1951, especially those in one particular area of the curriculum.[23]

In 1956 there were four full-time lecturers in Women's Subjects. Miss McGee, the Head of Department, had been appointed two years before as Head of Commerce, General Education and Women's Subjects. Now, women's crafts were so popular that a separate department had been created with Miss McGee in charge. With her were Jessie Searle; Mabel Dinwoodie, lecturer in cookery, who had joined in 1953; and Miss Barnes who became full time in 1956, having worked part time for many years. Another seven staff – five women and two men – were employed part time.[24] The Department ran the full-time courses in domestic science and the 30-plus part-time classes in cookery and a panoply of craft subjects.

It was important that the second instalment included rooms for these activities. This meant not only a change in the plans, which had to be agreed by the Inspectors, but also an increase in the cost. The revised estimate was over £150,000. This included money for a staff car park.[25]

Again there was some delay before building started. The Ministry did not give the go-ahead for 1956-57, but the project was included in the schedule for the following year. The governors were worried, however, that by the time the county architect had completed the revised plans, the year would be almost over before

---

[23] *Ibid.*, 25 February 1955.

[24] These were Mrs B E Davis (Needlework and Dressmaking Diploma, Bath Training College); Mrs A Farmer (Berkshire Branch Embroiderer's Guild); Mrs R S J Hards (City & Guilds Dressmaking); Mrs C J Lovelock (Trade School Needlework); Mrs N Runham (City & Guilds Dressmaking); W Allison and G Stanley.

[25] BEC 4 January 1957. The estimated cost of the buildings was £150,713, the quantity surveyor's fees £5,000 and the clerk of works salary £1,420 – giving an estimated total of £157,133.

work could start. Yet there was little they could do.[26] At the Speech Day held at Speenhamland School in February 1958, Eric Lansley spoke of the building work which was now imminent:

> 'Work on the second instalment is due to start next month', he said, 'and is hoped to be completed by September 1960. We will then be in a position to concentrate all our Newbury classes on one site instead of having them distributed over five centres in the town. I feel this concentration, together with the provision of a College hall, a library and dining and common room accommodation will go far towards fostering a corporate spirit among our students and staff.'[27]

Tenders were put out and again E A Bance was awarded the contract. Building began in March 1958. The project would take at least two years and it was not expected to be finished until July 1960.

There was some activity before the main building was started. A gravel car park was laid out at the front of the house and as the vehicles came straight out of the college on to the main Oxford Road, adequate sight lines had to be provided.[28] Two years later, there was more work at the front of the college. In 1960 the cottage at the south-west corner of the site known as Wayside, 36 Oxford Road, came up for sale. The County Council bought the house and garden, 0.057 acres, for £2,200. 'This purchase was made in order to complete the frontage of the college on to Oxford Road and the Newbury bypass, thus leaving the county architect full scope in planning the overall layout of the site and the proposed third instalment of the college.' It was intended to move Harry Whiting and his family into Wayside as his cottage was likely to be demolished to make way for the next building instalment. As it turned out, the Whitings did not move in. Number 36 Oxford Road was demolished, 'to improve the general appearance of the site', and the car park extended.[29]

---

[26] FESC 11 May 1956.

· [27] *NWN* 27 February 1958.

[28] BEC 3 May 1957, 13 September 1957.

[29] Ormonde House Deeds, Conveyance 14 March 1960; FESC 16 September 1960, 11 November 1960.

Work also started at the back of the house, where the greenhouse, which had played a central part in the drama of a few years before, was knocked down to make way for the new building. As a separate project, a detached brickwork shop was put up near the northern boundary of the site. This new workshop 'stimulated interest' in bricklaying and the Principal felt that the quality of the students' work consequently improved.[30]

While the second instalment was coming into view, there was major construction work going on along the college's southern boundary. This was the first Newbury bypass. We have seen how all the traffic going south on the Oxford Road went down through Speenhamland to the Clock Tower and into the town. In 1948 there were around two-million private cars and vans on Britain's roads. By 1955 there were 3.6-million, and the great expansion of private car ownership had begun. By 1960 there were almost six-million cars, and the volume of heavy loads travelling by road had also multiplied. Newbury's local answer to a national problem was a relief road scheme to divert through traffic away from Speenhamland and the town centre. The East-West relief road was built first, in 1958, 'to take traffic round the town via Shaw'. This was Western Avenue which ran along the college boundary and sliced the Shaw estate in two. Speenhamland School lost part of its playing field. A roundabout was built where Western Avenue met the Oxford Road; beyond, to the west, a new length of Bath Road was laid out. A small area of land, 0.12 acres, was left between the college boundary and the fence line of the new relief road. The County Council bought this for £5 in 1959, a small extension to the college site.[31] In 1965 the town's relief road scheme was completed with the opening of the Eastern relief road from Western Avenue to St John's Road.

The imposing second instalment was built behind Ormonde House. The main entrance to the complex was through a double set of double doors which opened into a spacious foyer. To the south were rooms on three storeys enclosed in a steel-framed structure with brick cladding. There were lots of windows and

---

[30] FESC 16 November 1956; *NWN* 27 February 1958. This was the fifth – and, as it turned out, final – brickwork shop.

[31] Education Finance Subcommittee 6 February 1959.

light and airy classrooms, including a practice office and rooms for typewriting.

The foyer was the focus from which radiated the communal facilities. There were two storeys on the north side and a single-storey extension by the main entrance. This was the students' common room. Next to it, on the ground floor, was the refectory, the windows of its large commercial kitchen looking out over the side drive. Its 'heavy equipment' cost £1,500. The refectory was for both staff and students, and in December 1960, Miss Bellamy Law was appointed manageress. There followed an assistant cook, a cashier and a number of general assistants. The Ministry of Education was pleased. Refectories had 'important social and educational functions' in the world of further education.[32]

The hall, with its windows set high in the walls, was next to the refectory. It was separated from it by a wooden partition which opened to produce a larger seating area. At the opposite end of the hall was a raised stage with its long grey curtains. Beyond this was a corridor of smaller rooms, including a somewhat grandly named Green Room as well as changing rooms equipped with showers.[33] The hall was spacious – there was room for 200 chairs – and it was used particularly for examinations in the years that followed. It was also a venue for social events, for student activities and for staff badminton and table tennis matches.

Above the refectory, on the first floor, was the library. The importance of libraries was the subject of Ministry of Education Circular 322 in 1957. 'Too many technical colleges are still poorly equipped with libraries, and too few libraries are in the charge of qualified librarians.' The original library in Ormonde House was not untypical, a few shelves in an office with the book holdings listed on a notice board. It was run by the staff and it was only open for fifty minutes a day, 'from 4.40 to 5 pm for day students and 6.45 to 7.15 pm for evening students'.[34] In marked contrast, Circular 322 gave detailed guidance as to the service to be expected, at least 3,000 volumes with an 'adequate range' of

---

[32] FESC 10 March 1961, 9 November 1962.

[33] A 'green room' is one in which performers can relax when they are not performing.

[34] SBCFE Prospectus 1951-52, p.14.

periodicals. To develop the library, a generous annual allowance was recommended, 'ranging from £500 for a small College with a book stock of 3,000 to £2,000 in a College of Advanced Technology'. The Circular concluded with sentiments which would not be out of place today, in a world in which students have become active learners who are taught the skills of information retrieval in what is now a knowledge-based society:

> The maintenance of an adequate library service is comparatively expensive, but the service is essential if students are to be trained to seek up to date information, to become independent workers rather than passive recipients of lecture notes, and to keep pace with scientific developments after they have passed their examinations. It is important, therefore, that the library should have the support of the teaching staff of the College ... The work of the lecture room and the library should be integrated, and the library should be a central point in the programme of each course of study at every College.[35]

New books were bought for the new library, £500 worth in 1957-58, and another £500 was spent in the following year.[36] In the summer of 1960, Pete White was appointed as the college's first librarian.[37]

Beyond the foyer were another two storeys, the main corridor linking with the workshops and laboratories along the eastern perimeter of the site. Here there was a lecture theatre with rows of raised seating for 60 people. This soon became the venue for classes to enjoy that audio-visual teaching aid of the '60s, the cine-film. Further along were a science laboratory and more workshops. There was also a second drawing office. 'Industry wanted people who knew drawing office work. It doesn't apply today because we've got computers doing all this, but in those

---

[35] BEC 21 June 1957.

[36] BEC 1 March 1957; FESC 15 November 1957.

[37] 'Pete White built up a cheerful atmosphere in a very comprehensive library and was the main instigator of the college weekly Newsletter.' SBCFE 25 Years.

days the drawing office was an important aspect of industry.'[38] Above were the rooms for the women's subjects, including, at last, a kitchen for cookery classes.

'The greater part of the second instalment of the college will be available for occupation in September 1960, and the remainder will come into use at the end of the year.'[39] Most of the rooms were ready by the first day of the Autumn Term on 12 September 1960. The refectory opened a term later, on 9 January 1961. The final cost was £125,479 with another £35,000 for furniture and equipment.[40]

The second instalment provided 'some relief' to the problem of 'insufficient accommodation'; but it was not the end of the story. The LEA was keen to start a third project for the proposed HNC work and to meet 'other requirements' in the area.[41]

At the other end of the county, the East Berks College also had new buildings. The first instalment at Windsor was completed in September 1955. An instalment at Maidenhead – workshops, laboratories, drawing offices – opened in January 1959 and the second instalment at Windsor was finished six months later. Prefabricated structures were replaced, communal facilities made available. As at Newbury, further instalments were anticipated for the 1960s. With new colleges planned for Abingdon and Bracknell, these were good years for the 'Cinderella' of Berkshire education.

'We had over 100 personnel on it'

Peter Mason was one of the young men working on the site on the Oxford Road.

> I started my apprenticeship with Bance at East Woodhay on 10th August 1959, and the first job was at the college. Bance's had a good standing locally in order to get the

---

[38] Interview with Len Hoyland.

[39] SRCFE Thirteenth Annual Report October 1960, p.3.

[40] FESC 4 March 1960; Education Development and Works Subcommittee 28 September 1962.

[41] Education in the Royal County of Berkshire 1959-60, Report by the Director of Education, p.31.

college contract and at its height, we had over 100 personnel on it. It certainly was a big job and gave us a good insight. It was a steel-framed building and it was basically straight brickwork for us. The bricks were nice and regular, machine-made of course. The canteen and student area looked into the back of Ormonde House – there were students in there when we were building it. The road was under construction – it was put in to service the building initially – and the line of it was marginally altered. The greenhouse which went along the back of the house was taken down, and while we were there, the conservatory was taken away. The expected completion date was well into 1960. They didn't occupy the main extension before the start of the academic year.

I was working under the general foreman, Rayner Palmer. He was well renowned in the area, a local lad from Inkpen. He was a really first class bricklayer, a very, very clever chap. In today's world, he would have gone much further than just a general foreman. We had a guy there, Mr Clark, the clerk of works. He was a dear old soul, a really nice old boy. He was very good at what he did and I could always go and ask him things. You always felt comfortable asking if something went by you in the lecture. Either Rayner Palmer or Mr Clark would always help you out.

The steel frame at the front of the college was going up when I started. It was fascinating to watch. They had the cranes there to drop all the steelwork into place, and these laddies would run along the four-inch sections of steel, bolting the next bits on, no harness, no nothing. They were super-fit people. They would climb up the stanchions and run along, bolting all the sections together so that they fitted. The Health & Safety Executive would have a heart attack now! And you know how long it takes us to put putty in a window – if you do it yourself it takes ages and ages. There was a guy there who worked for A G Glazing, who did the glazing at the front of the college. He had two handfuls of putty. He would start at the bottom of the frame in the middle. He'd go up and round and pick the glass and put it in, and then face putty it. Whoosh – whoosh – whoosh – he was as quick as that. It really was something else.

Harry Whiting used to have a shuffle round the buildings, the new bits, to see what was going on. We used to have a lot of fun. All the way through the corridors there's all the heating ducts, and the heating pipes were absolutely massive. Up the centre of the corridors you've got duct covers under the floor, and they were screeded over. Periodically you get access ways in, for inspection and maintenance. Come firework night, we used to crawl down these ducts, put the fireworks in, nip back out the other end and wait for the bang and the net results!

'*Every member of staff in the Engineering Department had contact with industry at some time or another*'

Although the unfortunate events of 1955 were something of a watershed, they were soon forgotten. Before long, Eric Lansley was looking out of the window in his office to see the bricks of the new college rising from the gardens of the old. Across the landing, there were a lot of new faces in the staff room. Full-time lecturers increased from 22 in 1956 to 30 a year later. To the experience of Charles Sully, Arthur Owen, Roy Pocock, Eric Carr and Dick Edwards was added the new blood of people who knew little about Albert Owthwaite's departure. So many appointments were made during 1956 and 1957 that, from the perspective of the staff room at least, this was the beginning of a new era. J W Ballard (electronics), Mervyn Cowie (plumbing), E L Donnelly, Miss Elson, W E Freebury (engineering), Eric Gardner (engineering), Don Heywood (chemistry), Bill Holt (engineering), Len Hoyland (engineering), W C E Jakins (commerce), I M R Jenkins (science), J H Newlands, J Petherbridge (engineering) and J H Scott (science) were all teaching by September 1957. So were Miss Barnes (needlecraft) and Fred Pizzey (English, liberal studies), who had previously been employed part-time, and Vera Garlick, who had returned after her two years away.

By 1960 there were more new faces, including those of Lionel Bernard (engineering), Eddie Irwing (electronics), Les Sugden (engineering), Daphne Loasby (liberal studies), Mrs Blake and Mrs Potter (needlework).

Len Hoyland stands at the beginning of this new chapter. It was the summer of 1956. Thirty-nine years old, a Lancastrian who loved his cricket, Len brought with him experience from the factory floor, the drawing office and the classroom. He came to Newbury to look after the workshops – the new ones were almost finished when he arrived – and to teach technical drawing. Len's journey was typical of many of those who taught in colleges in the '50s, leaving school at 14, working in industry, studying at night school. This is his account of his FE adventure.

> My background was Manchester. I left school when I was 14, as most people did. Not many went to grammar school in 1931. None of my friends did. They all left school at 14. It was in the depression and there were no jobs. Nobody could get a job unless they knew somebody. I happened to have a father who worked for Ferranti. He could say, 'I can get you a job,' and I went in as an apprentice at Ferranti. Going to work, there was always a long queue of people outside the main entrance. They were unemployed, waiting to see if someone had died in the night or if someone hadn't turned in because they were ill, and they would be taken on. There were no jobs, so unless they went to report to the big factories, they wouldn't get a job – and of course for years they didn't.

> I did what a lot of my friends did – I continued my further education at night school. Ferranti were a very good firm. When they took me on as an apprentice, they said, 'You are going to night school for two or three years.' I went to Oldham Tech for five years and by the time I was 21, I had taken an ONC and an HNC, and I realised the value of education. At 14, you don't know anything about it. Towards the end of my HNC, I was going one day a week and two evenings; before that it was all evenings. There were only five students in the class. Firms did not give day

release in the '30s, they wouldn't do it. Ferranti gave it to me as a concession.

When you were an apprentice, they first of all put you in the workshop and give you all sorts of things to do. You get your hands dirty, that's the main thing. Unless you dirty your hands, you can't be an engineer. The only way you can learn about materials is to handle them, and they're dirty and they're oily and they're greasy. When I was about 17, they moved their apprentices around. Vacancies would occur in the drawing office. Everybody wants to go and work in the drawing office. They would select a dozen 16-, 17-year-olds and they'd say, 'Report to the drawing office. The chief draughtsman wants to interview you.' You would go into his office.

'You want to be a draughtsman do you?'

'Yes, we'd love that.'

'Right, we'll see what you're made of then.'

He would pass the paper round.

'I want you to draw a right-angled triangle and put the letters A, B and C on the sides. Let's say the base angle there is 35 degrees. Write down the sine of that 35 degrees.' Sine is the opposite side over the hypotenuse, B over C or whatever.

'Tell me what the cosine is.'

The cosine is the adjacent side of the hypotenuse.

'Tell me what the tangent is.'

These three things, that's all he wanted to know. And I knew it. It wasn't very advanced information for a 16-year-old. He took the papers in and a short time after I got an invitation to say you start in the drawing office at such and such a day. And that was it.

I was a drawing office apprentice until I was 21. I'd got an HNC then. They offered me 30 shillings (£1.50) a week to stay. I belonged to the draughtsmen's union, and I knew the union rate for 21 was £3/5/- (£3.25), which was a fortune! Ferranti weren't in line there, so I said to my father, 'I'm going to leave. I can find a job for £3/5/- a week.'

He said, 'How do you know you can find a job?'

I said, 'I've already written to a firm in Oldham and they'll take me on for £3/5/- a week.'

He said, 'I don't think you're being very loyal. Ferranti have trained you, they've given you the opportunity of becoming a draughtsman and now you're leaving them.'

I said, 'If they'll give me £3/5/-, I'll stay.'

So I went to the chief draughtsman and said,

'I want to offer my notice in.'

'Leave? What on earth do you want to leave for?'

I said, 'I happen to have got a job which pays much more money than you're paying.'

'How much are they paying you?'

'£3/5/-.'

'£3/5/- a week? We can't do that.'

I said, 'That's why I'm leaving.'

The chief draughtsman went straight down to get hold of my dad.

'What's all this about your boy wanting to leave? It's disgraceful. We've brought him up, we've taught him all he knows, and now he's off. Can't you stop him?'

Dad said, 'No, I can't stop him.'

Len left Ferranti – 'that was alright' – but there was a much bigger cloud approaching as the international situation deteriorated and war broke out. Within a couple of years, Len found himself working for the Ford Motor Company making aero engines for the RAF.

A Merlin engine was an aero engine designed by Rolls Royce, used on Spitfires, Lancasters and Hurricanes. Rolls Royce were making one at a time, a couple of dozen a month. This was no good. It was wartime and they wanted more. Only one firm could do that – Ford Motor Company could make hundreds in a week. A greenfield site started, and within less than a year, hundreds of Merlin engines were coming off the line. I worked for Ford in the drawing office for five years. That was a wonderful experience. I couldn't have joined the forces if I'd wanted because

I was in a reserved occupation. It was very satisfying because we were doing a very useful job. It was jolly hard, seven days a week, no holidays. We were making better engines than Rolls Royce. On the test bed they were more efficient. The most important thing was that each part was interchangeable with the Ford Merlin. You could take a piece out of one engine and it would work in another. Rolls Royce made it different altogether. Each part was fitted to a particular engine. When that part had to be replaced, you couldn't get one out of stock because it wouldn't fit – it had to be made especially for that. All the engines were slightly different so there was no interchangeability.

When the war was over, Len stayed in the Manchester area and went to work for Reynolds, 'the chain people'. It was during this time in his life that he started to think about moving out of the drawing office and into the classroom. A friend of his was teaching in a technical college and one day when he was indisposed, he asked the draughtsman to take his place. The experience was to be a turning point in Len's life.

I stood in for him one evening and I thoroughly enjoyed it. I thought, I'd like to do this. It opened my eyes to the prospect of a new career. I remembered the teachers at Oldham Tech. I was inspired by two people. They must have made such an impact that I wanted to become a teacher because of their attitudes to the class. I didn't realise it at the time, but I realised it later. They were so marvellous. They had the time to do their material on the board. Then, they didn't just sit down reading a book; they came round and sat with you and gave you additional instruction. I thought, how rewarding a job like that must be, for them as well as for the students. It intrigued me. This is really better than working as a draughtsman. So that's what gave me the push into teaching.

I did evening school work regularly for two or three years, drawing and maths. I was nearly 30. Before I got a full-time job, I took a one-year course, one night a week, on teacher-training. That was sufficient. I'd already done evening work so I had some idea of what to expect. I got great benefit from that course when I think about it all now. It was like a new world for me.

There were two technical schools in Manchester. The technical school took pupils at the age of 11 or 13, to 16, and they would be taught technical subjects for the benefit of local industry. They were absolutely wonderful feed-ins to industry because they were staffed by people with industrial experience. The teachers were not straight from training college. A lot came from Ferranti teaching specialised subjects. The pupils benefited from this. I saw advertisements in the press inviting applicants for teaching in technical schools. I did that part time at Newton Heath, and eventually, I got a full-time job in 1948. I never regretted it, yet when I made the change from industry to teaching, I went down in money. I took a financial sacrifice, and that was hard; I had to wait many years before I caught up. But I enjoyed the work, more than just making drawings in industry. I really enjoyed working with young people. The only way you can discover this is to do it in the evening and say, 'Well, if I don't like it, I can throw it up.' I was teaching drawing 'cos I'd been in a drawing office and I knew what industry wanted and I could teach the pupils to do this. They would take O-levels in engineering drawing and then they would all get jobs in the drawing office in local industry because they had had the help from the technical schools. It doesn't apply now because we've got computers doing all this, but in those days, the drawing office was an important aspect of industry. The nearest thing we've got to technical schools today is the city technological colleges. They've been frowned at by people who suggest that it's a very narrow education, but it's intended to feed into industry.

I worked in the technical school for seven years, then I went into further education. I was at Salford for a year as an assistant lecturer. I didn't like Salford – it was much too big. There must have been 20 or 30 new people.

When they were appointed, they had to go into the Principal's office, and he would say, 'Good morning everybody. My name is so-and-so. We'll probably never meet again but I thought we ought to assemble for one occasion. At least you know what I look like. I may well pass you tomorrow in the corridor because I won't remember you.' And that was it. I never saw him again. It was vast, it really was, and terribly unfriendly. So I put in for a job at Newbury and got an interview.[42]

It was 1956, and I didn't have a car so I'd come down from Manchester on the train. Ron Spiller said, 'How are you going to get back?'
I said, 'I'm going on the train.'
'Oh', he said, 'I'll take you to the station.'
I never spoke to him again since that day, but he struck me as a nice bloke.

The reason I got the job at Newbury wasn't just the fact that I was an apprentice in Ferranti. I had two Higher National Certificates. I took the electrical one when I was at Oldham and later, after the war, I went to Manchester to study for the mechanical one. That's exactly what they wanted at Newbury because they had an electrical and a mechanical workshop. They wanted someone to establish them, and I got there just in time for that. Everybody else on the shortlist was either electrical or mechanical. They were not both.

The extensions to the college included engineering workshops, electrical workshops and drawing offices. I was in charge of the mechanical and the electrical engineering workshops for technicians and craftsmen. It was part of my job to establish these and to select the machines that we needed. I was also in charge of the drawing office. Drawing was my principal subject and I used to teach engineering drawing at all the levels. I used to be very

---

[42] The interviewing panel was made up of Eric Lansley, Roy Pocock and Ron Spiller.

meticulous. I spent a long time in my own time, before the class arrived, putting up on the board drawings to which I could refer. I did them in chalk. Gear wheels are not very easy to draw, or to teach. I put those on. In the prospectus there's a picture of the drawing office and I'm standing at the board with the gear wheels on it.

The craft apprentices from Plenty and other firms needed a little bit of coaxing, or coercing, in order to get them interested. When you get a good class and they want to learn, they are well behaved, making our job easy. If the class is riotous and they don't want to know, at the extreme level it makes the job impossible. We had those as well, fortunately not many, but just one or two students in the classroom can disrupt. Yet I found that, by and large, the great majority of the apprentices whether craft or otherwise, were quite sound and gave no trouble. And there were some jolly good chaps as well, who were very good indeed. But one day a week was very limited, and the day that they attended started at nine o'clock and went through to seven. They were covering four subjects in that time, so it was a full day. The alternative was to have a day and one evening, but they preferred to make it one day rather than to break into their evenings, so they had all their evenings more or less free.

There are some students who are very easy to get on with, easy to teach. I meet students of course, over the years. Once we were on the M6 going north and we stopped at one of those busy transport places. We were sitting there having a cup of tea and this young man came up to us and said, 'You don't know me, do you? I remember you – you're Mr Hoyland aren't you? You taught me drawing.' He gave me his name. I couldn't remember him. This was in a crowded motorway place, and he'd picked me out. He came with a view to being friendly, not critical, and I thought, that's nice. It happens to all teachers, doesn't it? Some make an impact and some don't, and some make an impact for the wrong reasons.

'I'm steeped in industry and the staff was selected because they'd all got engineering backgrounds.' Len's colleagues included Bill Holt. 'He had a similar background to me. He was an apprentice at Mather and Platt in Manchester – he went to college as well.' Eric Gardner had a 'similar experience to mine, an industrial apprentice, and an HNC man. He got his hands dirty, and that's the test of a real apprentice.' Les Sugden arrived in 1960. 'He was in the next drawing office to me and between the two of us, we used to handle all the drawing at the college.' And of course, there was Charles Sully.

> Charlie was a Londoner originally, a real character. He was very good, very well qualified. A Labour man, absolutely, and he had a go at everybody at different times. He could be abrasive and he could be sharp at times, but he was a very kind-hearted man. The stories I've heard about the number of occasions in the early years, before I went to the college. He'd be walking along the Oxford Road and somebody, a total stranger, would break down – in those days cars were always breaking down – and Charlie would offer his assistance. Or they might have stopped him and said, 'Would you mind having a look at this?' And Charlie would. He enjoyed doing it. He liked helping. I've heard of cases where he'd say, 'I can't do it here but if you help me push it back into the college, I'll do it.' It might have been a Sunday, it didn't make any difference. He said, 'I'll see what I can do for you', and he'd work on it. He had only one method of treatment – the bonnet would be up and everything had to come out. He'd get to the bare bones of it. Even if it was only something to do with the radiator he would say, 'I think you'll have to take the engine out.' He would spend hours of his own time to repair a car. That's remarkable, isn't it?

'At lunchtime you had to get out'

On one day each week, between 1956 and 1959, **Peter Lomax** walked to Ormonde House from his home in Craven Road. When he started his motor vehicle course, the workshops were not finished and for his first term, the practical lessons were in Charles Sully's garage. Soon after Christmas, however, the motor engineering workshop was ready.

> I was about seven when my family moved to Newbury. I lived in Craven Road and went to St Nicolas' Church of England School, on the corner of Enborne Road and Rockingham Road. Sometimes I stayed for school dinners, but there were no catering facilities in the school and we had to go down to the Community Centre. We used to be taken down there in the traditional school crocodile. It only needed one or two teachers to go with us because we were much better behaved than they are now. We were more frightened of the teachers, so there was a bit of discipline. Sometimes we were late back to school because we had to sit until we'd finished. I remember diced carrots which weren't properly cooked, and they were crunchy and took a long time to eat. They didn't improve when they got cold. I passed the eleven-plus and went to the Grammar School, and at 16, just after O-levels, I applied direct to Marchant's Garage and I was accepted. There was some contact between a branch of my family and the old man Marchant.

> It was just something that I wanted to do. I was apprenticed at the garage, which was down on the corner of Queen's Road. It later became Gowrings and is now one of those burger places. Marchant's were an important garage in this area. They were Vauxhall Bedford main dealers, which meant more than just being a dealer. And they were Rover dealers. And through their taking over Green and Whincup, they became Volkswagen and Land Rover dealers. And they were Jaguar dealers, so we saw the exciting XK120 in the workshops. That's the first car I ever did more than a hundred miles an hour in. It was out on road test – somebody else was driving.

> Garages of any reasonable size sent their apprentices to college – it was a general thing. They thought they were investing in their future, and anyway, apprentices were

cheap. A garage would only take on one at a time, so they would have two or three progressing through at different stages. They weren't all the same age and they would go to college on different days.

I was on day release for three years. It was a full day, nine till seven o'clock. There were three apprentices from the garage at the time I was at college. Marchant was a governor and took an interest in what I was doing. He checked up on me from time to time and I got called upstairs, 'to see how you're getting on'. There was a lot of homework. The course took in a lot of things, but they were all related to motor vehicles. There wasn't anything completely separate, such as English or maths or whatever, but they certainly came into it, much more than they do now. There was a weighty book which was called *Science and Calculations for Motor Vehicle*. Technical drawing was virtually a separate subject – they don't do drawing now. And there was welding but we didn't do that much – it was only very basic. Everyone remembers Charlie Sully. He was the course tutor. He was a good teacher and I learned a lot from him. He was a bit of a character as well.

At lunchtime you had to get out. We went down town because there were several coffee bars. There was one called the Tea Bar, which was about where Millets is now, and there was one on the corner up in the Broadway with bow windows. There was another one on the corner of Park Way, so there was a choice of snack places. I left with the Mechanics' Certificate, first class. In those days in the City & Guilds, you did the first three years in Newbury. Then I was sent on day release to Reading for another two years, which gave me the higher level Technicians' Certificate. I enjoyed my time at college because it was what I wanted to do.

13

THE SUMMER OF 1960

T he second phase of building finished in 1960. South Berks
College, with its several rectangular blocks with flat roofs
and walls more glass than brick, was now a prominent
feature in the topography on the northern rim of the town.

The refectory did not open for business until January 1961.[1]
Everything else was ready by the end of the summer of 1960. 'At
last the college had all its departments in new buildings on the
one site, although there were still classes in Ormonde House.'[2]
General and commercial subjects were in the three-storey extension
soon to be known as A-Block. The hall was used for drama, music
and physical education. Domestic science and women's subjects
were taught upstairs, room 17 the permanent home for cookery.
The Community Centre was no longer needed; neither was the
Technical Institute. Its equipment was brought up to Ormonde
House, a property company bought the building and it became
a branch of the National Westminster Bank. Further along
Northbrook Street, the rooms over E Hill & Sons were vacated,
as were the premises in Bartholomew Street.

The college's governing body in 1960 was new. With up to 30
members since 1951, it had been one of the largest in the Southern

---

[1] During the first two months of the Spring Term 1961, sales averaged £120
a week. 40% of the takings were for lunches, the rest during mid-morning
and afternoon breaks. FESC 10 March 1961.

[2] SBCFE 25 Years.

Region, but now its membership was reduced to 16, a smaller body 'more likely to be an effective instrument of the College government than a large one'. The new board had to have 'strong industrial representation' with half of its members coming from local industry.[3]

Ron Spiller continued as chairman. Revd Gerald Matthews, who had succeeded Revd Russell at St Nicolas' Church, was vice-chairman. Didge Marchant, Maurice Paine, Marjorie Showers and Mark Wakeley were all pleased to continue. Marjorie Showers was one of two women on the board; the other was Mrs Cox. Both had been on the women's advisory committee. Similarly Charles Brown, district organiser of the National Union of Agricultural Workers, had been on the committee for agriculture, and S Goldstein the one for science. Other governors included H A Stradling the builder and Northbrook Street garage owner J Pass.

Eric Lansley was now in his fifth year as Principal, with a full-time academic staff of 28 men and women, five of whom were heads of department. One of the heads, Roy Pocock, was in his eighth year as Vice-Principal. There was 11 full-time support staff. Five of these worked in the offices, including registrar R W Tucker (appointed 1956) who took the photographs for the college prospectuses. The other four were women, with Betty Ward the most experienced. There were four technical staff and two caretakers.[4]

Table 21 South Berks College: Heads of Department 1960

Department	Head	Appointment to College
Building	Arthur Owen	January 1949
Commerce and General Subjects	Vera Garlick	September 1952 September 1956
Engineering	Roy Pocock	September 1949
Science	Eric Carr	September 1952
Women's Subjects	Mabel Dinwoodie	September 1953

---

[3] *Ibid.*, 6 March 1959.

[4] The technical staff in 1960 included Jeff Jeffery (workshop technician), John Humphries (workshop storekeeper) and Brian Salmon and Ruth Brown (laboratory assistants).

Building had some claim to be the oldest department. There were three full-time lecturers in 1960: Arthur Owen (carpentry), Bill Parrot (bricklaying) and Mervyn Cowie (plumbing). The demand for courses had remained steady since 1948 but there had been no significant growth – 100 students from 40 firms in 1957 – and few new courses were introduced. There were 45 employers listed in *The Newbury and District Association of Building Trades* in 1960, in Bucklebury, Chieveley, East Ilsley, Great Shefford, Heath End, Hungerford, Kintbury, Lambourn, Newbury, Speen and Thatcham. Each one supported the National Joint Apprenticeship Scheme. 'The apprenticeship comprises of practical training at the employers' workshops and building sites and technical education at the local technical college.' All the apprentices were encouraged to work for City & Guilds certificates at South Berks.[5]

Vera Garlick became Head of Commerce and General Subjects in 1958. She was responsible for more full-time students than any other department and the courses for school leavers meant lots of contact with Joan Marks and the Youth Employment Service.[6] There were also day-release courses for shop assistants, and numerous evening classes. Shorthand and typewriting were taught most evenings, there were accounts and bookkeeping classes, and courses in management had recently been introduced.[7] General subjects included O-level English, foreign languages – Dutch, French, German, Italian and Spanish – and classes in choral music, display, drama, elocution, musical appreciation and physical education (for women).

Roy Pocock's Engineering Department had the most full-time staff and although there were a handful of youngsters doing the Pre-Apprenticeship, most of his students remained apprentices on

---

[5] *Commonwealth Technical Training Week, 29 May-3 June 1961, Handbook for Newbury and District*, p.29.

[6] Joan Marks became Newbury's youth employment officer in 1957. The office was above a shop at 94a Northbrook Street.

[7] There were four courses in shorthand, from beginners to 120 wpm, and five in typewriting, from beginners to RSA III. Management Studies included principles of management, evolution of industrial organisation, office organisation, statistical method, work measurement and financial and cost accounting.

day release. In 1960 the Education Committee reported that 'over the county the apprenticeship vacancies were sufficient in number and variety to satisfy those able to take advantage of them and the training opportunities they give.'[8] Courses included the ONCs in Engineering and the City & Guilds in Electrical Installations and Electrical Technicians, and Machine Shop, Mechanical and Motor Vehicle Engineering. The annual flow of students from the SEB was important. This organisation was proud of its 'full range' of training schemes for school leavers and its 'more advanced' schemes for those already employed. Its craft apprenticeship trained electricians, electrical fitters, jointers, meter mechanics and motor vehicle fitters.[9] Many of the mechanical engineers came from Plenty where the training supervisor organised indentured apprenticeships with 'paid day release every week' and all examination and college fees paid. There were opportunities at the Eagle Iron Works for core makers, electricians, fitters and turners, millers and drillers, moulders, pattern makers, sheet metal workers, toolmakers and welders.[10]

Most important of all, as long as the stream of students from Harwell and Aldermaston kept coming, engineering courses would flourish. Moreover, it was these students who kept Eric Carr's Science Department going as well with the ONC in Applied Physics, the A-level programme and the City & Guilds for Laboratory Technicians. The Medical Laboratory Technologists' course was for those working at Compton's Agricultural Research Station.

'Don't forget that Newbury is still – for all the Harwell and Aldermaston – a great agricultural centre'

Alongside the departments were two smaller areas of work organised into sections. By 1960, Dick Edwards had been in charge of handicraft courses for eight years. For 16 hours each week he taught small groups of dedicated men and women how to make things out of wood and metal. There was always a sense of

---

[8] Education in the Royal County of Berkshire 1959-60, Report by the Director of Education, p.45.

[9] *Commonwealth Technical Training Week Handbook*, p.33.

[10] *Ibid.*, p.1.

urgency about getting a place in one of Dick's classes and they were so popular that many of his students came back year after year. There were courses on every night of the week, and in 1960, four evenings were devoted to woodwork. From the use of basic tools 'for the fundamental joints and processes', the students moved on to work of their own choosing, provided that it was 'within their capabilities'. The work was organised on 'individual lines' and could include 'turning, veneering and carving'. The fifth evening was beaten metalwork, in copper, brass, gilding metal and silver, from serviette rings and ashtrays to fruit bowls, vases, spoons, and chalices 'as skill is acquired'. The classes were also suitable for those who wanted general metalwork, as long as they had access to a machine shop.

The other section was responsible for agriculture. Most of this sort of work was done at the Berkshire Institute but some courses were organised at Hungerford, Lambourn and in other villages. In 1955, P L Hay (BSc Agriculture) was appointed full-time lecturer at the South Berks College and it was around this time that the advisory committee for agriculture was set up.[11]

These initiatives encouraged curriculum development. During 1955/56 the college put on block-release courses to instruct young farmers in the operation of agricultural machinery. One of these was organised on a farm at Faringdon using the owner's machinery – for which he made no charge – and included the Young Farmers' tractor drivers' proficiency test.[12] Motorised vehicles were replacing horses on Berkshire's farms and in the summer of 1956, the college became the proud owner of a second-hand tractor – 'with hydraulic lift, power take-off, belt pulley, starter and lighting' – generously donated by a local firm.[13]

Day-release courses in agricultural mechanics and farm welding were organised and at Harwell fruit-growing was put on

---

[11] There was some discussion with the Berkshire Institute over responsibility for agricultural courses. 'I ran an Agricultural Mechanics course at Newbury and we had a full-time agricultural lecturer before a new Principal insisted that agricultural classes should be run by the College of Agriculture.' (Roy Pocock)

[12] Agricultural Education Subcommittee 11 May 1956.

[13] *NWN* 13 September 1956.

for the commercial horticultural workers. In night school there was a steady demand for poultry husbandry – it was reckoned that there were twice as many head of poultry in the county as before the war – and there were also classes in bee-keeping and fruit-growing.[14]

In the later '50s, there were still more than 2,000 farm workers in Berkshire under the age of 21. A day-release programme was offered but failed through lack of support. Hence Anthony Hurd's plea in 1958:

> Don't forget that Newbury is still – for all the Harwell and Aldermaston – a great agricultural centre. As a farmer, I know there is a great need for that extra topping up, for getting that extra technical education. I do hope you will be able to get full co-operation and support for your agricultural courses here.[15]

Day release was an alternative to the full-time residential course at the Berkshire Institute. In 1960 a City & Guilds in crop and animal husbandry and farm machinery was organised; and there was also a programme in horticulture with UEI and RHS examinations. Berkshire farmers, however, were not supportive. 'It is regrettable that more advantage is not taken by the farming community of the opportunity ... It may be that the absence of the student for a whole day from the farm is too much of a handicap.' There were only 67 agricultural students in Berkshire on day release in 1960.[16]

The core of Newbury's agricultural work, then, was at night, a comprehensive two-year programme in general agriculture. First offered in 1957 – at Newbury, Reading and Wantage – with much interest shown by the rural community, farm workers were given the opportunity 'to add basic facts of land production to the practical experience gained in their job'. The syllabus was broad and divided

---

[14] Agricultural Education Subcommittee 1 March 1957, 23 May 1958, 20 November 1958, 19 November 1959.

[15] *NWN* 27 February 1958.

[16] Education in the Royal County of Berkshire 1959-60, Report by the Director of Education, p.36.

into four sections, each taught over one term: agricultural science (grass and crop husbandry), farm and barn machinery, animal husbandry and farm organisation and management. There was an examination at the end of each term and at the end of the course a county certificate was awarded to those successful overall. In 1960 there were 142 students on the course, which was organised at Newbury, Buckland, Pangbourne, Reading and Windsor.[17]

It was the growth of agricultural education at Newbury which encouraged the governors to ask the LEA for a minibus to encourage students to come to classes. It could take them to and from their homes, which were often in isolated areas poorly served by public transport, and enable them to visit farms and the Institute at Burchett's Green. Moreover, the vehicle could be used by other students for educational visits and by staff attending conferences. The LEA agreed and a 12-seater vehicle was purchased in 1962.[18]

The minibus was used by other students. When the Didcot-Newbury railway line was closed, six full-time students, five girls and a boy, had to travel from Didcot by bus. This entailed a change and a wait of 45 minutes. Eric Lansley was concerned about the waiting time in a 'relatively isolated' area and because it was taking them two hours to get home. The LEA asked the bus company to change the timetable but in the meantime, the students were taken home by minibus. In spite of Berkshire's request, the company did not change the timetable and the minibus continued to be used on the Didcot run, although this meant 'serious limitations' on its use by the agricultural students.[19]

'Teaching calculus to brickies wasn't exactly the best thing'

Peter Mason can trace his family history back to the time of Queen Elizabeth I. 'In the 1590s, one of my forebears was mayor of Newbury, so we have been in the area a long, long time. We're part of the John and Frances West gifts. We've all got pedigree numbers, so we can apply to go to Christ's Hospital or apply for

---

[17] *Ibid.*.

[18] Education in the Royal County of Berkshire 1961-62, Report by the Director of Education, p.39.

[19] FESC 14 September 1962, 9 November 1962.

the pension or whatever.' Peter was brought up in Woolton Hill and went to Park House School. When he was 15, he knew exactly what he wanted to do for a living.

I was working in the building industry before I left school – weekends and high days and holidays – with A A Beaver. I used to do odds and sods for them to earn a bit of pin money, totally illegal now of course. That gave me a very good insight, and I could have had an apprenticeship with them, but they didn't specialise much on the building side. Their main work was sanitary engineering, and it was bricklaying I wanted to do.

I was lucky enough to get an apprenticeship with Bob Bance. My father was a master mason, and he used to work with Osborne, and it was through his work there that I got the apprenticeship with Bob Bance, because he was a well known craftsman in the area. Bance was a big builder in those days. I didn't go through the careers master at school. I told him that I'd already got a job because I knew what I wanted to do. With a name like mine, you couldn't do anything other than building could you? He knew Bob Bance ever so well and he said to him, 'I've got better lads than him.' And Bob Bance wrote a letter to him. He used to write like he used to speak and there was quite a few expletives. The careers master was also my form master, and he read the letter out in class.

I started my bricklayer's apprenticeship on 10th August 1959. My apprenticeship was five years. I got my indentures from the Southern Counties. 'Thou shalt not consort with women 'til you've completed' and all that sort of thing. It was very much old form. All that's changed now. I started on £2/5/4 (£2.27) a week and some of that was tool money. That was not only for the provision of your tools, but also to replace those that were worn out. You got as many as you could possibly afford. The first thing a brickie needs is a trowel and a spirit level, and you carried on then, lines and pins and all the basic stuff.

My first job was helping build the college extension. I was given day release to undertake the City & Guilds course. First off, it was one day and one evening a week, then it went to one day and two evenings; so I was spending a great deal of time on site, both working and studying. After attaining the City & Guilds craft certificate, I continued my studies and gained the advanced certificate. We did a four-year course. Bill Parrott let us undertake the advanced craft a year after we had taken the ordinary craft. He was hopeful that most of us would take the full Technological Certificate; that was building maths, building construction, building services and surveying. Most of us did, and after we had done that we were exempt from a proportion of the Ordinary National – but that had to be done at Reading.

The members of staff who guided me through these courses were Bill Parrott, Mervyn Cowie, Arthur Owen and Mr Lane. Arthur Owen was the chippy and Head of Department. He lived in Thatcham and used to drive a little powder blue Standard Eight or Ten. Bill Parrott taught the brickwork. He did some of the academic side of it as well, like building science. Mervyn Cowie was the plumber master. Other tutors were brought in to take the Technological Certificate. There were lots of tradesmen at the college, but there was no one to do the more academic side of things. We had a man from the SEB took building maths, a fantastically nice chap. Teaching calculus to brickies wasn't exactly the best thing. As a separate entity, a filler subject, I chose to do an RSA course in English. I felt it would be wise. If I was going to do a lot more written exams, it would pay me to be a better wordsmith than I was. We used to have to do presentations for all sorts of things. And I did quantity surveying in the evening with a guy Daniels; he used to do it in his spare time. Charlie Sully didn't teach me, but you could always see him on the campus trying to convert somebody or other. He was very much the local Labour Party, a very distinctive sort of character who used to stand out in a crowd.

There were eight or nine of us, all apprentices, and all local lads fresh out of school, either Park House or Hungerford. Strangely enough, we didn't attract too many from St Bart's. We had an increase after the first year because the ones that failed were put back into the year to do it again. Certainly one of them came back down and did it again and I'm very pleased I didn't suffer from that. Some of them are still around the area now. An apprentice with me used to work for A J Chivers and is now a director of Ballast Wiltshire. One was with J W Palmer down the London Road – he now runs his own company. There was one from Lambourn, another from Shalbourne and one particularly good bricklayer – he's been at it all his life and he's still on the tools.

Building was really big, oh yes. Straight after the war, all the local companies had quite a few apprentices. There was a consortium – Hoskings & Pond, Smallbone, Cooke, Bance, and Wooldridge – and they all joined together and did housing estates. Shaw was built by the Newbury consortium, as was Elizabeth Avenue and Valley Road and the Ministry houses. At Bance, I was the only bricklayer in my year, but we had a plumber and a couple or three chippies. In any one year, we would have three, four or five apprentices. There were more building students at college than most anything else. Every company had apprentices and they would all do their training at South Berks College. In this way, we knew some of the lads from the other companies. The small plumbing companies also used to send one or two to college.

The guy that used to look after all the apprentices was Bates from Camp Hopson; he used to be the local chairman of the apprentice board. Hence the prize I was lucky enough to be awarded in 1964. It had a wonderful title, 'The Camp Hopson Prize for Building Students for Consistent Effort'. It was in the form of book tokens, and I bought myself a series of core brickwork books – they outlined all sorts of obscure bonds and bits and pieces – and some very useful building science books that were needed for the Technological Certificate and later on for the Ordinary and Higher Nationals. There was no presentation. They just gave it me and said, 'Here you are.'

We were working a 48-hour week, including the Saturday morning. It was slightly less in winter because of the light. We used to have to work from either 7.00 or 7.30 am to twelve o'clock midday on Saturdays. Five o'clock was the knock-off time, so when it was a college evening, seven till nine, we didn't have to waste a lot of time – after working there all day, going back home, change and have tea, and then cycling back into Newbury. Everything had to be done by pushbike. It was hard days. We used to stretch it out sometimes till half-past seven because it was accepted that you did have quite a difficult task. I was lucky because I was only at Woodhay. Some of them were in Hungerford and Lambourn. Some had motorbikes which made it much easier. You'd leave your bike round the front, except if you had all your tools, when you'd ride on down to the brickwork shop and park it outside. The brickwork shop was a separate block. We also used to have to go to Ormonde House for some lessons, not many, mainly theory-type. Packed lunches for me were the norm and I would eat outside, or in the brickwork shop, or wherever I was. In my first year I was lucky because I went to the mess hut with the builders.

We used to have to do homework, and that was very much an increasing thing: the farther you got on, the more you had. It was hard and there were internal assessment exams for each year. They wouldn't let you go on unless you had passed all the exams, and that included every subject you did. So you would have a practical test, and maths and science and design and all sorts of bits and pieces. You did the written exams in the classroom and all the practicals in the brickwork shop. When it came to the practical exams, you had to take your own tools. The college had tools but we used to hate using the damn things, because they were never like your own – it was completely different. That was why you were encouraged to bring your tools for your examinations. You were more familiar with them. You get quite an affiliation with your tools if you are handling them all day every day. Biking in from Woolton Hill, you had these strapped to your back, and bricklayers' tools are pretty heavy. The first practical exam in '62 was the six-hour, and then it was the seven-hour for the advanced, and they always planned it on Cup Final day, much to our disappointment!

Just before the completion of the college's second extension, I was transferred over to the other side of the Oxford Road where we were building the meter room for the SEB. That was a different style of building, with different bricks, the old pinewood bricks from Hermitage, ever so irregular. We had some tradesmen who were in the First World War. It was a complete experience for me because they brought a lot with them from their past work. If an apprentice went to a building today, he would just see the modern way of doing everything. We didn't. After we left the college we were altering older houses, and this is where these older boys shone because they were brought up with the older style buildings. So our practical side was very much all-embracing – and we were expected not only just to lay bricks. You used to have to do the tiling and drain-laying and all sorts of other bits and pieces. Today you get a ground worker to do the drains and the roads and the sewers, and the brickie just lays bricks. But then there weren't separate people to do that sort of thing. We were in the transition between what the brickie does today and what he did in the past. So from that point of view, it was an all-embracing apprenticeship. It gave us lots of knowledge about the way things used to happen and the way things were evolving.

Most of the older tradesmen used to build in sand and lime but we were building in cement mortar. Now you put pipes together with a plastic joint in between them. In those days you used to have a stick, three or four feet

440

long, and wrap it round with a piece of sack to fit inside the pipe. You then used to joint the pipes physically with a very high grade mortar, cork it in with gaskin and then fill it up with cement. These all used to have to be trowelled up. They didn't have to weep at all. It was all done in wet form, and you used to draw what we call the dolly through the pipework to take all the excess mortar or jointing compound from inside the pipes. The pipes were two foot long. They were all foreglazed, but not all of them were round. Today you could lay a mile of pipes, but you'd be lucky if you could lay ten or 12 feet a day in those days. For the lead pipes, they used to get the moleskins out and wipe the joints. All these skills are lost, but is there any need of them now? We were taught all sorts of bits and pieces as well, with regard to rubbing arches and things like that. You used to rub the bricks down to shape on a big flat stone and make them into arches, things that you would never think of doing today.

The college was basically straight brickwork for us because it was a steel-framed building. When we went from there to do other works, everything was very different. We weren't building steel-framed structures with brick cladding very much at all. It was all sorts of different systems which gave a wealth of experience which you could always draw on. I still do all my own building at home. We had to have sufficient expertise to do all these other sorts of works. Some of the bricklayers today wouldn't know what all the bonds were. They only build in single thickness or half-brick thickness, cavity construction. We were building solid walls to match all sorts of patterns that went before – all the bonds. It was a complete experience.

The training at the college was very useful because we were getting a very good background with the firm because of the quality and diversity of the work they were undertaking. The college and my firm gave me a wonderful experience in all aspects of building for which I am most grateful.

*'I was pleased to pass and to be able to wear a college blazer –
my sister sewed my badge on to the breast pocket'*

In the midsummer of 1960, **Roland Wise** was enjoying the last few
weeks of his Pre-Apprenticeship course. By the end of the summer,
the lad from Lambourn had signed his indentures and was getting
ready to start work at AERE Harwell.

> It was an all-age school at Lambourn. There was the
> juniors and the seniors there.[20] 15 was the age to leave and
> I was born in September so I could leave at Christmas. I
> was not sure what I wanted to do. I hadn't got a job and
> I tried knocking on the door at the local post office. 'Have
> you got a job as a postman?' I was quickly dismissed, very
> disappointed I had been turned down.
>
> I really wanted to do woodwork, but like all good parents,
> mine said, you had to have an apprenticeship. I couldn't
> get a good apprenticeship as a carpenter. Miss Marks was
> the careers lady and she used to visit all the schools and
> interview each one of us as to what we wanted to do. She
> did her best to find you appointments. I remember being
> called into the headmaster's office.
> 'You are staying on, my boy.'
> 'Oh yes? I thought I was leaving.'
> 'No, you are staying on because you are going to join this
> course at South Berks College in September.'
> It had been suggested by Miss Marks. There had obviously
> been a prior discussion between my parents, the headmaster
> and Miss Marks, and I was just told, in a nice way, that
> that was where I was going. My parents had obviously
> been briefed because money was short and they had to
> subsidise me at school for another two terms. I became
> head boy because my curriculum had finished. I was the
> odd-job boy. I was keen on engineering, and although we

---

[20] Lambourn was one of the last of the all-age schools in the Newbury
district. Those pupils over 11 were transferred to the John O'Gaunt
secondary modern school in Hungerford in 1963-64.

didn't have an engineering workshop at school, someone recognised that I had a forte for it.

I had failed the eleven-plus, and that was disappointing to me. So it pleased me that I was going to college. I always wanted further education, not knowing what I was going to find when I arrived.

We had to sit an entrance exam – that was very early on. We were met in the 'greenhouse' as we called it, in Ormonde House. It was an attachment on the side. We had this initial gathering. It was general about the college, and the next thing was, we were called in for an exam, and it was a Saturday morning. We were paraded along the new part of the building that was being built – it was still in a very early stage. There was banging and clattering and a lot of brickwork going on. We were put into this room – it was bleak and brickwork – and we sat this exam. It was under strict exam conditions, high pressure, no talking or things on the table. We could see builders all around, and the noise of the drilling was going on. It was a long exam, two or three hours, and there must have been a bit of everything in it. Typically, one young man gets up after an hour and walks out, and you think, 'Am I that thick?' I had always been taught to stay right to the end, even if you twiddle your thumbs, because you never know, by doodling and flicking through your paper you might think of something. So I stayed right to the bitter end.

There must have been 20 or 30 in this room, but on the course itself, there were only about 15. The others didn't get in. I was pleased to pass and to be able to wear a college blazer – my sister sewed my badge on to the breast pocket. The blazer was black. It fitted the black and yellow striped tie. We had to travel on the bus with St Bart's pupils. It was caps in those days and if the boys were caught outside of school without one, they were reported. We also had black and yellow scarves, longitudinal stripes. I wouldn't say it was compulsory, but quite a few people attended with a blazer, badge and tie – many of my Pre-Apprentice group did.

The course started in September 1959. There weren't that many students around. I came not knowing what I was coming for. Students came by bus – we had a bus pass from Lambourn – and there was a lot of hitching as well. You would stand and thumb and get a lift. We weren't earning, but my brother was very generous. He was working and he was giving me ten shillings a week (50 pence). That was a lot of money and I was very grateful. We had to work Saturdays to get more income, either down the greengrocers or car washing.

The Pre-Apprenticeship was well organised. We didn't want for a lot. It was a general educational experience, a varied course. It wasn't just engineering; they were preparing us for the world as well. There was a lot of that in it, and communication with not only our peers but our seniors as well. The course was good for me. It had value, and still has value today. All the classes were taught on the college site. We weren't down in the town at all. They were all boys and we were together all the time. We didn't separate, so we knew each other quite well. You started in your little group and then at lunchtime you'd go off with someone you wanted to. There was good camaraderie within the group, which was developed by the lecturers.

We had English, writing letters and applications, things that you do in GNVQ now. Fred Pizzey took us for that. Roy Pocock took us for maths. He was quite a character – no one could forget him. He called me 'Willie' Wise – that was his style – but he knew exactly what you were doing and what you were up to. He had the respect, perhaps because of his standing, because you didn't mess about. He had that way with him. He was a great person, a people's person who helped an individual. Don Heywood took us for science. We did a lot of experiments, but I didn't take to chemistry at all. It was the fear of pouring something or doing something wrong. It wouldn't happen because we were very closely monitored. We did woodwork with Dick Edwards. We produced this bowl, which I've still got at home. We were taught in the chicken hut, long and wooden, standing on its own. Len Hoyland was the drawing man. He was another gentleman. If we behaved in the class we were allowed to listen to the Derby – we actually brought the wireless out. He wasn't a bit interested, but he allowed us to have this race on. We had a little sweep of course.

We did engineering in the workshops; that was the direction we were being manoeuvred into. We had Arthur Bedford. Motor vehicle wasn't part of the course, but Charlie Sully came into the workshop occasionally. He was a staunch communist, but he didn't try and convert you. He would relate some misdemeanour or other, or he would explain what went on in other countries. We tried to stay clear if we could, but if we didn't particularly want the subject taught us, we would get him onto communism and he would be away. He was good at that. We spent many hours down in the workshops, yet the course was not all about us going to an engineering establishment. I know of two guys who went into the commercial field, accountancy and secretarial.

You had to do recreation on one afternoon a week. Roy was a great cricketer and I remember playing against the teachers down at Northcroft. We got annihilated. During the summer Fred Pizzey would take us to Northcroft, open-air swimming. He was a good swimmer. We wanted to play football, but we had no facilities until we were charged with going down to a grassed area that we'd spied upon. 'It needs cutting down boys!' So a group of us were down there, with our shirts off and our rip hooks. That's all we had and we cut this area for a football ground, team building at lunchtime. We were desperate to get it because we wanted to play football.

There was a lot of homework, and you had to do it. We were cajoled and pushed. They kept good records, where we were and what we were up to. They were very particular; everything was marked and comments made. They had the energy and enthusiasm. Once my sister had a serious accident and I couldn't do the homework. My parents wrote a letter to Mr Pizzey, explaining that she had had this accident and I was distressed. I got away from homework for an evening, but it was quickly recovered.

We went down town to get our lunch. Sometimes it was a bottle of Tizer and fish and chips in a bag. One day three or four of us were walking along the riverside by the American bridge.[21] We had finished our fish and chips. This guy was a bit of a lad and he rolled his paper up, threw it down on the floor and used it as a football. He kicked it, but he had slip-on shoes on, and his shoe went into the river. We followed it all the way up to the sluice gate. What could we do? Time was getting on and we had to be back. We managed to get it, but we had a terrible time. We thought we were going to fall in. We went back and we had Fred Pizzey. I don't know whether he believed us or not.

I seemed to be geared towards engineering. I don't know how I found out; it was an individual thing that Roy Pocock developed. We had our interviews about what we were going to do, and it was suggested that we apply for apprenticeships and there was this application form thrust under our noses. 'Roland, you ought to do this.' There was this application form for Harwell. I filled it in and the next thing I know, I'm going along for a test and an interview and I'm in. I had very little to do with it and didn't know what I was applying for, but we knew of its standing.

---

[21] This was the emergency bridge erected over the River Kennet at the southern end of Park Way at the beginning of the Second World War in case the stone bridge in Northbrook Street was destroyed by enemy action. It was also used as an alternative river crossing for heavy tanks. The bridge was replaced in 2001.

'It was a super atmosphere in those days – there was fun to be had and we had fun'

The summer of 1960 and **Sid Dixon** had been at college for a year. He had come from Park House where good teaching had given him a solid foundation when he started work. He was a Plenty's apprentice and he had completed his first year in mechanical engineering. He had enjoyed it, and was looking forward to the start of the new term. He was on Miss Garlick's 'approved list' and was allowed to talk to 'her girls doing RSA'. A country lad from Hamstead Marshall – 'we go back to the middle of the 19th century' – Sid and his family were now living in Stoke, close by Hurstbourne Tarrant in Hampshire. He had been coming into Newbury on the bus but now he was 17 and excited about the prospect of learning to drive and getting his own car.

> I went to Enborne primary, a little country school with about 30 kids in two classrooms. Maths was never a problem and we did tables every day. We used to have these cards to work from and I used to have to wait for the kids to catch me up. I passed the first part of the eleven-plus but I didn't pass part two. You had no preparation; you just walked into the exam. It was a nightmare for a kid in the country.

> I went to Park House at the age of 11. We lived midway between there and Hungerford. We used to have a taxi 'cos there wasn't the transport. Then we came in on the bus from Hamstead to Kimber's Corner by Blackboys Bridge, crossed over the road and caught the school bus up to Park House.[22] That was a nightmare! Fights, and that was within Park House, without the fights that used to take place between Park House and the Grammar School. They used to defend the Girls' High School territory on the Andover Road, which they thought was their's – but

---

[22] The Kimber family were high class grocers who traded from Bartholomew House on the corner of Bartholomew Street and Pound Street, a junction known as Kimber's Corner.

fortunately not all the girls thought that the best boys came from the Grammar School. There were some tough nuts, oh yes, and there were disputes.

It was a great time to be at Park House. There were two masters in particular. Mr Fox taught me the basics of maths and algebra; he put the spark there. Titchie Allen took it on, and it developed at college into applied maths for the calculations of the speeds and the powers for the lathes and whatnot. In engineering drawing, Mr Hughson was the one, a great man and a great master. He set the foundations and Len Hoyland built on them when he took over.

There was maths and English – six subjects was the most you could take at school. It was UEI. Then a new exam came in which was called UEI School Leavers, which was the forerunner to CSEs (Certificate of Secondary Education). I stayed on an extra year and did the new one at 16. There was a small group of us. Six started, five finished and one got expelled. 1959 was a gorgeous summer weather-wise. We finished the exams and a group of us worked with Mr Sharp, the science master, and fitted out the intercom system. We used to play cricket and tennis – lovely tennis courts we had – and we used to go down to the open-air swimming pool. That was a brilliant summer.

Miss Marks used to come to the school, but I did not get the apprenticeship through her. There was a lot of employment. There's always been high employment in the town. In the late '50s and '60s, if you were fed up with your job, you just left, went down the road and got another one. I applied to Plenty through the paper and went for an interview with John Hall-Craggs.[23] He was very much involved with youth and was always encouraging. He went on to be chairman of the company after I'd left.

---

[23] John Hall-Craggs joined Plenty in 1955 and became sales director. He was a member of the college governing body – and its chairman – in the 1970s.

I started at Plenty on Monday, October 5th, 1959. They sent me to college on day release, one day a week, through the day and evening as well. I expected to go home at five o'clock and catch the bus back to Stoke, only to be told that we needed to be at college till seven. I thought it was worse than being at work. There were several other characters, lads from Park House and from schools around. Newbury had a lot of the industry of the day, engineering and mechanical engineering. There were other people from Plenty on the course. We all came to college and then we went off in different directions. And we had students from Harwell and craft apprentices from Newbury Diesel and Opperman Gears. There was a lot happening around Newbury, and it wasn't just the engineering. There were several electrical contractors, and there was a hive of building. You had all the building trades at college, the carpentry and the bricklaying.

I did maths, engineering drawing, workshop technology and science. It was all vocational, all tied in with your work. It was about engineering and the sciences, full stop. There were some really very good, very dedicated tutors. I learnt more and received more academic education after leaving school than I had learnt at school. We didn't go down to the workshop very often, only occasionally on whatever was needed for a test piece, the lathes or milling machines. Mr Bedford was very good, been in industry, knew about workshop practice, a very knowledgeable guy. But it was a theory rather than a practical course and we spent most of the time in the classroom. Science, in the science lab, was electrics, mechanics and physics, three subjects all in one. Charlie Sully took us, but he was a very good mechanical engineer, a very good auto mechanic. What he didn't know about motor vehicles, not only the practical but also the technical side! He was a character, very down to earth but very good.

One of the most brilliant tutors that I came across and had the pleasure to be a student of was Len Hoyland. Len taught me engineering drawing – that was his main subject - but he could teach me anything. He was a brilliant freehand drawer as well. I had some very good maths teachers that raised the algebra, the geometry, the trigonometry. We did the maths which applied to engineering, such as lathe speeds and horsepowers. They came into science as well. Mr Pocock was the Vice-Principal. He was involved in the teaching, but you would see him a lot around college. He was known by all the boys, a well respected member of staff. Lansley was someone we had little contact with. You learnt a lot by coming to college. I certainly did. It hasn't got me anywhere, but I learnt a lot. It is a centre of excellence now, but it was then. It certainly raised my standard of maths. Some of the geometry that we had was quite involved. And engineering drawing, well, Len was just the tops.

There were no clubs at the college, and it's never been a sporting place because of the lack of space. But it was a super atmosphere in those days. The refectory – it was termed the common room then – was alive. There was fun to be had and we had fun. There were a lot of great characters around. The students got together and we knew who was in on whatever day we were. Miss Garlick was policing the girls doing RSA. There were a few of us in my class that were on the approved list – we were actually allowed to talk to them. We were honoured to be on Miss Garlick's list. There was one lass; her name was Jennifer Monroe-Ashman. She used to live at Cold Ash, and she was gorgeous. I often wonder where that girl went.

There was always banter but never rudeness. There was fun and high jinks but there wasn't vandalism. You wouldn't ever get anything smashed up. We were involved in all sorts of pranks. Our last Christmas at college, we were a small class, six or seven of us. We'd been to the Bacon Arms for lunch. One lad when he came back just crawled up on the desk and went to sleep. The rest of us, every time the lecturer turned to the blackboard, we moved one seat. So continually through the afternoon, every time he looked back there would be a different face looking at him. And he didn't say a word. He just ignored us. It was totally stupid, but at the time it was hilarious.

The first part of A-Block was finished – we were some of the first students in there – and the engineering workshops were in operation. There was a lot of fir trees around, far more than there were later. The car park was at the front. There weren't many cars but the types of vehicle you had then are the classics of today. The old Riley Pathfinders, and Len Hoyland had a Riley 1.5, a very sleek machine. Us poor old apprentices managed to keep a car on the road; literally, they were just kept on the road. That was sometimes a weekend job. That was the brilliance of the Morris Minor 'cos there was nothing that you couldn't do between Friday night and Monday morning. And even if it was a new or reconditioned engine, that was out and back in for eight o'clock Monday morning. There were no MOTs and as an apprentice you kept your vehicle on the road. Exhaust pipes went around with all sorts of tape and wire to keep them on.

I was living at Stoke and I always seemed to be late and we had maths first thing. I came to college on the bus, and that was a long day because you had to wait for the bus down at the Wharf in all winds and weathers. Fortunately, I passed my test within a few weeks of being 17. Then I had a little Austin Seven, with a notorious, now a very valuable, number plate. It didn't have a starter motor, it had a starter cam, and I sold it for £6/10/- (£6.50) to the local gamekeeper for his son to trundle round the woods in. In 1962-63 we had that abominable winter. It started snowing on Boxing Day, and there was still snow in the fields in March. There were drifts on the road coming along from Hurstbourne Tarrant into Newbury. I used to come in early 'cos I used to drop my father off. Fortunately we had a Land Rover. One morning there was just a couple of tracks you could see, but we got through. The first job at work was to thaw out the pipes round the factory 'cos there was no heating and slurry in the lathe flows.

The skilled man was earning £20 a week but we were cheap labour. My first week's wages are indelibly printed on my mind, £2/13/10 (£2.69) for a 46-hour week. But it went up every year and I did better than most apprentices for money because I always kept a car on the road. It was Monday to Thursday, 8 till 6, Friday 8 till 5, and Saturday morning till lunchtime. We got our training on the technical side at college. There was no apprenticeship training as such; it wasn't a training school. You were put with one of the skilled guys from day one and you picked it up as you went along. That's how you learned – but it was a damn good apprenticeship.

There's an old saying: the apprentices from Plenty could turn their hand to anything. They turned out good craftsmen, and that is true, because there's a lot of guys who have come out of there and moved away from engineering and they are very good in their field. Some guys have gone into their own building companies – they're good practical people. Having been through an apprenticeship at Plenty, you can work anywhere.

Shoosmith and Walford were the joint managing directors. Shooey was the top dog, and he was very good. He had little contact with the men but he would walk round the factory every day. He knew everything that was going on on the shop floor. Then he would go back to the works manager, Mr Jones, and he would pick up points. Jonah's office was a few stairs up – it was very much upstairs and downstairs at Plenty. After he'd gone, the door would go flying open and Jonah would inevitably fall halfway down the stairs and then trundle off into the factory. In best builders' language, he would persuade somebody that something wasn't done or something needed moving. He would then go to the foreman, who would go to the chargehand, someone at the bottom. There was always the bottom of the pecking order.

There was a little route that went from the back of Plenty, across behind Fisher the fruiterer's into Bert Austin's pie shop. Saturdays we would wait to see where the foreman was and then somebody would be detailed with cash in hand to fly through to Bert Austin for a number of pasties before the foreman came back. Next to Plenty's front entrance was a shoe shop and then a pub. At Christmas, that was a jaunt to the Catherine Wheel. Having got thoroughly tanked up at lunchtime, we would take trolley jacks round the town with apprentices being tugged on these damn metal things. We would hurl them round the town with cans and string tied to them. It was great. It was the done thing, the way of life.

In the summer we played cricket. We used to have the use of a Morris Oxford pickup with a canvas roof – three in the front and the team in the back with the bag and all the bits and pieces. Peasemore, Brightwalton, an inter-factory match against Sigmund up at Reading, all over we used to play. We used to play against the Shoosmith XI at St Mary Bourne. That was a big do – a bus, tea, lots of beer, and lots of people got drunk.

There was a social life and people valued their social time. People had breaks in the morning and had a lunch hour, a whole hour. They had time, or they made time. There was hard work and there was hardship, but there wasn't the stress, there wasn't the rat race. People were born into the working-class bracket and that's where they had their fun. There was little clamour to get to the top.

It was a five-year apprenticeship and I left college in 1964. It was all exams. We had exams during the year and at the end of every year. I didn't leave with the certificate, and I disappeared out of education after that. You had to pass the lot and there was one subject that bugged me and that was the electrical side of science. I never was able to come to grips with that. I didn't have any interest in it. If I went back to it now, with a different attitude to study, it would

453

not present the problems it did at the time. Another big factor was self-confidence. We were very young and self-confidence was something that was lacking, a big barrier to learning. If you think you can, then very often you can. If you think you can't, then that is a way to failure. You have to come to grips with that, sometimes the very hard way.

If you failed your course, two things happened. First, you would have to sit the exam again. The second thing was, working in a factory, everybody knew you'd failed. There was no hiding place. You had to live through that. That could be difficult and there wasn't a lot of sympathy around to encourage you, to help you to pass. At the end, if you passed, you went through the magic gate and you were hotfoot up through the office. If you failed, then you remained as one of the 'dirties', and that was it.

Into the '60s ... and Miss Garlick has to cope with the miniskirt

In the autumn of 1960 **David Jones** was taken on as the college's laboratory assistant. He lived in Stockcross but he only went to school there for 18 months. 'I was chasing a young lady and ran into her sister coming the other way with a kettle of boiling water.' David was badly scalded and ended up in hospital. After the accident, his parents sent him to a private school in Craven Road in Newbury and he stayed there until he went to the Grammar School. This was where Roy Pocock first came across him. 'Eric Carr and I substituted for the deputy head of St Bart's in about 1957 – while there I taught David Jones in maths.' By the time David reached the fifth form, in which he spent two years, he wanted a job in technical drawing 'because it was being advertised in the paper all the time'. However, a fortuitous visit to the youth employment officer caused him to change his mind.

I was sat in her office and the 'phone rang and it was Eric Lansley. 'We have a position for a lab assistant. Could you put it on the notice board?' Miss Marks looked at me and said, 'How about going for that?'

I said, 'Fine. Where's South Berks College?'

I lived at Stockcross and didn't come into Newbury very often. I saw a policeman and asked him where the college was. He said, 'All I can tell you, mate, is that there is a lot of new buildings going up.' I got an interview and went to the receptionist in Ormonde House. 'Oh, somebody else has come for that job as well.' It was a chap called Ben Hartson. He had come out of the medical labs, where his boss was Sir Alexander Fleming. We were interviewed by Lansley, Pocock and the Head of Science, Eric Carr – three of them, a bit daunting at 16, 17; but that was the era when things were done properly. They appointed both of us as lab assistants, me full time and Ben part time. I started in October 1960.

When I came, there was the first and second instalments, the horsa huts, the chicken houses and the brickwork shop. At the end of the first instalment was the tennis court. It was still played on – Harry Whiting used to have a knock on it. The blue noticeboard was there and when that was demolished it went to Stockcross. You would come out of the back door of the machine shop and face the chain-link fencing for the tennis court. The other side of that was a tiny allotment, a cabbage patch. Between the two horsa huts there was a boiler house and behind them there was a field with a horse in it. The steel shed on the end of the chicken houses was Dick Edwards' woodstore, 'cos he went through the store into the chicken house and then into the other one. There were two of them end to end, woodwork and machinery, and there was Miford lathes in there as well. I used to turn bowls in the chicken hut in my dinner hour till Pocock came in and caught me about quarter-past one one day, and that was that. On the north end of the chicken houses was the brickwork shop and on the west side were the two cottages for Harry Whiting and Charlie Sully. To the south of the cottages was a shed which had welding and bits and pieces in it. Then there was what appeared to be a chapel, which had furniture stored in it when I came. The conservatory had gone, but there was fresh paint on the side of Ormonde House where it had been. A cottage was in the corner by the car park, but it wasn't there for very long as the space was needed for car parking. Marlborough House was next door and it was very much taboo. It was bigger than Ormonde House, absolutely immaculate inside with a fabulous staircase. If you went over the hedge, the old gardener would hit you with a shovel. The apples and the plums were on the trees until they fell, but God help you if you got in there and he was about.

I came as a lab assistant, very green basically. I took home something like £15 a week, which was what my father was getting as a mechanic. I had a science background, albeit general science as I failed the individual sciences. I was appointed to engineering science and I became Eddie Irwing's lab assistant for part of the time. The rest of the time, thankfully, Jeff Jeffery was training me. Jeff was my boss and he trained me as I went along.[24] He and his wife treated me like a son for seven years until he retired. They both took a shine to me. I got a very good friend in Jeff.

I learned because I'm a practical and not a theory person. I picked up welding very quickly, seeing I did all the welding, gas and electric, right across the college. I started to do the machine shop repairs because Jeff taught me to use the lathes and the milling machines. I became more use on that side than stuck in an office or a lab. John Humphries was storekeeper, Ruth Brown was chemistry, and Brian Salmon was general. But in those days we all did each other's jobs. If Ruth was out, I did chemistry or Salmon did chemistry.

I worked with Don Heywood in chemistry. I did preparation work, 'cos we did everything in those days. Only when you get into the last 20 years did it get so technical. I got day release and did laboratory techniques

---

[24] 'David Jones had a very good teacher – Jeff Jeffery could do anything.'(Dick Edwards)

through the '60s. I passed all the practicals and failed all the theory, which is bloody typical. I did this for four years. I did a rerun and still didn't pass the theory. Ray Harraway took all the laboratory techniques side of it, and we had a big practical. The other students in the class were from Harwell and Aldermaston.

In the first two or three years I used to do laboratory techniques, the practical part of it, with Jeff in the evening. He and I made this shadow board in the science workshop with about 50 tools on it, with the white shadow of the tool behind each one. At about half-past seven, when we were due to finish and the students were due to catch their bus back to Harwell, he would go in the storeroom.

'Everything back, lads?'

'Yes Mr Jeffery.'

And he said, 'Well, I'm sorry to inform you, but there's 12 six-inch rules, 14 screwdrivers, three pairs of tin snips, and two pairs of pliers missing, and until they're back, you aren't going.' At quarter to eight they had missed the bus and they were still arguing the toss.

'Who put these in my lunch box?'

And out came two pairs of pliers. That went on for about three weeks. The second week it was down to about ten tools missing. The third week it was down to two. The following week they were all on the bus at half-past seven. They had missed the bus three weeks running.

I also did a 12-week course at nights with the chief glass-blower at Harwell, which is why I did all the glass-blowing at college as well. Jeff and I designed the course, and Dick Edwards, Don Heywood and I were the staff on it. When Jeff retired, glass-blowing was still in fashion. It had not been ousted by commercially-built stuff, but it more or less vanished at the end of the '70s. I built the glass-blowing workshop and I destroyed it eventually because it had to make way for art.

Ballard was electronics, brilliant.[25] He was one of the only people that's taught electronics that could actually build it as well. The open days in those days were real open days. It was absolutely fantastic in the early '60s. Hundreds and hundreds of people came, mainly because Mrs Potter had all her ecclesiastical embroidery and whatnot in the hall, and Dick Edwards had all his beaten metalwork, silverwork, turning and woodwork. Nobody ever went anywhere else. They just used to come to the hall. The college decided they wanted to know how many people were coming in. They went to Mr Ballard and he made a counter in the workshop, four valves, stuck it over the door and counted all the people in there. Eventually he went to Street College in Somerset as deputy head and finished up as head.

Bill Holt was electrical engineering. He was very good. It wasn't part of my job but I used to fill in as a practical technician all over the place. Bill was the only lecturer I worked for who knew exactly what he had, where he had it and where he wanted it. It was all written down, and it was always there because he bloody checked it himself. Not many people do that. He was absolutely immaculate to work for. He started off in the horsa hut with the electrical machinery and all that sort of thing. He had a Triumph Mayflower, grey, absolutely immaculate. He used to drive it in first and second gear. He never went above second.

Len Hoyland was in the workshop superintendent's office. You had overload, and the alarm bells for the machine shop were situated in there. Arc welding was in the machine shop as well, and the machine shop was working flat out every day of the week. If I needed to use a machine I'd book it a fortnight in advance. Jeff and I moved the entire workshop in the first six years because it was underfloor-wired and the water used to come up through the drains. That was not a good idea, so we overwired it. All the

---

[25] 'J W Ballard contributed much to the Applied Physics course before leaving to become Principal at Street.' SBCFE 25 Years.

machines were bolted down and one of the first things I did was jack 'em up and take some of the bolts off, so they were all free-mounted and wired overhead. It was all individual, glass-enclosed tucks and bolts overhead.

The drawing office was in between the chemistry and physics labs, and Len Hoyland used to teach up there. That was the era when you had ammonia-sensitive paper, before photocopying and that sort of thing. You did an ordinary pencil drawing, put the sensitised paper over the top of it and fired it up with mercury vapour lamps under a big glass dome. Then you put the paper in the fume cupboard – I used to get called to put the drawings in the cupboard – and expose your ammonia. The drawings used to come out as blue prints.

There was also a drawing office next to the lab, what became the biology lab, on the ground floor of A-Block. Les Sugden taught in there. He had a Triumph Herald, as clean under the bonnet as above it. He used to polish the engine as well.

I did a lot of work for Eric Gardner. I was his technician as well for a while. We dabbled in encapsulating steel in plastic for hedging in metallurgy and I did a lot of that with him. Also with him I dabbled in stresses and strains in perspex. We used a denizen tensile tester for plastic. Whereas the engineers used it all the time, we used to vary 'cos Eric was interested in strains and stresses.

Lionel Bernard was at the college when I came. He was light years ahead of his subject. I was encapsulating electronic components in perspex for him in the '60s, and that didn't come in until 15 years later. Jeff and I made six-inch squares of perspex, with holes all the way over, so you could put all the components on a matrix board.

Plumbing was off the machine shop and the gas and arc welding was in there. Jeff taught me to weld, the staff picked it up off me, and then they started teaching it. They had a two-day lightning course with BOC, and that's how welding started. Mervyn Cowie was a plumber extraordinary, a brilliant plumber. He taught me to weld lead, and he always called me 'Dai the Welder'. He used to do lead burning, lead flashings, duralite – a thick felt-like substance – BSP pipes, copper-soldered fittings. We used to recycle the lead on site, melt it into blocks and sell it back and get sheets. We also used to recycle the lead into strips for lead welding. We used to pour the melted lead into trays, an inch wide, three sixteenths deep, so you got strips to do your lead welding.

Another thing I used to do was stand in the stores, Friday nights, right through till half-past nine. I did just about everything. Building was big and we used to do concrete tube testing and lintel testing for the industry. They sent us a handful of concrete in a cube and we'd let it go 24 hours or seven days, or whatever it was, testing it by instruction. We'd have a number of cubes and then we'd destroy them. Arthur Owen was carpentry, bloody brilliant, but he was a theoretical and not a practical crafter. I sat in on a lecture by him one day. He talked for half an hour on a wood chisel without repeating himself, and it was interesting.

Charlie Sully was always doing engines. There was a pit in the floor of the motor vehicle workshop. He made a case that he needed a technician, and I was seconded to him. The only stipulation was he had to provide me with a full timetable every week. He couldn't do that, and the only thing I used to do on a regular basis for him was start the diesel engine. We had a single cylinder diesel engine in one of the horsa huts and heat treatment used to be done in there. You used to put a cartridge in it, set it alight, get the flywheel in a certain position and turn it. You had to have your hand in the right place because it used to bite back. Jeff got thrown out there a couple of times.

Eric Lansley was a perfect gentleman. He would have made a wonderful diplomat. Nothing was too much trouble for him. I was in trouble in the hall one day with about 30 sheets of board. He came in.

'Do you need a hand?'

Timid 18-year-old, I said, 'You're joking.'

'No' he said, 'I'll give you a hand. Got another saw?'

Then he said, 'Hang on, I'll get Poke.'

And it finished up I had the Principal and the Vice-Principal in there. Pocock didn't mind 'cos he was practical anyway. He wore his smock more often than he did anything else.

Mrs Potter was Flemish, a lovely lady. She was upstairs in the domestic science rooms, all sewing machines and cutting-out tables. When she got excited down the 'phone I used to say, 'Hang on – I'll come up and see you.' She taught dressmaking and ecclesiastical embroidery, wonderful stuff with gold and silver thread. I dabbled in photography for her. Honor Blackman appeared in *Vogue* dressed in leather, and I divided the picture into 12, blew it up to 24 by 24 in the darkroom, and pieced it together to get her life-size for an open day.

Miss Garlick and I crossed swords quite early on. Straight from school, I saw her as a martinet. It was the era of vinyl records, and she asked me to put a Dansette record player in the library. Pete White was there, running the library, and I went and put the record player out. It was for an RAF officer, respectable in his uniform with gold braid, come to give a careers lecture. Half an hour into this, I was in the workshop with Jeff and the 'phone was ringing. 'Jones? Miss Garlick here. What the bloody hell do you mean by providing me with a record player that doesn't work? I want you up here, now!' And the 'phone went down.

'Right, my dear.'

I'm 18, white as a sheet, goes up, creeps in. The class was all girls, all my age. I was frightened to bloody death.

I goes up to the wall, puts the switch on and walks out 'cos the light comes on. The following morning at ten o'clock Jeff said, 'I've got a packet of fags here from Vera and you've got a little box and a note.' The note said how grateful she was that I hadn't bawled her out in front of an élite member of the RAF. Would I please accept a box of chocolates – and she'd enclosed a packet of fags for the brilliant teacher I had in Jeff.

I also did all the projecting, 16mm projectors, nine till five, every day of the week. We had so much of it, we built on the back of the lecture theatre to cut the noise of the projector down. We used to store about 40 chairs, 20 each side, because a lot of people used to go in and watch films.

Miss Garlick came in one day and said, 'Whenever I come past the lecture theatre, you're either in there showing a film or you're just coming out with a film under your arm.' 'Yes,' I said, 'I show films nine till five. It's all recorded in the diary.'
She said, 'Well, before you do anything else, I need to know who you are doing it for. I am going to stop it, because that's not teaching.'
And I'm looking a bit bloody nonplussed and she obviously noticed it.
She said, 'Is there a problem?'
I said, 'Well, do you really want to know? I don't need to look in the book. It's you, Business Studies, nine till five, four days out of the five.'
'I don't believe it!' she said.
But it was in my diary. She was as good as her word. It stopped within a week and I went down from nine to five and square eyes, which I'd had for three years, to three films a day. Then videos came in and stopped it dead. Miss Garlick also had to cope with the miniskirt, 'cos that was just coming in. She took it in good heart, but it was a different world.

One of the biggest changes since 1960 has been from chalk and talk to handouts and OHP work. I struggled through laboratory techniques theory for four years and I still remember some of it 'cos I had to write the damn stuff down quickly off the board. It spoilt my handwriting. I left Craven School with copperplate handwriting, but to keep up with the Don Heywoods and the Ray Harraways of this world, it came to the point where I finished up printing because I could print faster than I could write. We had an electronics lecturer who used to stand up the first day of term and tell his class, 'I start at nine o'clock, which is when you must be here. If you come in at five past, and I'm on my second board, you've missed a board full.' And he used to teach like that. I've seen him do it with nobody in there, even taking it to that extreme to make a point, and as they've walked in the door, 'Well, I'm sorry lads if you can't get here on time. That's the second board full.'

It was all chalk and talk then, and you learnt something from that, whereas now you listen to a lecture with a handout and it's too easy. My handout from a Red Cross lecture goes into a folder at home, and if I do a lecture, I go to the folder and take it out. I don't read the bloody thing until I do the lecture.

Another change is, at the Grammar School we used to get two projector films twice a term. You looked forward to it, and I can still see those black-and-white pictures. Then I came to the college, and you're getting 16mm films every damn day of the week. And now it's gone to video, I don't think it's appreciated any more.

If I thought that coming straight from school there was very little discipline at college, there certainly isn't any now. There wasn't corporal punishment as such, but nobody heard too much about it if somebody's ear got clipped. The ultimate was, 'We'll 'phone your firm.' They did that and it was a deterrent, but they don't bother with that now.

14

LOOSE ENDS

Vera Garlick did not have to cope with the miniskirt for very long. She retired as Head of Business Studies in 1964, one of the first to retire from the college rather than leave. Fortunately her wealth of experience was not lost to further education as she became a governor, worked on the committee for liberal and social studies and taught for the WEA. Yet retirement gave her the time to indulge her passion for local history and she became an accomplished author of books about Newbury.

Of the staff voices heard again in this volume, **Eric Carr** retired as Head of Science in 1966. He had spent a lifetime in teaching and for a short time he went to work at Mary Hare School. 'Somebody had left to get married and I taught physics there for a few months. I enjoyed that.' Both Vera Garlick and Eric Carr had left their mark at Ormonde House. 'Each had built up a new department and the close contacts with industry and commerce which this entailed but had never lost contact with their students.'[1]

Roy Pocock continued as Vice-Principal and Head of Engineering in the '60s. When national concern was expressed about the high failure rate among FE students, the college developed a selection procedure for applicants, and in 1962, tests were introduced to distinguish potential craft students from the technicians.[2]

---

[1] *Ibid.*.

[2] Education in the Royal County of Berkshire 1961-62, Report by the Director of Education, p.35.

Roy Pocock continued to work with the apprentice manager at AERE and 'a lot of the Harwell set-up continued because of the personal relationship between Jock Wallace and me'. A unique experiment started in 1966. Block release replaced day release for many of the atomic apprentices and the training was reduced from five years to four.

Roy Pocock and John Wallace were the architects of this change. It was tried out with electrical apprentices and when the merits of day and block release were compared, it was found that the examination results of block-release students were better than the others.[3] So in the autumn of 1966, the electrical and mechanical apprentices spent one week in three at college with lecturers visiting the training schools at Harwell and Aldermaston to give additional instruction. This way of training was accepted by City & Guilds and eventually by the Southern Regional Council.

> This last was the most difficult hurdle because many local colleges were reluctant to lose students from their area, while others were quite emphatic that they could run the same course for Harwell equally well, and while this was almost certainly the case, no other college was in the same geographic location to Aldermaston and Harwell, and any sub-division of the course would have destroyed its viability.[4]

Roy Pocock became Principal of South Berks College in 1970. 'One has to be extremely lucky to move from Assistant Lecturer to Principal within the one establishment.'[5] The new Principal was responsible for 43 lecturers, which had increased to 68 by the time he retired.

Roy spent a lot of time in meetings with the LEA at Shire Hall in Reading. 'I encouraged a lot of activities between the schools and the college, and also between the FE Officers and the Principals. Lansley was not keen on that sort of thing – I had the

---

[3] Education in the Royal County of Berkshire 1963-64, Report by the Director of Education, p.36.

[4] The First Thirty Years of Apprentice Training at Harwell, *op.cit.*,p.9.3.

[5] SBCFE 25 Years.

facilities to do it. When Edwards was made Director of Education, I invited him down to lunch at home. He came with Colin James and one or two others. I used to keep ducks and chickens and such like on the farm, wring one's neck and put it in the pot.'

John Wallace retired in 1978. The departure of the last founder member still working for Harwell's training board meant that one of the last links with 1948 was severed. As many as 800 apprentices had passed through his hands in 30 years. A year later, in 1979, after 30 years at Ormonde House, Roy Pocock also retired. Yet he still came to the college, joined a craft class and made a table. His tutor was Dick Edwards.

'I had some good people who were interested, and they will always get on'

Dick Edwards also retired in 1979, but he continued as a part-time tutor. By the time he finished, he had worked for five Principals, a unique achievement. Albert Owthwaite appointed him and he worked under Eric Lansley and Roy Pocock, 'entertaining students of all ages in rather adverse conditions in woodwork and metalwork in one of the original pre-fabs'. He continued part-time under Eric Memmot (1979-92) and finally left the college in 1996 during Gordon Bull's time as Principal (1993-2000). He was 80 years old.

Dick always remained modest about his work. He produced professional silverwork with his own silver mark and as for his expertise as a tutor, 'I had some good people'. During our conversations he could still recall the names of many of his students, and two of them he remembered particularly well.

> Roy was a good Principal, but he once told me to do something he couldn't do himself. He came to me one afternoon and said, 'Look at those two over there. Can't you control them better than that?'
> And I said, 'Well, you try. And if you can do any better than I can, good for you.'
> His remark to me was, 'My God! You don't expect me to deal with those two do you?'

The 'two over there' were their wives. 'Connie and Olive used to work together – or natter together – on the same bench.'

'ONCs and HNCs had such a long history dating way back to before the war – they served a very, very useful service'

When a person's time at the college drew to a close, it was customary for their colleagues to gather in the staff room in Ormonde House to say their goodbyes. **Len Hoyland** retired at the same time as Roy Pocock. 'We both made our farewell speeches. He was the senior man of course, and therefore he took precedence.' Len had spent half his working life at Newbury. For more than 20 years he had taught technical drawing to apprentices, and from the mid-'60s, many of these came on block release.

> The apprentice would come to us one week in three. Block release was something unique in further education in those days, and Mr Pocock, give him the credit, he instigated it. It took a lot of organising, of that I am sure, because it wasn't generally accepted. Further education, generally, was day release. If you could persuade an employer to release you for one day per week, that's all he could manage. He didn't want to know about block. Local industries wouldn't let you go for one week in three; only Harwell and Aldermaston could allow one week in three.
>
> You might say, what's the advantage of block release? One week in three was obviously more student hours than just one day a week. Consequently progress could be more rapid. Imagine five days instead of one. It meant you could cover the work in a much shorter time, and that suited Harwell and Aldermaston. They welcomed that, so it was very satisfactory, and I'm sure that the students benefited.
>
> It was very complicated to get the timetables to interlock. It had to be arranged whereby one group from Harwell would come and they would attend for one week. It was a block of three and the second week in the block of three there would be another group from Aldermaston. And

then the third week there'd be another one from Harwell. There were three different groups, all working together to the same syllabus. So you would teach for a week, then the next week it would be the same subjects again.

The Engineering Department never looked back. The links were extended because members of the staff at Newbury would go to Harwell and Aldermaston half a day a week to teach on their premises, to help with homework or anything else that was felt appropriate. So it was a two-way process: they came to us and we went to them. That again was Pocock's idea. He was determined that once he'd made the contacts, he wasn't going to lose them, and if it meant some of his staff having to go to the sites, he permitted that, he encouraged it. I remember going to both places and being confronted with the same students that I'd have in college. We weren't strangers; we'd got a bond between us and we got to know them well.

Away from the drawing office, Len had the opportunity to share one of his interests with a wider public.

Long-case clocks were a hobby when I was working, and we ran a clock course at the college. It was an evening course and I was the instructor. It was put in the prospectus, 'People interested in repairing their clocks', only grandfather clocks, nothing else. I had taught myself over the last 30 or 40 years. Twenty students came for the first one. They were coming in with long-case clocks over their shoulders. They brought the movements in. They all had problems, and I knew where to get the spares and how to fit them together. Roy Pocock joined the group and I did enjoy that clock course.

Miss Garlick had a clock and she rang me and said, 'Look, I've got a grandfather clock here. Will you come and see it?'
I said, 'Yes, I certainly will. What's wrong with it?'
'Oh', she said, 'It won't strike.'

So I said, 'Well, I'll come and have a look at it.'
I went and looked at the clock and I said, 'Well, it wants repairing, so-and-so and so-and-so.'
I took the movement away, repaired it and brought it back again. She had it in the hall at the bottom of the stairs. I said, 'Why did it bother you when it wouldn't strike?'
She said, 'I couldn't sleep. I couldn't sleep unless it struck.'
'What's with the silence?'
She said, 'I couldn't do with the silence. I want it to strike through the night. I can't go to sleep unless I hear the strike.'

Miss Garlick was a remarkable lady. At meetings, you can imagine, she was very outspoken. She was a very clever lady and she's written one or two books. I was very respectful of her learning.

Len's final years in the drawing office were a time of major curriculum change and his career came to a close tinged with sadness and not a little disillusionment. 'I was within three or four years of retiring when this change came in.' Many of the engineering courses, the National Certificates and the City & Guilds, were replaced by TEC Certificate courses run by the Technician Education Council. This was a significant change. The ONC and City & Guilds, with their long established national reputations, had been at the heart of Newbury's vocational education since 1948. Len himself, when a young man, had studied for the National Certificate in night school, and many of his FE colleagues had travelled along the same road.[6]
The new courses, the first of which started in 1977, were quite different from the ones they replaced. The TEC syllabus was broken down into units, 'with credit obtained for units completed at any time'. Assessment was at intervals through the year, with the subjects 'examined by phased tests during the study of the

---

[6] Lecturers in the 1950s with ONC/HNCs included Lionel Bernard, W Freebury, Eric Gardner, Len Hoyland, R C J Ireson, Bill Parrott, C Taylor and John Trodden. PT assistants with ONC/HNCs included J S Bill, W J Garland, H P Lidiard and F J Stevenson.

unit'. Homework and practical coursework counted towards the overall assessment.[7] No longer, then, was the student's future determined by the performance in an end-of-year examination.

In the mid-'70s, National Certificates, that is ONC and HNC, and City & Guilds Technicians' Certificates, were phased out and replaced by the TEC and Higher TEC Certificates. That was a big milestone. ONCs and HNCs had such a long history, dating way back to before the war. They served a very, very useful service. They were regarded as being the escape route from the workshop into the drawing office certainly, and beyond the drawing office maybe. If you were mentally adapted to teaching, you could go up that route. They did superb work in helping people who wanted to educate themselves. Their target was the HNC. That was the highest they could go, in their own time, in the evenings. This is what I set myself out to get. I was very sorry about the phasing out.

The new TEC certificate was unit-based. There was an exam after so many weeks on each unit, based on what had been done the previous three or four weeks. It was only a short hour's test. The student had to pass. If they didn't pass, they didn't fail either. You would set another test and they would sit it the next week. This could go on for ever – there was no limit to the attempts they could take – they all had to get through. They passed all the units, some of them after two or three attempts. Then, to reach an overall assessment, homework and coursework were taken into account.

No final exam – they don't even have that now in some universities. With no final exam, everyone is a winner. This was the first instance of dumbing down on record, a process which has since affected all branches of education at all levels. It certainly takes place in schools. In the comprehensive schools they dumb down. It takes place even

---

[7] Newbury College Prospectus 1977-78, p.31.

in universities. One word springs to mind – catastrophic! When it comes to choosing the syllabus for the A-levels, the mathematics syllabus is dumbed down because the students find the calculus part of it very difficult. 'Do we need the calculus? Of course we don't. Take it out.' That's dumbing down. Anything that you find really difficult, do we really need it? I don't think so – so we don't have it.

A-level nowadays is not what it was because this dumbing down has proceeded over the last few years. If you compare the recent A-level papers with those of 30 or 40 years ago, they are totally different. The rigour – this is the thing we're talking about – is absent.

Some people are of the opinion that change is always good, but it's not true. It's not that I'm a stick-in-the-mud or anything like that. I'm not one to say that there should never be any change – of course there should be – but things can change for the worse. I couldn't consider the TEC scheme to be an improvement. I couldn't see the justice in arranging for no one to fail. If everybody passes, it doesn't mean anything does it? It seemed to me that they were more concerned about the people who were slightly dim. They wanted to make sure that they were elevated. The bright ones have been sold down the river because the dim ones were given the same certificates. That can't be right. Do we want everyone to pass? It would be a wonderful world if everyone was enthusiastic and wanted to learn, and wanted the rigour, and wanted the challenge, and were prepared to devote energy to it. But we're not all like that, are we? Are we all equal? Politics comes in here somewhere, peeping its head over the top. 'We're all equal. We're all the same.' Wouldn't it be a dull world if we were? We never will be anyway, no matter how much you wish it. And yet despite the changes which seem to have taken root, that doesn't mean to say that in ten years time they will still be holding sway. Someone will stand up one day and say, 'Hold on, where are we going?' It's the pendulum – it swings and it comes back again.

'Oh yes, the badminton was good'

A young **Betty Ward** arrived in Ormonde House in the early
'50s and stayed for the rest of her working life. She was made
assistant registrar in the mid-'70s. More and more people were
taking examinations and this took up a lot of her time. If Betty
had any time left over, she was organising the Staff Association
and enjoying her badminton.

> There was a big Staff Association in those days, mid-'60s
> onwards. I was treasurer for years, simply as I had access
> to the safe and the money and everything else. Thursday
> night was staff sports night in the hall. We used to play
> badminton. We used to go down to the Congregational
> Hall and play somebody from somewhere else. There was
> a table tennis team – they went out playing – and there
> used to be darts in the hall. Roy was keen on the Staff
> Association and we used to have dances out at his barn at
> Boxford. We also went up to London to the theatre.
>
> You had the ones who joined in and those who didn't;
> it's always the same with these things. But, oh yes, the
> badminton was good.

It was with some relief, perhaps, that Betty retired in 1986.
She was 60 years old and had been at the college for 34 years.

> I was pleased I got out. Computers came a year after I
> had left. They used to send me to Reading, to Shire Hall.
> I used to sit there and didn't know what the hell they
> were talking about. I hadn't a clue. My poor little brain
> wouldn't take in computers. It leaves me cold, and when
> they talk about getting into the internet, I don't even know
> what it is. The only thing modern I get into is a mobile
> 'phone. I have been nagged and nagged to get one. I do a
> lot of motorway driving on my own, and my friend said,
> 'It's utterly ridiculous. You must get yourself a mobile
> 'phone.' It's purely for an emergency.

The college's youthful laboratory assistant **David Jones** soon found himself involved in a variety of work. 'I was appointed first aid officer jointly with Ray Harraway in '64 and I've still got that.' When E-Block was built in 1966, 'Bill Holt got put into the ground floor and Jeff and I made all the display stands for him and all the electrical stuff was put in it.'[8] When it was decided to start an audio-visual aids department, 'I graduated to 14 OHPs, half a dozen slide projectors, two 16mm projectors and a Dansette record player.' Chief Technician Jeff Jeffery remained his boss and once Jeff had retired (1967), David was eventually promoted.

> Jeff announced his retirement and they didn't want to appoint internally. Although I was doing the work, they decided that they would appoint externally. They employed a lad who was an electrician, and he came in not knowing anything about the college at all. He carried on as he was, so I actually did the job for the next seven months. He then gave it up and went to South Africa, to Groote Schuur Hospital as an electrician at the time of Dr Christiaan Barnard's heart transplants, and the college appointed me.[9] I hadn't stopped doing the job. He wasn't really the sort of person they were looking for. They appointed me and I just took straight over as chief technician. When we went self-financing in 1993 we were up to about 25 technicians.

---

[8] The third building instalment was in two phases, B-Block and E-Block, and cost around £150,000, plus £62,000 for furniture and equipment. Ormonde Cottages and the legendary chicken hut were demolished to make way for B-Block, built by Wooldridge of Hungerford. 1.2 acres of land was bought from neighbour Robert Kidd of Marlborough House for £1,250. Charles Sully moved away from Oxford Road, Harry Whiting moved to a new bungalow on site. The three storeys of E-Block were built in the north-east corner of the grounds next to the caretaker's bungalow. A J Dunning of Andover built E-Block and the bungalow. See Ormonde House Deeds, Conveyance 20 October 1960; FESC 10 May 1963, 20 November 1964; Education Development and Works Subcommittee 27 September 1963, 22 May 1964, 2 October 1964.

[9] Christiaan Barnard (1922-2001), South African cardiac surgeon who performed the world's first successful heart transplant operation in 1967.

The college has missed a lot of opportunities over the years. We're supposed to be in 'Silicon Valley' from the end of the '70s, but only recently have we dabbled in any practical electronics. Never have we run practical electronics, when you think of all the electronics firms round here. Similarly Business Studies was very slow to become updated with computer stuff. That's why you've got all these business schools in the area. Again, we were reckoned to be about third in the country in Outdoor Education, but the lecturer was stopped from expanding it. You've got missed opportunities all the way down the line.

'They gave a lot – they gave helluvalot'

In the spring of 1973, the local newspaper informed its readers that one of the town's 'Labour stalwarts' was leaving the area.[10] **Ron Spiller** had retired from Aldermaston and was moving to Devon. For some time he had been going to night school where 'he did two or three years art classes'. **Barry Spiller** also came to the college in the '60s.

> I went in 1961, for a year, doing an engineering course. Then I went and worked at a garage for a time and then I took an electrical apprenticeship course, City & Guilds. When I was there, South Berks College was pulling people from as far away as Wallingford. It had an enormous catchment area.

Ron and Aileen Spiller did not regard their move to the South West of England as retirement; rather, they were 'starting anew under different circumstances'. They were looking forward to getting involved in the community, and this is exactly what happened.

> When they moved to Devon, mum was quickly approached to become a magistrate on the Axminster bench. They had very few Socialists on the bench and she was to make the balance a bit more equal. She was also on the Exeter and

---

[10] *NWN* 12 April 1973.

Devon Health Authority, and she joined the University of the Third Age. My father was very much a political animal and he was involved in quite a few things down there even though he was retired. He was chairman of the local Inshore Fishermen's Association and he twice stood as candidate for the East Devon ward. He was heavily involved all the way through, right up to his death. They gave a lot – they gave helluvalot.

'We've never been out of work – you could pack up a job and go somewhere else all our lifetime really'

Some of the student voices heard in this volume spent all their working lives with the same employer, but the majority moved on to new situations. Finding work locally was not difficult and almost all of them stayed in the Newbury area.

Many of the young men at the college in its early years were liable for National Service. An alternative was to enlist in the regular army, and carpenter **Roy Crocker** signed up in February 1952. King George VI had just died; the young Queen Elizabeth was now head of the nation's armed forces. 'Three days earlier, and we could have said we were a King's soldier.' Roy had to report to a camp in Goodge Street in London.

> Originally it was a station and part of the underground, but that particular section had been closed down and the army used it as a transit camp. Sweets were still on the ration, but when we went up to London, they were selling sweets and you didn't need a ration book for them. You could buy whatever you wanted. We thought this was wonderful.

After three years serving Queen and country, Roy returned to builders Eggleton & Tallin, stayed there for a couple of years, and then went to work for F J Reynolds in Thatcham. One of his first jobs was in Croft Road in Newbury where lecturers Bill Parrott and Mervyn Cowie were building their own houses. 'They were putting the footings in and I put the roof on for one pair of houses.' Dick Edwards remembers the building causing 'a bit of bother' amongst the neighbours.

People were having houses built on the opposite side of the road, and on the same side, and they were coming and looking at their's, and looking at Bill's and Mervyn's, and saying to the builder, 'Why isn't ours being done like that?' Their's were built; there was no cutting corners. One instance was their staircase. The stair had a joint mortise and tenon properly done – down the road they were just two pieces nailed together. 'Why have they got a joint like that, and why isn't ours done like that?'

Plumber **George Milsom** was also working for F J Reynolds. He was called up, joined the Oxfordshire and Buckinghamshire Light Infantry and went with Roy to the camp in London. 'They used to kick us out in the morning at six o'clock. They said we don't want to see you till midnight.' A few weeks later, and George was on a plane to Egypt and flying into a tense political situation.

> We took off from Blackbushe airport. We were stationed at Suez, right at the top, and guarded the different filtration plants. It was when they had trouble and strife. Neguib ousted Farouk, and Neguib was the front man for Nasser. Had Nasser ousted Farouk, we would have gone in. We were all on the backs of Centurion tanks, all the tents rolled up. We were ready for the off. Then it was suddenly, 'Stand down!' Neguib was thought of as a dove not a hawk. Things settled down, but if you went out, you had to go in fours, with one of you carrying a Sten gun, because they were stabbing you in the back.

It was with some relief that George came home to the peace and quiet of Thatcham. A few years later he was training apprentices and he decided to go back to night school. This time round the college was 'all pukka'.

> The apprentice said to me, ''Course you've never done any lead burning, have you?' We never did lead burning when I was an apprentice, so I thought, I'd better get my finger out and go back up to Ormonde House. So I went and did

a course in welding and lead burning.[11] That was 1958 and Mervyn Cowie took us. They had everything – they got it more organised. You could get there at seven and there's all the welding equipment. Yet some things, perhaps, had not changed. Mervyn Cowie was the one. If you got there one night, and didn't feel like it, and got him talking, that was it. He'd say, 'Well, time to pack up lads,' and we hadn't done sod all! He was on the ships. He could spin a yarn, all where he'd been and what he'd done. If he had done all what he told us, he would have been 160! But I'm not saying we didn't learn anything.

A few more years passed and George changed his job. There were lots of employment opportunities and many of the erstwhile apprentices took advantage of this. 'A helluva lot left the building over the years and got into more lucrative jobs. I've always said we came into work at the right time. We've never been out of work – you could pack up a job and go somewhere else all our lifetime really.' George left the building, went to work on oil-fired boilers for Foster in Hambridge Road, and stayed there until he retired. The company was later taken over by Hartwell (Oxford), 'and now BP owns the lot'.

During his time in National Service, **Graham Tillen** followed the football whenever he could.

> I was in the Royal Artillery, the heavy ac-ac. I didn't go out the country. I went to bloody Oswestry for four months, which was a dump, and then I went to Newcastle-on-Tyne. There I watched a lot of football, and I played a bit as well. You've got St James' Park there, when Milburn, Mitchell and all them played. Milburn had an electric turn of speed. We used to watch them one week and Sunderland, in the old stadium at Roker Park, the next. If we were desperate, and they were both away, we did watch Gateshead a couple of times – they were in the old Third Division North. You used to go up there with the old Geordies with the cloth caps. There was no aggro or anything like that. You paid

---

[11] The evening course Lead Burning and Welding for Plumbers started in 1957.

one shilling and three pence (6p.). Then I had to go to Essex, an ex-POW camp near Gray's, a primitive place compared to Newcastle. And I had three months down in Cornwall as well – that was in a TA place at Holyrood Bay near Newquay.

After the artillery, Graham went back to Camp Hopson, but not long afterwards he decided to leave the 'old firm' and go self-employed.

In 1954 I went up to Valley Road, the main Valley Road beyond the AWE houses. That's where we were building when I came out of the army. Blake of Padworth got the second phase of that estate, up Barn Crescent at the top of the hill. I was self-employed – it had just started to come in. The brickwork was let out. It was 'on the lump' as the saying is. So I worked up there, on the council houses, subcontracted to Blake. John Rankin School went up round about that time – you get to that through those atomic houses as I call them.

For many years Graham worked as a self-employed bricklayer, living in Thatcham and filling his spare time with cricket and football. The work became less demanding as he got older.

Building used to be all physical. They've modernised it as much as they can. They've got the power saw and the power tools, which is good, and even the bloody screwdrivers now are battery operated. They've got their hard hats and the hard toecaps and all the guys now have got mobile 'phones.

In the years after the war, once you got a job you got your wages and that and you stuck at it. But now it's all harum-scarum, racing about like bloody clockwork soldiers. Man has become more like a bloody robot.

I've served on a lot of committees in my time. I've been a member of the town cricket club for 40 years, secretary for 23. I used to keep wicket for them. I'm known on the circuit, the old bugger in the red hat. I also kept goal for Thatcham.

Graham 'retired' in the summer of 1998, but a few months later, he was still laying bricks.

> Somebody said to me at work, 'Look you old bugger, you should be at home. You're doing someone out of a job.'
> I said, 'Look, you can't do my bloody job. That's why I'm here.' That was the end of that conversation.

'I went down to Harwell – you could work all the hours you wanted down there'

Like Graham, painter and decorator **Alan Lawrence** also trained at Camp Hopson, but he chose not to go back there after National Service. He returned to the 'old firm' eventually, but when Camp Hopson closed down its building department in the '60s, he too became self-employed.

> I just finished my apprenticeship and I was a qualified decorator then. I had two or three weeks on top money before I went into the services, which was about ten pounds a week. Then I was back down to three pounds a week. You got your food and keep of course in the services. I joined the air force but I didn't go abroad. They didn't seem to send the two-year people abroad. I did my training at Wilmslow and then at Sutton Coldfield in Birmingham.
>
> When I came out I wanted to get married. The money was nothing really. It was good money if you were taking home £10 a week as a full tradesman. So I went down to Harwell and worked for W A Chivers, from Devizes. Chivers built Harwell – a lot of people say that's what made the firm. You could work all the hours you wanted down there – Saturdays, Sundays – and the money was good. It wasn't really decorating, what I was used to. I was just industrial painting. I stuck that for two and a half years, and then I

said, this is no good. It was one winter time. It was cold.
I was in one of those reactors right under the hills at the
bottom. Damn this! I don't have to do this any more.

Mr Bates was still the building manager at Camp's. He
was there when I was apprenticed. I said, 'Any chance of
coming back?'
He said, 'Come back Monday, whenever you like.'
So I went back to Camp's and I was there until they closed
down the building side of it. Prices got too expensive; they
were getting short of work and cutting down on the staff.
They called me in and said, 'We're a bit short of decorating.
I suppose you wouldn't mind helping out on removals for
a day or two, would you?'
I said, 'I don't mind as long as I get the same money.'
Removal people weren't paid all that well. The hourly rate
was poor although they used to put the hours in.
'Well,' he said, 'they're pretty busy and they're just ticking
over, but you might give them a hand.' Being the youngest
one there, I suppose they thought I was the fittest. That
was a change – I used to enjoy it. I did it for three months
one winter. It's hard work at times – it's a young man's
job. They tried cutting the staff down, whittling it down,
whittling it down. When they finished, there were three
painters left. The foreman painter had been there 40-odd
years. They called us into the shop one day and said they
couldn't go on any longer. They'd tried all things; they'd
decided to close it down. We were retired. They paid us a
bit of redundancy and we called it a day.

Alan went to work for a decorator in Speen; but a couple of
years later he decided to go out and work for himself.

I used to do a lot of private work in the evenings and
weekends. I thought I might as well start doing it for
myself. I've been working for myself since 1967. I've
never been out of work. I've never advertised; it's all
recommendation by word of mouth, which is the best way
to go on. With our trade, round Christmas is the quiet time

'cos people don't want you about. There's been times when I've thought, what am I going to do for the next fortnight? But something always comes up. It might be a day here, a couple of days there, a little job you promised to do. I've very seldom had any time at home.

Some of Alan's work came by way of Roy Crocker. 'If he had any decorating to do, I used to go and do it for him. And if I had anybody that wanted a bit of carpentry done, I used to get Roy to go and do it for me.' When not working, Alan enjoyed playing golf in Devon and Cornwall with his friend George Milsom.

Years later and Alan returned to Ormonde House, but this time to meet his daughter. 'She worked for Plenty and was going in for accountancy. She went to the college for a couple of evening courses. I used to go in there and pick her up. It was amazing. What a size it is now compared to what it used to be.'

'Building apprentices came to college and then they all disappeared, and the strange thing is, the housing boom didn't make any difference'

George Abraham managed to avoid the military call-up. After college he continued working with his father and then with his eldest son. 'I've passed the fancy stuff on to my son and we are still using it.' Building fashions have come and gone, but the Abrahams have continued to build new houses and helped transform a lot of old ones.

The army was there at the end of your apprenticeship to cheer you up. I should have gone in. I was marvellous, just the man they wanted. I went and had a medical, but I had had bad experiences before. I couldn't eat in public and silly things like that. So after they passed me, I went and saw my doctor and said, 'I've got on well, but how do I go on if I can't eat with anybody?'
He said, 'It's a bit of a waste of time training you.'
And so they gave me another medical and at the end of that they more or less said, 'When we have got shot of everybody else, we'll probably call you in.' I wasn't called.

The family thing's been going now since 1936. We had six or eight of us altogether. Two or three carpenters and bricklayers came into college after me. When I'd finished, they took it up. We taught the people that worked for us. My eldest son worked for his grandfather and we always work together now. He's self-taught with us. We've always worked as a family. My cousins came to work for us. We were showing them our methods and how we built, which was traditional. My cousin at the time was teaching brickwork in Swindon College. We were showing him and he was showing the students in the evenings.

We couldn't see any point in doing brickwork the way we were being taught at college because it was disappearing. When we look back now, I suppose we wasted our time. In the '60s and '70s we built cavity walls, then suddenly people started filling them up with foam and insulation, which is a bit defeatist.

The stuff of the '60s and '70s, it's not to be proud of, is it? We ought to knock most of it down. I'm ashamed of it when I think I was part of that. The stuff before was good and it's getting better again now, but some of it really shouldn't have been left.

Apprentices came to college and then they all disappeared, and the strange thing is, the housing boom didn't make any difference.[12] You would assume you wanted to train a lot of people, but everyone picked up a trowel and went building. It is sad that it should disappear in a boom time.

---

[12] In the later 1960s, builders ceased to recruit many apprentices and craftsmen increasingly became self-employed. All over the Southern Region building courses in FE were undersubscribed and the SRCFE had no choice but to restrict the number of colleges providing the curriculum. In 1970 the Building Department at South Berks College was closed down. Four lecturers were affected. Arthur Owen, with a protected salary, stayed on; the others were offered jobs at Reading College where the courses were to continue. The brick workshop at Newbury was used for heavy vehicles. FESC 13 November 1970

I don't think you can hand on knowledge that way – it's only how fast you can do it. Eventually we shall run short of building technicians – you mustn't call them bricklayers now. If we wanted a bricklayer, we would know one already. You'd just ring up. It's very much word of mouth now. We only do this area, so it's not a problem, but if you had a job at Slough or somewhere like that, you would have to get somebody from Slough. The development in the '70s and '80s was so big, there was never enough, so anybody who could lay a brick laid a brick. It didn't really take that long – it's only when you get to the more decorative stuff.

I notice how many houses Hoskings & Pond built in the Newbury area in the '30s. They packed up about ten years ago – Smallbone bought them out. They were down by West Mills. There must have been a tremendous boom in houses in the '30s, masses and masses of the same style, good quality houses with bay windows. It seemed to be the thing to be doing. Now we have forgotten all about things like that. We just build ones with square corners on. It may be quicker, but there's not much pleasure in it, not for the people doing it, which is a shame. The people that we work for want traditional buildings. We convert houses to look older than what they are. People don't want it to look like it did when they bought it. We find there's a good market for that. People are buying the site and converting the house into what they want. We always get the customer involved. Most of my customers are still feet and inches, not metric. We don't work with an architect, so we have to educate them into the game of building, and they've got to try and convey to us what they want even though they can't picture it too well. We are supposed to end up doing what they want. In some ways, if there was a course they could go to, it would be nice. The sort of building we do, we'll get another generation out of this. People are wanting Victorian and Edwardian houses again.

484

The bricklaying side is only a small part of building. That was a trade, and you had to have a trade, but nowadays you've got to be able to do any part of building to be a builder. For the brickwork in a house, you're only there for two or three weeks. You've got to have a lot in a year. Our way, we probably stop for six months at a time on the conversions. There's only two or three of us at the moment and it suits us fine. Hopefully we shall carry on.

Building's going to go on. It's an interesting job. It's not like some jobs where you never see the end product. Building is unique because you actually see and achieve at the end of a day's work. At the end of the year, you can say, 'Well, that looks good.' There's not many jobs that allow you to do that.

'We are not training anybody now'

Bricklayer **Peter Mason** finished at Ormonde House in the mid-'60s and went on to Reading for the ONC. 'Quite a few of us after qualifying at Newbury went on to Reading.' He already had the Technological Certificate so he was exempted from part of the ONC. Peter was also taken on as an examiner.

All the lads who got a reasonable pass were invited to join the Guild of Bricklayers. I was invited to join, and from the Guild they drew the examiners for the City and Guilds wet trades. I did a two-year stint, '65 to '67. The first college I had to go to was Oxford College of Technology. I had to do the Ordinary and Advanced there, two separate weekends. The next time I had to go to High Wycombe. Then all the exams changed and it was continuous assessment.

Many of Peter's friends from Ormonde House stayed on the tools while others went on to run their own companies. One became a gamekeeper, another emigrated to Australia, and Peter became a building inspector with Newbury Council. Still in his early 20s, he was surprised to get the job. It was 1965.

I was building at Sir William Cook's property at Hampstead Norreys. There was a shortage of work and all the gangs were put together to get this job done for a racehorse trainer. The foreman chippy says, 'Look in the *Newbury Weekly News*. There's a good job for you. The Borough Council want a clerk of works.'

I said, 'I might go for that.'

He said, 'Don't be so bloody silly. I was only joking.'

I thought about it, and not being the wordsmith I am today, I went to the chappy next door. He was an engineering graduate.

I says, 'I have been toying with the idea.'

And he says, 'Have a go.'

So we sat down and cobbled a letter together and sent it off as a no-hoper. A couple or three weeks went by and nothing happened. Then one morning the letter came inviting me for interview.

I had a little scooter to get about on, which was a lot easier than the bike, so on the back of the scooter we put the case and the suit and all the rest of it. It was late morning the interviews, so I thought I would work first part of the day, go into Newbury for the interview, and then come back to work. We were interviewed and Charlie Hyde, an old craftsman, said, 'And I want you to stay and I want you to stay.' And they said, 'You've not got the job, but we're very impressed with what you've done and where you've been and how far you've got in the period of time. What we would like you to do, and I don't want you to give me your answer now, is to think about becoming assistant building inspector. So I want to see you next week, same time, to see whether you will accept.'

Now that was quite dramatic that was. I'd just started to buy a house, but the money was £25 a year less than what I was getting on site, so it had to be thought about.

They're all piss-takers in the building industry. When I got back from the interview, they could hear the scooter grinding up the hill to Hampstead Norreys. They all scurried about. It was just like a wedding, with an arch of scaffold tubes. We had to drive through this archway – we couldn't go anywhere else – with the foreman, the general, standing there.

And he said, 'Did you get it?'

'No.'

Of course they all fell about laughing.

'But,' I said, 'they offered me another job.'

'I know – dustman, road sweeper,' all the usual bits were coming out.

'No,' I said, 'assistant building inspector.'

A few weeks after Peter had started his new job, he had to inspect some houses on Fifth Road. Coincidentally, the 'general' from Hampstead Norreys was in charge of the site. 'One of my first jobs was to go and have a look at his foundations, which didn't get approved. So that was something else – but we were the best of mates and I still see him now.'

For more than 30 years, Peter Mason worked for the local authority in Newbury, during which it 'changed three times', from Borough Council to District Council (1974) to West Berkshire Council (1998). He continued to be involved in education and training, as an assessor on the Technical Education Board for RICS. 'I do a lot with them running all sorts of bits and pieces.' He retired in 1998, Acting Principal Building Control Officer for West Berkshire 'looking after all aspects of building legislation and works within the area'.

> Looking back, it was a worthwhile apprenticeship, because even now I can still draw on my experiences from then, especially if you are altering the old structures and things like that. Anybody entering my profession now has come through A-levels, ONC, the full-time OND courses, and then they've gone into Institute examinations and qualified that way. They haven't got a great deal of practical experience. This is one of the problems.

'The plutonium building had just gone active'

When **Alan Gibbs** started night school, he was working as an electrician for the House of Toomer. By early 1952 he was at AWE Aldermaston and a few months later, he finished his ONC. He had worked hard for four years and it had paid off. 'It was rather embarrassing because my boss at Aldermaston was in the same class. He failed, and I got a distinction.' In the autumn, Alan started the HNC at Reading. This time he was given day release but unfortunately, after a year, he had to drop out. 'My eye problems got worse. It was just too much studying and I had to pack it in, but it didn't affect the job.'

The job was making weapons. 'The plutonium building had just gone active and we were getting the plutonium in and producing the nuclear part of the weapon. You were working alongside chemists and metallurgists, in a team, wearing pressure suits and everything, really involved. It was very interesting work, something new every day.' Alan did this for five years, before moving on to 'high voltage work, particle accelerators'. He left Aldermaston for Harwell, working as a high voltage technician in the Rutherford Laboratory, a job which took him to CERN in Switzerland.[13] 'It's the central European nuclear physics place near Geneva. The accelerator goes under the mountains in a massive great tunnel. The particles go round this great circuit, 80 kilometres in diameter. They fire them in opposite directions at each other, so you get fantastic results.' Alan stayed at Rutherford until he was 65. He had worked for more than 50 years.

As a young man, Alan had been interested in college. 'It's something that everybody should take up.' Not surprisingly, once retired, he made his way to night school. When the windows of his house needed replacing, he was keen to do the work himself. He enrolled for carpentry and around the same time his wife started dressmaking and cookery classes. In 1998 Alan and Kay Gibbs celebrated their golden wedding anniversary with their three daughters, two grandchildren and six great-grandchildren.

SEB employee **Graham Curtis** had also been at night school

---

[13] European Organisation for Nuclear Research.

in 1948. He studied engineering for a year but then left. Twelve months later he came back, but this time for bookkeeping. His career had changed. Graham was now an office worker.

> Rates of pay for the clerical grades were very diluted compared to the skills. They are still marginally different today, but in those days there was a big gap. Mr Creed took me for bookkeeping; he worked for the SEB. I got the post in the finance department at Harwell 'cos I'd done bookkeeping and the person that was with me hadn't. We were next door to the Apprentice School. I did the time cards and I used to pay the apprentices. Business is the best thing that ever happened to me.

> We had a young lad at Harwell who was a mechanic's mate. He hadn't served his time. He did S1, S2, and he got as far as S3 but he was sick for the exams and he had to do it again – he had to do another year. To him it meant more than most because there was a rule, that if a mechanic got an ONC, he became a skilled man automatically, which meant a terrific amount, more money and promotions. He's the only mechanic's mate I've ever known that's made it.

Graham continued at Harwell, picking up more clerical qualifications. At work he was regraded and at college he completed an ONC in Commerce, 'background as far as the organisation was concerned', and an RSA in Secretarial Duties, 'office procedure really'. Fifteen years went by and then, in 1966, he left and set off along a very different path.

> I went to college as a mature student, teacher training for three years. This was at the time when everybody went in, when Crosland expanded during the mid-'60s.[14] All these married women came in, and there were a few mature men. We were a new college. It was interesting. It had been a ladies' training college, all girls. It had had one pregnancy

---

[14] Tony Crosland (1918-77), Labour politician, Secretary of State for Education and Science 1965-67 in Harold Wilson's Labour Government.

in 13 years, not that I approve, but to get only one in 13
years, imagine what the discipline was like!

The Principal picked these 90 students. They were all men.
We had a very wide range: a gravedigger, a professional
cyclist, librarians, trainee accountants. We were dropouts;
nobody else wanted us. We had the greatest number of
rejection slips of any lot of students anywhere in Britain
– no one had less than six rejections. They weren't over-
academic and they were possibly a bit bolshie. I was the
oldest, 44, and looking back, I must have been mad.

We turned up at nine o'clock in the hall, the 90 of us, and
everybody was in a suit. The Principal came in.
'Good morning, gentlemen.'
He got his tape recorder up there and played the song *Little
Boxes*. That was his thing – but education isn't little boxes.
'What about subjects?'
'I like geography.'
'Well', he said, 'we'll have that. What's your hobby?'
'Gardening.'
'Oh, you can do biology.'
My 'biology' was taking a Brussel sprout to pieces the first
year at the Grammar School. So I failed, and I had to do
it twice.

Going to teacher-training college was the next best thing
I ever did. I taught for 11 years. The ladies cost less – I
wasn't the only married man that had this trouble. Teachers
got increments for war service plus industrial service. The
women didn't get increments for bringing up children,
which was wrong. So you could be a lavatory cleaner
and get an increment, and you could have triplets and not
get one. I came out of teaching with 13 increments on a
16-point scale. Newbury didn't want to employ me and
I finished up in Brent. Can you imagine a primary school
of eight-year-olds, where if you go 20 minutes without
one hitting another, you've had an easy day? Where the
head's idea of discipline is to send them to the vicar? Just

imagine what the atmosphere in that school was like. In the playground, it was no use just blowing the whistle. The whole staff had to go out and fetch them in.

I went up to John Rankin on supply. It was a lovely school. They were so well disciplined. Every time I did supply, I always got dinner duty, playground duty. It was always me. This particular day the head came looking for me. He found me out in the playground. He said, 'You're not in London now.' In London, the duty teacher had to be out in the playground before the first child got out.

Graham eventually left teaching because 'there wasn't enough supply work'. Yet he had few regrets. 'I'm glad I'm not teaching now; they're nothing but record keepers.' In the early '80s, he started what turned out to be his last job, at AWE Aldermaston. 'Because I was a teacher, they put me in the training school. The first thing I had to do was write the previous year's reports and I'd never even seen the people.'

Graham had started going to evening classes originally to help him get on at work; later on, he went for fun. He did woodwork with Dick Edwards and also cookery, which was very good. 'The only snag was the time scale. She had to demonstrate, you had to cook it and wash up all in two hours, which is pretty grim.' He also went to the WEA. 'I did some very interesting classes on buildings and we had one gentleman that came and talked about windmills. He could talk for hours on windmills.'

'Most of the electricians in the Newbury area did their training with the SEB'

Pete Hutchins joined the electricity industry when he left school, and stayed in it until he retired. 'I worked for three different companies but the same organisation. At 14 I went to the Wessex Electricity Company. Then it was nationalised and became the Southern Electricity Board, and two years before I took early retirement, it was privatised again, as Southern Electricity PLC.' After Ormonde House, the SEB apprentice was called up. A keen member of the Air Training Corps, Pete had already had a taste of adventure. The ATC started in Newbury in 1941 to provide training for those young boys who wanted to join the RAF.

When I was with the ATC I got a flight to Kenya with the RAF in 1950. I had to report to an address in London and we were to go by RAF coach to Lyneham in Wiltshire. Today you could go from London to Wiltshire in a couple of hours but we had an overnight stop in Reading in a hotel and then went to Lyneham. The next morning we boarded an aircraft and I was made assistant quartermaster for the two-week trip. We went to Malta the first day. It was seven hours fifteen minutes. The next day we went from Malta to Egypt, on the Canal Zone. Then an overnight stop, and the next day we went to Khartoum in the Sudan. Another overnight stop, and eventually the next day to Kenya, an RAF base near Nairobi. We had a long weekend there – the stay was extended by one day. We boarded the aircraft. They started up the four engines, inner port, inner starboard, outer port. The last engine they started, the propeller part went over the aircraft and damaged the fuselage. So we had to get off and we had an extra day's wait there. Then back the reverse to what we went out. I liked it there. Malta was beautiful.

I finished at the college about April 1953 and I joined up in June. It was only a matter of a few weeks. I had had very good results from my City & Guilds, but it was well known that you seldom got where you wanted to in National Service. If you wanted to go in the RAF you usually ended up in the army and things like that. I joined the RAF, and I think it was because of my association with the Air Training Corps.

When I was selected for trade training, I got the electrical course as well. I enlisted up near Warrington – that's where I had to report to. Then I came down to Cannock Chase and did my eight weeks square-bashing. For trade training, I was sent to Melksham. I did a 20-week training there, which was virtually the same as what I had done at college.

I didn't have a mark under 95 per cent. And we all lined up this morning with postings. I particularly wanted to go to Germany, or abroad. In them days we were worldwide, and when they read out the names, there was people going to Singapore, Germany ... and Melksham. I was transferred over to permanent staff and helped on the training side. I did all my National Service at Melksham.

I went in on 10th June 1953 and came out on 9th June 1955 and went back to the SEB. I was qualified and after a period of three months refresher with other electricians, I went on my own and had an apprentice with me. And that's what I did 'til I retired in '92. From about '71 to when I finished, I was on the management side. My successor, who took over from me, says they haven't taken any apprentices since '93. To show how numbers have fallen, the total number of Southern Electric employees today is about 3,000. In our day, there was that many at Reading alone. The shop's gone; it's a furniture shop now. In recent years before it closed it was Powerhouse. We were there until 1968, and then we moved to Hambridge Road, new offices down there, but they retained the shop right up to privatisation.

Most of the electricians in the area that are either self-employed or working for firms did their training with Southern Electricity Board. Two or three people in the area that I know are self-employed and were trained at our company. It was recognised as an extremely good tip-top training. After their apprenticeship was finished, they went their own ways. A lot stayed, but there was always a good percentage that went. All my working life was with one company. You won't get it today. I've got three sons and they've all had more than one job. The days of one job for life are gone.

Plenty's pattern makers **Pete Tidbury** and **Ron Mead** were both called up. Pete did not go, 'owing to a hearing problem'; Ron joined the Royal Berkshire Infantry.

After doing the training at Reading, I finished up in Germany. We took an ex-Luftwaffe airfield base and it was a fabulous place. It was never detected during the war and it was never bombed or interfered with. There was no British fire of any sort. Each billet-block was double-glazed, parquet floor, two to a room. It was fabulous. We had showers and bathrooms. The cookhouse – the mess – was a distance away, as was each other building. Each company had their own building and between each building was a wood. On top of each building was big hooks. During the war they had camouflage nets hooked on the top of the buildings and on to the trees; so the buildings were under camouflage nets. The runways were grass on mesh and the hangars were in the hillside. All you could see was the control tower. It was a super place. It was in Goslar, in the Harz Mountains, skiing and all that stuff. I was there all the time, and I only did two guard duties in two years. I was company carpenter out there. I took woodwork and I had my own workshop. I was making these plywood boxes to go in the kit bags and kit pouches so that everybody looked smart. You used to put a board in the bed blanket pack, so everything was dead neat, square and sharp. They were giving me half-a-crown (12 pence) a set for these boxes.

When the two years were up, Ron returned to the pattern shop, and stayed, although there was one occasion when he almost left.

Elliott's advertised for a jig and tools manager. I went down to see them. I got the job, so I hands the notice in at Plenty. I'm due to leave on the Friday, and a chap who was in the pay office came up on the Thursday with my cards and my pay. We were up at King's Road. They used to bring it up so you didn't have to traipse all the way down to the main works.
'You going to Elliott's? Don't go. My wife works there. They've been taken over and they're closing.'
So I went and asked for my job back at Plenty, and I've been there ever since.

Ron Mead had gone to night school in the early '50s. Years later, Plenty's pattern makers went to Gloucestershire for their training. Later still, they went to Oxford.

> Going back 30 years, they used to send apprentices to Stroud. They lived down there for a bit and they came home weekends. They used to do the course down there because that was genuine pattern-making courses. Then Pressed Steel at Oxford took it on. They had a massive pattern-making shop because of the body formers and pressed dies and stuff, and so they used to take our pattern makers from Plenty and they used to go to Oxford to college. It was day release. Plenty were paying for the courses.

> Now you've got this NVQ business. What a load of rubbish! You get some bloke come round with virtually no experience, and he comes in and he assesses somebody. He comes in and assesses a pattern maker – and he don't even know what a pattern maker is. I mean, how can he assess?

Plenty were keen on organising social events for their workforce, parties at Christmas and special dinners for those with 25 years service.

> They had what they call the 'Golden Trough' – that was the management's dining room. You had the canteen, they had the 'Golden Trough', and if you were in the drawing office, at Christmas party time or anything, you were segregated. There was one place where we went – they even had one of these rope-on-pole things like you get down the middle of a church – and the drawing office was in there, and the workers were out here.

> For the 25-year service people, they started doing dinners once a year and they still do it to this day. They take you out to dinner – they are having it now at Newbury Racecourse. I went to the first one. There wasn't that many people then that had done 25 years; there were about a couple of dozen there. You were invited into the 'Golden

Trough' for a meal. It was darned good – roast potatoes, Brussels and a bit of steak. It was a cracking meal, and they would give you a bottle of spirits as a present.

I stayed at Plenty and I worked 49 years and 11 months. I wanted to do my 50 years, but the pattern shop closed down. The place was redundant – otherwise I would have got my gold watch. I mean, 50 years, you ought to have a bloody palace! People used to have a gold watch. It used to be worth £600, which was a lot of money going back a few years. They always used to buy Benson's, and they used to have them inscribed. People then could do 50 years. Now it's only the 49 as they start later from school at 16.

While working in the foundry, Ron also managed a newsagent shop in the town. 'Maths at college was useful because I had a shop. My wife ran it but I used to do the early mornings, half-past five, so I was a glutton for punishment. I used to do all the rounds, mark all the papers up, and get all the boys off. I had 16 boys, a fair few. I still own the shop but have nothing to do with it.'

Like Ron, Pete Tidbury almost managed to complete 50 years with the company. He missed it by a few months 'because my birthday's in June and I started in the September.' Once retired, Pete continued working, making wheelchairs at Greenham for non-mobile children. 'Whizz-kidz, that's the charity who we work for. They're for these invalid children who can't support their backs. We build the basic, but after that it's customised, with all the different controls. If they can't move anything else but just one foot, we put switches so they can get along in their wheelchairs. They go abroad, America and whatsit.'

Sheila Smith left Ormonde House, completed her ONC at Reading and went on to the HNC, the only woman in her group. She travelled to Reading by train with three young men, one from Plenty, the others from Aldermaston. 'We used to have to catch the half-past six from Newbury, get off at Reading and have a coffee. Then we used to have to go out to the aerodrome at Woodley – that's where the Engineering Department of the college was in those days. I did my last year at Reading in the new building, when they moved to King's Road.'[15]

By the time she had finished at Reading, Sheila had completed her apprenticeship at Plenty and left. She had been earning £6 a week in the drawing office. Lansing Bagnall at Basingstoke offered her £10 a week, an offer she could not refuse, especially as they were willing to let her continue with the HNC and help her with the bus fares to and from work. 'They were a very generous firm in all sorts of ways.' Two years later, and Sheila moved again. Some of her friends worked for Isotope Developments at Beenham, later known as Nuclear Enterprises. Housed in Beenham Grange between Newbury and Reading, the 200 employees (in 1961) designed and manufactured scientific and electronic instruments for 'medical, research and industrial applications of radio activity'.[16] The wages were attractive, £13 a week; so was the prospect of travelling by train. So Sheila went to Beenham and became a design engineer. She left to raise a family and then, in the early '70s, she returned to work – as a laboratory technician at Park House School. She had only been there a few months when an opportunity arose to teach technical drawing – and she did this for ten years. 'Everybody at Park House did technical drawing.' In the early '80s she retraced her steps to Ormonde House and taught drawing there. A few years went by and she moved again, this time to the Abbey School in Reading.

'We have got full-time students at college now who were excluded from school and have come back into education via what we do'

Engineer **Sid Dixon** left South Berks College in the summer of 1964. One of his first priorities was a holiday with one of his friends. 'We saved for the whole year and then blew it in two weeks.' His friend worked for Opperman Gears and while at college with Sid, he had somehow got to know an au pair from Sweden. So the two young men decided to go to Stockholm. 'We were completely ignorant of the country and the culture. Some of the old boys from the factory came and talked to me before I left

---

[15] Reading College of Technology opened on King's Road in 1955.

[16] *Commonwealth Technical Training Week Handbook*, p.18.

'cos Sweden had quite a reputation in those days.' They took a boat from Harwich, a train through Holland and Denmark, and a ferry to Malmo. They were planning to hitchhike to Stockholm, but they never arrived.

> We tried twice to get to Stockholm, but they'd stopped picking up people and giving lifts. We camped in a pine wood at a little place on the Baltic. We were there for a fortnight and came back. We never did get to Stockholm – I've still never been to Stockholm. The last night we slept on a park bench in Malmo, with all the characters that were trailing around out there. We had hassle, oh yes, we had hassle. They didn't take to me but they took to my friend, much to his annoyance. We got out of there very quickly, little country boys back home to the sticks.

After college Sid stayed with Plenty for another 18 months. 'I went to Germany with them for a spell in 1965.' When the company moved out of the town centre, he did six months in the new factory in Hambridge Road. Then, in the spring of 1966, he handed in his notice and went off, somewhat bravely, to start his own business in steel fabrication. He was 22 years old. 'As the workshop manager said when I went into the office and gave my notice in, you've got a lot to learn my boy. And he was quite right. I did have a lot to learn.' Sid took over a forge in the village of Shefford Woodlands and within a few years he was making gates and ornamental ironwork, all to his own designs and all the time using what he had been taught at college. 'Maths comes into fabrication, geometry for the different angles you need. Engineering drawing is used a lot in sheet metal work. You draw and cut out the different sections and then build the component.'

Some years later, and the urge to travel returned. 'I just packed up, locked the door and kept some of the plant.' It was 1973 and this time Sid got further than Malmo. 'I took off round the world.' On his return, he started up his business again, this time in a scrapyard in Fifth Road in Newbury.

> When I came back I picked up the reins, the old customers, and started again. I expanded and went into steel

stockholding as well as fabrication and sheet metal. That really took off as there was a lot of building going on. Steel girders 42 foot long used to come into the yard on a flatbed with the steel hanging over the back of the lorry and over the rads at the front. I had sleepers either side with an alleyway down between. The steel would go over on to the sleepers to keep it off the ground. It was all wrapped up. Father used to come in and paint them with lead oxide. Then I'd cut them, a whole range of steel. I would cut the girders as the builders wanted them. I used to have one driver who wore no socks, just shoes.
'Where do you want it, guv'nor?'
This guy used to line himself up with this alleyway, and then reverse and slam on the brakes. Forty-two foot of steel would hurtle like a javelin through the air off the back of the lorry. Then he would select first gear and drive forward and it would come crashing down.

Sid Dixon ran his stockholding business for more than 20 years. Then, in the 1990s came a change of direction which brought him back to Ormonde House and vocational education with an overt social purpose. Sid began the Newbury Motor Project providing opportunities for young people, including juvenile offenders, to get involved in working with motor cars. 'I see youngsters with learning problems, with dyslexia and what have you, and I am able to sympathise with them. But I also have the advantage of the other side of the fence when I can say, success is available to you. Just don't write them off. We have got full-time students at college now that were excluded from school and have come back into education via what we do.'

Mechanics Mick Terry, Ray Claridge and Ron Pontin were called up for National Service as soon as they had finished their apprenticeships. **Ray Claridge** did six weeks basic training at Blandford Forum in Dorset and was then sent to Ashford in Middlesex where he continued his vehicle work and completed the National Craftsman Certificate.

It must have been about the first year of the army. They let me off for the time to do it. I did it at Chiswick bus garage. What they gave us was a plain washer and a nut, and you had to file the inside of the plain washer so the nut fitted in exactly. If you didn't mark the nut and the washer, he wouldn't fit anywhere, 'cos the nut was not true size. They had different sizes. If you didn't mark the nut and the washer, you was filing and filing; so you had to make sure you'd got it right. One of the other jobs was valve-timing on a big bus engine that was on a stand; another was to do something like an MOT on an old Morris.

In 1955 Ray went back to Nias – 'the job was kept open' – got married and bought a house in Thatcham. 'When you took your first mortgage, your repayment per month was equivalent to your wages for a week. Your wife's earnings didn't come into it. My wages were about £11/-/- a week because my first mortgage was £11/13/4 (£11.67) per month.' Ray stayed at Nias for 25 years. When he left, it was to work as receptionist at Wheeler's Garage on the Broadway; but he was only there for a year.

A job came up at South Berks College. Charlie Mankin asked me if I was interested in doing lecturing up at the college on Links. It must have been about 1973.[17] Pocock and Jim Gearing were the ones who interviewed me. It was teaching on the Links courses, schoolchildren who came to the college for half a day. Then I was moved over to the motor vehicle section. The man in charge was Vince

---

[17] The Links courses started in the late 1960s, the beginning of that relationship between schools and the vocational specialists in FE colleges which is encouraged by the government today. Forty years ago school pupils, usually, but not exclusively, in their final year of compulsory education, came to South Berks College for a few hours a week to study a vocational subject. In the 1970s the trickle became a flood and by 1976 there were 600 boys and girls coming to the college each week. With the raising of the school-leaving age to 16 in 1975, the Links provided an alternative curriculum for those young people who found that they had to stay on at school for an extra year. The courses were popular with the schools, so much so that they paid for the staff as well as the extension at the front of A-Block in 1975. This extension, known as the ROSLA building, was built as a specialist room for girls' Links courses. It later became the committee room.

Pearmain – Pearmain's Garage in the Bracknell area. They were garage people.

When the college needed another lecturer, Ray thought of one of his friends from Wheeler's. 'I introduced Mick Palmer to the college. When they wanted somebody, I asked him if he was interested, and he came up.' Ray taught in the motor vehicle section until he retired in 1993.

'My life has been travelling in all directions'

National Service for **Mick Terry** was also in the army – in Honiton in Devon and Stirling in Scotland – and like Ray, he was pleased to be able to continue his work with vehicles.

> I went into the REME. You could take three courses if you wanted to – third, second, and first class engineer. I passed the third and second while I was in the army. I used to go round with the staff sergeant, a smashing chap, and we used to do vehicle inspection. Vehicles had to be inspected every six months. I passed my second class trade test and he was thrilled to bits because I'd been with him. It was a fortnight's test and they really put you through your paces. In the workshops I went to, they were very strict. It was chassis alignment and all this business. They had the complete workshop and they used to put faults into engines and you had to find out what was the fault. It was tough stuff, all the theory. Without the college tuition I don't think I would have done it; some of it must have gone in without me realising. At the end of it there was the driving test in a ten-ton lorry.

When Mick came out the army he decided not to go back to Nias; instead he chose a smaller garage in the town, 'a tinpot affair, not much prospects'. He was not there for very long before he decided to leave the motor industry altogether. He found a new job, as an engineer with Opperman Gears in Hambridge Road.

> I was just trying to find my feet. I was disillusioned with the car trade. There wasn't a lot of money in garage work.

We had some friends who were dead keen on buying their own house. I thought, this sounds like a good idea, because we had got married and were unable to buy. We rented a mobile home in Thatcham. I got to thinking, I'm spending all this money and I'm never going to own a stick of this. So I thought I ought to try and buy a house, and Opperman were offering more money, building gear boxes of all different shapes and sizes. It was piecework and you could earn a lot more money than in a garage. That was my driving force, really, and I never regretted it.

Life at work was strict in those days. Major Opperman would walk round every morning looking at all the benches. Then the works manager would walk round, and if you weren't working, or if you were doing something they didn't think you ought to be doing, you were soon questioned. 'What are you doing?' They wouldn't have you hanging about or mucking about. They were getting their money's worth out of people.

Then the chief draughtsman at Opperman Gears, Jim Pike, left and set up his own business. Before he left, he came in and said, 'Mick, would you come and work for me if I get my business going?'
I said, 'Yes, if things are right.'
He said, 'When things get going, I'll come and see you.'
The business was Tormatique. I kept in touch with him and one night he came in and said, 'Will you come and work for me?'
We started work in his garage, building gearboxes. Fifteen hours a day we were working to get this business going. Then it got too big and we moved out of his garage and went up to Reading, right by the hospital. Then we came back to Newbury, to two places. I became works manager. He took over three or four businesses. Tormatique grew and grew and then he sold it to Limitorque of America.

In the '70s Mick moved on again, to Beenham's Nuclear Enterprises where he spent 20 happy years. 'I've done nuclear radiation detector equipment and I was lucky enough to get a good name for my work up there.'

Mick Terry had moved a long way from motor engineering, and yet much of the groundwork for his later career was done at Ormonde House.

> I'm sure it was, I'm absolutely convinced. As with anything, you need a theory and a practical; it's the basis of anything. This is what is sad now. They're not doing the proper apprenticeships and training that they should be. It's all very well doing all theory, but you need some hands-on experience. In those days, they made you do it, and you didn't answer back and say, 'I'm not going to do it'. You did it. If only the young people were privileged to go back and live in our younger days. You didn't have televisions and all the rest of it, but you appreciated things more.

'I don't think cars were really me, and they were short of machinists, so I moved more into that side'

Ron Pontin spent two years in the air force, at Abingdon in Berkshire, Bridgnorth in Shropshire and Cardigan in Wales. He moved around a lot, but this did not prolong his decision to get married. 'We said we would get married when we were 21.' When he came out of the RAF, he went back to the garage in Lambourn and took his National Craftsman Certificate at Reading – where Didge Marchant was one of the examiners. Ron stayed at Lambourn, but his job changed as he moved away from vehicle repairs and became more involved in machine engineering.

> We did a lot of work for a company at Ogbourne St George. They spread lime on the farms and they also did crop-spraying and we used to make the equipment for the booms and everything. What happened was, the machinist at Lambourn had an ulcer. Before I went into the air force, the machinist had an awful lot of work to do. Besides doing tractors and stationary engines and cars, they also did panel beating. There were also haycockers and we used to make those. They used to go along when the grass was

laying, pick it up, bring the basket, trip it, and put it in a big heap. That was spring and summer months. We used to send a lot off to Ireland, being damp over there.

They said, if there's anybody interested, you could go on machines and do machinery. I don't think cars were really me, and they were short of machinists. So I said I wouldn't mind having a go, and I moved more into that side. Building haycockers meant a lot of machining, especially cast iron. You used to go to work all spruced up in the morning and when you came back home, your shirt was black. I learnt welding and I spent more time on that side than I did on motor vehicle. I did machining and welding. It's more constructive, it's more interesting. By that time I'd got my National Craftsman, and I was also married and we were expecting our first child. It was November 1958. June left work in January '59. Frank Thatcher was my boss. I got called into his office. You know how it goes through your mind, 'What have I done? What have I done?'
He said, 'I've been talking to Wally Stagg, and we've decided to give you the foreman's job. We don't want any drastic changes.'
And that's how I got the foreman's job. Though the money was good for Lambourn, outside it was better.

I got called to this combine one day at Middle Bockhampton Farm. It's a work of art to change the plugs because you had to get right underneath. I took the plugs out to clean them, and they had put the leads on wrong. Of course, it missed. I just swapped them over, and there you were. We used to get stationary engines used on the farms, for milking, bailing and things like that. There was one at Lambourn Woodlands that drove a generator. That used to be a late afternoon job – a little spec of carbon under the valve and it wouldn't drive the generator. One of the machining jobs we had was for the farm at Welford Manor. They had some international tractors and they couldn't get any spares, so we used to build them up. One of the most interesting jobs was the valves we used to make for a company which did crop-spraying. That was a Wally Stagg design. The valve hinges at first were cast iron, which you had to machine. We also used to make all the components for the horseboxes.

I stayed at Lambourn Garages until 1980, when I got made redundant. Frank Thatcher had retired by then. I'd been there for years. It's funny how things happen. I took my wife to hospital for an operation on the Wednesday and Friday I got made redundant. It was a great week! There weren't the jobs about. I went to Earley for a job and I'm glad I didn't get it 'cos it would have been a nightmare getting there and back. There was nothing local, in engineering or anything.

Fortunately for Ron, there occurred a chance meeting with his friend and college registrar, Ewart Morris.[18]

Ewart happened to say, there's a job going at the college as a driver. Was I interested? That was August 1980. I turned up and I walked round and saw Dave Jones and talked through the driving job. There was also a job going as technician and they said, 'Which job do you want?' I said, 'I'll have the workshop job.'

The money was not as good as in the garage, but Ron stayed at the college for 15 years.

'I abandoned motor vehicle work completely – I didn't want a dirty job all my life'

By the time **Peter Lomax** finished at Ormonde House he was earning around £12 a week as a qualified mechanic. He stayed at Marchant's Garages for another three years, did more training at Reading and then, surprisingly, 'abandoned motor vehicle work completely'. He went to work for Proofed Packings on the London

---

[18] Ewart Morris was registrar at South Berks College from 1966 to 1991, following in the footsteps of R W Tucker, appointed in 1956, and J H Brooks, appointed in 1961.

Road, a company which specialised in 'printing, paper converting and flexible packaging'.

Marchant's had the first Crypton engine analysing machine in the area, the first one in Newbury and I don't know how far. They decided I was bright enough to use this machine and I went up to London to learn how to use it. That was after my apprenticeship and I was allowed to wear a white coat. I had my picture in the *Newbury Weekly News*. It was an event that this thing had arrived in Newbury, and I was standing there twiddling a knob on it and wearing my white coat.

The City & Guilds Motor Vehicle Technicians' Certificate at Reading was a more advanced course than the one at Newbury, a progression from one to the other. I wanted to do it. Marchant's paid the fees, but they didn't pay transport and they certainly didn't pay me any overtime for setting off at 7.30 in the morning and getting back about 9.00 at night. We did more welding – they had ARC and things – and more technical drawing than at Newbury. I used to travel backwards and forwards on the bus with my T-square and a complete set of spring clips to hold the paper on the drawing board – you always had to remember to take those. We also did the grandly called National Craftsman Certificate. This was a practical examination, a full day on practical tasks. Welding came into it, fitting and all those sorts of things.

Then I abandoned motor vehicle work completely. When I left school, that was what I had wanted to do, but I changed my mind having seen a bit more of the big world, and I didn't want that as a career. The work didn't seem to have prospects. There were two sons and a daughter in the business, so prospects were limited as far as I went. I was getting dirty, and I didn't want a dirty job all my life. I realised that I could do better – 'I'm too good for this place' – which may be conceited but I think it turned out to be true. History proves that I was right. Marchant's were disappointed and I know I did feel guilty at the time.

I went to work for Proofed Packings, a complete change of direction. I did very well, progressed, and ended up senior management. Then everything started changing. Ownership changed, people changed, existing directors went and were replaced by other people. They seemed to have their own contacts and friends outside. They seemed to be set on getting rid of anyone who'd been there a long time. Several other people went either shortly before or after I did. I ended up being unemployed for the first time in my life, for about a week. I had to find something else, and I was fortunate, but I didn't know it was going to turn out like this.

The good fortune was an opportunity at the college which he had left 30 years before; and in 1989 Peter returned as a technician with the motor vehicle lecturers. 'I had been to the college and I had done an apprenticeship, so I had a second profession to fall back on, which was a good thing as it turned out.'

'Ray got in touch with me – do you fancy teaching?'

Mick Palmer finished his apprenticeship in Hungerford and his wages were put up to the improver's rate. Shortly afterwards, he was in the last cohort of the young men to be conscripted and was put in the infantry. His father was not happy and wrote to the War Office, pointing out that the infantry was not the best place for a qualified mechanic. A week later, Mick had a letter to say that he would be transferred into the REME – if he passed a trade test.

The annoying thing about it, I did a month's training with the Gloucesters, enjoyed it and made some good mates. They were going to Hong Kong for the duration of their service and I would like to have gone. I passed the trade test, got into the REME and went to Blandford Forum. I did six weeks basic training with them and then I had a month in between finishing training and being posted abroad.

I went to Germany, a small town called Hamelin [now Hameln], about the size of Newbury, and stayed there for 20-odd months. I did a trade test and got a higher qualification in the trade. That put me into a craftsman, third class. I then took a diesel course in Germany and I went to Dusseldorf for six weeks on craftsman two, which was equivalent to the National Craftsman. We had a wide range of vehicles. I worked on motorbikes, dispatch rider stuff, up to 26-ton cranes, but in the last six months I was more involved in the cranes. I was stationed with the REME as part of a bridging company. The drivers – the service corps – drove the vehicles; the engineers built the bridges; and REME kept the vehicles and everything running. We used to go out on site when they were bridge training and repair them in our workshop.

I came out in '61. I decided I would have a rest from doing anything mechanical, so I went down to Colthrop, forklift driving. The reason I went down there was they were the only place in the area that was paying good money, and I had been underpaid for six or seven years. I decided that I would get some money. For about ten months, I was doing shifts, 12 hours on, 12 hours off. I got married in the meantime, and then my wife June got fed up with me being away on shifts. I didn't want to stay in a factory all my life anyway, so I went back into garage work.

I followed a similar trail to dad, servicing a fleet. I worked for House of Toomer. They were a hardware store and builders' merchant and they had a television department, an electrical department and the shop. Dick Greet was Toomer's – before him his father owned it. He lived on the Andover Road and eventually moved to Kintbury. They had a workshop down the back of the shop and I was maintaining the fleet of delivery vehicles. I did all the repairs. They had these big 15-ton wagons that used to do the big deliveries, several 15-cwt and 12-cwt vans and some small five-cwt ones. They delivered anything and everything. If they were going to Kintbury on Thursday, and you wanted a box of screws, they would put it on the lorry and take it. Anything you wanted delivered, they would deliver.

I went to Wheeler's in 1968 and I left there in '70. They were Vauxhall and Bedford; then the last 18 months I was there they went Renault. I was on the shop floor repairing cars. I was workshop foreman for 18 months. I was there with Ray Claridge. I did a course at college in '69, in the evening. I was amazed at how fast the college had grown. I hadn't been there for ten years, and W-Block was up.[19]

Then I left Wheeler's and went over to Tenoplast at Basildon. They were a plastics-producing firm that were working on extrusion. I was on the inspection side, quality control, to make sure their product was up to scratch. I was working 12-hour nights and 12-hour days, alternate. Again, it was really money-orientated. Being on the staff at Wheeler's, you were only getting a fixed wage – you were working all the hours God made and you weren't getting paid for it. Having a family at the time who were growing up, I decided, if they're not going to pay the money, I'm going to get out the motor trade and see what I can earn.

That's when Ray got in touch with me and said, 'Do you fancy teaching? There's a part-time job if you want it, 26 hours a week, teaching motor vehicle.' I'd been teaching the apprentices down at Wheeler's. There must have been eight or nine that I was looking after and they all came to the college. The job was offered on condition that it would probably be a full-time post at the end of the year. I started in October 1974, teaching on City & Guilds and the RTITB training programme. This was my sole income, and my contract was up at the end of June '75. Then I was asked to come in for an interview and I got offered the post full time.

One of the first subjects I had to teach was 'moments and levers'. I thought, I've got to do something about getting my head round this. Charlie Sully was still teaching.

---

[19] W-Block was built in the 1960s as an extension to the first instalment of workshops after one of the horsa huts had been demolished.

'Come and ask me if you want anything', he says. 'Don't be frightened. There's no disgrace in asking for advice.' Ray had been working on the Links courses for about a year, and when I came full time in '75, because motor vehicle was expanding somewhat, Ray came over to teach with us. And Charlie had said, 'If you've got any problems, come and see me. We will spend a bit of time in the classroom before classes start, during Admin Week or prior to that.'

So I went to see Charlie and he spent about three or four half days in the first week. We were going in there, and we were sat down, and he was teaching us. Anything you wanted, Charlie would go out of his way to help you. He did it purely because he enjoyed teaching. He explained this 'moments' to me, and I thought, 'Why the hell couldn't I get this at the time?' But it was the way Charlie put it over. He started off so very basic even I could understand it. I've tried to base my style of teaching on what Charlie taught me, and what I noticed when Charlie was teaching.

The garages were dead keen on education, as long as they didn't have to pay for it. Marchant's were very heavily into education. We used to have regular meetings with the advisory committee. They put forward what they wanted, and it kept you in contact with the trade. It was useful to know who to contact and which people did what. I'm surprised it's been done away with; you lose your links with industry.

The indentured apprenticeship disappeared in the early '70s. They went on to training boards. Then they got disbanded and the managing agents came in, Thames Valley Enterprise and the TECs and that. Today we do progressive assessments. Every unit that we complete, we do an end test, and at the end of the year, we do underpinning knowledge tests on units. We found that homework was a hit-and-miss affair. People just wouldn't turn it in, no matter who you got in touch with. They didn't seem to bother, and the managing agents couldn't care whether they did the homework or not. So we decided two or three years back, rather than us hit our heads against the wall all the time, we would try this route. It seems to work and they know if they've got a test coming up they have to get a certain percentage.

'When I was at Colthrop it used to be full of youngsters – an intake every year'

One of the most prominent displays in the college's silver anniversary publication (1973) was that of Colthrop Board Mills, '25 years of association with the college and its many excellent facilities'. In 1956 Colthrop was taken over by the Reed Group, and the North Board Mill was built at a cost of five-million pounds. Reed's paper and packaging was sold worldwide and the mills remained one of the largest employers in the area with 2,000 people on the payroll in 1980.

The Board Mills could be relied on to send apprentices to Ormonde House every year. **Robin Morris** was one of them and once qualified, he looked forward to being paid the full rate for the job.

After the apprenticeship, the wage was about a fiver. The joke was, you finished your apprenticeship, you came out, got your indentures, and then you did a probationary period for six months – you was two pence below craft rate. When you had done your probationary period, you got the full craft rate. Then, in the fullness of time, if you was really, really good, you got what they call the extra two pence. That was technically called 'proficiency' pay. It didn't go up each year and you could wait two years for a wage increase.

A few years later, I went back to college and done an evening course in a workshop. But it was basic, and I went to my firm and said there's not much point. I finished up working as a tutor. A chap called Mr Hill was doing the tutoring in the evening. He did say to me, 'Really, you can tell me as much as I'm telling these people.' So I finished up helping him until the course ran out, and then there just wasn't any point.

I toyed with Aldermaston. I was getting fed up at Colthrop for various reasons. I had a lot of problems with certain management. I was always in trouble, personality clashes. My dad was there, and it created problems. My father was management. 'You're not like your father. Why don't you take after him?' Being called 'Young Bill' is alright at 16, but at 21, 22, it began to get to you. I had the chance and I thought I'll try Aldermaston. I kept thinking about their premises. They were expanding. I got the forms, and then I saw what was involved. They wanted to know the political beliefs of my grandparents. So I said, 'Sod this, I'm not having that', and I decided not to apply. Then somebody said to me, 'They want people at Culham, over Abingdon way.' I toyed. Somebody said, 'It's a white-coat job.'
I thought, 'Will I or won't I?'
Then I thought, 'How the devil do I get to Culham?'
I didn't have a car, I was terrified of motorbikes, and it would be a long bike ride in the middle of December over Ilsley downs. So in the end I thought, 'I won't bother.'

Then another chief engineer arrived at Colthrop and the problems just went out the window. Him and I hit it off without too many set-tos. And yet he was a complete fireball, go up in the air, rant and rave. But we came to an understanding, we got on and in the end, I just soldiered on. I was in the South Mill then, always a rebel and involved in trade union activities. I've been a union member since I left school, for the last 50-odd years, the AEU, the cream of the cream. They rounded up two or three of us so-called troublemakers and sent us to the North Mill. I was transported to the colonies, and this was the best thing they ever did for me, it really was. For the first time I was on my own and left alone to do everything myself, in my own time, in my own way. I had my own department and I shut the doors when I felt like it.

So Robin worked on at the paper mill, for more than 40 years.

> We took apprentices in as electricians and then, later, on instrumentation. It was a bit restricted at South Berks and they started to go to London for the day. Then Basingstoke got to grips with it and some of our lads went there.

> They still have apprentices at Colthrop today, but it has changed. Now they just have sheds with two or three machines in them; it's not a full-scale workshop where there's 100 turners and fitters. Engineering was the cream. It was only from the '80's onwards that you suddenly began to realise, why did you bother? You might just as well be a factory labourer and earn more money. It's a terrible indictment that engineering is still looked down upon. These firms in the early '80s, when problems were surrounding them, they cut back on apprentices here, they stopped them there. I always used to say they would pay for it, and it's coming true. They're screaming out for good engineers at all levels – fitters, turners, electricians. The problem is, the keen ones in the 30 to 35 age group, those with two kids plus a mortgage, they're not there like they used to be. You've got youngsters or the older blokes like myself when I was working, and there's a bloody great gap. Up to the time I left work, any new project in the last ten years could be made in countries like bloody Spain. We used to scratch our heads. Spain? We thought all they could produce was shoddy, terrible stuff – but our companies have gone to the wall. Obviously it's a political thing, but it's happened, and without the companies, there aren't the youngsters going into it. When I was there, it used to be full of them, an intake every year.

'I had several jobs offered to me because I was well known in the trade'

Reliance Coaches, with offices on the Wharf in Newbury and at Brightwalton, had been set up after the First World War. It provided local bus services as well as tours and excursions.

Fitter **Bill Yates** had not been working there long when he went to night school to learn welding. He was with the bus company for 18 years. When he left he joined British Road Transport in Thatcham, staying until it closed down in 1981. Bill then got a job at Midwinter, the corn and seed merchants in Newbury. At the age of 62, he was made redundant. 'I was alright. I had several jobs offered to me because I was well known in the trade. I was only out of work five days and then went to the AA workshops at Thatcham until I retired.'

'I've only ever had one man in a class I've been to'

Teachers **Audrey Lewendon** and **Marjorie Fisher** were both enthusiastic students in the '50s – of cookery, dressmaking, leatherwork and woodwork. Audrey left Speenhamland School when her children were born and later on, she did some supply work. She continued with evening classes, one in pottery at Turnpike School and a lot in cookery at the college once the second instalment, 'the modern bit at the back', was built.

> One of those classes was interesting because it wasn't a practical class. It was watching somebody cooking. I didn't like that very much and I wouldn't have gone if I'd have known it wasn't hands-on. That was a very strange course. I wasn't the only one who was disappointed, but whether we didn't read it right when we said we'd go to it, I don't know.

Audrey's sewing machine remained idle for many years, until her daughter found a use for it, in A-level needlework at the County Girls' School.

Marjorie Fisher taught at Speenhamland for 15 years and then the infant school at Woolton Hill. She, too, continued with night classes, woodwork and pottery in the '60s, sewing in the '70s. Ever adventurous, she celebrated her retirement in 1975 with a trip round the world; and some years ago, she could be seen enjoying an aerobics class.

'We got started by the van'

In the mid-'50s **Mary Harte** was taken on by South Berks College as a typewriting instructor.

> Initially they wanted someone for a term, for a short period. Mr Owthwaite had been looking to see who was coming up here as he thought that was the best way to get someone. He said would I do it? At first I said no. It was his secretary Mabel Lord who came to see me. I said, 'Why can't you do it?'
> She said, 'No, I don't want to do it.'
> So I had an interview and Mr Owthwaite said, 'We will try it for a fortnight, but I think you can probably do the term. Mabel will sit in with you for the first evening.'
> She did sit in but she didn't say anything. She did her knitting.

This turned out to be the beginning of a long career in FE. Even after retiring, Mary came back to college to help out 'when someone was having a baby', and then came back again, but this time as a student to learn word-processing. In 45 years, the wheel had turned full circle; and her husband Pat came with her. They found out about the course from the Roadshow vehicle, a Berkshire county library van which had been converted into a mobile information unit for the college.

> We were doing some shopping in Thatcham. I went in the van and got some leaflets on computers and we found out what it was all about. The leaflets were put aside and forgotten for a while. Then we rang up Margaret Young and we had an interview. We thought we were too old.

'I failed my bookkeeping at college and here I am, years afterwards, doing it'

Most of the full-time 16-year-old girls who had learned shorthand and typewriting under the watchful eye of Gladys Sugg found work easily: with accountants and solicitors, in banks and building societies, in council offices, in shops and hotels, and in industry. Many of them came back to night school, first to improve their speeds and later to learn about the electronic revolution which was radically changing their work situations: the desktop computer, word-processing packages, the internet and the intranet, and communication by email. Many changed jobs during their working lives, as well as spending time at home bringing up children.

When **Vi Chandler** left school, she had wanted to become a nurse. By the time she left college, she had changed her mind. In the summer of 1953, she started work as a junior shorthand typist for W H Smith in Northbrook Street. 'Typex, anything like that, was taboo.' Vi had only been there a few months when she climbed the stairs up to the youth employment office and found another job, still as a typist but this time with the accountants A C Brading.[20] 'We used to do about six copies of things.' She went back to Ormonde House for shorthand, 'to get the speed up', and to the Community Centre for cookery. A few years later she was married and her husband enrolled for evening classes as well.

After working for Brading for many years, Vi decided to go self-employed. She had little trouble finding work in the Newbury-Lambourn-Hungerford triangle. 'I failed my bookkeeping at college and here I am, years afterwards, doing it.' She still preferred shorthand to typewriting. 'Although I don't use it a lot now, there is one man who will always dictate.' When some years ago she was asked to take the minutes at a meeting – an opportunity which she had not had for a long time – she was delighted.

'I'm not computer-literate, but I know what I'm doing'

Jill Delaney was pleased to find a job in the chemist's in her own village of Lambourn. 'I was to go and do the office work, the bookkeeping and all that.' Unfortunately it did not turn out as she had hoped. 'They just put me in the shop.' Fortunately, a few months later, her father heard that one of the veterinary practices was looking for someone; and Jill got the job. Forty-five years working for the vet's in Lambourn and the skills nurtured in the upstairs room in the somewhat drab building in Station Road were gradually extended.

---

[20] Accountants A C Brading had offices in Newbury and Hungerford.

I used to take dictation and use shorthand a lot at one time, but now they tend to write it out in longhand and give it to me to type out or put in on a computer. I'm now more on the accounts side than anything else – not that I use the bookkeeping now because it's all computerised. I was lucky. I did progress from a manual to an electric typewriter, so it was easy going on to a keyboard for a computer, 'cos it's very similar to an electric typewriter. I really enjoy doing my accounts on the computer, and typing in all the stuff that goes with it. I'm not computer-literate, as the expression goes, but I know what I'm doing.

'You never do that in an office – you are in the big wide world now!'

Rosemary Lambourn did not find a job straightaway at the end of her course and in September 1953, like other young people in her situation, she thought of going back to college. She decided against it, but she did go to one of Mrs Spackman's evening classes in Hungerford, in shorthand and typewriting. In November, Rosemary started work in A C Brading's Hungerford office. She earned £2 a week.

There were two men, the manager and the trainee, and I was doing whatever they wanted, typewriting, and shorthand and so on. I was using the typing skills very much. The first week I was at work, I remember typing this letter, terribly nervous. This woman in the office had to look at all my letters before they went into the boss for signing. She said, 'What do you think that is?'
The word was 'typewriter', and I had got 'type' on one end of the line, all uniform, then a dash, and I put 'writer' on the next line.
'You never do that in an office.'
And I can see her waving her arms.
And I said, 'Well, we were taught to do it like that at college.'
And she said, 'You never do it. You are in the big wide world now!'

After two years at the accountants, Rosemary moved to solicitors Charles, Lucas and Marshall. A few years later she moved again, this time to work as a secretary at Opperman Gears. 'I worked for the works director. I used to go to union meetings and so on. By that time shorthand was well and truly a second language to me. I had found it difficult at the beginning, but afterwards it wasn't.' In the early '60s, she went to evening classes in Reading. 'It was a more advanced course and I got up to 120 words a minute, which in those days was reasonable.' Rosemary was at Opperman Gears for 15 years. Then, in the early '70s, she moved to the Elcot Park Hotel where she worked as the conference banqueting coordinator.

> In those days when you got into work it was a job for life, more or less. That was the intention in your head and you weren't going to leave after six months and find something better. You had a certain amount of loyalty to your employers and you wouldn't dream of dropping them in it. Those disciplines were taught me, that you went to work, that you did a good day's work for a fair day's pay, that you were loyal, and that you thought they were going to be good to you as well. It has changed a lot, not altogether for the worse.

> I've been in the job I'm doing now for 24 years. I work part time, but it's actually seven o'clock till half-past two. We get paid a basic rate for the hours we do. The shorthand comes into play quite a bit when I'm doing show-rounds, but I don't have the typing to do or anything like that. We have people in the office to do that. If I were to try and find another job now, apart from my age being against me, I've been in the hotel industry for such a long time, people think you don't know anything else, and they wouldn't readily employ you.

'Goodness,' she said, 'You made it!'

Shirley Woodage was 17 when she left Ormonde House for the second time. She was still set on a career with the police but in the meantime she found work as an invoice clerk in the accounts department of the House of Toomer. Then it was a job as a copy typist at the School of Military Survey at Hermitage. It was here that she took civil service examinations and became a proficient typist. 'Now, of course, it's computers and word-processing. I couldn't get the hang of that. It's so different to a typewriter.'

In 1959 Shirley realised her long held ambition and joined the Berkshire Constabulary.

> You weren't allowed to be posted in Newbury in those days, so I did three years at Wokingham and then I came back to Newbury. The old police station used to be the big white building next to Speenhamland School in Pelican Lane – it's Social Services now.[21] In the early '60s I used to do the crossing in Oxford Road for the children going to Speenhamland and I used to see the college students. They had scarves and I can remember thinking, 'Lucky things! When we were there we had nothing like that.'

> When I got stationed back at Newbury, the first thing I did, I went and knocked on Miss Garlick's door.
> 'Is that Miss Garlick?'
> 'Goodness,' she said, 'You made it!

Shirley had made it. Eight years as a woman police constable and she was promoted to sergeant, working in Abingdon and Bracknell. 'I used to do all the Royal Ascot races, so I saw a lot of the Queen.'

'It was a grim place in those days, a bank. It was ever so strict'

Val Walters has vivid memories of her first day in Newbury's National Provincial Bank.

> I rode my bicycle up there. It's very strange for anybody going into a new job, isn't it? You feel absolutely lost, don't you? I hated the first morning, especially when I

---

[21] The new police station opened in Mill Lane in 1965.

had to go down in the dungeon and make the tea. I went home for lunch and remember saying to my dad, 'I'm not going back.'

He said, 'You bloomin' well are! Get on that bike!'

Val reluctantly cycled back to work. The weeks went by, but the job did not get any better. The work was monotonous and the atmosphere was strict, but Val stuck it for a year.

I couldn't stand it – it was so boring. I was not using the skills I had been taught on the course. I was in the back doing statements for people. Nowadays, money paid in and drawn out is put into a computer; then, everything had to be in longhand. The only machine we had to work on was an adding machine and a typewriter. They used to put a big piece of paper in the adding machine. You would have this pile of cheques and you would put the amounts in all the way along this paper. Then you took it out and you would look through the cheques again and memorise the signatures because you had to put them next to the money they had in or out. I would get very het up on a Saturday morning because I would be busy trying to get everything done and some person would come in and say, 'Can I have a statement please?' And you had to get it out and balance it and everything.

It was a grim place in those days, a bank. It was ever so strict. I will tell you why I left – this is my father coming out in me. I was going to go out somewhere special one Saturday afternoon. We had to work in the morning, so I thought I would put a bit of nail polish on my nails. This awful man cashier said, 'What dreadful nails!' And I stood up, I went straight to the manager and I said, 'I'm giving in my notice. I've had enough. Now!'

So Val left the bank and went to work for Clement Clarke, an optician in Cheap Street. She stayed there until she got married. 'I was happy there – I did all the office work. Dr Fawcett was the specialist then – we made all his appointments. You got to see all the doctor's paperwork and I found that interesting.' Val married Alan Walters. An AWE apprentice, Alan had studied engineering at the college while Val was a student. Their romance, however, did not begin in Ormonde House but at 'an old time dance in St Mary's church hall'.[22] A few years later Alan taught at the college and together the couple enjoyed a game of badminton with the Staff Association. Some years later, Val's father 'Chuck' Houghton worked at the college as a technician and her niece enrolled as a student. Then it was the turn of one of Val's daughters, who followed in her mother's footsteps and did a secretarial course.

'One of the biggest employers in Newbury – people at the SEB used the college a lot to further their careers'

Iris Matthews' job with New Brothers was the start of a full working life: five years at the seed company, seven years at the SEB and 25 years with Berkshire County Council. It was a career characterised by change and lifelong learning. 'I've had the opportunity to go right through from the old manual typewriters, the Remingtons and the Royals, to word-processing and computer skills.' A year or so after her secretarial course, she went back in the evening for more typewriting and shorthand. Years later, and it was word-processing. Then came more computer training, this time provided by her employer. She was also involved in youth work in Thatcham, where for many years she helped run the Boys' Brigade.

> My first job you had to work on a Saturday morning and because there was a shop attached to the business, every third Saturday you were expected to be there all day. We had to be there to type the orders as the shop people took them. You had the Wednesday afternoon off – the shop closed half-day. I was getting fed up with this because you wanted to go out on a Saturday and I had to work till one o'clock.

---

[22] In 1955 a 20-year-old AWE student, Alan Walters, was awarded the Student College Cup for the best technical report. St Mary's Church in London Road, and its church hall, was demolished in 1976.

Places like the Electricity Board, who employed a lot of people, didn't work Saturdays. They were a five-day week. I applied for a job there and got an interview but they wouldn't take me. I hadn't got my 100 words a minute shorthand and I had to go to evening classes to get it. I had to have that piece of paper. I achieved that and then they offered me a job. It was strict in those days and the standard of work had to be good. My time at the college put me right. I went back to evening classes in the late '50s, which were held above Hill the leather shop – it's just down below Dixon. We used to go down this alleyway and up the stairs. Mr Tucker took us; he used to work for the railway. Pitman shorthand – it was a speed class that I went to – 80 words a minute March 1957, 90 words a minute March 1960, 100 words a minute July 1960. We used to get the bus into Newbury from Thatcham and come home about nine o'clock and walk up the road. You were safe to do that sort of thing then.

I went to the SEB in May 1960. That was a big old house up the Bath Road; you could get in off the Oxford Road as well. They had a big extension built on the back, but when I first went there I was in the old house. They had departments – accounts, commercial, engineering – and you worked with your respective department. They had their departmental head and some of us that did secretarial work were in a little office with only three people. About two years after I was there they had this two-storey extension and they turned one part of it into a typing pool with our supervisor. It brought us all together. We didn't know some of the others. You might see them when you went into work or when you went home, but we didn't actually know them. We still worked for our departments. I was in the secretarial section which dealt with personnel and general staffing – a lot of typing and shorthand.

If you worked at the SEB you knew a lot of people. They employed about 200, one of the biggest employers in Newbury. People at the Electricity Board used the college a lot to further their careers. It was one of the places to work and the pay and conditions were good. I started paying my superannuation in those days, and now I've finished work, I'm very thankful I did. When you left the SEB you were careful where you went. You wanted the same conditions of employment, sick pay and all that, and if you'd got superannuation, you wanted to go somewhere where you could transfer it. It was still manual typewriters at the beginning of the '60s, and then they had one or two electric ones. I never had one but then the audio ones came in and that's one of the reasons why I left. You had no option; it was do that or get out.

So that's when I moved on again, and I joined Berkshire County Council. I went to the education department in Peake House – that was my home for a few years – and I've been in the audit department with Social Services. There's been change in the council over the years, but I stuck it out till I retired. When I first went to Social Services, interviews were held in Newbury, but somebody always came from Shire Hall to do them. Then as the years rolled by, a personnel department was created in Newbury. I was in personnel and that lasted for about ten years. Then it was all clawed back to Shire Hall, centralising and decentralising. I never worked in Reading. Several times jobs disappeared in Newbury. My job went to Reading so I got a job in another section. I've done typing all the time and I still use my shorthand; it's a second way of writing for me. At work you might have the occasion, if someone wanted to dictate a report from another office, and I used it if I was taking telephone messages. When I worked in personnel, and a reference hadn't come through, I'd often have to take it down over the 'phone on the day of the interview and then type it up before the person came.

I'm secretary of the WI in Thatcham, and I do the minutes in my shorthand notes at the meetings – so I kept my shorthand going right through. In personnel, that's when I really started learning on the computer side. Putting all the staff on – that was a mammoth task but we had to do it. In the 1980s I went to college for word-processing. They let me go in the daytime. It was a crash course in Word Star, a day a week for a month. Then over the years Berkshire had their own training suite. There was a lot of in-service training eventually, at Bracknell, at Shire Hall, at the Apex Plaza at the station in Reading. I went for word-processing 'cos they introduced the packages as well. There was no need to come to college because you had those courses offered you.

The last course I went on before I retired – having become West Berkshire Council – was an email course. They'd just introduced that within the council and I said, 'I'm going. I want to know what it's all about.' When you read about people going to computer courses, women in their 70s, it's good that they want to learn new skills. Some people, they just give up, don't they? Just going to work keeps you in touch with everything that's going on.

I've got a little part-time job now so I haven't finished completely. There's a social work agency in Newbury that supplies social workers to the office where I used to work, and many other offices in the Reading and Swindon areas. They do the supervised contacts. This lady set this business up and I got to know her through the duty system. I usually go the first week of the month and give a hand. I said to her, 'I don't want any responsibility. I'm just going to type up the reports on the supervised contacts.' I'm familiar with the content of the work, and again, it keeps me in touch.

Since I've been retired I've bought myself a computer. I've got a manual portable typewriter but I thought, 'It's no good; I can't live without a computer.' I never thought I'd hear myself say that.

'That's where I started my legal career'

Secretarial student **Jennifer Foster's** job with Thomas Turner the gunsmith lasted six months.

> The office was very old-fashioned, the way they dealt with invoices and things. Not much happened and there wasn't that much to do. I used to spend most of my time upstairs in the gun repair room and I found that quite fascinating. They used to expect you to serve a bit in the shop, just to fill in the time, which I didn't care for.

She moved on, to Plenty to type invoices – 'I couldn't stand that' – and to Mercantile Credit, an insurance company in West Street. This was much better, 'working for the branch manager, doing general correspondence, typing and shorthand.' Jennifer stayed in insurance for three years but when the manager moved, she moved as well, to work for the manager of Opperman Gears.

> I hardly ever saw him – he was in America a lot. It was a funny set-up. There was a big factory area, and the offices were up one side of the building. But to get to the ladies' loo you had to walk through the factory, hotfooting, and all these catcalls from the men on the shop floor.

Six months later, and she was on the move again, this time to Gardner Leader, the solicitors in White Hart House in the Market Place. 'That's where I started my legal career.' Jennifer had had five different jobs in as many years, but there was some continuity during this part of her working life: she kept enrolling for evening classes.

> I started going in the evening straightaway when I first went to work, to carry on my speeds. In 1958 I did shorthand in a room above the leather shop – handbags, brief cases, suitcases – in Northbrook Street. We went down a very narrow alleyway, then in towards the left, upstairs, three storeys. LMS is upstairs today, a recruitment agency. I did shorthand and typing, two evenings a week, one for

each subject, for quite a few years. It seemed to go on for ever. I eventually gained my RSA I, II and III in typing. The last certificate I took was the RSA shorthand 140 – that is very good. Considered good nowadays is 120 – that was always the thing to aim for. But I fancied doing court reporting, and in order to get on the course to train to be a court reporter, which was in London, you had to have 140. I didn't do the course because by then, my mother was an invalid. I was working all day, looking after the house and looking after her.

I used to love writing shorthand. Unfortunately it's not used today, not to the same extent. It's disappeared because of Dictaphones. They are so convenient. I've got a boss who works all hours, and he takes it in the car and on the train and dictates. I've got the one with an earpiece – I don't like the overhead business.

Miss Garlick was the one who tried to start a teacher-training course at college.[23] I thought I'd give it a whirl – hence my teaching practice. I taught evening classes once a week, Pitman shorthand for beginners. I did that for two years. I did not find it easy as I was then of a shy, retiring nature. In a way I found it pretty demoralising. The girls were only there because they had to be there because the employers paid for them to go. There were one or two willing to work but the rest just mucked about. I felt that a bit depressing. If anyone was prepared to work, that was fine, but not just to come and muck about because it disrupts the whole class. I would set them homework to do and they wouldn't do it. People dropped out and we didn't have enough to go on with it, so it never came to anything.

Jennifer's career progressed in legal work rather than in teaching. She stayed at Gardner Leader for three years or so, was married and worked part time until she had children. Years later she returned to work for a solicitor on the London Road.

---

[23] This was the RSA Shorthand Teachers' Certificate in 1957.

I was home for ten years but I did a bit of shorthand and kept my speeds up. I used to teach privately, three girls who used to come to me. I used to sit here thinking, 'What can I do next?' So I went out and found myself a job with Ward Bowey, now Penningtons Solicitors. I started off doing afternoons, typing and general dogsbody. That's when I first came in touch with an electric typewriter. Amazing when you think back; it's not that long ago, but how things have changed. One till five, and it generally spread. 'Can you do a bit extra? Can you start earlier?' And I became full time. My boss suggested I did the Institute of Legal Secretaries. I used to do it in my lunch hour, type all sorts of stuff, write essays, answer legal questions. It took me three or four months to complete it – I must have enjoyed it. In 1996 I became a fellow of the Institute of Legal Secretaries.

My early training stood me in good stead and has guaranteed me a good working life. I've never had to argue for a job. I have always had my choice.

'By then I was a design engineer'

Derek Loosen finished his AWE apprenticeship in 1960. Within a few months he had decided to leave Aldermaston and, somewhat surprisingly, move away from Newbury. He went into lodgings at Stevenage in Hertfordshire, where he had secured a job with English Electric.

When I finished my five years, Aldermaston offered me a job as an instrument maker. I didn't want to be an instrument maker. I tried to be a draughtsman because I was interested in engineering drawing, but they said, 'We've got other people better qualified.' So when I saw this advert for training to be a draughtsman at English Electric, I applied for it and went.

I did a year on their course, an intensive course, and I was given a job in the drawing office. Because I had been an instrument maker, I was put on instrumentation, where everything was drawn ten times full size. It was the Bloodhound surface-to-air missile. While I was there I went to college and did a Higher National in Mechanical. I stayed there for two years. I got married while I was there and my wife came from the Newbury area; but she didn't like Stevenage. I didn't like it very much either. We had a flat in the old town, but the new town was a horrible place.

So I came back to Newbury, to Opperman Gears. It was actually Limitorque Valve Controls, manufactured under license by Opperman Gears. I left in '66 and by then I was a design engineer. I was working for the chief engineer who started up his own company and I joined him. Mick Terry was one of our first employees, our first fitter. He came from Opperman Gears. The company was called Torcmatic, and we made gearboxes for opening and closing industrial valves. During the day I used to do all the design work and in the evening put the things together. We had people in Reading doing the machining for us. Then we got a workshop in Reading and we employed Mick and a couple of others. I was planning all the manufacturing. We were in Reading a few years then we took a lease of a building in Arnhem Road in Newbury, outgrew that and moved into one across the road as well, and then moved into another one further up the road.

At Aldermaston, Blacknest ceased to be a hostel and became their computer centre. When computers became fashionable in the '70s, we started using them as a bureau. They used it mainly for their own business but they had some spare capacity which they let out, and we were the first persons to use it. One of my old friends, who was an apprentice the year before me, helped run it; so I used to see him on a regular basis. I used to do all our production planning, submit the information once a week and then next day we'd get back all the printouts.

Derek worked for Torcmatic for many years. By the 1990s he was back in Ormonde House, but this time as an FE governor.

I look back now and I think, well, it didn't do me any harm
not passing the eleven-plus. I've got a lot of friends that
passed and not done anything with their lives at all. It's
like everything else in life – it's what you make of it.

'I was an instructor and then I went through to becoming apprentice scheme manager'

Aere Harwell opened their apprentice school at Winfrith in
Dorset in 1958 and all first-year training was moved there.[24]
Two years later, **Roland Wise** started his apprenticeship ... and
had to leave home.

> Because of the Pre-Apprenticeship, I was nearly 17 when I
> arrived at Harwell. I finished at college in June 1960 and
> started at AERE in September. It was daunting for all the
> apprentices, because the first year was spent away at a
> training centre in Dorset. That was something else. You
> hadn't been away from home, apart from holidays, and
> you packed your bags and went away for a year. Then
> we came back and we went right through at South Berks
> College. Mine was the full Tech Certificate.
>
> I remember assembling in the main lecture hall at Harwell
> to be told that some of us had been selected to run as guinea
> pigs on the block release, which was one week at college and
> two weeks at work. Block release was new; previously it
> had all been day release. Because we were two weeks away
> from college, the homework was packed in. Originally we
> couldn't cope with it, but it quickly settled down. We had
> meal tickets and this forced us into the refectory, which was
> up and running. It was popular. There were a lot of people
> queuing and you had to try and beat the queue.
>
> You finished your apprenticeship age-related – the day
> you hit 21 you became fully fledged and you were paid

---

[24] Harwell's first-year apprentice training was at Winfrith in Dorset from
1958 to 1970.

the going rate if you were given a job. So I did four years and one month.

Harwell offered Roland a job. 'We had to apply, and if we kept our noses clean, and if there was a vacancy – which always existed right through the years – then you were offered a post. Some were not offered jobs.' When he started, he had still to finish his ONC. He stopped studying for a while and then went on day release to Reading, one day and two evenings. 'It was quite tough. Travel was paid for day release but the evenings were your problem. There was no financial support for that.' It was worth the effort as the young apprentice of 1960 eventually ended up in charge of the much respected apprentice training programme. He worked at Harwell for 30 years. People like Roland, and there were many of them, were affectionately known as 'lifers'.

I had three hats: I was a pre-apprentice, an apprentice and then part of the management structure. I became a craftsman, a research engineer, and then I went into estimating. Harry Wells and John Wallace instigated all the apprenticeship scheme. I was in the building and they happened to see me at my desk. I saw them a couple of times wander backwards and forwards. The next thing I know, I had this 'phone call. Would I go and see them? There was a sickness problem. They had a temporary position for an instructor in the workshop. Would I like to go down? Talk about being in the right place at the right time. Would you believe it? Even when I was an apprentice, that's always what I wanted to do. I went down there for a couple of weeks, and then it was another couple of weeks, and then it was a six-month, and before I knew where I was, I was interviewed and got the job. And then I went through to becoming scheme manager. The duties took us to Newbury College and then on to the advisory committees. I knew Eddie Irwing well, and we had the staff come out to Harwell, Fred Veness and Bob Green for instance. They used to come out once a week to run the theory side, to get the number of hours in, but that link-up, that relationship, was a good thing.

530

I spent the rest of my working life at Harwell and worked in many different areas. When the apprentice scheme closed down, I moved on to the education and training department and ran that. Then they asked me to close that down. It's quite a task to say to your staff, 'I'm sorry – who of you choose to go first?' So I retired and took part-time work.

Part-time 'bits and pieces' included Abingdon College for two years as training scheme manager, and a return to Harwell as consultant for the Rutherford Laboratory. 'They were taking apprentices again, so I did their testing for them and advised them as to who should be for interview.' By this time, Rutherford apprentices studied at college in Abingdon, not Newbury.

Abingdon was always treated as the science college; Newbury was the technical college, engineering. There was the Berkshire link as well. It became very difficult when Harwell became part of Oxfordshire in 1974. There was a lot of pressure put to bear that they should go to Abingdon then, but they didn't have the facilities at the time, and the structure was at Newbury, so they continued there for a while.

Roland also worked at Newbury as the tutor of an abrasive wheels course and was once given the responsibility for putting together a college inventory. 'I had the opportunity to visit every room, every nook and cranny. I recorded what equipment was around, and how many chairs, and ironing boards would you believe – there was a lot of ironing boards around.'

The Pre-Apprenticeship programme was closed down in 1970. Yet Roland believes that there is still a need for such a course in FE. 'You have to go with the times; I'm a firm believer in that. But change for the sake of change, I'm not sure about that. Change for the right reasons, that's alright.'

'One of them became a scientific assistant – and that was me'

Apprentice **Ian Walker** had started his studies at Oxford and finished at Newbury. Once qualified, he stayed at Harwell for four or five years working in the research reactor division.

> If you look at the listings of what happened to the apprentices, most of them became technician grades in one way or another – drawing office, mechanical or something. One of them became a scientific assistant, and that was me. I didn't want to go into the technician grades. The drawing office at Harwell was a very prosaic organisation. I had been fortunate enough to work in the research reactor division, doing electronics for the various experiments they ran on Dido and Pluto. I was encouraged by them to apply for a job to carry on doing just that, but the only thing they could offer me was scientific assistant, which is a step down from the technician grade. I enjoyed doing it. I got made up by one grade to assistant experimental officer, but it was then very difficult to make any progress at Harwell because in that stream you had to be academic and you had to show you were doing research. Building electronics for experiments didn't seem to fit. If you went to a board, they were asking you all sorts of things about physics which you didn't know and nothing about electronics because they didn't have the discipline in that area.
>
> So I did eventually leave, but it was a very interesting time. I got a tremendous amount out of it in terms of learning about things and learning to understand electronics and mechanical engineering.

During this time, Ian returned to Oxford College, studied pulse electronics and completed an HNC. He then moved into electronics, went to work for Quantel in Newbury and stayed there for more than 30 years. He did go back to Ormonde House for an evening class.

> And I have some beaten metalwork at home to prove it. Dick Edwards took the class in the woodwork shop – a very, very nice chap, and very good and very knowledgeable, not

just in the theory but also the technique. The sort of person who knows exactly how to hit it – 'I'll show you how to do this' – and suddenly it's flat again. One chap came in and he would bring some chunks of wood with him, and all he would do is turn out bowls. He'd done the metalwork for a while, got fed up with it, and decided to work on wood instead. There was one lady who was a very regular person on the course; she did the coffee and biscuits at break. Mr Joyce, the Newbury surgeon, would take a whole packet of biscuits and put a tenon saw through the middle of them.

***'From instrument maintenance to management –
what you learn at college you gradually build on and change
around, and you're using it all the way through'***

Ken Hunt had left Ormonde House with his mechanical engineering certificate and was offered a job in one of Aldermaston's instrument workshops. He had been trained as an instrument maker, but now found he was working as an instrument mechanic. AWE was good on staff development, and Ken was given further training for his new work.

> I went one day a week to Harwell reactor training school, and did evening studies at home to keep up. They condensed a five-year City & Guilds into two years and I passed to get a full Tech City & Guilds in instrument maintenance.

Within a few years 'electronics was coming into instrument making'. Ken was determined to keep abreast of these developments and went back to Ormonde House to learn about electrical engineering. 'The endorsement was digital techniques, electronics and all those sorts of things.' It took three years, and in 1971 he completed the Electrical Engineering Technicians' Certificate (City & Guilds). 'Charlie Sully taught me the basics, and this guy on the Electrical was just like Charlie.'

Not long after this, Ken's work at Aldermaston changed again. He moved from the workshops into the laboratories as a laboratory technician, by 1980 he was workshop supervisor, and within a few years he was managing the workshops.

Then it was project management. All this meant more training, in business studies at Basingstoke College. He finished as manager of engineering support, 'all the engineering support for trials'.

Ken retired in 1997. By this time, the competition for places in the Apprentice School was nothing like it had been when he had filled in his application form 40 years before. 'When I left, they were still offering about 30 places. They couldn't get enough applicants – that's how it's changed – so very often we ended up with an intake of ten.' Ken had spent all his working life at Aldermaston, from instrument maintenance to engineering management with many steps in-between. His career was as varied as it was fulfilling, and much of the groundwork for it was done at Ormonde House. 'What you learn at college you gradually build on and change around, and you're using it all the way through, although you don't quite stick to your trade.' In the 1970s, he did an evening class – 'I thought I'd learn brickwork' – but since he retired he has enjoyed his fishing and his woodwork.

'I didn't do what I was trained to do for that long, but it has given me a good mechanical background'

Colin Roberts finished his Aldermaston apprenticeship, was offered a job as a mechanical instrument maker, stayed for two years and then began a new life on the other side of the world.

> We went to Australia in '63, the £10 assisted passage. We didn't even pay the £10 because I had a job to go to. They were always advertising for people – it was a nationwide advert. They had some jobs in the government, in the aircraft industry, for instrument makers. I applied and they jumped on it. The reason they picked my application out was because I had been an apprentice at Aldermaston. Its fame had spread out there.

> I was in Melbourne for nearly three years, then back to Newbury, but not to AWE. Aldermaston is a bit of a lifestyle. It was good while you were under the regime of the apprenticeship, but somehow I didn't think it was the place to spend the rest of my life. It felt very incarcerated,

showing your pass each day, clocking in and clocking out. The outside world, commerce and industry, seemed so different. Having gone to Australia, I didn't want to go back into that game – it felt very restricted somehow. I went to Versatec in Newbury – it became Xerox Engineering Systems. Gradually we were all made redundant. I was out of work in 1993 for almost a year; then I got a job with Compass down Bone Lane. They made computer systems and data storage systems. When they got taken over by another group called Forefront, I was redundant again. Now I work for a very small company in the town, as service manager for computer maintenance and sales.

Even though I did an apprenticeship in instrument making, I didn't do what I was trained to do for that long. But it has given me a good mechanical background. Where I am today, the biggest problem we have is printers; and printers are very mechanical, the way they handle paper. And fixing computers is very mechanical. I've not been on a lathe for a long time, but the background I have has helped.

And finally …

Vera Chandler left Ormonde House in 1943 just before the convent schoolgirls arrived. All around, Newbury families were doing their best to adapt to wartime conditions. Young men left to fight, and there was a notable presence in and around the town of vast numbers of service personnel. The Allied Club had moved from London and was occupying Donnington Grove, the imposing Georgian building in Grove Road, and Vera went to work in the canteen, 'taking tea to the officers and odd jobs like that.' She was not there for long. A year went by, and like thousands of other young women, Vera became a factory girl, a dramatic change for Mrs Waldron's former housemaid. Yet all over the country women were learning new skills, doing hard and sometimes dangerous jobs that had previously been regarded as men's work – and doing them well.

This was war work. I went to Vickers Armstrong. Vickers were very big. They had three factories – one at Mill Lane, one at Shaw, one at West Street. If they needed you at one of the others, they moved you around. I went to West Street first; then we were transferred up to Shaw.

Vera worked as a riveter on 12-hour shifts, drilling holes in Spitfire aircraft components. The contrast with her work 12 months before could not have been greater. She stayed at Vickers Armstrong until the war was over, and then moved to Elliott's. She left a year or so later. 'Once I was married, I didn't go to work until my children had left home.' When she eventually went back to work, it was at The Blackbird public house in Bagnor, the village where she had spent her childhood.

Not too many years ago, Vera could be seen going back to Ormonde House along the side drive down which she had cycled in 1942, past the scullery and the boot-house, the wall of red brick with its lean-to greenhouse, the chicken hut and the two cottages. But this was Sunday, and she was not going to work. Vera was on her way to a car boot sale.

1

APPENDIX ONE

THE PLACE

Newbury, situated at the crossing of main routes from east to west and from north to south, began as a settlement by a ford across the River Kennet. Soon after the Romans arrived in Britain, the road from London to Gloucester was built, crossing the river at Speen where the Romans built a military outpost. They stayed for four centuries. With the Saxons, river valleys became the best places to settle and the Newbury area became part of the kingdom of Wessex. There was a Saxon settlement at Ulvitrone at the southern end (Bartholomew Street) of the modern town. After the Norman Conquest (1066) the land was given to a Norman lord, Ernulf de Hesdin, and a new town for craftsmen and traders – 'Newbury' – was developed. Situated in a valley surrounded by good farming land and downland for sheep, Newbury's favourable position on the road network built up its prosperity. The town flourished with economic activity in Bartholomew Street and Cheap Street. In the 13th century, the town became one of the most prosperous places in the country and had two members of parliament. The manufacture of woollen cloth was important from the 15th century and Newbury grew to a centre of national significance. Wool was brought down the Wantage and Lambourn roads from the Cotswolds and spun and woven in Newbury. The principal business centres were south of the river, in the Market Place, Cheap Street and Bartholomew

Street. The cloth trade produced the town's greatest hero, Jack Winchcombe (Jack of Newbury, d.1519), who set up the first 'factory' in England, with 200 looms and a workforce of a thousand. Garments were carted over Greenham Common to south coast ports and on to Europe. The booming weaving trade financed the building of the Grammar School and the parish church of St Nicolas' in the early 16th century. Cloth production spread out to the villages such as Greenham, Shaw and Speen, and there were fulling mills at Benham Valence, Brimpton, Colthrop and Thatcham. Newbury's population increased from approximately 1,900 in the late 14th century to 2,690 by 1525. In 1596 the town was given the right to set up a market and craft guilds.

In the 17th century, Newbury was of strategic importance to both sides in the civil war. The king's headquarters were at Oxford and Newbury was on the route to the west from London, the centre of Parliament's power. The pragmatic commercial interests of the merchants, shopkeepers and tradesmen, and the influence of Puritanism, ensured that Newbury sympathised with the Parliamentary cause. There were two bloody engagements in the neighbouring countryside, around Wash Common (1643) and Donnington Castle (1644).

The cloth industry declined in the 18th century but Newbury remained a thriving market town serving the surrounding countryside and villages. The trade in corn was important and breweries, corn mills and maltings were part of the local economy. As the town of Bath became popular, visitors from London travelled along the Great Bath Road, the A4. The coach journey took two days. Newbury was halfway and became the main stopover. This encouraged the development of coaching inns in the Speenhamland area and the care of the thousands of horses passing through created job opportunities.

In the 1720s the River Kennet from Newbury to Reading, where it joined the River Thames, was straightened and made navigable for sailing barges. Newbury became a busy inland port, the Wharf area was developed and manufacturers and traders travelled great distances to load their products onto barges for transit to London. A wide range of goods – food, raw materials, stone and coal – was carried back from the capital. The Kennet and Avon Canal was completed in 1810 and provided an inland waterway link between the ports of Bristol and London. This brought further advantages to the town but the golden era of the canal came to an end in the 1840s with the advent of the railway. In 1847 a branch line of the Great Western Railway opened from Reading to Newbury and Hungerford; this was later extended to Westbury (Wiltshire) and Penzance (Cornwall). In the later 19th century, the north-south rail link was provided, from Newbury to Didcot, Winchester and Southampton (1885); and a line was opened to Lambourn (1898).

By the early 19th century, the population had grown to more than 4,000. The town continued as an agricultural centre serving the needs of the farmers of south-west Berkshire. The Corn Exchange was built in the Market Place in 1862. The weekly sale of sheep and cattle in the yards of town centre inns came to an end in 1873 with the opening of the cattle market in Market Street. New industries began to develop. Plenty's iron foundry was started in the late 18th century, the gasworks opened in 1825 and Elliott's joinery works began around 1870.

In the first half of the 20th century Newbury remained a market town, providing an outlet for the produce of local farms and a range of supplies and services for people living in the area. There were still a lot of family-owned businesses meeting people's day to day needs, but national companies – of booksellers, chemists and grocers – also had a foothold. There were fewer people living and working in the countryside, and more people were employed in the town in office-based work, as accountants, estate agents, secretaries and solicitors. This trend continued after the Second World War. The development of the Atomic Energy Research Establishment at Harwell (1946) and the Atomic Weapons Research Establishment at Aldermaston (1950) brought many scientists and technicians to the district and provided jobs and training opportunities for local people.

There were rapid changes in the town in the latter half of the 20th century. Newbury grew into a business, commercial and distribution centre and the market town was subsumed. Between 1950 and 1970, the flour mills, the breweries and the cattle market closed and farm traffic disappeared. From 1970, the town was transformed by the development of the computer industry. The number of scientifically trained people encouraged the development of the electronics industry in and around the town with companies such as Bayer, Kerridge, Quantel and Vodafone. The media industry also expanded with television and radio studios. At the same time, the position of the town, in the centre of southern England and at the intersection of main trunk roads, allied with changes in transport patterns, led to the area developing as a major distribution point. Both Newbury and Thatcham have growing commercial areas and redistribution depots. The main factors here were the opening of the M4 motorway (1971), and the development of Portsmouth as a cross-channel commercial port and Southampton as an international container port. The traffic generated by these developments led to the Newbury bypass (1998), the improvement of the A34 as a link between the south coast and the Midlands. These economic developments have led to Newbury becoming, again, one of the most prosperous towns in the country, with a low level of unemployment. Its mixed economy status has made it popular to incomers.

LOCAL GOVERNMENT

Although there was some sort of independent town government in the Middle Ages, Newbury was granted a charter of incorporation by Elizabeth I in 1596. The borough was to be governed by a council which was to include the mayor, aldermen and representatives of the principal trades. An extension of the area of the borough took place in 1878 when part of the parish of Speen, including Donnington Square and Speenhamland, and part of Greenham, were brought within its boundaries.

In 1878 new municipal buildings were opened facing the Market Place, housing offices and a council chamber; a clock tower completed the building in 1881. The old town hall, or mansion house, was demolished.

It was during Queen Victoria's reign that local government of the modern type was established. County councils were created by an act of 1888 and by the following year Berkshire County Council was operational.

In 1934 the boundaries of the borough were extended again to include parts of Cold Ash and Thatcham. A smaller area was taken from Enborne.

In 1948 Newbury Borough Council consisted of 24 members – six aldermen and 18 councillors – presided over by the mayor. The borough was divided into three municipal wards, each returning six councillors. The councillors served for three years (one third retiring each year) and were then subject to re-election. The aldermen were elected by the councillors and served for six years, half of their number retiring every three years. The mayor in 1948 was Councillor Oliver Brown. Newbury Borough Council was responsible for running the town's services, with Berkshire County Council providing education, social services, the police and fire services.

Local government reorganisation in 1974 resulted in the abolition of borough, rural district and urban district councils. Larger local authorities replaced them and Newbury District Council took on duties for the western half of Berkshire. The County Council retained the services it had previously provided and took over some others, including libraries. A new and larger police authority, Thames Valley Police, was formed covering Buckinghamshire and Oxfordshire in addition to Berkshire. Thames Water took over the former civic functions of water supply and sewage treatment. 1974 also saw the incorporation into Oxfordshire of some of the north-western parts of Berkshire, including Abingdon and Harwell.

Further reorganisation in 1998 resulted in the abolition of Berkshire County Council and the formation of six unitary authorities to provide all the services (except police) in the county area. West Berkshire Council is the unitary authority covering the area previously managed by Newbury District Council.

POPULATION AND HOUSING
Area of Newbury Borough in 1948: 2,612 acres

Population:

1901	10,061
1911	12,107
1921	12,295
1931	13,340
1951	17,772
1961	20,386

Council House Building pre-1939

In 1920 the first council houses were built in St George's Avenue. These were modern houses for rent by the poorer members of the community and were to rehouse those displaced from the courts and yards in the town centre. By 1939 Newbury Borough Council had built over 400: in Camp Close, Cromwell Road, Essex Street, Monks Lane, Remembrance Road, St George's Avenue, St Michael's Road, Skyllings and Speenhamland.

Council House Building 1945 to 1960

'All the houses constructed since the war have hot and cold running water, bathrooms and all modern conveniences, and are of the traditional brick and tile construction. The layout of the new estates is a considerable improvement on the old type of council houses, and every endeavour has been made to construct them on attractive lines.' (*Civic Week Handbook 1948*).

There was much council house building after the Second World War and by 1961 more than 1,000 had been built.

The 100-acre Shaw estate was the biggest housing estate in the town. It included 302 houses with an additional 120 in Love Lane. Building started in 1946 and was finished in 1953. Newbury Borough Council was responsible for the houses south of Love Lane; those to the north were the responsibility of Newbury Rural District Council.

Building began on the Valley Road estate in 1952, on land extending from the Ministry of Supply site in Valley Road, to Essex Street: Barn Crescent, Elizabeth Avenue, Hill Close, Middle Close, Pond Close and Wood Side. 240 houses had been completed by 1960.

Building on the Bath Road estate started in 1956.

Council houses were also built in Craven Road, Cromwell Road, Doveton Way, Enborne Road, Hutton Close, Kendrick Road, Newport Road, Queen's Road and Western End (temporary prefabricated bungalows).

Ministry of Supply House Building

Houses in the Valley Road and Wendan Road areas were built by the government in the 1950s for Aldermaston and Harwell employees.

Valley Road estate: Garford Crescent, Henshaw Crescent, Home Mead Close, Sidestrand Road and Valley Road.

Wendan Road estate: Chandos Road, Culver Road, Roebut's Close, The Glade, Three Acre Road, Upper Meadow and Wendan Road.

WHERE PEOPLE WORKED

Significant Industrial Employers in 1948

Colthrop Board Mills, Thatcham.   Folding Box Manufacturers

Elliott's of Newbury, Albert Works, Albert Road. Furniture Manufacturers

Newbury Diesel, Kings Road.   Engineering and Marine Engineering

Opperman Gears, Hambridge Road.   Engineering - Gear Cutters

Plenty & Son, Eagle Iron Works, Cheap Street and (foundry) King's Road.   Engineering and Marine Engineering

Vickers Armstrong, Turnpike Road, Shaw. Engineering

Significant Building Contractors in 1948

E A Bance & Sons, Ball Hill, Woolton Hill

Camp Hopson & Co., Northbrook Street

A J Chivers, 63 Cheap Street; workshops in Winchcombe Road

Cooke Bros., 20 Northbrook Street and (yard) Park Way

Eggleton & Tallin, Berkeley Road

Hoskings & Pond, 32 West Mills

Love & Brown, Park Street

J W Palmer & Sons, London Road

T C Pembroke, 22 Park Street

F J Reynolds, 1 Bath Road, Thatcham

Newbury and District Association of Building Trades Employers 1960

Members provide facilities for training apprentices in various building crafts and indenture apprentices under the National Joint Apprenticeship Scheme for the Building Industry administered by the National Joint Apprenticeship Board.

R C Abraham, Kintbury	Hoskings & Pond, Newbury
W T Adams & Co., Lambourn	F J Lewis & Son, Great Shefford
W Ansell & Sons, Newbury	E Lipscomb & Sons, Newbury
W J Ayres & Co., Newbury	W Martin, Chieveley
E A Bance & Sons, Newbury	W Meadham, Newbury
A A Beaver, Heath End	W G Middleton, Newbury
Brooks Plastering, Newbury	A W Milson, Bucklebury
Brown & Cleverley, Newbury	D Molloy, Thatcham
Camp Hopson & Co., Newbury	J Morley & Sons, Hungerford
C W Cann, Chieveley	G C Osborne & Son, Newbury
A J Chivers, Newbury	J W Palmer & Sons, Newbury
Cooke Bros., Newbury	F Paulin & Son, Newbury
C A Denton & Sons, Newbury	Payne Bros., Newbury
L G Durnford & Sons, Newbury	T C Pembroke, Newbury
F A Eacott, East Ilsley	A E Rawlings & Son, Newbury
Gibbs & Son, Hungerford	F J Reynolds, Thatcham
J T Gibbs & Co., Hungerford	R C Smallbone, Newbury
D S Giles, Speen	H A Stradling, Thatcham
Harris Bros., Lambourn	C W Tillett, Wash Water
E J Hassell, Newbury	Vockins & Taylor, Newbury
G W Hastings, Newbury	H G Wells & Sons, Newbury
H J Hedges, Newbury	J C Wooldridge & Son, Hungerford
Hitchman, Newbury	

Newbury Garages in 1948

Green & Whincup (Marchant's Garages proprietors), 61 Northbrook Street and (garage) West Street. (Rover, Jowett, Citroen, Hillman)

Marchant's Garages, 24 and 26 Greenham Road; commercial vehicle works Queen's Road and (garage) Swan Bridge, London Road. (Bedford, Jaguar, Singer, Austin, Standard)

Martin & Chillingworth, 21, 23 and 25 The Broadway and (garage) 42 London Road.

Murray & Whittaker, St John's Garage, Newtown Road and Monks Lane filling station. (Renault)

Nias, Herborough House, 122 and 123 Bartholomew Street. (Humber, Hillman, Sunbeam-Talbot cars; Commer, Karrier trucks)

Pass & Co., West Street and (showrooms) 84 Northbrook Street. (Ford, Fordson Tractors)

Stradling's, 79 Northbrook Street; (garages) 4 London Road. (Wolseley, Rover, MG, Morris, Riley)

Wheeler's, (showrooms and offices) 4 - 8 The Broadway; main workshops 192 London Road; motorcycles 11 - 13 The Broadway. (Vauxhall, Daimler, Lea-Francis, Guy)

Other Significant Employers

Atomic energy establishments **AERE Harwell** (1946) and **AWE Aldermaston** (1950).

Southern Electricity Board, 7 Oxford Road and 39 Northbrook Street. The nationalised SEB was set up in 1948 when it took over 48 concerns, both privately and publicly owned, engaged in selling and distributing electricity.

MARKETS, SHOPS, etc

Market Day, Thursday.

The **cattle market** was held on Thursday in Market Street.

The **wool market,** established 1862, was held annually on the first Saturday in July.

The **Michaelmas Fair** was originally a hiring fair where those looking for work would assemble in the Market Place on the first Thursday after Michaelmas Day, traditionally wearing a symbol of their trade in the hope of attracting the attention of a prospective employer. By the 20th century this practice had been dropped and the fair had become purely an annual entertainment. It was held in the Market Place, the Wharf area and Bear Lane but in 1945 it was moved to Northcroft as it was considered too disruptive for the town centre.

Northbrook Street was the main shopping thoroughfare. It included three department stores: Camp Hopson, Marks & Spencer and F W Woolworth. Its other shops in 1948 were:

Tailors, Outfitters, Drapers, Lingerie, Fashion	17
Grocers, Fishmongers, Game, Fruiterers, Provisions, Greengrocers, Dairy, Tea Merchants	11
Shoe Dealers, Boot Makers, Boot Repairers	8
Newsagents, Tobacconists, Confectioners	7
Hairdressers, Beauty Specialists, Masseuse, Chiropodists	5
Public Houses, Off-licence, Beer Retailer, Wine Merchant	5
Butchers, Bakers	4
Jewellers, Watchmakers	4
Booksellers, Printers, Publishers, Stationers	3
Chemists	3
Cleaners, Dyers	3
China Dealers	2
Cycle Dealers	2
Photographers	2
Wool Stores	2
Antiques	1
Baby Carriage Manufacturer	1
Fancy Goods Dealer	1
Government Supplies Dealer	1
Ironmonger	1
Leather Merchant	1
Musical Instrument Manufacturer	1
Sewing Machine Repairer	1
TV and Radio Dealer	1

Also in Northbrook Street: Insurance Agents (6), Accountants (3), Solicitors (3), Architects (2), Dentist (1), Optician (1), Physician (1) There were also numerous shops, south of the River Kennet, in the Market Place, Cheap Street and Bartholomew Street.

The **Newbury Chamber of Commerce** was founded in 1918. It had 250 members in 1948. 'This body is fully alive to its responsibilities, not only in commerce, but also in questions of importance for the general welfare of the borough and surrounding districts.' (1948 Newbury Guide)

CINEMAS, PUBLIC ESTABLISHMENTS

There were three **cinemas** in 1948:

The Carlton, 28 Cheap Street. On the site of Newbury's first cinema, it was destroyed by fire in 1950.

The Forum, Park Way. Opened in the 1930s with seating for over a thousand; closed in 1998.

The Regal, 10 Bartholomew Street. Opened around 1930, closed in 1962, demolished in 1968.

Public establishments in 1948 included:

Child Welfare Centre, Greenham House, Greenham Road.

Citizens' Advice Bureau (in the Public Library), Cheap Street. Opened in 1940. 'Its voluntary staff deals with enquiries of all kinds. Problems relating to National Insurance, housing, education, food, marriage and other personal matters are among the most numerous.' (*Civic Week Handbook 1948*)

Corn Exchange, Market Place. Built in 1862, this was where the farmers sold their grain. It also provided an indoor venue for the town's activities.

Corporation Public Swimming Baths, Northcroft Lane. An outdoor pool, at 240ft. long and 40ft. wide, it was the largest in the south of England in 1948.

General Post Office, Cheap Street. Opened in 1896.

Greenham House Pleasure Grounds, Greenham Road. 'Greenham House Grounds, unavoidably neglected for years, have now the benefit of a keen skilled gardener. With colourful flower beds and good green grass, the grounds are now quite attractive.' (*Civic Week Handbook 1948*)

Ministry of Labour and National Service, 2 Craven Road. This building was formerly the Oddfellows Hall.

Municipal Buildings, Market Place and Mansion House Street. Built 1878-81.

Museum, in the Jacobean Cloth Hall near the Market Place. 'The most interesting specimen of old buildings that connect the town of Newbury with the palmy days of the clothing trade.' (Kelly's Directory 1950). It was built in the 1620s as a municipal cloth-weaving workshop to give employment to the poor; later used as a warehouse and as a museum from 1902.

Newbury and District Gas Undertaking (Southern Gas Board), showrooms 18 Cheap Street; works in King's Road.

Plaza Theatre, Market Place. Built in 1925, acquired by Newbury Council in 1933, demolished in 1986.

Public Library, Cheap Street. Built in 1905-06 with a grant from the Carnegie Trust Fund, it had 9,000 books in stock in 1948.

Victoria Park Pleasure Grounds, Victoria Park. In the 1930s, Newbury Council organised the **Newbury Work Fund Scheme.** A new road – Park Way – was built and plans to improve the facilities at Victoria Park were carried out. 'Victoria Park, centrally situated, with its model-boating lake, paddling pool and other attractions, forms a valuable town asset.' (*Civic Week Handbook 1948*).

CLUBS, SOCIETIES

Political Clubs, Unions
National Farmers' Union (Newbury Branch), 22 Market Place
Newbury Conservative Club, 6 Cheap Street
Newbury Divisional Labour Party, Hon Sec 34 St George's Avenue
South Berks Liberal Association, 61 Northbrook Street
Sport
Newbury Bowling Club, Victoria Park
Newbury and Crookham Golf Club, Greenham Common
Newbury and District Angling Association. Headquarters: The Lamb public house
Newbury and District Junior Football League
Newbury Rugby Club
Newbury Squash Rackets Club, 86 Northbrook Street
Others
Boy Scouts, The Rovers' Den, The Wharf
Boys' Club, 60 Northbrook Street
British Legion, meet at Haig House, Albert Road
British Red Cross Society, 61 Northbrook Street
Christian Science Reading Room, Newtown Road
Craven Foxhounds
Freemasons: Loyal Berkshire Lodge of Hope (No. 574); St Bartholomew's Lodge (No. 6307); Victory Lodge (No. 3954)
Girl Guides, Girls' High School, Andover Road
Independent Order of Oddfellows: Newbury Female Lodge; Loyal Jack of Newbury Lodge

Independent Order of Rechabites, meet at Temperance Hall, Northcroft Lane

Inland Waterways Association (Kennet and Avon Branch)

Masonic Hall, Northbrook Street

National Federation of Women's Institutes (Wash Common Branch)

Newbury and District Allotment Holders' Association

Newbury and District Amateur Operatic Society

Newbury and District Gardeners' and Amateurs' Mutual Improvement Association

Newbury and District Grocers' Association

Newbury Chess Club

Newbury Choral Society, Lecture Hall, Cromwell Place

Newbury Community Centre, Station Road

Newbury Guildhall Club, 134 Bartholomew Street

Newbury P S A Brotherhood, meet at Congregational Church, Cromwell Place

Old Newburians Association (St Bartholomew's Grammar School)

Royal Air Force Association

Soldiers', Sailors' and Airmen's Families Association

South Berks Floral Society

Temperance Hall, Northcroft Lane

Toc H, Newbury Branch

Welsh Society

Winchcombe Club, Waldegrave Place

Workers Educational Association

WHERE PEOPLE WORSHIPPED

During the Reformation in the 16th century, Newbury was quick to embrace Protestantism and three martyrs were burned at the stake in 1556. In the 17th century the town supported the Parliamentary cause in the civil war and remained a nonconformist centre in the years that followed.

Baptist Church, Cheap Street. Built in 1940, this building replaced the Baptist Church in Northbrook Street.

Congregational Church, Cromwell Place, Northbrook Street.

Methodist Church, Northbrook Street. Built 1837-39.

Methodist Church, Bartholomew Street. Built 1878, demolished in 1960s.

There were also **Methodist Chapels** at Stroud Green, the City and Wash Common.

St George's, Church of England, Andover Road. Built 1933.

St John's, Church of England, Newtown Road. Built 1955-57, this church replaced the previous St John's Church (1860) destroyed by enemy action in 1943.

St Joseph's, Roman Catholic, London Road. Built 1923-28, its campanile is visible across the northern part of the town.

St Mary's, Church of England, London Road. Built for the parish of Speenhamland 1831, demolished in 1976.

St Mary's, Church of England, Shaw. Built close to Shaw House.

St Mary's, Church of England, Speen. A medieval foundation.

St Nicholas', Church of England, Bartholomew Street. Built c.1500-32.

Waterside Chapel, off Northbrook Street. Built for the Presbyterians on the northern bank of the River Kennet in 1697. The building was demolished in the early 1960s. The Waterside Youth Centre was built on the site, opened 1964.

TRANSPORT, COMMUNICATIONS

Newbury Railway Station, Western Region, Station Approach. The station was rebuilt 1908-10 as part of the upgrading of the line which had become the major rail link to the west of England. There were regular trains east to Reading and London (Paddington), and south-west, to Devon and Cornwall. There were also branch lines to Didcot and Winchester and the Lambourn Valley.

Reliance Motor Services, The Wharf, Newbury and Brightwalton. Established in 1919, this was the oldest independent operator of motor coaches in the district.

Newbury Weekly News, weekly newspaper, 34 Northbrook Street. Blacket, Turner & Co., proprietors and publishers. Published Thursday, price 2d. Thursday was market day; hence 'pig and paper' day. Started in 1867, its circulation in 1960 was 21,000.

2

APPENDIX TWO

THE COLLEGE

Table 22 South Berks College: Governors 1952 to 1961
* denotes chairman

Governors 1952 to 1955

Councillor O S Brown, Alderman H R Metcalf, Revd B Russell to 1954, Revd R R Woodfield from 1954 (BEC); A B V Brown, F Howes, Mrs M P Showers (Newbury Division); Councillor M W Paine (Borough Council); R L Spiller from 1953 (S-W Berks Youth Employment); W T Sugg to 1953, I A Webb from 1953 (Community Association); Alderman C A Hawker (Youth Advisory Committee); R H Radcliffe* (Building Employers); M H Wakeley (Mechanical Engineering Employers); A R Marchant (Motor Engineering Employers); D McMahon, W Winter (Trades Council); G P Hopson (Chamber of Commerce); G Suggett (WEA); Revd K Joyce (C of E); Canon A G McDonald to 1954, Revd A E Zollo from 1954 (RC); Revd C I Ward (Free Churches); C Audsley (Hungerford Advisory Committee); Revd E J Rumens (Lambourn Advisory Committee); Mrs C Hobbs (Thatcham Advisory Committee); Mrs G Pike (Women's Interests).

Governors 1955 to 1958

Councillor O S Brown, Dr G E Harrison to 1956, Revd G C Matthews from 1956, A H Willes (BEC); A B V Brown, F Howes, Mrs M P Showers (Newbury Division); Councillor A R Croker (Borough Council); R L Spiller* (S-W Berks Youth Employment); I A Webb (Community Association); Revd R R Woodfield to 1956, H Biddis from 1956 (Youth Advisory Committee); R H Radcliffe (Building Employers); F C Marsh (Electrical Engineering Employers); M H Wakeley (Mechanical Engineering Employers); A R Marchant (Motor Engineering Employers); G Rickard, W Winter (Trades Council); R E Moore to 1956, W C Franks from 1956 (Chamber of Commerce); S Goldstein (WEA); Revd K Joyce (C of E); Revd A E Zollo (RC); Revd C I Ward to 1956, Revd Crew from 1956 (Free Churches); C T Milsom (Hungerford Advisory Committee); Mrs C Hobbs to 1956, T G B Howe from 1956 (Thatcham Advisory Committee); Mrs S Cox, Mr R M Fishenden, Dr D T Lewis, Miss D L L Walters (Co-opted).

Governors 1959 to 1961

C Brown, Mrs S Cox, W C Franks, S Goldstein, A R Marchant, Revd G Matthews, M W Paine, J Pass, J Shackleton, Mrs M P Showers, J Southern, R L Spiller,* H A Stradling, M H Wakeley, I A Webb, A H Willes, (J Astor from 1960).

Table 23 Berkshire FE: Principal Salary Scales 1948 to 1960

From July 1948	£300 to £555
From September 1949	£700 to £850
From April 1951	£900 to £1,000 (SBCFE salary £940)
From April 1952	£1,050 to £1,150 (SBCFE salary £1,050)
From April 1953	£1,090 to £1,190
From April 1954	£1,115 to £1,215 (SBCFE salary £1,165)
From August 1954	£1,165 to £1,265 (SBCFE salary £1,223)
From October 1956	£1,550 to £1,770 (SBCFE salary £1,550)
From October 1959	£1,800 to £1,950 (SBCFE salary £1,950)

Table 24 South Berks College: Full-Time Lecturers 1948 to 1960

Lecturers	From	To
C Sully, Engineering	1948	1967
A Owen, Building (Carpentry)	1949	1978
W B R Pocock, Science and Mathematics	1949	1979
J W Whitham, Electrical Engineering	1949	1950
W Atkinson, Science	1949	1952
D W Mothersell, Mechanical Engineering	1950	1950
J Forster, Building (Brickwork)	1950	1951
R T Ritchie, Electrical Engineering	1950	1954
F W Tweddell, Mechanical Engineering	1951	1951
C A Taylor, Building (Brickwork)	1951	1952
J Trodden, General Technical Subjects	1951	1954
C L Cox, Engineering	1951	1956
P C Garlick, English and General Subjects	1951	1952
Miss E J Searle, Needlecraft	1951	1959
Miss V F M Garlick, English and General Subjects	1952	1954
W E Carr, Science	1952	1966
K Morton, Building (Brickwork)	1952	1953
Mrs P Y Silvester, Domestic Subjects	1952	1953
Mrs G E Sugg, Shorthand and Typing	1952	1967
R W T S Edwards, Maths and Woodwork	1952	1979
W J Parrott, Building (Brickwork)	1953	1967
F S Barnes, Science and Maths	1953	1965
N S Colquhoun, Engineering	1953	1954
Miss M B Dinwoodie, Women's Subjects (Cookery)	1953	1970

Lecturers	From	To
J S Theodorson, Engineering	1953	1955
L T Basketter	1954	1955
J E Wicklen	1954	1955
Miss A M B McGee, Women's Subjects	1954	1958
A M Bedford, Engineering	1954	1974
W J Ramshaw	1954	1955
R C J Ireson, Engineering Science and Maths	1952	1955
P L Hay, Agriculture	1955	1960
A G Elgood	1955	1956
M Cowie, Building (Plumbing)	1956	1965
J H Newlands	1956	1961
J H Scott, Science	1956	1960
L Hoyland, Superintendent of Workshops	1956	1979
J W Ballard, Science, Electronics	1956	1962
J Petherbridge, Engineering	1956	1958
Miss D A Barnes, Women's Subjects (Needlecraft)	1956	1960
Miss V F M Garlick, English and General Subjects	1956	1964
W Holt, Electrical Subjects	1955	1974
Miss M Elson	1957	1959
E L Donnelly	1957	1964
R D Heywood, Chemistry	1957	1989
I M R Jenkins, Science	1957	1960
E C Gardner, Engineering	1957	1982
W C E Jakins, Business Subjects	1957	1960
F J Pizzey, English and Liberal Studies	1957	1984
W E Freebury, Engineering	1957	1966
F L Bernard, Engineering	1958	1984
M J Keene	1958	1958
Mrs E Potter, Women's Subjects (Needlecraft)	1959	1979
Mrs D J C Loasby, Liberal Studies	1960	1969
L Sugden, Technical Drawing	1960	1982
Mrs M M C Blake	1960	1961
E A Irwing, Electronics and Physics	1960	1988

Table 25 Berkshire FE: Salary Scales from 1956

Note: Equal pay for men and women was to be operative by April 1961.

Head of Department		
Grade I	Men £1,250 to £1,400	Women £1,000 to £1,120
Grade II	Men £1,400 to £1,600	Women £1,120 to £1,280
Grade III	Men £1,600 to £1,750	Women £1,280 to £1,400
Grade IV	Men £1,750 to £1,900	Women £1,400 to £1,520
Grade V	Men £1,900 to £2,050	Women £1,520 to £1,640
Lecturer		
Assistant, Grade A	Men £475 to £900	Women £430 to £720
Assistant, Grade B	Men £650 to £1,025	Women £580 to £820
Lecturer	Men £1,200 to £1,350	Women £960 to £1,080

Table 26 South Berks College: Part-Time Instructors

1951/52	
L Airey BSc (Hons), ARIC	J G Alderman, BSc (Hons), ARIC
Miss D A Barnes, CGLI	T J Bashford, DipEHA
A Bates, BA	Miss I Brooks, FISTD
Mr E R Broadbent	Mrs H E R Le Cornu
Mrs I N Cox	S Creed, ACA
Mrs D Creed	Mrs M W Croker
R Daniels, FIBD	Miss E E H Day, M of E Cert
Mr P G Dyson	P A Einstein
G Evans	R L Evans, MA (Cantab)
Mrs K M Evans, DipPhysEd (London)	Mrs H Garlick, BA
Mrs R S J Hards	F Hards, BA
K P Harris, AMIMechE	D E Harry, M of E Cert
G Haskell	G I Hughson, M of E Cert
G B A Inglet, BA, ACA (Ireland)	H J Johns
A E Jones, PCT	Mrs E Jones
P A J Levi, ARAM	Mrs C Lovelock
W MacIlvride	Miss J Menard, MISTD
Miss G Moses	D R Mott, M of E Cert
E Newport, Registered Plumber	J Nicol, ARIBA
S Norwood	Miss Peters
Miss C Reid	L C Ronson

Revd E J Rumens	W L Seaborne, MA, FRGS
Mrs L B Sewter, M of E Cert	Mrs L E Shaw, CGLI
K Spackman	C H Stanley
A P Stubbington	Mrs G E Sugg, PCT
W J Sweetland	R Taylor, ACA, DPA
V C H Taylor	Mrs K M Turnbull, M of E Cert, CGLI
F C Vize	G Watkins
W C Wellstead	Miss E C White
R Wilson	Miss M Wingfield, FISTD
J P Wyatt	

1952/53 New Instructors

Bassett, BA, ABSM	Mrs R Bell, BA
Mrs L A Burgess, SRN, RCN	Mrs K Canning
Mrs I A E Dolan, RSA	Miss M M Dunbar
Mrs M H French	E H Hunt
Miss M O Maghie, RSA	F S Martin, MSc, ARCS, ARIC
Mrs M Ord	S N Rowe
Mrs V E Saunders, SRN, SCM	Mrs L Stratton
R W Tucker, PCT	

1956/57

Agriculture: W H Selbie, BA; F H Wiggins. **Building:** K E Fidler; F G Pizzey; N S Smith. **Commerce and General Education:** Miss L Brown, BA; Miss D Cole; S W Creed, ASAA; Mrs R Harte; A E Jones, PSTD; Miss G Moses, Diploma Handels, Oberlehrerin; Miss S Reed.
Engineering: E F Barber, AMIMechE; J S Bill, HNC(Mech); W J Garland, HNC(Mech), ONC(Elec); B C Hedge, IMechE; A Hill, ARB;D G Keevil; H P Lidiard, CGLI, ONC(Elec); D I Page, PhD, BSc; R L Page, CGLI; F J Pizzey; F J Stevenson, ONC(Mech). **Science:** P J Anderson, PhD, BSc; J Boyce, FIMLT; W J Ferguson, BSc; Miss D M Hasking, AIMLT. NDD; S E Jeffery; P C C Long, FIMLT, AIST; P R J Matthews, FIMLT: S W Osborne; G S Smith, AIMLT; F H Summerfield, ARPS; R J Taylor, AIMLT; M W Thompson, BSc. **Women's Subjects:** W Allinson, Art; Mrs B E Davis, Needlework and Dressmaking Diploma (Bath Training College); Mrs A Farmer, Berkshire Branch Embroiderer's Guild; Mrs R S J Hards, CGLI Dressmaking; Mrs C J Lovelock, Trade School Needlework; Mrs N Runham, CGLI Dressmaking; G Stanley, Art.

Table 27 Berkshire FE: Part-Time Instructor
Hourly Rates 1948 to 1960

Class	1948	1949	1950	1951	1956	1957	1960
Grade I	7/6 (37p.)	8/6 (42p.)	8/6 (42p.)	9/6 (47p.)	10/- (50p.)	12/6 (62p.)	15/- (75p.)
Grade II	8/6 (42p.)	9/6 (47p.)	9/6 (47p.)	10/6 (52p.)	11/6 (57p.)	15/- (75p.)	18/- (90p.)
Grade III	10/6 (52p.)	10/6 (52p.)	10/6 (52p.)	11/6 (57p.)	13/- (65p.)	17/6 (87p.)	21/- (£1.05)
Grade IV	–	–	–	–	15/- (75p.)	20/- (£1)	27/6 (£1.37)

Table 28 South Berks College:
Area Evening Institute Classes 1951/52

Subject	Compton	Hungerford	Lambourn	Thatcham
Art	–	–	X	–
Athletics Training	–	–	X	–
Ballroom Dancing	–	X	–	–
Brass Band	–	X	–	X
Building Construction	X	–	–	–
Cabinet Making	–	–	X	–
Choral Music	X	X	X	X
Cookery	–	–	X	–
Drama	X	X	–	–
Dressmaking	X	X	X	X
Embroidery	–	–	X	–
English	X	–	–	–
Folk Dancing	–	X	–	–
French	–	–	X	X
German	–	X	–	X
Keep Fit and Dancing (Women)	–	–	X	–
Mathematics	X	–	–	–
Music Appreciation	–	–	X	–
Old Time Dancing	–	–	–	X
Renovations and Alterations	–	–	X	–
Shorthand	X	–	–	X
Technical Drawing	X	–	–	–
Typewriting	–	–	–	X
Women's Handicrafts	–	X	–	X
Woodwork	–	X	–	X

SELECT BIBLIOGRAPHY

AWE Aldermaston

AWRE News

Berkshire County Record Office

Berkshire Education Committee, Minutes 1946 to 1961, C/CL/C4/3/21-25

Berkshire Education Committee, Minutes of Subcommittees 1947 to 1973, C/CL/C4/9/41-67. These include the Minutes of the Further Education Subcommittee; also the Minutes of Agricultural Education, Building and Works, Co-ordination, Education and Finance, Secondary Schools and Schools Management Subcommittees

Berkshire Education Committee, Regulations for Technical and Evening Institutes 1931-32, N/E2/1/2/3

Berkshire Education Committee, Technical and Evening School Section, Minutes 1910 to 1925, C/CL/C4/6C/1

Census 1901, 1911

Newbury Civilian Register of Electors 1945, C/CL/R1

Newbury Community Centre Records, C/Edn/12

Newbury Divisional Executive Minute Books, 1946 to 1968, C/Edn/2/1-3

Newbury Technical Institute Governors' Minutes 1910 to 1935, N/E2/1/1

Newbury Technical Institute Prospectuses 1929-30, 1931-32, 1933-34, N/E2/1/2/1-4

Secondary sources:

Harwell: The British Atomic Energy Research Establishment 1946-1951, (London: HMSO, 1952)

K E B Jay, *Atomic Energy Research at Harwell*, (London: Butterworths Scientific Publications, 1955)

Newbury College Library

Ormonde House Sales Brochure 1923

South Berks College and Newbury College Prospectuses

South Berks College Supplement in Newbury Weekly News, 6 September 1973

South Berkshire College of Further Education 25 Years, Anniversary Publication

Newbury Library

Commonwealth Technical Training Week, 29 May – 3 June 1961, Handbook for Newbury and District

Directories of Newbury: Blacket's 1923, 1936, 1942; Coburn's 1917; Kelly's 1930, 1932, 1936, 1937, 1941, 1942, 1947, 1950

Newbury Borough Council Minutes 1946 to 1960; Official Year Books, 1945-46 to 1963-64

Newbury Official Guide 1938; Newbury Rural District Guide c.1948

Newbury Weekly News

Secondary sources:

Clive Collier, *Southern Electric: A History*, (Maidenhead: Southern Electric, 1992)

Vera Garlick, *The Newbury Scrapbook*, (Newbury: *Newbury Weekly News*, 1970)

Nikolaus Pevsner, *The Buildings of England, Berkshire*, (Harmondsworth: Penguin, 1966)

John Porter, *John Porter of Kingsclere, An Autobiography*, (London: Grant Richards, 1919)

Newbury Museum

OS Berks Sheet 35.13, 25 inch series, 1933 edition

Reading Central Library

A Handbook for the Citizens of Newbury, Civic Week 1948

Berkshire Education Committee, Scheme of Further Education and Plan for County Colleges, September 1949

Berkshire Education Committee, Since 1945, Education in Berkshire, Report from 1945 to 1956 compiled by the Director of Education

Education in the Royal County of Berkshire, Report by the Director of Education, 1957-58, 1958-59, 1959-60, 1961-62, 1963-64, 1967-70

Southern Regional Council for Further Education, Ninth Annual Report October 1956; Tenth Annual Report October 1957; Thirteenth Annual Report October 1960

Southern Regional Council for Further Education 21st Anniversary 1947-1968

UK Atomic Energy Authority, Harwell

The First Thirty Years of Apprentice Training at Harwell, (Harwell: Education and Training Centre, 1978)

25th Anniversary of the Harwell Laboratory Trainee Scheme 1958-1983 (Souvenir Booklet)

Unpublished MSS

G.T.Shoosmith, *Mostly Plenty, Being a Continuation of the Reminiscences of GTS, Over the period 1952-1987*

Other Secondary Sources

Peter Allen, *A Popular History of Thatcham*, (Oxford: Foxhole Publishing, 1999)

John Betjeman, *Coming Home – An Anthology of Prose*, Selected and Introduced by Candida Lycett Green, (London: Vintage, 1998)

John Betjeman, *Letters, Volume Two, 1951 to 1984*, edited by Candida Lycett Green, (London: Minerva, 1996)

R A Butler, *The Art of the Possible*, (Harmondsworth: Penguin, 1973)

L M Cantor and I F Roberts, *Further Education Today*, (London: Routledge & Kegan Paul, 1979)

Creative History Group, *Newbury Roundabout*, (Newbury: 1989)

P Gill, *Cheltenham's Racing Heroes*, (Stroud: Sutton, 1998)

J F C Harrison, *Learning and Living 1790-1960*, (London: Routledge & Kegan Paul, 1961)

Peter Hennessy, *Never Again, Britain 1945-1951*, (London: Vintage, 1993)

Richard Hoggart, *The Way We Live Now*, (London: Pimlico, 1996)

Norman Longmate, *How We Lived Then*, (London: Pimlico, 2002)

Candida Lycett Green, *The Dangerous Edge of Things*, (London: Doubleday, 2005)

Arthur Marwick, *British Society Since 1945*, (London: Penguin, 2003)

Kenneth O Morgan, *The People's Peace*, (Oxford: Oxford University Press, 1992)

R Mortimer, R Onslow and P Willett, *The Biographical Encyclopaedia of British Flat Racing*, (London: MacDonald & Janes, 1978)

N Moss, *Klaus Fuchs, The Man Who Stole the Atom Bomb*, (London: Grafton Books, 1987)

Robin Oakley, *Valley of the Racehorse*, (London: Headline Book Publishing, 2000)

Michael Sanderson, *Education and Economic Decline in Britain, 1870 to the 1990s*, (Cambridge: Cambridge University Press, 1999)